THE HUNGRY WORLD

THE HUNGRY WORLD

AMERICA'S COLD WAR BATTLE AGAINST POVERTY IN ASIA

Nick Cullather

HARVARD UNIVERSITY PRESS

Cambridge, Massachusetts

London, England

First Harvard University Press paperback edition, 2013

Library of Congress Cataloging-in-Publication Data

Cullather, Nick, 1959–
  The hungry world : America's cold war battle against poverty in Asia / Nick Cullather.
    p. cm.
  Includes bibliographical references and index.
  ISBN 978-0-674-05078-5 (alk. paper)
  ISBN 978-0-674-72581-2 (pbk.)
    1. Agricultural assistance, American—Asia.   2. Economic assistance, American—Asia.
  3. Food supply—Asia.   4. Food relief—Asia.   5. United States—Foreign relations—Asia.
  6. Asia—Foreign relations—United States.   I. Title.
  HD2056.Z8C85   2010
  338.1'873095—dc22   2010010950

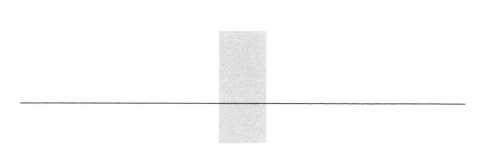

For Melanie, Isabel, and Joseph

sa pagiging kamanlalakbay

CONTENTS

ILLUSTRATIONS

(following page 158)

Polish children queue up for American food relief in 1919. Herbert Hoover Presidential Library.

Norman Borlaug shows the test plots at Chapingo to Elvin Stakman and Henry Wallace in 1946. Rockefeller Archive Center.

Agrónomo in training Ignacio Narvaez in 1950. Rockefeller Archive Center.

Horace Holmes demonstrates a steel plow in Etawah District in 1950. Special Collections Research Center, University of Chicago Library.

Morrison-Knudsen project manager Ted Johnston tours the Kajaki Dam with Afghan dignitaries in 1957. Lyman Wilbur Collection, Albertsons Library, Boise State University.

The Helmand Valley development. International Cooperation Administration, Report on Development of Helmand Valley, 1956.

President John F. Kennedy welcomes Prime Minister Jawaharlal Nehru to Washington in 1961. John F. Kennedy Library.

Walt W. Rostow, architect of modernization as theory and policy. Lyndon Baines Johnson Library.

Robert Chandler introduces Presidents Lyndon Johnson and Ferdinand Marcos to IR-8 at Los Baños in 1966. IRRI.

IRRI's glass and aluminum laboratories faced an experimental farm where rice was grown in "traditional" ways. IRRI.

This book started with a simple aim: to tell the story of the green revolution, the greatest success in the history of foreign aid since the Marshall Plan. In the late 1960s, stunning innovations in agricultural science, particularly dwarf strains of wheat and rice, allowed chronically poor and starvation-prone Asian countries to feed themselves for the first time, ushering in a new era of hope and economic dynamism. My project was soon complicated by recorded observations and experiences that refused to conform to this story. The first to go was the timeline, which by most accounts begins after World War II when scientists and aid officials realized the implications of a global population boom that foreshadowed an era of famine and conflict in the densely peopled countries of Asia. It became clear on my first visit to the U.S. National Archives that the plans already being implemented at that stage had been laid much earlier, when no population explosion was in sight. At the beginning of the twentieth century food emerged as a new instrument of diplomacy, and ambitions for a spiritual awakening of Asia took a scientific turn. The "traditional" agriculture over which American technology had triumphed turned out to be of recent design, using seeds developed at U.S. universities only a few years before "modern" varieties arrived to take their place.

But as each element of the legend dissolved, the outlines of a far more interesting and important story came into view, the birth of a new type of international politics. It goes by a variety of names—nation-building, humanitarian relief, foreign aid—but it is usually known simply as "development." It is the species of politics that speaks to humanity's greatest ambitions for progress and welfare and to its greatest fears of social collapse, and it is the politics where the demands of nations for security and prestige connect with the most personal of needs, for health, work, and food. Today it is such a part of diplomatic routine that it is seldom spoken of except in terms of budgets and targets, but there was a time when it was a bold new experiment in mankind's relationship to each other and to the land. It was a test that would decide the fate of a divided, nuclear-armed, and hungry world.

Tracing this story led many places and indebted me to many people. My most persevering collaborators have been archivists and librarians, especially Lou Malcomb, who has kept paper copies of the *Congressional Record* and the *Foreign Relations* series within easy reach at Indiana University's government publications collection. Anke Voss-Hubbard and Kenneth Rose guided me through the Rockefeller Foundation Archive on two occasions. Alan Divack cleared room for me in the tight space of the Ford Foundation Archives. I am also deeply grateful to Ian Wallace, the head of information at the International Rice Research Institute; Jane M. Wu and Gabriel Stergiou at the FAO Archive; and the staff at the Nehru Memorial Museum and Library. Linda Hanson and the archivists at the Lyndon B. Johnson Library have made it the most welcoming of all presidential libraries.

Many who have spent their lives working in Asian fields have shared their recollections with me, including Thomas R. Hargrove, Van Nguu Nguyen, and Dat Van Tran, who graciously hosted us at a memorable dinner in Rome. I am also grateful for invaluable advice from seminar groups, including the MIT Seminar on Science, Technology, and Society; the History Departmental Seminar at the University of British Columbia; The David Bruce Centre for American Studies at Keele; the International Center for Advanced Studies at New York University; the Mershon Center for International Security Studies at Ohio State University; the Miller Center at the University of Virginia; the Center for International History at Columbia University; the Netherlands Institute for Advanced Study; and the Contemporary History Institute at the Nehru Memorial Museum and Library. The editors of *Diplomatic History, India Review,* the *American Historical Review,* and the *Journal of American History* published early versions of this work and furnished valuable critical appraisals.

Several colleagues have been generous enough to read the manuscript in whole or part and offer helpful suggestions and corrections. I am particularly grateful to David Engerman for his friendship and guidance. Amy Staples prepared me for what I would find at the FAO Archives. Emily Rosenberg, Paul Kramer, David Ekbladh, John Krige, Marc Frey, Deborah Fitzgerald, Matthew Connelly, Marilyn Young, and Michael Adas each provided valuable criticism and counsel. Colleagues at the National

University of Singapore—Ryan Bishop, Tim Barnard, Greg Clancy, and Ian Gordon—supplied encouragement and advice at an early stage of the project, and those at Indiana—including Jeff Wasserstrom, Mark Roseman, Padraic Kenney, Sarah Knott, Dror Wahrman, Rob Schneider, and Joanne Meyerowitz—have furnished support and guidance from beginning to end. Chad Parker and John Baesler, once graduate students, now professors, have been required to reread many versions, and their thoughts have been of great value.

My editor, Joyce Seltzer, steadied this project and steered it into print, and I am thankful to her. Melanie supported this project in so many ways but especially by letting me keep the little room in the quietest part of the house. Isabel and Joey tried their best not to bother their dad when he was writing there, and mainly they succeeded.

INTRODUCTION

Lyndon Johnson glimpsed the Asian countryside for the first time during the four-hour drive from Delhi to the Taj Mahal, a flat stretch of dust and heat broken occasionally by thatch-roofed villages alive with barefoot children. To Johnson, reared on the arid plains of central Texas decades before the New Deal introduced running water, electricity, and a measure of prosperity, the scene was at once foreign and familiar. He felt he was looking into the past. He was dismayed that in 1961 "primitive plows hitched to water buffalo were still being used to till the soil." There was little or no irrigation, and he wondered how "India could ever feed its growing population under these circumstances." Dwight Eisenhower toured the same area just two years before and came away with similar impressions. The villages were "constructed of mud. Modern sewage, lighting, and running water were, of course, nonexistent," but far worse was the "hunger that emaciates the bodies of children, that sears the souls of their parents, that stirs the passions of those who toil endlessly and earn only scraps."[1]

The enigma of this landscape—crowded yet empty, timeless yet desperate for change—preoccupied American leaders for two decades after the Chinese revolution. From the high rangelands of the Hindu Kush to the rice paddies of Java, Asia contained nearly a billion people, a quarter of the earth's population. Outside of Japan, it was almost entirely rural. In this trackless interior, among millions of illiterate pastoralists and cultivators, a battle of ideologies would be lost or won. Communism had harnessed two powerful motivations: the desire to own land and the regime's "failure to provide China with enough to eat." In Vietnam, the Philippines, and Malaya, each harvest season meant a renewed battle between guerrillas and the army for control of the rice crop. Even democratic India had scant authority in the villages where four-fifths of the people lived.[2]

1

Americans were surprised by China's collapse and surprised again by the ferocity of the war in Korea, in which the U.S. Army that defeated Japan and Germany could achieve only a bloody stalemate. Election campaigns in 1950 and 1952 raged with charges that the administration misunderstood Asia, and that its mistakes had imperiled the national security. To explain the politics of the continent, the editors of *Life* turned to bestselling writer James Michener, whose first novel had just debuted as a musical, *South Pacific*. Asia had "exploded into the center of American life. Now it will stay there forever," Michener began. "What we do about the fact can make or crush us as a nation." He explained the fearsome ratios; Asia was five times as large as the United States and nine times as populous. Should it become an enemy, "strong as we are, we would be doomed." Although Asia hungered for progress and power, it was a place of pain and pathos, unable to feed its people not because there was insufficient land but because it lacked efficient methods of cultivation and distribution. Nonetheless, Asians would solve their problems in their own way. "The white man himself is finished in Asia" as a ruler, administrator, or missionary, Michener concluded. He could return only by devising a new type of diplomacy, geared to the continent's needs, so that "the white man, his money and his technical skills, will be invited back on the Asians' terms."[3]

Three challenges to the American vision of world order came together in the Asian heartland: communist expansionism, nationalist uprisings, and what social scientists called the revolution of rising expectations, a collective aspiration for land, food, and change fed by a growing consciousness of the outer world. In the "defensive arc" stretching from Pakistan through Thailand, the Philippines, and along the island chain to Japan, scarcely a single country remained unthreatened by insurrectionary or separatist movements. The Central Intelligence Agency warned alternately that the remnants of free Asia would join in a continent-wide communist monolith, or disintegrate into unstable and vulnerable fragments. For the United States, either possibility represented an existential danger. The perception of Asia's vastness, its population, and its poverty conjured images of Mongol hordes. "If we become the only fat duck in a hungry world," newspaper editor Gardner Cowles warned, "look out."[4]

While these apprehensions were deepened by the Cold War, rural Asia posed a separate and more fundamental challenge to American leadership. The image of the Asian peasant, shaking off his ancestral torpor and taking up modern arms, aroused primal fears. As early as 1900, theorists

2

warned that the peasant problem might ultimately defeat any global order the United States might try to construct. "The incorporation of this great mass of beings into our civilization," Alfred Thayer Mahan warned, "is one of the greatest problems that humanity has yet to solve." Halford MacKinder, the father of geopolitics, identified the Eurasian heartland as the "geographic pivot" of an approaching struggle among the great powers. In the twentieth century, dominance would belong to the empire that could command the allegiance of the "horse-men, camel-men, and plow-men" of the Asian interior. As Marx had a century earlier, Americans saw the peasant as a transitional figure, caught halfway between feudal serf-dom and capitalist proprietorship, but it remained an open question whether Asia could evolve into a market-based industrial society without bringing the world down in flames. Henry L. Stimson, dean of the foreign policy establishment, wondered if China could adapt and "whether the capitalist system may not break down on the problem of the peasant." Asia's rising aspirations amid chronic scarcities of food and land fore-shadowed an era of revolutions more violent and momentous than the one Europe had barely survived.[5]

But if farmers, food, and land were the problems, the United States might already have the answers. Scientists and philanthropists argued that feeding the hungry and reviving barren lands were challenges Ameri-cans were uniquely equipped to take on. Horticultural innovation was one of the perks of national expansion; nineteenth-century traders and naval expeditions combed six continents for crop varieties that could be grown commercially. Plant breeding made American farms the world's most productive even before mechanization and chemicals lengthened their lead. The United States routinely "performs the miracle of the loaves and fishes," the Reverend Josiah Strong counseled. It was the only nation in history that could make "a thousand civilized men thrive where a hundred savages starved." American organizational innovations after the turn of the century—nutritional science and demography—made it possible to ratio-nalize food supplies on a national or even a global scale. By the interwar years, the Rockefeller Foundation was testing the proposition in Mexico and China.[6]

The new style of diplomacy Americans devised to meet the crisis in Asia was called development. How and on what terms Asia's population would be integrated into the world economy, whether fragile postcolo-nial states could extend mechanisms of taxation and authority over vast ungoverned hinterlands, and whether poverty on this scale even could be ameliorated were all questions that lay outside of the customary conventions of international relations. As empires disintegrated in the wake of World War II, the concepts and institutions that supported the practice of international aid and humanitarian assistance came into operation worldwide, but most were constructed in and for the specific setting of rural Asia. Whereas Africa and the Middle East posed a seemingly straightforward challenge of tapping intact resources, Asia confronted developers with exhausted lands and ancient and intricate cultures in need of reform. It was the most underdeveloped place on earth. The U.S. government turned to scientists and private foundations for help in guiding the evolution of its poor, backward territories into modern, prospering nations. These advisers, drawn from academic and professional disciplines, expected an imminent break with the past—in Walt W. Rostow's image, a takeoff—which would mark "the transition of a society from a preponderantly agricultural to an industrialized basis." As conceived by economic theorists, development was a cure for the condition of rurality. "The first and very commonplace observation to be made about the underdeveloped and unprogressive countries is that they are all agricultural," John Kenneth Galbraith explained. "There is no industrialized country in the world which can be said to be stagnant." Tied to the land and owing his livelihood to the dictates of nature and custom, the peasant embodied the premodern personality. Material development would begin as a psychological process when the peasant abandoned his mud brick villages, primitive plows, and ancestral ways of life. China's revolution and the growing ferment throughout Asia signaled that the moment of takeoff was at hand.[7]

In the view of policymakers, the postwar revolt of Asia expressed not a repudiation of the West or its historical injustices, but the depth of popular aspiration for the material and social gains made by the West. Formerly isolated villagers wanted electric light, medicine, and motorbikes. It was a continent-wide awakening into the modern era. "There is in this vast area what we might call a developing Asian consciousness," Dean Acheson observed in 1950, "a revulsion against the acceptance of misery and poverty as the normal conditions of life." Communists had not created a hunger for change, but they were cunning enough "to ride this thing into victory and into power."[8]

In the early postwar years, "this thing" was a palpable force moving ahead with reckless momentum. Development projects were designed not to induce growth but to guide it and give it meaning. The purpose of aid, for Harry Truman, was "to keep human progress from going off the rails." It was crucial for material advances to symbolically affirm democratic values, property rights, and alignment with the United States and its allies. Theory and policy were driven by a quest for narratives to frame problems and forecast futures, and the performance of development was inseparable from this process of scripting and scenario building. A number of expository conventions recur across the development decades, but three had a formative role in schemes implemented in Asia. Projects were designed for "display" to produce statistical victories or as carefully staged spectacles dramatizing the fruits of modernity. They were also composed, usually from inception, as "models," formulas to be replicated at later times and other settings. Finally, narratives defined lines of conflict in developmental politics. Models were pitted against each other as tests of allegiance and modernizing prowess. If the Soviet system's appeal lay in its proven formula for industrial planning, the United States looked to agricultural technology for a different angle, better suited to the Asian environment. It sought scenarios that would discipline the region's unruly politics and shore up client regimes. In Dean Rusk's estimation, an India devoting its energies to problems of food and farming would be "the kind of India we want."[9]

American advisers were never able to settle on a single, consensus model of rural development. They disagreed on fundamental goals, such as whether improvement should empower the farmer, the consumer, or the government. Social science offered little practical guidance, largely because it conceptualized agriculture as a state of pre- or underdevelopment. Sociology and anthropology, for instance, defined "modernization" as a process of casting off the cultural forms of the village, of abandoning the farm either psychologically or physically. Economists used urbanization as an index of progress, and distinguished between the metropolitan "modern sector" and the rural "unorganized economy." Because the countryside could never be truly modern, there was considerable disagreement about what modern agriculture might look like. A surfeit of solutions drawn from the American experience added to the confusion. Domestic agriculture remained in persistent crisis from the 1930s through the 1970s. Scientific advances only intensified the "paradox of plenty" whereby increases in yields hurt crop prices and decreased farmers' earnings. New Deal reforms shored up incomes but generated huge, unsustainable surpluses. The continual need for fresh federal interventions might have led some to question the suitability of the United States as an example for

Asia, but in practice it multiplied the number of models. U.S. officials largely agreed, at least after 1940, that their system of agriculture ought to be the envy of the world, but they had different ideas about what made it enviable. They idealized the pattern of ownership, typified by the family farm, while recognizing that small farms were losing ground to corporate agribusiness. They admired the top-down regional planning of the Tennessee Valley Authority (TVA), but also the bottom-up cooperative ethic of farm communities. Asia served as a political Rorschach, a formless need into which conflicting ambitions could be projected.

By 1950 Americans were already at work settling nomads, rewriting tenancy laws, damming tributaries of the Ganges, and tinkering with plant genetics and the social architecture of villages. Professionals with specialized talents—hydrologists, urban planners, plant breeders, chemists, and sociologists—sacrificed careers and homes to practice their craft in remote and punishing latitudes. Their work remains controversial, and although they are remembered as unsung benefactors or shills for corporate agribusiness, their nation called them to serve. They went to Asia seeking adventure and a chance to fulfill their generation's responsibility to confront poverty. Thousands followed the Asian drama through the books and magazine stories of James Michener and Barbara Ward, or the radio appeals of jungle doctor Tom Dooley. From 1950 to 1971 the United States invested more than $20 billion in economic aid to countries in the region, a total that substantially understates the scale of the effort and its effects. Aid in the form of foodstuffs may have amounted to five times as much. Asian governments, multilateral lenders, and private foundations launched numerous initiatives with official U.S. support or guidance, each designed to reconstruct whole landscapes. They brought running water, new knowledge, and sometimes prosperity, but they also supervised the disruption or displacement of thousands of people.[10]

These projects amounted to a sustained confrontation with the physical and cultural environment of rural Asia. Although framed in a martial language of revolutions, conquests, and explosions, it is more fittingly described as an encounter because of the interchange of figures—American, Asian, and transnational—who molded developmental ambitions and narratives. In this context, power worked less through governments than between them, in the panoply of private and multilateral funding networks, research institutes, and freelancers who were inventing not just new policies but a new type of policy. Asian leaders hired the first foreign engineers and advisors and launched their own programs before

President Truman initiated foreign aid in 1949. U.S. experts adapted their designs to already unfolding plans, to compete against Soviet or Chinese schemes, or to unfamiliar natural conditions. Instead of a First World imposing (or bestowing) its solutions on the Third, developmental politics pitted transnational coalitions of experts against each other. The one group rarely consulted, even in the world's two largest democracies, was the electorate.

Within this encounter, Americans pursued three conflicting goals. First, they aimed to restore a putatively lost "balance" between food supply and population. Experts saw revolutions and social turmoil as political manifestations of mankind's persistent struggle to wrest sustenance from the soil. In the increasingly stable pattern of international affairs, hunger remained an irrational element, turning citizens into mobs and giving demagogues license. Second, they sought to modify the psychology of the peasant. In the rural setting, science offered a unique medium for inculcating democratic and progressive values. The United States' clear lead in technology could have a telling effect, magnified by the intimate connection between culture and the cycle of planting and harvest. "When we introduce new techniques," Margaret Mead observed, "we make a break with the sustaining tradition . . . disrupting the patterns of relationship between man and wife, father and son." American advisers believed their innovations would have a catalytic effect, inspiring farmers to question the fundamental assumptions of the society around them. Finally, rural reconstruction was a technique of nation-building. Policies to assure balance between population and food supply authorized, even mandated, official intrusions into the most intimate of personal decisions. By asserting control over agriculture, nations defeated their internal enemies and gained a degree of authority over resources, territory, and people that colonial empires never had.[11]

The wave of development activity that peaked in the 1950s and 1960s is known today as the "green revolution," a name conferred in 1968 by U.S. Agency for International Development administrator William Gaud. The harvest that year had been dramatically large, and Gaud contrasted peaceful science-based development against the "red" guerrilla revolutions unsettling the Asian countryside. His term lent coherence to three decades of conflict, innovation, failure, and success, but he intended no retrospective judgment. Instead, he offered a template for future action, in other words, a model. The name "green revolution" stuck, and a substantial body of legend grew, following the narrative arc of the model. A heroic parable of

7

population, food, and science solidified into history. "Indeed, but for irrigation and the input of science through the so-called 'green revolution'," Eric Hobsbawm affirmed, "large parts of South and Southeast Asia would have been unable to feed a rapidly multiplying population." This synopsis conflates outcomes with motives and asserts a problematic counterfactual, but it also omits politics, the clash of ideas, cultures, and personalities that drew Eisenhower and Johnson to rural Asia. War and international rivalry were not incidental; they were not only the reason these events occurred but also why they are remembered in this way.[12]

An intrinsically forward-looking enterprise, development seldom has recourse to the past except as a decontextualized model or as a schematic baseline against which to measure progress. But the history of Asia and the United States has a great deal to do with development. Leaders understood the upheavals of the last century as the unfolding of an evolutionary process, and their decisions, made in this frame of reference, had lingering effects. The complex and often invisible bargains that went into the aid relationship dictated how millions would vote, eat, and earn a living. Crucial choices about food and famine became internationalized and removed from local political control, while Asians, at the moment of their emancipation, ceased to be colonial subjects only to become developmental subjects, mobilized, sterilized, and enlightened by foreign experts. The pattern of U.S. and international response to humanitarian crises, especially famine, was set during this period, as were the fundamentals of nation-building and counterinsurgency, which remain the favored strategies for subduing rural threats to the global order. Today, U.S. marines, the latest generation to struggle for Asian hearts and minds, confront the Taliban amid the ruins of irrigation works built in the 1950s by American engineers.

A reexamination of development as a historical influence expands the story of the green revolution in several directions. It begins with the emergence of a worldview in which hunger and poverty were no longer seen as the universal human condition but as a danger to international stability. The campaign to renovate isolated rural societies had specific origins at the start of the twentieth century with the invention of measures of nutrition that made the food needs of whole nations calculable. Through quantitative tools, Americans first perceived a world food problem that could be addressed by science and organization, while Asia's extent and population marked it as the site where new techniques would have greatest effect. By the 1930s, agriculture was the cornerstone of a new style of international welfare economics based on applying knowledge and resources from industrial countries to mitigate the needs of poorer countries.

The global economic crisis lent urgency to this project, but also shifted its priorities. The Roosevelt administration located the origins of the Depression in the isolation of farm communities from a growing city-based consumer economy. New Deal reforms—the Agricultural Adjustment Act, the TVA, and the Wagner Steagall Act—each aimed to restore a lost balance between the country's rural and urban halves. These schemes offered prototypes for agricultural modernization overseas, but foreign fields also served as proving grounds for methods that had fallen from favor in Washington. Mexico's Depression-era experiment with agricultural revitalization, aided by the Rockefeller Foundation, set a new pattern in which Americans would project domestic conflicts over resources, science, and land onto distant settings.

"Modernization," a term that entered the policy discussion in the 1930s, had more than one sense, and the New Deal afforded more than one way to carry it out. Innovation was driven by debates among technocrats over the meaning of progress. The history of development is incomplete without a consideration of these trade-offs and the lost possibilities they contained. Modernizers imagined many attainable futures for Asia, and the alternatives of land reform, community development, TVA-style river valley development, farm-industry integration, and the "new strategy" based on high-yielding varieties of wheat and rice each represented a distinct interpretation of the Asian condition and the goals to be sought. Scientific breakthroughs brought only an ambivalent triumph, not over tradition but over rival ambitions for improving the human condition.

A history of development must, finally, consider the politics of memory through which projects are retrospectively given meaning. The practice of modeling, of translating experience into remedies to be taken from one part of the world and implemented in another, was itself a signal innovation in global planning. References to the Argentine model of floating exchange rates or the British model of socialized medicine represent a style of comparative empiricism indispensable to policy discussions today but largely unthinkable before World War I. It required a relativistic view of human problems that began to emerge at mid-century as American and Soviet advisers sought to translate images of modernity onto the Asian landscape. It is a limiting perspective, blind to local contexts and contingencies; it sees past obstacles but also overlooks opportunities, and

9

it has proven irresistible to leaders seeking certainty in a dangerous world.

Just five years after Johnson's visit, another future president gazed through a car window at an Asian landscape, "brown and green uninterrupted, villages falling back into forest, the smell of diesel oil and wood smoke." Barack Obama lived in a village surrounded by rice paddies and came to know the "empty look on the faces of farmers" when the rains never came and the vagaries of a world that was "violent . . . unpredictable, and often cruel." He saw, from a child's perspective, the futility of his mother's "New Deal, Peace Corps, position paper liberalism," but as president he renewed his country's commitment to the people of poor nations "to make your farms flourish . . . to nourish starved bodies and feed hungry minds." Africa has provided yet another opportunity for the United States to demonstrate what it has learned from a century of experience in confronting hunger. On the eve of his first official visit, Obama proposed to bring the troubled continent a new green revolution.[13]

1

THE WORLD FOOD PROBLEM

The work of measuring just how much food the human race needed to survive began after breakfast on Monday, March 23, 1896, when Wilbur O. Atwater sealed a graduate student into an airtight chamber in the basement of Judd Hall on the Wesleyan University campus. News reports likened the apparatus to a meat locker, a room "about as large as an ordinary convict's cell" lined with copper and zinc, its interior visible through a triple-paned glass aperture. Its occupant, A. W. Smith, took measured quantities of bread, baked beans, hamburger, milk, and mashed potatoes through an airlock during rest periods that alternated with intervals of weightlifting and mental exertion, "studying German treatises on physics and the like." Meanwhile, thermometers, hygrometers and electrically powered condensers, pumps, and fans precisely measured the movement of heat, air, and matter into and out of the chamber. Smith was inside a calorimeter, a device previously used to measure the combustive efficiency of explosives and engines. It recorded his food intake and labor output in units of thermal energy.[1]

The national penny press found a Chekhovian parable in the "Wesleyan glass cage," printing sensational reports on the voluntary captivity of Smith, alternately described as "the man in the box" and "the prisoner of science." On the second day of the experiment, Atwater had to turn away a young New York woman who appeared at the lab asking to be allowed to take Smith's place in the chamber, but despite distractions, the calorimeter's first run was an enormous success, generating pages of data and a $10,000 congressional appropriation to continue the work. The U.S. Department of Agriculture (USDA) built a copy of Atwater's device in Washington, D.C., and Francis Benedict, an Atwater student, persuaded the Carnegie Institute to construct a larger version at Harvard.[2]

Subsequent experiments also attracted keen interest. Atwater locked champion cyclist Nat Butler in the calorimeter to establish "how far a man ought to ride a bicycle on one egg." Wesleyan's football captain volunteered to take his French final inside it to determine the quantum of heat generated by an hour of cogitation. But it was the statistical results—tables that assigned calorie counts to specific foods and tasks—that stirred national controversy and made Atwater a household name. Clergymen applauded the discovery that the body created in the divine image produced energy more efficiently than a locomotive. The Women's Christian Temperance Union organized an anti-Atwater campaign when the lab confirmed that liquor was nutritious (after an experiment in which a test subject was sustained in the calorimeter for six days on a diet "largely composed of alcohol"). But most sensational of all was Atwater's pronouncement that mathematical laws governed the mundane act of eating.[3]

As federal officials recognized, the calorimeter had ramifications for the management of factories, prisons, and schools, as well as the provisioning of armies. It could reduce the cost of rations, and test their suitability for the tropics and for varying conditions of work. Atwater expected an even greater benefit. For the first time, scientists would be able to make exact comparisons between diets of different nations. The need for this kind of statistic was apparent to Secretary of State Elihu Root. In the midst of tense negotiations with Japan in November 1908 he went to Boston for the "express purpose" of seeing the Carnegie calorimeter, which he judged an "invaluable invention." Journalists anticipated that its greatest impact would be on the "Asiatic races" whose improvement could begin by bringing their diet up to an American standard. Economic and social progress in Asia would have to wait for nutritional progress, the *Review of Reviews* observed, because "what can we expect either of physical or moral vigor from communities who live on the physical plane of millions in the Orient?" With a numerical gauge, Americans could begin to imagine the influence to be gained by manipulating the diets of distant peoples. The calorie, Atwater declared, would determine the "food supply of the future."[4]

Before the calorie, the notion that "food supply" could be managed at a national or global level was practically inconceivable. Thomas Malthus, who coined the term, regarded food supply as fixed, an inevitable check on the growing population and wealth of each country. State efforts at agricultural "improvement" focused on the raw materials of imperial trade—tobacco, leather, cotton, sugar, and spices—rather than on locally consumed staples. Americans seized on Justus von Liebig's discovery of plant nutrition to grow more on each acre, but the total *national* capacity remained theoretical because nearly all food was consumed within a few miles of where it was produced. It required the telegraph and the railroad to unify a national market, and even then it was decades before standard weights and grades were worked out. The Chicago Board of Trade, which gained a position as a national exchange in the 1880s, generated a cloud of statistics tracking individual commodities as fluctuating values, bets on future volumes and prices. The calorie offered something more solid. It conceptually rolled all commodities, all farms into one big farm and all markets into an aggregate national or even world market, as if all people were drawing provisions from a single larder. It made the abstract idea of food supply tangible, taking a hypothetical limit on human potential and distilling it into a political problem that had scientific and organizational solutions. The possibility that individuals could systematically regulate their appetites, and that total food production and consumption could be balanced at an international level, awakened Americans to new personal and political obligations. Thanks to Atwater, every schoolchild who refused to eat his peas would be sternly reminded of the starving children in China.[5]

A Global Mission Encoded in Numbers

The concepts of food supply and balance expressed a new consciousness of connections between the physical vitality of other countries—health, living standards, and agriculture—and the security of the United States. The practice of diplomacy had always involved taking stock of material conditions, including diet and agriculture, in foreign lands. Thomas Jefferson, who admired Italian horticulture enough to bring back fruit and grain varieties (using diplomatic cover to purloin seeds), considered European agriculture not to be more evolved but *differently* evolved from that of Virginia. Europeans adapted to a scarcity of land, whereas Americans used land to compensate for a shortage of labor. Commodore Matthew Perry's expedition to Japan collected samples of plants and agricultural implements and took note that markets in Hokkaido offered "neither beef nor pork nor mutton" but mainly "vegetables, and a preparation of beans and rice flour which has the consistency and appearance of cheese." Such exchanges promoted trade and domestic cultivation. Abundance pointed to natural endowments or native skills that might be appropriated; situations of scarcity, being more common, attracted less notice. Touring China in 1878 in the midst of a famine that killed between 8 and 10 million people, former President Grant attributed the catastrophe to an absence of railroads. A growing sense of control over production and consumption, enhanced by technology, lent diet and agriculture a new and sinister significance. Scarcity came to be seen as evidence of societal failure and, after World War I, as a threat to peace. By 1942 "freedom from want" became a war aim, and in the context of the Cold War, Asia's inability to balance its food supply and population became a vital concern for the United States.[6]

While often associated with Malthusianism, the awareness of the "world food problem" that peaked in the 1960s and remains central to international humanitarianism today owes less to eighteenth-century inheritances than to twentieth-century methods of reading the social and physical world by the numbers. Amid the growth (and collapse) of global consumer markets between 1900 and 1950, the arithmetic of standards of living, national incomes, resources, and population gained significance in assessments of the relative status of countries. Increasingly, "development" rather than civilization or power served as the chief gauge of attainment. As articulated by such figures as Albert Beveridge, Sun Yat-sen, and Subhas Chandra Bose, development expressed an ambition to engineer progress on a national scale, and a belief that technology and scientific planning could initiate a historic transformation of timeless agrarian societies into dynamic modern nations. Numbers lent a sense of certainty and method to this process. As imperialism's rigid racial and civilizational hierarchies gave way to a more fluid, universalistic vision of social evolution, statistics provided the only stable ground on which to base theories and predictions. They formalized loose cultural suppositions about the fundamental nature of "backward" societies and the preconditions for modernization. By the interwar years, developmental assumptions guided all aspects of international economic and political relations. Development, according to Herbert Hoover, was the "dominating fact" of the century, a concept that embraced "the whole spiritual, social, and political life of our country and the world."[7]

Memorializing Atwater in 1974, J. George Harrar, president of the Rockefeller Foundation, wrote that the discovery of the calorie mobilized an "informal alliance" of "scientists, farmers, government agencies, educators and processors" with a mission to feed the world. The path

14

from knowledge to organization and action was not nearly so straight-forward, but the calorie did help Americans envisage a world food problem that scientists and diplomats could confront. To be used as a social resource, food had to be detached from customs and tastes. Above all, a plan for the future of food, a picture of what an ideal *modern* food policy would look like had to be imagined. In a century dazzled by the pace of technological change, statesmen asserted claims to legitimacy and authority in the form of formulas for development. The calorie supplied the first half of a formula; the other element was population. A new science, demography, challenged the prevailing idea that population grew in a fixed, geometric curve. With American encouragement, governments around the world came to recognize food and population as controllable variables that held the key to human consumption and reproduction. Progress would be defined as a balance between them.

Numerical indicators prepared the way for a broad consensus on development, jumping linguistic boundaries and displacing local knowledge. The calorie spread quickly around the world. By 1909 Ernest Shackleton was rationing his Antarctic expedition by the calorie. Wherever it went it carried a number of linked ideas. These included a conviction that food was fundamentally uniform and comparable between nations and time periods, that the state had an obligation to assure a "balance" between the supply of food and the dietary needs of the nation, that wheat was uniquely important as an international conveyor of bulk food value, and that the interests of world peace might ultimately require a global food balance rationalized through some form of international regulation. At the time, these ideas did not constitute a policy but only a direction for policy, a notion of which way progress was headed and where the United States could lead.

Official enthusiasm for Atwater's experiments indicated the degree to which the need for an index of food consumption had already been recognized. Before the invention of a quantitative measure, it was difficult to speak of food in competitive evolutionary terms or to foresee the direction improvements might take. While mechanical efficiency could be measured by mechanical means, no scale had yet been devised to assess human fuel. The very notion of efficiency seemed inapplicable to agriculture, which relied on uncontrolled inputs, such as sunshine and rainfall. The "science" of nutrition was largely the domain of vegetarians and iconoclasts such as Horace Fletcher and John Harvey Kellogg, who judged diet by moral and aesthetic criteria. The son of a Methodist minister, Atwater began his

15

nutritional research at Yale in this vein, but graduate work in Berlin and Leipzig introduced him to the chemical and physiological studies of Carl von Voit and Ludwig Max Rubner in Germany and Armand Gautier in Paris. The handful of biochemists conducting dietary observations in Europe in the 1880s formed a scientific avant-garde, working with little official support in the face of skepticism from leading biologists and physicians, but Atwater, on returning to the United States, found industrialists and government agencies eager to fund nutritional research.[8]

Atwater framed his investigations as a tool of "scientific management," allied with Frederick Winslow Taylor's efforts to resolve industrial unrest through the methodical study of time and motion. Labor organizers argued for leisure, meat, and bread as issues of justice, but scientific reformers presented them instead as factors of efficiency and cost. Proceeding from a Taylorist conception of a mechanomorphic body, Atwater led an effort by manufacturers, municipalities, and the federal government to set scientific "standards of living" that could be used to contain wage levels while maintaining a healthy and contented workforce. Between 1885 and 1910, nutritionists conducted more than 500 investigations of the eating habits of inmates of slums, boarding schools, Indian reservations, Chinese railroad camps, and Georgia plantations, but researchers were unsatisfied with their findings. Predictably, unions and individual subjects resisted efforts to locate their wage floor. More disturbingly, the growing pile of surveys documented an almost unclassifiable diversity of food customs, yielding data that only complicated the reformist argument for enforcing norms. Atwater, in collaboration with Rubner and Gautier, began experimenting with a process for rendering food and labor into thermal units.[9]

The need for a standard gauge was evident at the 1893 Columbian Exposition in Chicago. Among the least visited but most impressive exhibits was the Agricultural Building, a glass-domed arcade housing nineteen acres of edibles: French cheeses, Indian curries, Javanese coffees, Greek oils, and an eleven-foot statue of Germania carved from a solid block of chocolate. "In walking through the corridors of this Agricultural Building, the earth and its nations seem drawn up for martial review," commented one juror. "The history of the older nations, the customs of the new, the social status of all, are revealed." But the terms of comparison were unclear. Although exhibit spaces imposed a taxonomic order, the effect on the viewer was of a culinary Babel. Mechanical displays excited "wonder and admiration" for being "more typical of the genius of America," a *New*

York Times reporter noted, the Agricultural Building was more apt to evoke "a strain of idealistic poetry." The raw variety of comestibles impelled exhibitors to identify underlying principles that supported their claims to advancement. The United States backed its displays with statistical charts showing the volume of grain production, while France mounted diagrams tracking the price of bread from 1830 to 1891, and Ceylon illustrated its share of Asian and European tea markets. At Chicago, "the line of triangulation into the future," Henry Adams observed, was measured in units of "power, tonnage, and speed," but in the Agricultural Building the heterogeneity of flavor, color, and custom simply yielded to an equally ambiguous surfeit of numbers.[10]

This metrical handicap excluded food from the turn toward statistical reasoning that was altering social debate in the United States. Americans increasingly digested their information in numerical form. In 1898 the U.S. Bureau of Statistics reformatted its publications to increase their influence and circulation, issuing weekly bulletins instead of annual compilations. The Census Bureau followed suit, releasing serialized highlights from its decennial reports. Official figures only augmented a growing stream of private data. The public learned its risks of accident, typhoid, and homicide from monthly actuarial digests issued by insurance companies. After 1905, gamblers judged horses by the statistical portents in the *Racing Form* and baseball fans sized up hitters by the box scores in *The Sporting News*. Newspapers published an avalanche of statistics evaluating business acumen by quarterly earnings, literature by copies sold, and drama by the number of weeks on Broadway. The metric revolution was nurtured by European *bureaux statistiques* throughout the nineteenth century, but to contemporary observers in the twentieth century this shift toward mass consumption of statistics appeared to be a new and not altogether positive development.[11]

Numerical expression fostered an altered worldwiew both more definite about solutions to complex problems and more attuned to indicators of rising and falling fortunes, especially among nations. Moral and legal argument had lost authority, Princeton historian Winthrop More Daniels remarked in 1902, "today the man of average intelligence . . . has in his mental make-up a numerical frame-work, more or less exact, in which unconsciously the main facts of political and economic geography comfortably pigeonhole themselves." Instead of holding a fixed place in a hierarchy of races and nations, Americans could track their country's movement along a sliding scale of humanity on any number of axes of advancement. Carroll D. Wright, a Labor Department statistician, noted that "it is nothing rare for a public man to ask an official statistician to give him offhand the average wages paid in the United States or the wages paid in half a dozen designated countries, or to state in a few lines the criminal conditions or . . . the cost of producing various articles in different countries." Official discourse consisted in such comparisons, which defined problems and ranked the severity of commercial and military threats. Many observers considered quantitative reasoning a modern and distinctly American trait. "If the English are a nation of shopkeepers, Americans are a nation of expert accountants," critic and playwright Eugene Richard White observed. "We go about reforming and purifying the world with a committee report at elbow and a statistical compilation in each hand."[12]

The calorimeter translated the vernacular customs of food into the numerical language of empire. Atwater revolutionized nutritional science, as historian Hillel Schwartz observes, by theorizing food "without reference to taste, ethnic tradition, or social context," but he changed his field in other ways, too. Under his direction the emergent discipline of nutrition left its descriptive, reformist roots and became a quantitative, technocratic specialization. Where diet experts had formerly directed advice at individual patients, they now studied whole populations at the behest of the state. Their terms of analysis adapted to the new calculative logic; the critique of working class diets receded, and the notion of an "American diet" to be compared with other national diets assumed prominence. The calorie lent food a conceptual coherence and established boundaries and hierarchies that defined it as a social object. Atwater's schedules ranked grain, meat, and dairy goods as important national resources; while fruits, leafy vegetables, and fish registered such slight nutritional value they could scarcely be classified as food. Tea, coffee, and spices, on which whole imperial systems had once flourished, had no value at all.[13]

The calorie represented food as uniform, composed of interchangeable parts, and comparable across time and between nations and races. In 1911 C. F. Langworthy, who succeeded Atwater as head of nutrition investigations at the USDA, compiled surveys undertaken by missionaries and ethnographers into a ranked list of the peoples of "each country and each epoch" on a scale of daily caloric consumption, with the "native laborer" of the Congo at the bottom (2,812 calories) and the American athlete at the top (4,510 calories). Challenging dietary theories of racial difference,

18

Langworthy stressed that the human diet was far less diverse than had formerly been thought. Broken down into chemicals, the potatoes and cheese that fed the Irish laborer were identical, except in quantity, to the rice and ghee that nourished an Indian coolie. The central component in every diet was nitrogen, the element that lent "energy value" to meat, milk, and wheat. The thermodynamic theory of nutrition superseded whole systems of colonial knowledge of "useful plants," native diets, and tropical nutrition. Langworthy could also reassure Americans that their nitrogen-rich diet was the "finest food supply of any country in the world."[14]

Treating societies as closed systems, nutritionists suggested that a "physiological economy" of food governed institutions and nations, and that "scientific eating" based on caloric "bookkeeping" would increase national efficiency. Langworthy and Atwater identified "balance" as characteristic of a progressive diet, and enumerated several ways that personal and market behavior could be modified to square the food ledger: Individuals should balance physical exertion and caloric consumption; meals should balance luxury proteins against necessary carbohydrates; and economic policies should match supplies, on the basis of calories, to the needs of populations. As a measure of *optimization,* the calorie represented a significant advance over the kinds of statistics used since the eighteenth century. Officials had searched tables of tax receipts, birth rates, harvests, mortality, and crime for natural laws and constants that would serve as foundations for policy, but the calorie revealed a wide discrepancy between "natural" behavior and the ideal balance that might be achieved through social regulation. As Atwater and Langworthy never tired of pointing out, people of all classes and educations ate the wrong things in the wrong amounts, and neither the appetite nor the market could accurately assess needs. So while nineteenth-century statistics guided and limited the state, the calorie went further. It authorized government to tell people what was best for them.[15]

Calories presented a thin simplification of nutrition better suited to gauging large populations than to guiding personal habits, as physicians repeatedly pointed out. In 1917 the American Medical Association warned against the "unwise domination" of the calorie in the popular mind, but its use persisted through the enthusiasm of advertisers, who emblazoned calorie counts on cereal boxes and instructed consumers that "calories measure food energy the same as dollars measure money." The federal government also eagerly seized the calorie to fill a need for statistical information on consumption. After war broke out in Europe, speculative runs on commodities and food panics in major U.S. cities revealed the inadequacy of both the market and official knowledge. The Agriculture Department needed to balance Europe's requirements against the danger of domestic scarcity, but as the secretary admitted, it had no information on which to base such judgments. "Where the food supply is located, who owns it, what may be the difficulties of securing it, whether the local market conditions are due to shortage, whether there can be artificial manipulation or control, no one can state with certainty." Combined with censuses, caloric tables could be used to estimate rations for cities, armies, or even nations. Military rather than hygienic necessity made the calorie an international standard measure of food.[16]

Under pressure of war, the successful marshalling of food consumption and production became a state responsibility. American observers paid anxious attention to the warring powers' use of blockades to starve their adversaries to defeat. Using calories as a gauge, war correspondents assessed the offerings of restaurants and meat markets and the content of soldiers' rations. The *New York Times* suggested that Germany, with its ports sealed, represented a closed chamber within which national energy and food production would have to balance. When a group of American engineers organized a massive food drive for occupied Belgium, they turned to the "science of dietetics" which, newly rescued from "the hands of vegetarians and other extremists, seem[ed] at last to have arrived upon solid ground." The commission calculated purchases and rations on the basis of calories, which it considered "almost the only thing to be considered" in managing famine relief. As U.S. supplies became critical on both sides of the Western Front, Europeans learned to calculate food by American numbers.[17]

In the United States, mobilization for war began in 1917 when President Woodrow Wilson created a national food authority under the leadership of Herbert Hoover, a mining engineer and chief organizer of the Belgium relief. From his headquarters at the Willard Hotel, Hoover launched a drive to conserve sugar, fats, and grain for export to the front. Administrators took immediate steps to expand the cultivation of wheat, "by far" the most essential commodity because of its portability, abundance, and destabilizing potential. Dry and calorie dense, wheat could "stand shipment" better than other staples. Despite a poor 1917 crop, "our stock of wheat offered the largest supply of calories available from any single raw food material," officials noted. More importantly, riots in American cities and Hoover's own experience in Belgium confirmed that bread shortages led to unrest. The "industrial classes" especially valued wheat as an affordable luxury and consequently "bread affects the morale of a people more quickly than any other food." European governments had long recognized this requirement for domestic order, but Hoover stressed its symbolic and practical ramifications for U.S. strategy. In the midst of war, he told his staff, "the wheat loaf has ascended in the imagination of men, women, and children as the emblem of national survival and national tranquility."[18]

In Hoover's view, the net outflow of 20 million bushels would leave a morale deficit in the United States that could only be filled by social discipline. Over the heads of striking farmers and protesting millers and bakers, Hoover appealed to his "police force—the American woman" to enforce wheatless Wednesdays and flourless "victory meals." As an instructional tool, the calorie was indispensable for setting rations, identifying substitutes, and defining the self-control expected of citizens. "You should know and also use the word calorie as frequently, or more frequently, than you use the words foot, yard, quart, [or] gallon," instructed one guidebook, "Instead of saying one slice of bread, or a piece of pie, you will say 100 calories of bread, 350 calories of pie." Consuming surplus calories amounted to "overeating" which sapped personal and national efficiency. Manhattan restaurants helpfully listed calorie counts next to each item along with the recommended quantities for each "walk of life."[19]

The conscription of individual appetites disturbed conventional distinctions between public duty and personal conduct. Leading churchman Lyman Abbot disparaged calorie counting as "spiritual hypochondria," while another critic complained that "formerly the highest science known to eating was to be able to balance green peas on a knife," but Hoover deployed "higher mathematics . . . to order your lives and grub." An unnamed Philadelphia poet lampooned the specter Hoovering over every American hearth:

An' all us other children when our scanty meal is done,
We gather round the fire and has the mostest fun
A-listnin' to the proteins that Herbie tells about
An' the Calories that git you ef you don't watch out![20]

Historians have described the enduring effect war rationing had on perceptions of diet and body image, and social theorists have associated the emergence of modern sovereignty with a move from "wholesale" methods of policing to "retail" forms in which individuals internalize state demands as rules of personal behavior. Hoover summed up the point in the slogan "centralize ideas but decentralize execution." He stressed an intimate connection between the "test" of bodily discipline and the trials facing the nation during the war emergency and after. Personal dietary sacrifice indicated the United States' arrival at a "stage of development" at which it was prepared to "protect its own institutions and those of Europe." Russia had never attained that stage, he argued, "and the result has been a massacre." He urged Americans to seek "victory over ourselves; victory over the enemy of freedom."[21]

Hoover defined food as both a core vulnerability in the international order and an instrument of U.S. influence. Food Administration experts created a ledger of global food resources and caloric requirements and shortly before the armistice, Hoover informed Wilson that the United States would have to undertake relief efforts in forty-five nations "if we are to preserve these countries from Bolshevism and rank anarchy." Britain and France continued the blockade after the armistice, but U.S. officials, with Hoover in the lead, pressured them to lift it. The new American Relief Administration (ARA) then poured food through every German port. Hoover's men took control of telegraph offices, ports, and railways. Allied and enemy governments received aid on equal terms, and the ARA dealt even with Bela Kun's Soviet regime in Hungary while U.S. agents conspired to overthrow it. Distinctions between enemies and allies offered only temporary security, Hoover insisted; ultimately, resources and distribution would make the difference between war and peace, order and revolution.[22]

In defining security, Hoover rejected traditional balance-of-power concerns as well as Wilson's reliance on international law and world opinion. Among the earliest proponents of a strategic concept that linked security to welfare, he located the germ of future wars in mass resentments incubated by scarcity. Material abundance reinforced stability, he argued, but "famine breeds anarchy. Anarchy is infectious, the infections of such a cess-pool will jeopardize France and Britain, [and] will yet spread to the United States." Hunger and unemployment "will not be cured at all by law or by legalistic processes," he warned, nor by nationalism or Bolshevism, although desperate populations would take up radical creeds. To forestall war, he believed, the United States would have to provide, in example and theory, an alternative route to progress, a progress measured by increases in standards of living.[23]

Hoover disdained the "indescribable malignity" of Paris, often feeling alone in his conviction that safety could not be assured by treaties, plebiscites, or borders. But he was not alone. Influential delegates, including leading socialists and economists, shared his hope for a peace based on social and material improvement. British economist John Maynard Keynes and French planners Jean Monnet and Albert Thomas advocated planned production and consumption as an alternative to the instability inherent in the prewar laissez-faire economy. European labor unions and industrialists hoped Taylorist and Fordist methods might quell class conflict. But Hoover seemed more interested in defining an exceptional mission than in finding allies. He sought to position scientific management as a uniquely American answer to Leninism.[24]

The appeal of radical doctrines, he believed, lay in their ability to explain the mystifying peaks and valleys of twentieth-century civilization. The marvels of capitalist industry—airplanes, instant communication, modern chemistry, and the assembly line—promised, at first, to link the world together in prosperity, but then threatened to destroy it. Vladimir I. Lenin, the Marxist theorist who seized control of Russia at the head of the Bolshevik Party, predicted more crises to come and pointed to laws of history and economics that accounted for the cyclical fortunes of capitalism. Hoover set out to define an "American substitute" for "these disintegrating theories of Europe." His *American Individualism* (1922) laid out a stage theory of history, modeled on Marx, but culminating in an era of "high pitch" mass consumption. Transitions between Hoover's phases were marked, not by crisis, but by innovations in cooperation. He looked to developments in social engineering to "enable us to synchronize socially and economically this gigantic machine which we have built out of applied science." Techniques of social optimization—such as advertising, standardization, market research, and dietetics—would harmonize wages, production, consumption, labor, and health. More importantly, they converted the Bolshevik's violent demands for peace, land, and bread into a neutral statistical language of entitlement. Optimization opened pathways to progress that bypassed the developmental dead-ends predicted by Marx and Malthus. Poverty represented not the crisis of capitalism but the open frontier of the market without limits. In the modern age, security would rest on an ability to dominate the strategic terrain of global consumption. "There

23

are continents of human welfare," he affirmed, "of which we have pene-
trated only the coastal plane."[25]

Hoover's vision played on enduring myths of American benevolence and
regeneration, but the red scare and the congressional revolt against the Versailles settlement momentarily dulled enthusiasm for schemes of global
management. In popular and official discourse, however, the notion of a
global food supply linked to America's future security had assumed a permanent place. Calories added a measure of certitude to assessments of current threats or dangers farther off, in Asia or in the distant future. A national conference on world food supply convened by the American Academy
of Political and Social Science noted that accurate estimates of how many
people could be sustained by the potential agricultural capacity of the earth
could now be made. Within decades, the delegates agreed, a balance would
have to be regulated by a system of international rationing. A 1925 survey
by Agriculture Department economist O. E. Baker estimated the outer limits of global wheat production and suggested two possible futures for the
United States: its population could stabilize at a "Chinese" standard of diet
by the end of the century or it could use the intervening grace period to
voluntarily check population growth.[26]

The global calculus shifted attention away from the conflict zones of
Europe and toward the vast concentration of population and resources
in Asia. Halford Mackinder, the founder of geopolitics as a field of study
and policy, predicted that dominance in the coming century would belong to the power that could command the allegiance of the horse-men,
plow-men, and camel-men of the Eurasian "Heartland" stretching from
the Vistula to the China Sea. Russia and Germany were likely contenders, but a U.S.-China alliance was also a possibility. In a widely discussed
1930 study, John Lossing Buck, who conducted the first caloric surveys
in China, explained that China's farming patterns were the reverse of the
United States'. The "pressure of population" compelled peasants to practice an intensive agriculture that produced a larger number of calories
per acre, chiefly in the form of grain. In the United States, a meat-based
diet supported expansive farming patterns that used technology to compensate for inefficient land use. As land grew scarce, Buck predicted, Americans would farm and eat more like the Chinese, and as China modernized,
American technology would allow cultivators to reap more from their tiny
plots.[27]

The theme of a natural partnership between American engineers and
Chinese peasants reached a broad audience through Pearl Buck's 1931

best seller *The Good Earth*. Buck's husband's tabulations outlined in broad terms an agenda for joint action: preserving China's food balance would ultimately require "some method of population control," but a short-range solution could be found in "more intensive methods of raising crops." By the interwar years, the narrative components of what would later come to be called the "green revolution" were already circulating—the imperative of balance, the centrality of Asia, and the solutions offered by intensified grain production and birth control—but it was unclear how such an agenda could be put into motion. Those arrangements would be worked out not in the halls of government but by a private foundation.[28]

The Elements of Progress

The newly organized Rockefeller Foundation was one of the first backers of Hoover's Belgian relief, and in the interwar years it institutionalized its own version of welfare internationalism. Much like the calorie, the foundation arose from an impulse to use scientific expertise to contain and steer progressive reform. In 1911 John D. Rockefeller's Standard Oil Trust had been broken up by the courts into thirty-four hugely profitable corporations. Rockefeller owned substantial shares in all of them, but no longer having a direct hand in management, he turned his attention to philanthropy. He endowed Spelman College in Atlanta and built the University of Chicago into a leader in medical research. He was concerned about his public image, but he also deplored what he saw as a trend toward "radical and ill-digested legislation, and thought and speech." The foundation would be a way of displaying his generosity and "setting forth the best modern thought" on social problems. The foundation has been fairly characterized as a guardian of corporate interests and as a scientific auxiliary of the federal government, but neither description fully captures its unique preoccupations with globalism and technology. In the interwar years, it specialized in managing connections between international security, science, and social change that would remain outside of official and commercial discourse until the Cold War era. Rockefeller's first concern was not to feed the world but to cure it. Assembling a group of leading doctors in his Manhattan office, he asked them to name "a disease affecting large numbers of people" with a cure that remained unavailable solely for want of funds. The dramatic success of the hookworm campaign was followed by campaigns against malaria, tuberculosis, and yellow fever that stretched from the Yucatan to the Gobi Desert. From the outset, it displayed a formidable global reach along with a capacity to "solve" pervasive problems through large-scale applications of scientific resources. Just a few years after it was chartered in 1913 with an initial endowment of $125 million, the foundation directed operations on six continents from its headquarters in New York.[29]

Frederick Taylor Gates, the Baptist minister charged with designing Rockefeller's "plans of world benefaction" described his task as "studying civilization, its origins and history, trying to analyze it, separate it into its elements, and find out as best I might, in what human progress really consists, and in what ways progress is to be promoted." Branching out into education, hygiene, labor, agriculture, and security issues, foundation officials saw their mission as addressing underlying sources of social turmoil, and they developed an in-house understanding of this special category of problems. The guiding principles of Rockefeller giving stressed avoiding merely ameliorative projects and attacking the "root of individual or social ill-being and misery." Fundamental conditions—deprivation, disease, ignorance, instability—were "international in character," connected to evolutionary forces of industrialism and social change too complex for any one nation to control, but nonetheless manageable through planned scientific interventions. Foundation officials viewed "applied science," particularly medicine, as a catalyst for the spread of problem-solving aptitudes, but they viewed progress as neither linear nor inevitable. The outbreak of World War I and the global influenza pandemic that struck just as the foundation was declaring success against infectious disease, reinforced apprehensions that civilizational decay, even collapse, remained possible unless human needs could be properly managed.[30]

In its early years, the foundation developed protocols for administering progress that stressed statistical inquiry and the cultivation of institutions and personnel. It directed grants toward efforts to standardize international measurements, to replace local knowledge with what one trustee referred to as "a body of substantiated and widely accepted generalizations as to human capacities and motives." The starting point of any project was a survey to distinguish the "local background" from generic, and presumably global, norms and goals. The investigating mission aimed next to identify men and institutions with "reliable" (that is, statistical) knowledge, as well as the professional and political clout to direct official attention toward a problem that could be conclusively and dramatically resolved. Symbolism was important. The resulting projects, cures, and reforms did not amount to progress themselves but only to models of

26

the techniques by which progress might be achieved. Foundation officials designed their investments to represent a pragmatic problem-solving mentality they believed would accelerate human advancement. President George E. Vincent valued hookworm because "the disease can readily be used as a means of educating the public in the possibilities of preventive medicine," and the Pasteur Institute for its "demonstration of organized team-play" in the heart of Paris. Displays of this type would convert governments and publics to the managerial, rationalistic worldview that offered the only salvation from conflict and social atavism. The foundation's most important work, a commentator suggested, was its "demonstration that mankind, when properly organized, can dominate its environment instead of being enslaved by it."[31]

The foundation's practices—its accent on measurement, demonstration, and conversion—refined the motifs of official discourses on development. Measurement was the principal innovation of interwar diplomacy, which consisted in setting calculable relations between powers: ratios of warship construction, quotas on immigration and trade, currency rates, and reparations. The practice extended to standards of social well-being, and as the chief creditor nation, the United States took the lead in developing new indexes of growth. "Our latest symbol is not the big stick," the New York Times diplomatic correspondent wrote in 1929, "but the irrefutable and passionless yardstick." But while momentum could be gauged by a steady accretion of value, the impulse for progress was more often regarded as a kind of conversion experience, a wholesale adoption of an instrumental, scientific outlook. The characteristic of "modern civilized peoples," according to economist Thorstein Veblen, was their capacity for "impersonal dispassionate insight into the material facts with which mankind has to deal." Anthropologists and ethnographers at the Rockefeller-funded University of Chicago were among the first social scientists to use the term "modernization" to describe a link between processes of urbanization, literacy, secularization, and reproduction. In a pivotal 1930 study of a Mexican village, Robert Redfield noted that modernization was fundamentally a cognitive, even spiritual event. On seeing a new technique or artifact demonstrated for the first time, a peasant "develops a correspondingly new organ, a new mind." Over the next two decades the problem of modernization would move to the center of academic debate, but while social scientists spun their earliest hypotheses, the Rockefeller Foundation already had practical experience with the ironies of modernization.[32]

The most influential single figure in shaping the foundation's ambitions was Raymond B. Fosdick, whose approach reflected his vocations as reformer, internationalist, and moralist. Born in Buffalo, New York, the son of a liberal high school principal, he inherited his parents' progressive politics. At the age of nineteen he transferred from Colgate to Princeton to study under Woodrow Wilson, a relationship that launched a career as a municipal crusader and then as an aide to General John Pershing at the head of the expeditionary force in France. In the nine months between the signing of the Versailles treaty and the Senate's rejection, he served as undersecretary general of the League of Nations, the only American to hold the position. Working alongside Sir Eric Drummond of Britain and Jean Monnet of France, Fosdick sought to "humanize" the Versailles system and win congressional support for the League by displacing balance-of-power politics with "a systematic approach to international problems where everybody has everything to gain and nothing to lose." License for this "new technique" of international activism was contained in League articles 23 and 24, which authorized international commissions for disease prevention, opium control, transit, and weights and measures. These "non-political" functions would create an organization that could address the root sources of international conflict by adjusting systems of labor, migration, production, and consumption. "It is not boundaries or indemnities, but food and coal and health, which concern the League authorities," Fosdick explained. They had the task "of discovering and applying the remedial measures necessary to keep a shattered world alive."[33]

Fosdick left the League when the Democrats and the treaty went down to defeat in 1920, but his groundwork had a lasting impact. Beginning in 1925, the League Health Organization and the International Labor Office (ILO), headed by Albert Thomas, initiated a series of national nutritional surveys based on the Atwater method. By 1935 the League had set a global dietary standard of 2,500 calories per day for a laboring adult. Like the eight-hour day advocated by the ILO, this represented an unenforced, unlegislated ideal, but it set a benchmark for school lunch programs, famine relief, and wage comparisons around the world. To Thomas, this represented a radically new way of conducting the world's business. The process of debating and fixing uniform social standards threw "into relief the common ideal to which we are all advancing" and established a common vocabulary for supranational governance.[34]

Fosdick returned to New York in 1920 and transferred his agenda to the philanthropic sector, presiding on the boards of all of the Rockefeller charities before assuming the presidency of the foundation in 1936. He shared Hoover's dark view of the potential for civilizational unraveling in the face of scarcity and inflammatory ideologies, although his familial experience (his brother, the renowned Protestant clergyman Harry Emerson Fosdick, fought a losing battle against fundamentalism in the 1920s) gave him less assurance that rationality would prevail. A persistent theme in his writing and stewardship was "cultural lag," the failure of human intelligence to keep pace with the disruptive tempo of technological change. Paradoxically information-rich and knowledge-poor, industrial society was in danger of being overwhelmed by the runaway capacities of physical science. Despite an outward triumphalism, Fosdick warned, Americans were "wandering in heartbreaking perplexity, swamped with the paraphernalia of living, weighed down by mountains of facts, trying to find some sure way out of this jungle of machinery and untamed powers." Restoring cultural balance, he judged, urgently required compensating advances in "the science of man," the natural and human sciences that would enable social engineering of a scale and ambition to match twentieth-century feats of physical engineering.[35]

To Fosdick, the world food supply presented an immediate opportunity for a demonstration of the type of world-scale scientific reform he had in mind. Innovations in measurement already allowed the identification of areas of surplus and deficiency, while Hoover's experience provided a practical model of how it could be done. In a commencement address at the University of Iowa in June 1924, he espoused a generational mission to "take stock of our planetary resources . . . to develop the method by which the population of the globe can best be sustained." The most pressing project was "the matter of the world's food." There was no immediate scarcity, nor did he subscribe to Malthus's theory of an inevitable limit. The newly acquired knowledge of the world's food supply gave Americans a moral obligation to act. "Through modern statistics we are able, in our generation, to get a complete picture of supply and demand in relation to the world's food," he explained. Modern censuses covered enough of the globe to allow a rough estimate of the total population—1.6 billion—as well as the rate at which it was rising. By joining national censuses with figures on food output and number of calories required, a statistician could work out a practical plan of global distribution. "The field has been surveyed and the factors are known," Fosdick told the class of 1924. "What we need now is synthetic thinking, constructive brains, and a plan, laid down in world terms."[36]

The Iowa speech signaled a shift from the foundation's traditional concentrations on medicine and education toward a widening arc of "science of man" initiatives related to agriculture, nutrition, biochemistry, and human reproduction. Foundation funds endowed Elmer V. McCollum's studies at the Johns Hopkins School of Hygiene, which set international standards for measuring vitamins, minerals, and amino acids. McCollum recognized that the absence of these micronutrients induced disorders such as pellagra, rickets, and beriberi, even in subjects receiving adequate calories. His discovery of "malnutrition" elevated dietetics to a level of clinical accuracy Atwater had unsuccessfully sought. New investments went into collecting social data, refining techniques of comparative statistical analysis of races and nations, and developing the Pacific islands as "racial laboratories" for the study of primitive societies. The International Education Board created an agriculture division in 1924 that poured grants into plant breeding, farm demonstration, and fellowships in Europe, Mexico, and China. Fosdick directed a thorough reorganization of the Rockefeller charities in 1927, consolidating agriculture and nutrition programs within the foundation's Natural Sciences Division (NSD). A particular focus was China, where the NSD funded rural extension projects through Nankai University and created a National Agricultural Research Bureau in Nanjing. The quantitative logic of the food supply made China an obvious choice. The foundation followed the numbers.[37]

The economic slump that deepened into the Great Depression hit first and hardest in the rural areas of the world, particularly in the single-crop regions—the Nile cotton belt, the coffee highlands of Brazil, Australian sheep stations, the cane fields of the Ganges plain—economies vulnerable to fluctuations in demand or currency values. In the colonial and semi-colonial half of the world, the industrial crisis was experienced as a farm crisis, often accompanied by droughts or floods, disasters amplified by neglect of the land. The economic emergency challenged the legitimacy of imperial regimes built around commodity exchanges that were drying up. To compensate, Britain reformulated its imperial project around a mission of development and welfare known as the dual policy. It would be an early test of social scientific expertise as a tool for maintaining dominance amid social turmoil. The successive hammer blows of Wilson's Fourteen Points, the Russian Revolution, and price deflation made it imperative, according to Sir Keith Hancock, to lend "positive economic and social content to the philosophy of colonial trusteeship by affirming the need for minimum standards of nutrition, health, and education." The dual policy, which accorded equal weight "to European enterprise and native development," adjusted colonial policy to meet an upsurge of nationalist agitation as well as the requirements of an emerging empire-wide consumer economy. The British viceroy in India cracked down on the Congress movement with one hand while promising a more responsive administration and rising living standards with the other. The restoration of mass production in the home economy required reliable outlets for the branded toiletries, appliances, and canned goods issuing from assembly lines, and the colonies contained Britain's largest sales territory. Reimagining subject populations as customers opened new possibilities and goals for imperial development.[38]

Official investigations into native health suggested that improved diets might enhance the labor efficiency and buying power of rural populations. In a pivotal 1927 study, Robert Boyd-Orr found that the "meat, milk, and blood" diet of Kenya's Masai produced more energy and a stronger physique than the largely vegetarian cuisine of the Kikuyu, and the same year Lt. Col. Robert McCarrison, who studied under McCollum at Johns Hopkins, confirmed the "remarkable difference in physical efficiency of different Indian races" owing to variations in diet. Imperial officials now recognized formerly tolerable rates of disease and mortality as "a heavy drag upon prosperity," while raising living standards could stimulate "demand for food, clothing, and every form of manufacture." Dietary statistics identified areas of deficiency and guided investment. Nutrition was thus critical to the implementation of the dual policy, the key to the linked problems of public health and agricultural revitalization. It gave British officials a broad injunction to plan the "development" of India's markets, agriculture, and social services in the name of health.[39]

Mohandas K. Gandhi and other Indian nationalists recognized that food planning furnished an expansive justification for Britain's continuing stewardship. Gandhi explicitly placed diet at the center of nationalist resistance, categorically challenging universalist claims inherent in the calorie and espousing the importance of unquantified "physical and spiritual values" in each food as well as the singularity of appetites and health of individual human bodies. Polished rice, starchy and vitamin deficient, turned out by "these hideous rice mills" represented the empty abundance of mass production. In crafting a link between diet and nationalism, Gandhi used food as a potent symbol of the value of the particular, the local, and the individual under assault from homogenizing logic of science and the market.[40]

An influential faction of Congress leaders, however, embraced science and the market, and seized the initiative from the British by drafting their own development plan. A national planning commission, chaired by Jawaharlal Nehru, began work in October 1938. Subhas Chandra Bose, president of the Congress, directed the commission to give special attention to the problems of poverty and "increasing population." The subcommittee on population, headed by Radhakamal Mukherjee, assembled figures showing that while the population was 25 percent larger than in 1915, the food supply had grown only 10 percent, leaving a deficit of 42 billion calories, or in human terms, 42 million "average men" without food. Having statistically disproved Britain's claims to stewardship of public health, the commission laid out the "features of a progressive planned food supply," beginning with a shift from export crops, such as cotton, tea, and jute, toward soybeans, peas, and "the more esteemed cereals," rice and wheat.[41]

The founding document of what would become the United Nations (UN) Food and Agriculture Organization (FAO) was the 1936 report of the League commission on nutrition, a compilation of research on nutritional requirements, dietetic surveys, and policy comparisons. Reading it today, it is difficult to see why this abstruse document inspired such editorial enthusiasm. Its findings were "little short of revolutionary," according to the *Spectator*, a sober-minded London weekly. For the *New York Times* the commission had laid bare "the challenge underlying the disorders of this epoch, the pretext for modern wars." The power of the report's message was conveyed less by the official prose than by a juxtaposition of three categories of numbers previously considered in separate contexts: figures on the minimum caloric requirements for mothers and children, per capita consumption of food in various countries, and total volume of food produced. The parallelism implied ("irrefutably," commentators agreed) an intimate connection between the crisis of agricultural overproduction in some countries and the problem of malnutrition in others, or in Australian delegate Stanley Bruce's celebrated phrase, "a marriage of health to agriculture."[42]

The nutrition report was the first venture in international Keynesianism. League officials noted that it broke with the production-centered prescriptions followed since Adam Smith and presented an entirely new agenda for "consumer economics." Intensified national efforts at food self-sufficiency coupled with an international push for food redistribution would spearhead a demand-driven expansion of global trade. Decreeing a universal entitlement to 2,500 calories per day, the report noted that advances in statistics made it possible to predict "the probable increase in demand which would follow on the adoption of an optimum regime of nutrition." The gains were potentially huge; Asia, for instance, could easily absorb surplus stocks of milk and wheat that the United States, Canada, and Australia were destroying to shore up farm prices. Moreover, the commission anticipated, transfers would provide a durable solution to instability. Because shortfalls were not episodic but chronic, food transfers would carve out permanent new markets and channels of trade, the commission anticipated. "Generally speaking," the report found, "most Chinese are in a state of malnutrition all of the time."[43]

Ideally, the "marriage" could halt the grim triage going on in the rural districts of the industrial countries. In Nebraska and Oklahoma, government men were buying cows for $16 each and then shooting them on the spot. The goal was to eliminate 8 million cattle, and get them off the market, in order to keep beef prices from sliding further. In England they were killing pigs, and in Brazil dried coffee beans were shoveled into the boilers of locomotives. In every country that once exported wheat, farmers now sold their grain to the government. The overhang—13 million quintals in France, 40 million bushels in Argentina, 200 million bushels in Canada, 240 million bushels in the United States—sat in silos and grain elevators with no buyers and no foreseeable buyers. Governments had agreed not to dump the surplus on the world market, but if it could be given away free to a demonstrably undernourished country—as what would later be called concessional, or "tied" food aid—the costly subsidy schemes could be justified as a sacrifice for world peace.[44]

Britain's Parliament hailed the strategy as a subtle assault on economic nationalism that could win over both the Germans and the Americans. Hitler was unresponsive, but the United States lent increasing support out of a conviction, urged by agriculture secretary Henry Wallace, that optimizing consumption in low-income areas of Latin America and Asia could solve the economic crisis. As the dangers of war grew more immediate, President Franklin D. Roosevelt restated the link between food and open door trade as the third of the Four Freedoms, "freedom from want, which, translated into world terms, means economic understandings which will secure to every nation a healthy peacetime life for

33

its inhabitants." The construction of a postwar order began with food. In 1943 the administration gathered seventy-seven nations to institute the first component of a new UN system, the FAO, with the aim of balancing mass production against the "mass buying power" of the world's farmers. Atwater's "food supply of the future" had become a political reality.[45]

Quantification only partly explains why hunger management suddenly became an issue for high-level statecraft. Coupled with a modernizing agenda (welfare internationalism) and a framework of interpretation (Keynesianism), food came to be seen as a tool for managing processes of change on a global scale. Although nearly every demarcated territory had a census by the end of the nineteenth century, and although an international movement of scientists and reformers had tried to draw attention to the issue, no similar consensus emerged around the issue of population. Four international conferences between 1927 and 1931 failed to reach agreement on whether humanity was reproducing too quickly, too slowly, in the wrong places, or with the wrong quality. As long as population figures remained a source of uncertainty, rather than a tool for managing uncertainty, they had little political utility. But in the two decades between 1930 and 1949, new theories of demography radically revised the strategic meaning of population growth. Census figures could be read—alongside figures on the harvest—as vital indicators, potential determinants of growth, instability, or war.[46]

Rescuing Malthusianism from Malthus

If reflections on food in the future tense could inspire alternating premonitions of revolutionary contagion and global consumerism, the subject of population excited even more vivid forebodings. When the 1930 U.S. census indicated for the first time a sharp decline in the white birth rate, and censuses throughout industrialized northern Europe (but not agrarian eastern and southern Europe) produced the same disturbing result, experts were able to forecast an assortment of equally plausible trends: racial decline, shrinking markets, rising wages, decreasing crime, increasing crime, softening international tensions, and resurgent militarism. Swedish economist Gunnar Myrdal noted that although the revival of the population question was likely to "dominate our whole economic and social policy," no area of economic thinking was more fraught with fundamental disagreement. Analysis of population figures was constrained by an

34

eighteenth-century language of natural laws and limits out of tune with the twentieth-century concern for scientific efficiency. Economist A. B. Wolfe attributed the failure to develop a theory of *optimal* population to the "stranglehold which the Malthusian logic had on the thought patterns of the orthodox economists." To analysts of the new Keynesian school, trends portended a "disastrous" drop in demand unless domestic and foreign consumption could be stimulated by planned interventions; "we have another devil at our elbow at least as fierce as the Malthusian," Keynes observed, "namely the devil of unemployment." The link between fertility decline and the Depression seemed more than coincidental, and economists wrote in uncharacteristically elegiac tones of the days when census and production figures moved upward together. John R. Hicks concluded his 1938 text with "the thought that perhaps the whole Industrial Revolution of the past two hundred years has been nothing else but a vast secular boom, largely induced by the unparalleled rise in population."[47]

Fear of a baby bust stimulated a search for conceptual tools for interpreting population dynamics. Members of the Population Association of America, an organization of birth control advocates, eugenists, anti-immigration activists, actuaries, and statisticians founded in 1931, could agree on the need for a science of population but on little else, not even a name for the new discipline, alternately called demometry, human ecology, larithmics, or population biology. The Rockefeller Foundation took the lead in developing demography as a profession, separating it from nativism and eugenics, and elevating it to the level of an international policy science. A pivotal figure was Frank Notestein, whose theory of demographic transition, formulated in the early postwar years, provided the first reliable index of modernization. But an earlier, less-noted figure illustrates the difficulties the foundation faced in reducing population dynamics to "widely accepted generalizations" of practical use to policymakers.[48]

The foundation aimed to transform census-taking from a national function into a practical tool of international social engineering. Its first venture was the Scripps Foundation for Research in Population Problems at Miami University in Ohio. Warren Thompson, a respected sociologist with a reputation as "America's best-known Malthusian," directed Scripps and led U.S. delegations to League conferences on world population in the interwar years. In *Danger Spots in World Population* (1929) and updated editions in 1943 and 1946 he sketched out a model for forecasting conflict based on the relative reproductive energy of nations grouped into three categories: high-fertility, high-mortality "C" countries; high-fertility, low-mortality (therefore rapidly expanding) "B" countries; and stable, low-mortality, low-fertility "A" countries. For Thompson, the critical scarcity was not food but land. Population pressure exerted itself spatially through inexorable forces of migration and territorial expansion rather than economically through consumer demand. Lasting peace, he argued, could be assured only by forced contraception and adjustments of imperial borders in favor of "dynamic" B nations such as Italy, Germany, and Japan. Thompson equated the professionalization of demography with the introduction of objective statistical methods, but his deterministic model left diplomats with little room to maneuver. By 1939 *Danger Spots* earned him a reputation as a modern prophet, but authorities on foreign policy naturally resisted conclusions that lent scientific legitimacy to Axis conquests.[49]

Until population came to be seen as an indicator of possibility and risk rather than a constraint, it seldom intruded into policy discussions. The press's agitation over population trends barely disturbed policymakers' focus on immediate geopolitical and economic worries. Roosevelt's only reaction to the census report was to quip that Southern senators would soon have to cater to the "descendants of the sharecroppers" who would hold most of the ballots in the South. On a strategic level, diplomatic officials recognized population and fertility differentials as exacerbating but not determining factors in conflict, particularly in Asia. Henry L. Stimson, who served Hoover as secretary of state and Roosevelt as secretary of war, characterized the Far Eastern crisis as a confrontation between "overcrowded Japan" and China's "great sluggish population," but judged that the outcome would depend on which side could employ its political program, organization, finance, and technology most effectively in Manchuria. As they watched a succession of disasters unfold in Europe and Asia, Roosevelt and his advisers had little use for single-variable forecasting or indeed prediction of any kind. "Up until last summer I was willing to make mental bets that such and such a thing would happen and such and such a thing would not happen," the president said in March 1939, but with nations collapsing across the globe he was less inclined to play the odds. A new awareness that borders and distance had been annihilated by modern technology reinforced the conclusion that the international system had lost its linear logic; distinctions that once separated local from global issues, social problems from security risks had been erased. In the emerging view, dangers came not from the steady accumulation of social pressures, but from unpredictable convergences—of psychology, economic distress, technology, and military opportunity—which with modern velocity would enflame small conflicts, render large states passive, or forge coalitions capable of projecting power across continents and oceans.[50]

The Rockefeller Foundation, too, was adjusting to an era of radical uncertainty. In 1939 a series of studies on defense problems concluded that U.S. postwar security would require, at minimum, holding an area comprising the entire British Empire plus the Far East and South America. Meanwhile, executives in New York watched helplessly as foundation programs in China and Europe disappeared behind fighting fronts. Fosdick was particularly disturbed that foundation-funded intellectuals in Germany eagerly took part in "the progressive disintegration of creative scholarship." It was dawning on foundation executives that the vectors of modernity they valued for solidifying world order—communications, research, technology—could also accelerate the drift toward chaos. The Medical Division, for example, agonized that its malaria and yellow fever eradication efforts were opening areas in the deep tropics to commercial activity, thereby releasing locally contained pathogens, such as the West Nile virus, into the global population. Fosdick worried that health programs in nations such as India only intensified overpopulation, meaning that "the result of our work is merely to substitute one form of death for another." Hidden and automatic—in the foundation's terminology "underlying"—processes could nullify effort or even turn benevolence into unintended catastrophe.[51]

Demography gained policy authority by abandoning prediction in favor of analyzing these dimly understood processes of change. Beginning in 1935, the Office of Population Research at Princeton, directed by two economists, Notestein and Irene B. Taeuber, and supported by the Milbank Memorial Fund and the Carnegie Institute, trained a generation of demographers who would have far reaching influence on government policy, including Dudley Kirk, Ansley Coale, and Kingsley Davis. The Princeton demographers elaborated on an approach first explored by Louis I. Dublin and Alfred J. Lotka in the statistical office of the Metropolitan Life Insurance Company. Rather than concentrating on fertility and mortality as binary variables, they positioned population within a spreadsheet of social indicators—incomes, education, distribution, socioeconomic status, and a host of psychological and political factors—and looked for patterns, an approach that reflected their own uncertainty about the processes they were exploring.[52]

Changes in demography reflected an important theoretical shift affecting all the social sciences in the years before World War II. Where scientists had formerly sought to simplify problems by reducing them to one or two variables they now used analytical methods capable of handling dozens, sometimes thousands, of factors. Warren Weaver, the new director of the NSD, observed that probability theory and new statistical methods mounted "an attack on nature of an essentially and dramatically new kind." Scientists tackled complexity, investigating the dynamics of large systems with a combination of uncertainty and confidence. "We did not know whether to be worried about overriding population growth or incipient population decline," Notestein later recalled, "but we were quite sure that we should be worried." As Princeton emerged as a center of research and training, the Rockefeller Foundation became its principal benefactor. Fosdick arranged for the League of Nations Economic Office to relocate to Princeton and the two statistical offices became a locus of postwar planning, developing extensive studies of population in Europe and Asia, and refining a distinctive, probabilistic methodology.[53]

Rather than straight-line trends, Notestein stressed potentialities stemming from still-undefined relationships between fertility, mortality, and a mix of determinants loosely connected to modernization: education, sanitation, food supply, political awareness, income levels, and industrialization. Differential fertility could neither be pegged to intrinsic racial characteristics nor repaired by contraception, but was rooted in "the different interests, values and motives of a changing culture." His articulation of transition theory, first publicly formulated in 1944, fit neatly with the style of realist thought emerging in the diplomatic and defense community. It offered clues for reading an inherently illegible international environment, suggesting ranges of possibility and points of potential influence, and invited policymakers to supply courses of action. Transition theory held that a sharp drop in death rates indicated the onset of modernization, as urbanization and improvements in health care took hold. A decline in birth rates followed, but more slowly because the requisite psychological adjustments—growing individualism, a consumerist outlook, and changing functions of the family—contradicted customs and religious codes deeply rooted in agrarian, traditional societies. In the transition be-

38

tween "premodern" and "mature" stability, population would grow dramatically, such as in Europe where it tripled in a single century. Notestein suggested a range of possibilities for Asia, from the "European" transition that appeared to be under way in Japan, to an "Oriental" pattern, evident in India, where mortality decline was not accompanied by either urbanization or cultural change, leading to a steep growth in the rural population that could only be checked by "repeated catastrophes." Demographic evolution should be viewed as an indicator, a variable, or a check on related processes of economic and social evolution.[54]

Transition theory released policymakers and foundation officials from a stark choice between dismissing population as an imponderable or building plans around dark mechanistic assumptions. Notestein dismissed natural laws and inexorable trends and suggested ranges of population outcomes that depended on policy choices in the future. Dudley Kirk, who left Princeton to become the State Department's first official demographer in 1947, explained that transition theory rescued malthusianism from Malthus. Where once "the writings of demography were filled with the dangers of overpopulation" they could now present "a re-evaluation of the relationship between population growth and economic development in the modern world." Weaver observed that it was now possible to transcend "limited" approaches "picturing all mankind as necessarily starving to death some years hence" and speak instead of the "possibilities" available through science.[55]

Foreign policy officials immediately grasped the new demography's value for assessing the highly contingent policy environment of the early Cold War. When the Foundation organized a "reconnaissance" of population in Asia known as the Balfour Mission in 1948, W. Walton Butterworth, the assistant secretary of state for the Far East, gave Notestein and Taeuber specific instructions on contingencies he wanted investigated. Butterworth was concerned about the American forward defense line in the "island fringe" of Southeast Asia, a region plagued by insurrection and fragile governments, but he had other concerns as well. The success of the Marshall Plan hinged on continued importation of rubber, cotton, and other plantation crops from Java and Malaya. The United States could either break the colonial trade patterns or restore them, but either choice would have ramifications for population growth and in turn affect economic and political stability on either or both of the two containment fronts. Butterworth solicited Notestein's opinion not merely on population problems but also on trade, agriculture, and the strategic situation, using demography as a tool of analysis.[56]

Within that analysis, improvements in agriculture gained new functions and importance. Because high fertility derived from practices, incentives, and customs associated with "the agricultural way of life," Notestein stressed that contraception could offer no effective check on population growth without the reorientation of values that came from urbanization. The Balfour Mission visited occupied Japan and Korea, coastal footholds of China still held by the Guomindang, the newly independent Philippines, and parts of Indonesia that the Dutch were struggling to control. For most of the survey area, particularly the vast Asian interior, no actual population counts, current or historical, could be found, but through sampling (substituting Taiwan for the whole of China, for example) the mission could map the dynamics of growth with a semblance of precision. On its return, the State Department's most urgent questions related to "whether there is any hope for reduction of the growth potential of the overpopulated Asiatic countries." Taeuber noted that although little effect could be expected from urbanization in overwhelmingly rural Asia, the motivations of peasants could be changed through social engineering. Education, legal rights for women, and especially "an improvement in agricultural techniques" could produce the instrumental outlook necessary to lower the birth rate. Notestein stressed that simply boosting production would only set conditions for scarcity at a higher level of population. Development should aim instead to modify attitudes. He recommended a structured program of industrial, legal, and social advancement coupled with crucial steps to improve rural conditions through irrigation and crop improvement, a process he called "balanced modernization."[57]

A subtle but discernible difference between the way Notestein, Taeuber, and Butterworth used the word "development" and the concept that Hoover or Fosdick wrote about marked an expansion of American ambition in the wake of military victory. Rather than a contingent process unfolding in history by its own rules and on its own schedule, "development" by 1948 had acquired a transitive meaning, as a procedure performed by one country upon another. In the emerging context of imperial disintegration and U.S. economic and technological predominance, it made sense for Notestein to prescribe a developmental regimen for all of Asia and for State Department officials to weigh plans for managing the historical transition of a continent. This reconceptualization had profound implications for the practice of foreign relations. Truman's Point

Four address in 1949 made modernization an instrument of Cold War strategy. The evolution of economies, social relations, and the natural environment would advance policy goals. This transitive sense appeared first in numerical language: demographic theory presented development not as Hoover saw it—as a "force which dominates the whole spiritual, social, and political life of our country"—but as a force the United States could dominate and use for its own ends.[58]

The histories of the calorie and demography tell us several things about the influence of quantification on developmental thought. The ideals of modernization were embedded in the numbers from the outset. Originating in a nexus of social reform, science, and public administration, the calorie encapsulated notions of food as a reserve of national energy, a salve for revolutionary discontent, and a gauge of civilizational status. Likewise, demography designated human fertility as a barometer of the psychological awakening to modernity. The distinction between objective quantitative needs and orientalist assertions is far less clear than might be supposed. Numbers cannot be regarded as the reality against which human agency is explained, but instead as an expression of the intentions and assumptions of historical actors. But they were not *simply* an expression. Just as revisions of accounting rules affect corporate behavior, new metrics changed the calculus of development. Where the improvers of the nineteenth century valued quantitative maxima (units of "power, tonnage and speed"), twentieth-century modernizers favored coefficients of optimization and efficiency, numbers gauged against other numbers. Demography and nutritional science identified progress with the rational organization of resources rather than the pursuit of outer limits. This carried the debate beyond Malthus. It also encoded an ecological sensibility into modernizing projects, an isolation of problems into contained spheres ("the agricultural sector"), a rejection of uncontrolled change, a search for equilibrium. Numbers drew attention to the importance of balance—between deficits and surpluses, industry and agriculture, population and food—implying that parities were natural and desirable and that unmeasured factors were extraneous.

To a substantial degree, the agenda for postwar development had already been set before anyone defined the specific strategic problems it was to address. The postwar baby boom had not yet shown up on censuses, and the Cold War had not yet begun. Atwater's vision of a rationalized food supply, Hoover's link between welfare and security, Buck's yearning for a partnership of American science and Chinese husbandry, Fosdick's concerns about imbalance between industrial and social capital, and Notestein's expectation that technology would adjust peasants' psychology (and birth rate) would all reappear as developmental themes in the coming decades. In the 1940s the Rockefeller Foundation assembled these elements into a program that aimed to transform the economy of one country, Mexico, as a staging area for the conquest of hunger in Asia.

2

MEXICO'S WAY OUT

Raymond B. Fosdick chose Mexico as a laboratory for "synthetic thinking" on the world food problem mainly because of war in Europe and Asia. It nonetheless proved a fortuitous setting. Mexico had already invested in agricultural training and research, and the war would make its farm economy a major supplier to U.S. industry by furnishing rubber, hemp, quinine, and other vital war goods. The foundation's offer of help was welcomed, and in July 1941 three Rockefeller Foundation scientists rendezvoused at the Plaza Hotel in Laredo, boarded a green Chevrolet Suburban, and drove across the international bridge to begin a month-long, 5,000-mile "reconnaissance" of Mexican agriculture. The journey of the "three ancients"—Elvin Stakman, Paul Manglesdorf, and Richard Bradfield—was the beginning of the Mexican Agricultural Program (MAP). Years later it would be regarded as the starting point of a worldwide agricultural transformation.

The Rockefeller program has been described as a response to fears that Mexico's population was outrunning its food supply. A 1961 documentary opens with aerial shots of a dark, teeming Mexico City "adding half a million people a year." The narrator adds up the dismal disparity between poor harvests and large families. "No hay sufficiente," he concludes. "There isn't enough." In 1972 Rockefeller executive Kenneth Thompson explained why the MAP was so widely copied around the world. It unfolded like a well-run experiment, first defining "a clear, evident, and identifiable problem"—the food/population gap—then building consensus around a "sharply focused" solution.[1]

The foundation and the U.S. government had many identifiable problems in Mexico in 1941, but a food/population gap was not one of them. Mexico exported food—including live cattle, vegetables, bananas, and coffee—to the United States, and the U.S. Department of Agriculture

(USDA), which surveyed foreign markets, deemed Mexico "largely self-sufficient" in food and fiber. Its population had been stable from 1910 to 1930 at roughly 16 million. The next census, which would not be published until 1943, would show an increase of 4 million, but Mexico was still less densely populated than the United States. The "ancients" reported that there were fewer inhabitants per square mile, but they were poorly clad and housed, illiterate, and inadequately nourished, giving Mexico "many of the aspects of an over-populated land." Their observation hinted at the real reason for the foundation's interest; Mexico epitomized, in their view, a type of backwardness that could be found throughout the colonial areas of the world. Solutions worked out there could be transferred to countries with similar "aspects" in Africa, or Asia. Mexico was to be a model.[2]

In the 1930s Mexico came to represent an ensemble of problems that were both particular to its postrevolutionary condition and ubiquitous throughout the unindustrialized world. Its reportedly stagnant agriculture, incipient violence, stoic peasantry, overpopulation, and feeble central government merged into a syndrome that defined national poverty as a strategic problem. Roosevelt administration officials saw Mexico as a preindustrial space in which they could build an idealized New Deal, minus the imperfections of the original. In the 1940s, as wartime spending fueled an economic revival, Mexico presented a successful formula for surmounting problems of agrarian change. It embodied a transformation from bucolic tradition to urban modernity that other countries on other continents would soon experience. This generic view of foreign backwardness might be called orientalist, but although nineteenth-century stereotypes persisted, the figurative Mexico evolved in response to New Deal innovations in science, economic policy, and diplomacy. Its adaptations were later projected onto the rice and wheat fields of Asia. Mexico was a surrogate for a category of nations we now call the Third World.

MAP staff were aware they were creating a prototype. From the start their research vision looked past the local circumstances before them toward distant, universal challenges. "We were consciously, and very early—we were doing it consciously—discarding those things that fit only one environment," Norman Borlaug later explained. "This was fundamental to being able to move thousands of tons of seed produced in Mexico to areas halfway around the world." After only two years, the foundation predicted that "the Mexican experiment will point the way to similar opportunities in other parts of the world." By 1950 it was recognized as "a blueprint for hungry nations," a prototype for the U.S. government's Point Four initiative and the Ford Foundation's modernization projects in Asia. In 1953 John Foster Dulles cited it as "the type of thing" that the United States should use to pacify the countryside in Indo-China.[3]

Models are a form of selective forgetting. When an analyst refers to the Taiwan model of export-led development or the Chilean model of monetary reform, history is displaced by a capsule narrative, part fact, part fiction, designed to convey a formula for development. Context and motives are stripped away, leaving an image of outside experts isolating problems and then introducing sharply focused solutions. What actually happened in Mexico was something different. Neither the problems nor the solutions were obvious at first. The project matured initially in the context of two great national renovation schemes—the New Deal and Lázaro Cárdenas's agrarian reforms—and later in reaction to war and the looming Cold War. Goals and techniques were not imposed from on top or determined by trial and error, but arrived at through collaboration, accident, and turns of events. What this history suggests is that the lessons of Mexico might have pointed to an entirely different course of development for Asia. The Malthusian agenda the model came to represent was a product of the foundation's anxieties for the future, rather than its hard-won experience. The model's script papered over the MAP's original design for a Keynesian green revolution, based not on increasing food supply but on raising incomes and living standards for farmers. It also suggests that the methodical, scientific sequence Thompson admired—problem, hypothesis, experiment, solution—was actually reversed. Development advisers in Mexico began with solutions and worked through a process of experimentation toward a suitable problem.[4]

In the late 1930s it was not hard to find agricultural scientists willing to leave their professional posts in the United States to go to Mexico. Although theirs was among the first of the sciences to receive systematic federal support—through land grant colleges and experiment stations—by the 1920s the field's conspicuous success had damaged its prestige. Revolutionary advances in disease control and Mendelian genetics yielded an abundance of bread and meat, fueling the consumer economy of the cities but depressing prices and land values in the countryside.

No one was more acutely aware of the agricultural scientist's dilemma than Elvin C. Stakman, a plant pathologist at the University of Minnesota. As a USDA researcher in the 1920s he had read news stories celebrating

"strengthened" wheat prices caused by an epidemic of stem rust, a disease
he had built a reputation for fighting. Rust was the nemesis of the plains
wheat grower, a fungus that waited until the farmer brought the crop
nearly to maturity before shriveling stalks into a blackened tangle of decay.
Using aircraft, Stakman discovered its deadly, brick-red spores wafting
16,000 feet over Oklahoma, carried on winds from the central Mexican
plateau. An ornamental shrub, the barberry, common throughout the
United States and Canada, sheltered the parasite in winter and released it
for a fresh season of devastation. Stakman's discovery of the continental
ecology of wheat diseases led to an international campaign, sponsored by
Pillsbury Flour Mills, to eradicate the barberry, and then to schedule regular inspection tours of Mexico to identify emerging rust varieties. He
viewed agricultural research as an international mission, a biological cor-
ollary to the Good Neighbor policy. But when barberry legislation reached
Congress in 1932, Rep. Miles Allgood of Alabama pointed out that disease
control only helped farmers produce more and earn less. Wheat had bene-
fited more than any crop from mechanization and scientific breeding. Before World War I, U.S. output never approached 800 million bushels, but
in the 1920s it rarely sank below that figure, and nearly a quarter of the
stock went unsold. Congress, Algood suggested, should fund a program to
"disseminate this disease that comes from these bushes throughout the
wheat district."[5]

More than other disasters of the Depression, the rolling crisis of agriculture shook the national faith in free markets and technological progress. With encouragement from university and federal experts, farmers
had aggressively expanded wheat, corn, beef, and pork production in the
1920s, only to watch, in the wake of the Wall Street crash, as plummeting
prices rendered their crops worthless. Observers linked the industrial collapse to the decline of agriculture. Deserted farms, overcrowded cities, and
a widening gap between factory and farm wages symptomized the decay at
the rural foundations of national prosperity. Addressing a conference of
party leaders at French Lick, Indiana, in 1931, New York's governor, Franklin D. Roosevelt, attributed the Depression to "the dislocation of a proper
balance between urban and rural life." While population and wealth concentrated in the cities, the productive heartland was abandoned and neglected. Opening his bid for the presidency, he maintained that rebalanc-
ing farm and factory required more than Hoover's emergency measures; it
called for "something deeper and far more important for the future—in
other words state planning."[6]

The disintegration of the farm economy seemed to confirm Roosevelt's diagnosis. In 1932 half a million farmers across the Midwest went on strike, blocking highways with felled telephone poles, destroying grain and milk, and pledging to "sell nothing" to the cities. Across Kansas, Nebraska, and the Oklahoma and Texas panhandles a five-year drought created a new desert, a "dust bowl." Federal investigators blamed the disaster on modern factory agriculture and the overextension of wheat growing into arid regions. Yielding to the artificial demands of urban markets, growers had failed to recognize that nature was "essentially an organism" rather than a machine, an organism that could exact a terrible retribution. Witnessing a Great Plains sandstorm, reporter Ernie Pyle was appalled by the "stupendousness of it. You can see the whole backward evolution into oblivion of a great land, and the destruction of a people."[7]

The Depression clarified the gap between the requirements of industrial production and rural values. Market logic parodied the myth of hardy individualism; ingenuity and hard work were repaid by diminishing returns and, ultimately, catastrophe. The anthropologist Robert Redfield, who coined the term "modernization" in his seminal study of a Mexican village, noted that U.S. agriculture's "problems are a function of our bigness, our rapid change, and the extension of urban characteristics over large parts of our nation." The complex division of labor had led to a breakdown of the "moral understandings" that governed an intrinsically primitive occupation. Federal efforts to contain the crisis through an improvised system of subsidies and production limits exposed the underlying paradox; while government hired urban workers to build bridges and libraries, farmers were paid to destroy crops.[8]

Roosevelt began his presidency, according to brains truster Raymond Moley, with a focus on "the central problem of agriculture—the paradox of scarcity in the midst of plenty." He identified the lack of rural purchasing power as the economy's main weakness, and he sought to promote rural industries, electrification, and managed prices to boost incomes. The first major legislative act of the New Deal equipped the agriculture secretary, Henry A. Wallace, with emergency powers. Chairman of the Pioneer Hi-Bred Corn Company and editor of the nationally distributed *Wallace's Farmer,* the new secretary personified the brand of innovative, science-based agribusiness whose possibilities had been cut short by failing markets. Together with David Lilienthal, director of the Tennessee Valley Authority (TVA), and Harold Ickes, who as interior secretary supervised forestry, conservation, and public works, Wallace espoused a rural-based agenda for national recovery. Rationalized planning of supply and consumption would replace the arbitrary dictates of prices and demand. In the first 100 days the Agriculture Department was an idea factory, churning out proposals for school lunch programs, credit schemes, and food relief. Wallace cultivated policy with scientific thoroughness. He "thought in exact quantities," Rexford Tugwell observed, "and his mind moved outward to the enlarged consequences of small facts."[9]

A New Deal for the World

Although his initial moves were ad hoc, Wallace gradually formulated an analysis that located the sources of the Depression in the problem of confining expanding markets within national borders. He identified industry, labor, and agriculture as competing rather than complimentary sectors. Artificially contained by the disappearance of empty lands, they preyed on each other, each seeking a larger share of resources and profit. The great modern ideologies—imperialism, fascism, and communism—offered alternative ways to suppress the market's centrifugal tendencies through expansionism or regimentation. The United States could follow suit by controlling internal production and demand, or it could join with other countries and manage economic expansion on a global scale "to balance our productive forces to the kind of world we want to live in." This meant exporting the New Deal's vision of rural reconstruction. Data showed that Europe, with its declining populations, could never absorb the U.S. surplus, but systematic efforts to expand "foreign purchasing power" in Latin America and Asia could stimulate a long-term revival. International development would be particularly important for the future of science, for until foreign markets could absorb expanding production, the public would demand "a halt in technical progress until consumption catches up."[10]

Until they could find a new use for their talents, the paradox of plenty condemned agricultural scientists to irrelevance. Wallace denounced laissez-faire incentives that made "a mockery" of efforts to "free mankind from the fear of scarcity." There was a "grave danger," he warned, "that our great body of men trained in the agricultural sciences, already standing by and discouraged with inadequate tools and operating funds with which to work, will become disrupted and scattered to other tasks." The Department of Agriculture faulted the discipline for its own marginalization. "Overspecialization" and an "erudite isolationism" had encouraged "distrust of scientists and the popular tendency to deride 'fool professors' or to ridicule 'scientific cranks.'" For the practitioners of scientific agriculture, the university offered no respite. Despite Minnesota's reliance on farming, the state university shortchanged agricultural science, even denying "cow college" students the scholastic honors of cum laude and summa cum laude.[11]

Stakman defended his discipline's economic value and claims to scientific standing by positioning agricultural research as an essential bridge between the physical and social sciences. "Botany is the most important of all sciences, and plant pathology is one of its most essential branches," he declared in 1937. Humanity's fundamental dependence on agriculture for food, resources, and trade situated the discipline literally at the root of all social problems. Scarcity had "far reaching sociologic and even political implications" that required "a deeper and more widely diffused sense of obligation to science" on the part of the public. He warned audiences already alarmed by events in Europe and Asia of the moral duties imposed by the pressure of human numbers against world resources. Norman Borlaug, an undergraduate up from Iowa on a wrestling scholarship, first heard him speak in 1938. He was struck by Stakman's ability to link the study of plants to the looming world crisis: "Science, diseases, food, population, world hunger, all were interwoven." Despite the poor job prospects for plant pathologists, Borlaug and J. George Harrar, a graduate student from Oberlin, elected to study under Stakman. Additional students came from overseas, through the auspices of the Rockefeller Foundation. As with medicine, demography, and other client disciplines, the foundation used grants to agricultural research to professionalize the field and redirect it toward the investigation of international problems. Stakman joined the natural science division as an adviser in the late 1930s, and when a proposal for Mexico came forward he seized the chance to demonstrate what agricultural science could do.[12]

Josephus Daniels began lobbying for foundation aid soon after he was posted to Mexico as U.S. ambassador in 1932. As publisher of the Raleigh News and Observer, he had written about Rockefeller hygiene and educational work in his native North Carolina. He was convinced that the foundation could offer a measure of economic guidance the embassy was in no position to give. In 1938 President Lázaro Cárdenas had expropriated American-owned agricultural lands and oil fields. His move to enforce Article 27 of the 1917 constitution produced an outpouring of public passion; thousands rallied in Mexico City's main square, the Zocalo, in support of nationalization. But the seizures locked diplomacy into a fruit-less cycle of property disputes just as Mexico launched social reforms that would dramatically affect the terms of its relationship with the United States. Despite the confrontation, Daniels and U.S. officials preferred Cárdenas over the rightist and leftist *caudillos* who periodically threat-ened to reignite revolutionary violence. Sporadic insurrections invariably originated in the countryside, and U.S. officials identified agriculture as the part of Cárdenas's program most critical to his political survival. Irri-gation, rural outreach, village health programs, and the organization of peasants into self-sufficient communal *ejidos* were elements of a *cardeni-sta* program to assimilate indigenous communities into the national pol-ity. Daniels proposed a broad initiative, incorporating foundation exper-tise in public health and education as well as agriculture, in support of Cárdenas's efforts to win over the peasantry and prevent Mexico from becoming "another Spain."[13]

Mexico offered a set of developmental problems at once foreign and familiar. Cárdenas's administration overlapped with Roosevelt's first two terms in office, and Daniels was one of many observers who drew paral-lels. The emphasis placed by *el FDR mexicano* on technocratic manage-ment, deficit financing, and systematic reform of health, labor, and agricul-ture struck both the administration and its critics as the first application of the new U.S. economic program in a foreign setting, and in the wake of the Spanish Civil War, ideological debates about liberalism's future increas-ingly revolved around Mexico. The Foreign Policy Association identified it as a capitalist answer to the Soviet experiment, while Frank Tannenbaum, a Brookings analyst, appraised the agrarian movement as a moderate ver-sion of "the general series of phenomena which includes the Turkish, the Chinese and the Russian revolutions."[14] Cárdenas, according to the *New York Times,* was inventing a nationalist economy favoring "a new group of small capitalists on farms."[15]

In policy debates Mexico appeared as a harbinger of the New Deal's destiny. Cracks in liberalism's façade widened after 1935, and the advo-cates of planning and redistribution, including Ickes, Lilienthal, Wallace, and Harry Hopkins, increasingly found their initiatives blocked by a conservative "Gladstonian" faction within the administration who urged a moratorium on regulation and a recommitment to free trade and the sanctity of property. These included Jesse Jones, the conservative Texan who led the Commerce Department, as well as three top officials at the State Department, Cordell Hull, Sumner Welles, and William Clayton. To

Wallace, Mexico was a testing ground for a new liberalism of abundance, a political third way between communist and fascist extremes, while for Hull, *cárdenismo* only illustrated statism's inexorable tendency toward mob rule.[16] He denounced confiscations and "suicidal" attempts at regulating consumption and output, even as Wallace acclaimed Mexico's program as a mini–New Deal that "backward countries" could emulate.[17]

To Americans who traveled, read, or went to the movies in the 1930s, Mexico was the prototypical backward country. Mexican westerns such as *Viva Villa!* (1933) and *Juarez* (1939) cast Mexico as mythic space into which filmmakers projected the eternal struggle to build a modern civilization from imperfect human material. The Pan American Highway, completed between Laredo and Mexico City in 1936, opened an escape route for tourists deterred by war clouds in Asia and Europe. A popular guidebook reassured travelers there was no need to cross an ocean to find the attractions "of the cold north and the lower tropics; of Persia, India, Arabia, Spain, and the Holy Land."[18]

Americans discovered in Mexico a baseline against which to gauge their modernity. At the turn southward from Texas 96 onto the Pan American Highway, "the swift-moving mechanized patter of a modern society gives way to a simple, less regulated, earlier stage of development," observed Ernest Gruening, editor of *The Nation*. Downshifting for the ascent into the Sierra Madre, the motorist traveled "backward also, through the long reaches of the past." The indigenous inhabitants, he explained, were "original Americans" preserving traditions of craft and artistry "rejected and neglected by us." Americans in the 1930s devoured Stuart Chase's bestselling travel diary and flocked to Abby Aldrich Rockefeller's touring collection of Mexican folk art. Chase, the economist who gave the New Deal its name, positioned the two countries as mile markers on a timeline of industrial evolution: the United States as "the outstanding exhibit of the power age" and Mexico as "the outstanding exhibit of the handicraft age." An ultimate solution to the ravages of the business cycle, he proposed, might be found in a merger of old and new cultures.[19]

The Mexico of imagination was fixed in an hour of emergence, an eternal morning into which Americans could project their own aspirations for renewal. Mexicans, wrote John Steinbeck, "live in the long moment when the past slips reluctantly into the future." But it was a fragile state, made even more precarious by the intrusion of Yankee Buicks and the daily Sunset Limited from Los Angeles. The irresistible pull of consumerism and the vast market just across the border could be felt in the remotest pueblos.

For well or ill, the *New York Times* warned, the time had nearly arrived when "the 'sad indian' has thrown away his oriental mask of resignation" and "become an occidental man with bourgeois ambitions."[20]

Roosevelt administration officials had more immediate concerns about the precariousness of the Mexican experiment. Cárdenas's expropriations had disrupted production and stoked unemployment and labor unrest. Chronically short of funds of every category—tax revenue, exchange reserves, and investment capital—the government relied on oil sales to the German and Japanese navies to stave off default. J. Edgar Hoover's persistent reports of Axis and Soviet fifth columnists heightened the general alarm. Senator Martin Dies found "incontrovertible evidence" that German engineers had laid out twenty-six secret airfields along the border. The approaching end of Cárdenas's term in 1940 touched off a succession crisis and revived religious and regional frictions. The urgency of shoring up hemispheric defenses grew acute after France collapsed in May 1940. Administration officials shelved their differences, offered to dismiss the outstanding property claims, and sought ways to solidify relations. Roosevelt moved to shore up Mexico's cash reserves by purchasing Mexican silver. He appointed Nelson Rockefeller to direct efforts against Axis propaganda in Latin America, and as a goodwill gesture dispatched Wallace, now vice-president-elect, to attend the inauguration of Cárdenas's successor.[21]

Mexico's capacity to withstand the threats of revolt and Axis subversion depended, many observers warned, on the success of the *ejido* experiment in domesticating the Indian majority and revitalizing the Mexican countryside. In his first four years, Cárdenas moved decisively to realize the demands of the Revolution, seizing private estates and distributing more than 15 million hectares to nearly a million landless families. Eventually half of Mexico's agricultural lands, much of it previously untilled, would be parceled out to village communes known as *ejidos*. Petroleum revenues paid for schools, irrigation canals, clinics, tractors, credit, pumps, and teams of researchers and advisers for communities that had previously had little contact with the government. Despite the confiscation of U.S. properties, the goal of acquainting rural Indians with scientific progress attracted sympathetic interest in the United States. John Steinbeck's film *The Forgotten Village* dramatized one pueblo's struggle to banish ancestral superstition and accept the authority of expert technicians. Daniels compared the land reform to the TVA, which had brought the civilizing energy of electricity into remote pockets of the rural South. *Ejidatarios* were "the stabilizing influence," noted *The New Republic*. "A sufficiently great proportion of peasants have been given land to serve as a bulwark should the crisis become desperately acute. . . . There can be no retreating from the land reform without causing chaos and disaster."[22]

Few doubted the potential for chaos. Diagnoses of the Mexican condition highlighted the social gulf separating the showy European civilization of the cities from the overwhelming majority of destitute, armed peasants who demonstrated by sporadic raids on railroad junctions and tourist caravans that they could control the countryside whenever prompted by their own mysterious inclinations. "Violence seems just around the corner," George Kennan worried during a visit to the Mexican capital. "The city sleeps the uneasy sleep of the threatened animal, and its dreams are troubled." To American liberals, the *ejido* symbolized a reconciliation between urban elites and a resentful peasantry. Redfield's studies and Steinbeck's film depicted the Indian's emergence as an epic journey from the village to the city. Encounters with hospitals, skyscrapers, and machines instilled a changed mentality, "a new mind." The diffusion of urban habits and ideas would contain indigenous aspirations within approved bounds. "Millions of dispossessed men and women" would be rooted "in organized, autonomous communities served by federal banks," Waldo Franks told readers of *Foreign Affairs,* while Mexico's elites would learn techniques of social justice. "The constellated life of the Republic, by economic law and national psychology, must obey the 'natural law' of the *ejido*."[23]

U.S. officials considered the small peasant-owned plots and communal commons less efficient than the commercial haciendas they replaced, but they recognized their primary value in socializing the peasant and curtailing Mexico's dependence on European capital. The land reform was "highly important," Nelson Rockefeller explained. "Under the ejidal system, profits, though less, stayed in and were spent in Mexico. The financial structure is considered an important experiment in exploring solutions for the world-wide agrarian problem." The *ejido* served as a vehicle for inculcating the profit motive and drawing peasants into medical and educational programs under government auspices. Recent historical accounts have eulogized it as a lost alternative to commercial agriculture, but American observers saw the difference as mainly a matter of scale. After a crucial tutelary phase, they expected communal properties to be parceled out among *ejidatarios* as homesteads, creating a class of competitive small producers whose incomes and consumption would feed an expanding network of retail and social services.[24]

As concerns about security grew, U.S. observers paid closer attention to the agrarian program, regarding the *ejido* not as the end point of a revolutionary struggle (or even a violation of property rights) but as a tenuous opening toward an industrial future. They shifted terms of evaluation as well, judging it as a temporary expedient rather than as a settled feature of the Mexican polity. Foundation officials drew their understanding of Mexico's agrarian politics from an authoritative study, *The Ejido: Mexico's Way Out,* by Eyler N. Simpson, a University of Chicago dean. Simpson forecast an impending "break-down of the folk culture" accelerated by film, radio, the automobile, and the tractor. The *ejido* would serve as an indispensable tool for managing change and introducing peasants to new habits of work, consumption, and clock time. He portrayed Mexico as a neutral terrain ideal for social experimentation, a "clear and unencumbered" ground without the "vested interests and antiquated institutional structures" that beset planners in industrial countries. Sharing Roosevelt's concerns about the balkanization of space in an industrial economy, he sought a middle way between urban congestion and bucolic poverty. "Properly conceived and developed" *ejidos* would grow into balanced farming and manufacturing villages interlinked by highways and power lines, creating an economy both spiritually fulfilling and resistant to fluctuations of the business cycle. Simpson aimed his research at revising the agenda of land reform to discount the goals of subsistence and village autonomy and urge instead faster capital accumulation through increased productivity. This seminal study introduced a number of narrative conventions that would later typify the branding of a development model, associating a social innovation—the *ejido*—with a widening circle of problems (rural unrest, cultural disintegration, congestion, economic collapse) while narrowing the criteria of evaluation to a single gauge. The measure of the *ejido*'s success would be its "performance" measured in the production of commercial crops.[25]

The Mexican Century

Wallace made security and agricultural productivity the twin motifs of his extended official visit in December 1940 on the occasion of the inauguration of Manuel Ávila Camacho, Cárdenas's handpicked successor. The vice president told reporters his ulterior goals were to investigate the "association known as an 'ejido'" and to keep Hitler from "starting anything on this continent." The visit was risky. Rioters, allegedly incited by fascist provocateurs, stoned the official motorcade, and Wallace was eventually flown out of Mexico City after an assassination threat. Nonetheless, it was choreographed to set a tone of folksy neighborliness. Wallace drove his own car from Washington, D.C., and newspapers in both countries tracked his progress across Tennessee and Arkansas. Briefly reported missing after an ice storm outside Dallas, he reappeared in Laredo and crossed the international bridge trailed by a carload of photographers. Crowds stretched for two miles along the highway at Monterrey, where Wallace paused to inspect factories and pick up the new secretary of agriculture, Marte Gómez. When the cavalcade was stopped by a rockslide in the Sierra Madre, the vice president joined soldiers in hefting boulders over the embankment. He arranged with Gómez to pay several visits to *ejidal* villages along the highway, where Wallace climbed into feed bins, sifted soil though his fingers, questioned farmers about fertilizer and prices, and collected ears of corn that he later classified and stacked in the hallways of the U.S. embassy. His statements underscored the need for a unified military and economic block in the "quartersphere" stretching from Canada to the Yucatan.[26]

Following the inaugural, Wallace remained on for three weeks to conduct a personal survey of the country's vulnerabilities and potential. He found the atmosphere of rural areas "amazingly like that of Bible times," but he struggled to link the sources of backwardness to deficiencies of agriculture. Many larger *ejidos* employed skilled agronomists, some trained at U.S. colleges. Farmers were able to plant on steeper slopes than in the United States; their uniquely designed corn cribs provided "perfect ventilation"; the *ejidal* schools were "better constructed than most of our rural schools in the United States," and in places "the soil was black and rich just like in that of northern Iowa." Using a wooden peg, Mexicans shucked corn "more completely than our huskers do." While observing the use of this tool, he was surprised to be addressed in English by a husker who told him that he had just come back from working the harvest in Illinois. The peasant's ingenuity and diligence could not be faulted for Mexico's rural poverty, Wallace concluded. The difference must lay in the corn, a low-yielding cousin of the Pioneer Hi-Bred varieties produced by his family firm. Moving outward to the enlarged consequences, he estimated that compared with Iowa, the Mexican farm used twenty times the labor to produce one eighth of the corn. This shortfall depressed wage rates, consumption, and prices; made Mexico dangerously reliant on foreign grain and cash; and produced the inequities that fed unrest. Wallace met with Rockefeller Foundation executives on February 3, 1941, shortly after his return to Washington, and urged them to undertake a technical mission to improve "inefficient and even primitive agricultural practices" in Mexico. If the "yield per acre" could be increased, he told Fosdick, "it would have a greater effect on the national life of Mexico than anything that could be done."[27]

Fosdick agreed to dispatch a team of scientists to survey Mexico later that spring. By reformulating the agrarian problem as a food problem, and the food problem as a matter of yields, Wallace had dispelled the foundation's lingering reservations. His analysis "cut through the details and irrelevancies," according to an official historian, straight to a "central idea" behind all foundation initiatives: the application of scientific methods to produce immediate gains. Wallace had conceptually separated the technical problem of food production from its political and economic context. His observations were limited to *ejidos,* which while politically crucial, represented a minor share of all agriculture in terms of cash value or land use. While *ejidos* comprised some 30 million hectares, 80 million of the most fertile and best-watered hectares belonged to haciendas, many producing non-food crops such as cotton, henequen (a rope fiber), and chicle, which along with gold and silver were the country's leading exports.[28]

Although haciendas were liable to expropriation under Article 27, the government had chosen to boost export revenues with high-value crops instead of putting more land into staple production. The low yields and food scarcity Wallace had observed were a symptom not of "backwardness" but of a rural economy in overdrive, straining to export as much as it could. Following the oil expropriation, Cárdenas's interests shifted away from agrarian reform and toward industry, a change reflected in efforts to contain food prices in order to hold down wages. In 1939 alone some 360 new industries were launched. Labor unrest was the biggest impediment to expansion, and Cárdenas bargained with unions to limit strikes in return for government restrictions on inflation. By 1939 State Department officials noted an emphasis on developing "productive capacity" instead of "the non-productive and apparently inefficient system set up by the *ejidos.*"[29]

Of greater consequence was Cárdenas's decision to import corn, beans, and wheat from the United States to undersell private wholesalers. Food prices quickly fell below production costs, a situation that touched off strikes by campesino unions. The principal form of resistance, however, was passive. Cultivators switched to the more profitable export crops and shifted grain production onto marginal lands: the steep hillsides Wallace had seen. Dwindling production forced the government to import even larger quantities the following year. The practices Wallace interpreted as signs of a moribund culture indicated the breakneck pace of Mexico's economic transformation.[30]

Fosdick's handpicked team of plant biologists—Maglesdorf, a corn specialist; Bradfield, an expert on plant nutrition; and Stakman—began their reconnaissance five months after the Washington meeting. After driving through a "kaleidoscopic" variety of climates and crops between Sonora and the Guatemalan border, they returned to lay out a clear plan of action and, almost as an afterthought, a problem. The solution was improved agricultural efficiency, hastened by "higher yielding and higher quality crop varieties," disease control, and experimentation. The team noted that Mexico, with its stock of unused talent and resources, was poised at the moment of emergence, a time when "substantial improvement could be accomplished with even a moderate amount of help." The commission identified the problem as one of low standards of living, a deficiency that all backward countries had in common. The commission suggested that the connection between agricultural efficiency and social welfare was not "simple" but nonetheless "obvious." Because 77 percent of Mexicans earned a living from agriculture, raising farm productivity had to be "at least part of the answer." The report had touched upon, and then evaded, a question that would bother development experts for the next forty years: how, or even if, improved agriculture translated into an improved society. Fertilizer and plant breeding could cause two stalks of corn to grow where one grew before, but as Stakman sensed, that could not be the end of the story. For Mexico to have a larger meaning, abundant harvests would have to trigger more permanent, far-reaching changes.[31]

While the agronomists were still puzzling about what they could achieve in Mexico, Wallace was raising the political stakes. At the peak of his influence in 1941, the "assistant president" put forward the administration's answer to Henry Luce's appeal for an "American century." In a February *Life* editorial Luce urged the United States to recognize its preeminence and use its power to dispense its laws, constitution, and "magnificent industrial products" to the world. Adopting Luce's evangelical tone, Wallace articulated an alternate vision of the postwar world he called "the century of the common man." In a series of speeches in 1941 and 1942 he argued that modern science had "made it technologically

possible to see that all of the people of the world get enough to eat." Scarcity fueled rivalry and war, and abundance would cement an international
order. To give all nations a stake, "peace must mean a better standard of
living for the common man, not merely in the United States and England,
but also in India, Russia, China, and Latin America." He explicitly rejected Luce's advocacy of the United States as a universal model, noting
the persistence of unemployment, malnutrition, and slums. Instead, he
pointed to developments "south of the Rio Grande" advancing with U.S.
technical and financial aid. This planned, balanced growth would "avoid
the mistakes we in the United States made" and serve as a model of the
full-employment economies promised by the Atlantic Charter. Under American stewardship, victory would usher in an era of economic renewal and
development, a destiny already unfolding in Mexico.[32]

The election of Manuel Ávila Camacho appeared to close Mexico's
revolutionary phase and to promise a mature, conservative course for the
party and the state. The unanimity of this hope among U.S. observers at
the time created an unprecedented era of good feelings. The period of liberal experimentation had ended for the New Deal, too, and the gravity of
the international crisis called for the sober, middle-of-the-road characteristics attributed to the new leader. "Curiously, through parallel historical
development," the *Washington Post* noted, Mexico "is moving into a period of consolidation and conciliation similar to that in the United States."
Ávila Camacho made development the keynote of his administration—
promising at his inaugural "an era of construction, of abundant life, of
economic expansion"—a theme American officials and investors welcomed.
"No more are we yanquis and gringos, but buenos amigos and fellow pan-
Americans," noted George Creel, a journalist and sometime Roosevelt adviser. Ávila Camacho had brought a "definite halt" to the "violent left
swing" of *cardenismo*. Creel organized a $100 million loan and invest-
ment scheme, but other sources of funds were rapidly pouring in. The
United States bought nearly all of Mexico's gold and silver output, as well
as new "strategic minerals"—lead, zinc, manganese, and feldspar—to feed
expanding war industries. The Export-Import Bank loaned $36 million to
upgrade railroads, highways and steel plants. Even before Pearl Harbor,
Mexico had become part of the military supply chain, a status that would
affect all its economic sectors, including agriculture.[33]

Soon after Mexico declared war in May 1942, the Roosevelt administration moved to integrate continental economic and defensive planning.
Lend Lease aid equipped the Mexican army and a new air corps. The

War Production Board surveyed Mexican industry and agriculture, U.S. advisers moved into key ministries, and joint technical committees supervised petroleum and irrigation projects. An urgent priority was to replace sources of tropical commodities lost to Japanese conquests; and the Office of Economic Warfare placed large orders for quinine, rubber, rope fibers, and castor oil. The USDA recruited 70,000 *bracero* farm workers to work fields in the United States. The resulting drop in grain cultivation, loss of labor, and influx of dollars had a predictable effect on food markets. Mexico imported wheat in ever larger quantities even as it shipped record volumes of beef, sugar, butter, and cheese to the United States. Scarcity and wealth were both signs of the wartime boom. As the price of corn quintupled, Mexico added $50 million per year to its positive trade balance. In September 1943, food riots in Durango prompted emergency decrees requiring planters to set aside lands for corn. In Frida Kahlo's portrait of Marte Gómez from this period, the agriculture minister is downcast and unsmiling, struggling to cope with the mounting crisis. Concentrating its efforts on maize and wheat, the ministry eagerly sought help from U.S. scientists and chemical companies.[34]

Gómez and Stakman signed an agreement establishing the Mexican Agricultural Program in October 1943. Stakman, who took charge of setting up the office, reported that the ministry had a proper appreciation for the value of science, particularly "the need for basic research." The authorization stipulated that research would focus on corn and wheat, but the foundation sent a variety of specialists. To lead the team, Stakman chose one of his own students, J. George "Dutch" Harrar, an energetic first-year professor and one of the few in the group who could speak Spanish. A plant pathologist, Harrar's research was in fungal diseases. He helped recruit John J. McKelvey, an entomologist, William Colwell, a soil scientist, and two corn breeders, Edwin Wellhausen and Lewis Roberts.[35]

Norman Borlaug, who headed the wheat program despite having only a forestry degree, had trouble getting permission to go. The United States was pressing its own scientists into the war effort, and Borlaug had a draft deferment that enabled him to work outside of Philadelphia at a DuPont laboratory that was developing a precursor to napalm. Stakman first had to get both the War Manpower Administration and DuPont to agree to release Borlaug and then make a case to his draft board in St. Paul, each time arguing that farm research in Mexico represented a reasonable use of military assets. Permission to take an automobile, a used Pontiac, and the necessary gas out of the country required further authorizations.[36]

In the first months, the MAP leaned heavily on local knowledge and infrastructure. Edmondo Taboada's experiments on maize rust-resistant native wheats provided starting points for Wellhausen's and Borlaug's research. The project set up on land donated by the Chapingo Autonomous University, the country's most prestigious agricultural college, located just outside of Mexico City on the expropriated hacienda of a former president. Borlaug, Wellhausen, and Roberts staked out test plots and assembled a few working tractors from parts cannibalized from the ministry's sheds. The university was the focal point of Cárdenas's rural modernization drive, training ground for the elite *agrónomos* who staffed the federal extension service that brought science to the *ejidos*. The ministry's suggestions, and official policy, guided the MAP's research agenda. Colwell initially worked on nitrogen-fixing "green manure" crops, such as clover, fava beans, and mustard. The foundation advised the ministry that most farmers would not be able to afford fertilizers, and that central Mexico's soils and climate made nitrates less efficient. A visiting USDA scientist, William Vogt, also urged an emphasis on soil conservation and organic farming. Nonetheless, *agrónomos* and the ministry pushed for more chemicals and a grain-first strategy. Likewise, the corn program produced the first significant new hybrids, but feuding between the ministry and a separate Corn Commission, and the lack of subsidized prices for corn meant that by 1963 the new strains had not been widely adopted.[37]

The work of a plant breeder requires the skills of a master jeweler: good hands, single-mindedness in the pursuit of an ideal, and the patience to wait through seasons of growing time to find the right specimen. Only a small fraction of hundreds of "crosses" produce an interesting new line at year's end. Borlaug, who often had little patience with people, was an artist. He would select a stalk of ripe wheat for its lineage or characteristics and sit down next to it. Carefully opening each kernel with tweezers, he removed the tiny male parts, the anthers, then with scissors he cut away the bran, the kernel's outer skin, exposing the moist, green endosperm. Covering the (now female) head with a waxed paper envelope, he took another complimentary stalk, stripped the bran from its kernels, and snipped into the stem, removing the female parts, the stigma and pistil. If all went right, the masculated head swelled visibly, extruding yellow strands of pollen. Borlaug then thrust the head into the waxed paper and shook it, filling the envelope with a cloud of spores. Throwing the male stalk aside, he closed the envelope with a paper clip. After taking detailed notes he would then repeat the process dozens and dozens of times.[38]

Without hesitating, Borlaug chose a breeding strategy based on the deficiencies of the Mexican soil. He was struck by the absence of organic and mineral nutrients. "The earth is so lacking in life force; the plants just cling to existence," he wrote in one of his first letters to his wife. "No wonder the people are the way they are!" He identified nitrogen as the key element, around which habits of cultivation developed. In "traditional" agriculture, crops were bred to survive in meager soils; sparse plantings offered defense against pests and diseases. Cultivators adjusted their aspirations to what the land could provide. Raising yields required improving the soil but also developing varieties that could take the higher fertilizer load without succumbing to rust or other diseases, and giving planters a motive to make the change. He became adept at staging "field day" demonstrations, side-by-side comparisons of old and new methods, to awaken local farmers to the possibilities. He came to see modernization as a transition from lower to higher levels of soil nutrients, and as he often did, he universalized the rule. "In all traditional agricultures throughout the world, there is a deficiency of nitrogen," he later observed. "This goes without saying."[39]

Chemical fertilizer had only recently come into widespread use in the United States. By 1943 mass production of nitrogenous fertilizers, an outgrowth of the munitions industry, had begun to expand wartime grain production in the American Midwest. When chemical exports to Mexico resumed after 1945, the breeding program focused on adapting varieties to large applications of artificial nitrates. This suited the food ministry's needs. With U.S. encouragement, Mexican grain fields had been converted to the production of war materials. Rubber, medicines, fibers, and oilseeds brought in dollars, but as the end of the war approached they suddenly lost their market. Reconversion would take several seasons, during which Mexico would be unable to buy imported wheat or grow enough on its own. Leading *agrónomos* and industrialists pushed fertilizer as a stopgap solution to an increasingly severe grain shortage.[40]

It was in 1945 that Borlaug developed his signature innovation in the technique of plant breeding. Stakman had suggested that Mexico's climate offered enough variation that two crops a year might be grown at different elevations. As the February-to-May growing season closed in Chapingo, farmers on the Pacific Coast were just planting for an August harvest. Borlaug took the Pontiac for drives along the coast north through Nayarit and Sinaloa, looking for suitable sites. At Ciudad Obregón in Sonora, he met Ricardo Leon Manso, superintendent of the Yaqui experiment station. The station had no equipment and only a few sheds, but it had land in a climactic zone perfect for Borlaug's needs. Sonora was a commercial wheat district, with large irrigated farms. Two neighboring landowners, Rafael Angel Fierros and Aureliano Campoy, provided machinery and labor. Rodolfo Elías Calles, the state governor and son of the former president, lent financial and official assistance. Harrar and Warren Weaver, who oversaw the program from New York, opposed this diversion of effort, but local support made it possible. Soon Borlaug was trucking seeds over a thousand miles from Chapingo to Ciudad Obregón and back, halving the time required to mature new varieties. "Shuttle breeding" accelerated the turnaround of seed generations and produced strains that could be planted under widely varying conditions. When Borlaug's first rust-resistant *supertrigos,* super-wheats, were released in 1949, official encouragement and subsidized water made them an immediate hit across the northern wheat belt.[41]

The MAP gave priority to inculcating Mexican agronomists in hands-on research methods. Graduate students from Chapingo apprenticed in practical breeding and extension techniques, and the more promising graduates received fellowships to U.S. land grant colleges. A few of the early trainees joined the payroll, including Ignacio "Nacho" Narvaez, who collaborated with Borlaug in the experiments on dwarfs and later managed the Pakistan wheat program. Apprehensive that "overspecialized" experts would alienate farmers in Mexico as they had in the United States, MAP trainers were alert for elitist pretensions that might need breaking. Borlaug took particular delight in bringing new college recruits straight to the field and "ruining their only decent suit." Apprentice *agrónomos* were taught that prestige came from practical results measured in increased yields. Asian and Middle Eastern trainees, who arrived on FAO and foundation scholarships, received the same treatment. All aspects of the work carried an implicit precedent, a generalizable lesson; "Mexico would be one of the difficult countries," Stakman assured the staff. Successes there would help "the larger program."[42]

Arcadia and Apocalypse

Amid the technical preoccupations of the early years, MAP scientists wrote little about their motivations or ultimate goals, but their evolving strategy increasingly favored national self-sufficiency and pushed the welfare of peasant farmers and their communities into the background. The new U.S. ambassador, George Messersmith, regarded the *ejido* system as a drag on productivity, an opinion seconded by the Ávila Camacho government, which had declared self-sufficiency a national priority. Foundation officials in New York continued to pay lip service to rural livelihoods while discarding, bit by bit, their earlier concepts of what modernized agriculture would look like and whom it would benefit. The wartime experience of the United States, where farm productivity rose sharply even as rural areas were largely depopulated by the draft and industrial expansion, posed an alternative to the strategy of modernizing peasants in place. Weaver worried that uneconomically small *ejido* plots would "defeat efforts to raise the level of agriculture." Borlaug's decision to shift operations to Sonora, the center of large-scale wheat farming, as well as a growing emphasis on wheat over corn, signified a preference for commercial growers. Reviewing the program in 1945, consultant Carl Sauer of the University of California noted that the MAP's research had shifted "away from subsistence or village agriculture to the needs of the city with an attendant emphasis on standardization of product and on yield."[43]

The agronomists changing concerns reflected, rather than caused, the marginalization of the *ejido,* a policy revision already encoded in the numbers both countries used to measure progress. The reorganization of Mexico's wartime economy included a thorough reappraisal of statistical practices. Following the Bretton Woods conference of 1944, the United States universalized its systems of national income accounting, and with it, its definition of growth. Latin American governments, flush with war dollars, readily adapted to the new budgetary standards, but they cost Mexico the yardsticks that measured progress toward the goals of the revolution. Cárdenas-era figures recorded the relative efficiency of investments in collective farms as against industry or commercial farming, as well as indicators of social advancement, local ownership, and relative wages. The loss of these categories not only made it more difficult for *ejidos* to lay claim to resources but also made the sector statistically invisible. *Ejidos* were absorbed into an "agricultural sector" whose operative gauge was production for sale.[44]

To American observers, Mexico emerged from the war as a developmental success story and an exemplar for postwar reconstruction. New refineries, steel mills, hydroelectric dams, and copper mines fueled a surge in industrial employment and wages. A Westinghouse plant turning out appliances for upscale stores, and soaring, pastel-colored modernist office towers emblemized the prosperity of the capital city. *Reader's Digest* expressed hope that the "long-delayed industrial revolution" would alleviate lingering resentments against the United States, while the *New York Times* confirmed that "Mexico has finally settled down politically." In his 1945 review of foundation activities, Fosdick contrasted the hopeful picture in Mexico against the bleak prognosis for human progress elsewhere. Across the globe, libraries, hospitals, research facilities, and a generation of scientists had been lost to the war. The atomic bomb, whose development the foundation had unwittingly advanced, threatened to cast suspicion on all scientific endeavor, but the example of international cooperation against hunger in Mexico represented a contribution "to world peace and to the development of the arts of civilization." This "pioneer experiment" in constructive science, he predicted, would have "wide significance" in the postwar period.[45]

Even before the dream of a Mexican arcadia reached fruition, it was symbolically paired with an apocalyptic future. *Life* showcased Mexico's flashy urbanism in a February 1947 issue anticipating the first state visit by a U.S. president. Color images showed that the war had "pumped a big transfusion of money into Mexico's body economic, threaded its skies with air routes, stitched electric power lines across its barren mesa, and reared dramatically modern buildings." The national diet still lagged—at only 2,100 calories per day—but new irrigation projects and crop breeds would soon raise food production "by 500%." Shortly before his departure, Harry S Truman received the early drafts of a speech he would give before Congress on the urgent situation in Greece and Turkey. "If we do not extend aid," one version warned, "economic disorganization and human despair in large parts of Europe and Asia will inevitably lead to Communism." Truman used his trip to Mexico to contrast the benefits of an expanding sphere of prosperity ("a good neighborhood as wide as the world") against a future of continued conflict. Standing before the Toltec pyramids, he warned that the United States did not "want to be a passing civilization" but it had reached the "destructive point where we must have world peace or be just like these ruins."[46]

Truman foreshadowed an image of an apocalyptic Mexico that would dramatically revise the meaning of the MAP experiment. Americans learned on the cover of *Harper's* in June 1948 that they lived next door to a dangerously overpopulated country on the brink of famine. Unless birth rates and commercial farming could be curbed, the article predicted, "Mexico w[ould] be a desert within one hundred years, unable to supply even the fifteen hundred daily calories" on which its citizens subsisted. Its author held disturbingly authoritative credentials. William Vogt

64

was the USDA specialist who had visited the MAP offices at Chapingo four years earlier. The article forecast such dire repercussions from the program's work that foundation officials were relieved it did not mention the MAP by name.[47]

Nuclear age anxieties about runaway science fed the 1948 population scare, the first of several that would mark the last half of the twentieth century. Truman hailed "a new era in man's understanding of nature's forces," but Hiroshima also marked a turning point in official and public attitudes toward science. Polls taken a month after the war's end showed that 27 percent of the public expected nuclear experiments eventually to destroy "the entire world." Legislation to place all basic research under the supervision of a federal agency moved rapidly through Congress in 1946 and 1947, and the atomic scientists' movement headed by dissident physicist Leo Szilard gave voice to fears that practical research could have unforeseen and even catastrophic consequences.[48]

The public was primed for the alarming message of two nonfiction best sellers. Vogt's *Road to Survival* and Fairfield Osborn's *Our Plundered Planet* echoed Thompson's and Notestein's warnings that modern sanitation, medicine, and nutrition had lengthened life spans, contributing to a postwar spike in population growth. But rather than linking demographic shifts to human conflict, they stressed the "silent war" waged by technology against nature. Depleted soils, silted rivers, and new dust bowls across large areas of Asia, Africa, and Latin America demonstrated that efforts to wring more from the land only shrank the earth's biotic potential. The authors held out no hope of reprieve. They dismissed the claim that chemical fertilizers could close the calorie gap; the earth had a fixed "carrying capacity" that could not be artificially expanded, and the outer were looming. Even though Mexico remained in 1948 more thinly populated than the United States, both authors used it to showcase the dangers of "overpopulation." Vogt portrayed it as the nation furthest advanced toward despoliation, its deforested, eroded hillsides presaging an approaching ecological collapse. Osborn cited the Mayan Empire, victim of a pre-Columbian population explosion, as a harbinger of "nature's final retaliation."[49]

The warning could not be dismissed as idle pessimism. Food emergencies in Italy and India had led Truman to ask Americans to go meatless on Tuesdays. State Department analyst George Kennan assessed the deteriorating situation in China as "classically Malthusian—a teeming population pressing against the limits imposed by disease, poverty, and recurrent wars," while Dean Acheson, the secretary of state, identified hunger as the common characteristic of all Asian countries: "There are just too many people to be fed under their present system, their present organization, the struggle with nature." Scarcities also had a discernible influence on elections and civil disturbances throughout Europe. Occupation governor Lucius Clay warned that Germans would soon face a choice between "becoming a communist on 1,500 calories and a believer in democracy on 1,000 calories."[50]

Rockefeller Foundation officials had their own reasons to be anxious. A barrage of reports from the overseas health staff depicted an unprecedented surge in population growth under way in many of the poorest countries and speculated that earlier disease-eradication programs had been the trigger. Notestein's demographic survey revealed a startling picture of the crisis along the Cold War front lines: the introduction of modern medicine and nutrition in the vast Asian hinterland had caused rural populations "to uncoil" with disastrous political effects. At the September meeting of the American Association for the Advancement of Science (AAAS), the implicit charge came into the open as delegates blamed the Rockefeller Foundation's campaigns against malaria and yellow fever for unleashing runaway population growth.[51]

For the next two years the foundation struggled to reconcile its mission with a growing conviction that any improvement in health or agriculture would simply worsen the inevitable catastrophe. John D. Rockefeller III and supporters among the trustees urged the foundation to redirect its efforts toward birth control, an initiative Warren Weaver and other bureau chiefs found unpalatable. Chester Barnard, who replaced Fosdick as president in 1948, wavered between sympathy for population programs and concern that conservationist criticisms would nullify the foundation's core competencies. If one assumed that the earth had a limited carrying capacity, he asked Weaver, "how do we justify the Mexican agricultural program?"[52]

At the 1949 meeting of the AAAS Stakman ventured a defense, arguing that scientific advances would "stretch" the surface of the earth, making possible a more abundant life for an increased population. But it was Weaver, a mathematician, who articulated the post-Malthusian counterargument the foundation would use for the next thirty years. In a July 1949 internal memo he conceded the point that the earth was a closed system, but argued that its fixed limits were far larger than Vogt had recognized.

From a mathematical standpoint, the principal limitation was not crops or soil, but energy and the potential supply of energy was vast and largely unused. He estimated total daily human consumption of energy at 15 trillion calories, one ten-thousandth of the amount of radiant heat supplied by the sun. The problem was not limits, but distribution. The collapse of colonial systems and rising nationalist agitation meant that the international system could no longer "stably tolerate" wide differences in the ratios of population to resources. The "tragedy of regions (India is an example) where people are now growingly aware of the rest of the world" but unable to duplicate its wealth would be a source of increasing tension. The task for science was to tap the solar reservoir to grow more food, to "buy time" for population control programs to work in these critical regions. He estimated that with imagination and existing technologies, scientists could double food production, assuring a respite of a decade or more. Weaver's formulation, which he called "human ecology," co-opted the conservationists' arguments while defining a new urgent mission: to win a race between population growth and food supply.[53]

As the foundation reorganized its operations around the new concept, the meaning of the Mexico experience changed. Human ecology became the basis of a division of labor between a new fund—the Population Council, which supervised fertility control programs on an international scale—and the foundation's public health and agriculture programs. Food and population were inextricably paired, and the Mexico program came to be seen as part of the "solution to the over-all population problem." Notestein's transition theory suggested that advances in nutrition, education, and urbanization led to declines in fertility, and foundation doctrine increasingly fit agricultural improvement into this developmental sequence. An "important aspect" of rural reform, Barnard suggested, was "the modification through education of the habits and predilections of the peoples concerned." Together with Weaver, Stakman, and (later) Borlaug, Barnard valued rural revitalization not as a solution to poverty but as a route to demographic stability. The emerging view favored an "industrial revolution of agriculture, whereby agricultural personnel are taken off the land and put to work in factories to make farm machinery, as presently occurring in America."[54]

Beginning in 1950, the foundation launched an international campaign to publicize Mexico as a case study of successful agricultural modernization. In press releases, publications, and films it presented an uncomplicated history of population growth, scarcity, and scientific rescue. A 1948 bumper harvest—previously unnoticed by the press—marked the year when Mexico "achieved self-sufficiency" in corn. Wheat came next in 1955. Harvests continued to fluctuate and Mexico imported grain in some years, but in these narratives self-sufficiency was a fixed goalpost marking the completion of the development process. The model stressed two motivations: raising production to match population growth and liberating labor from the farm. The MAP's recipe for training and its "package" of modern agricultural practices—rust-resistant varieties, irrigation, and chemical fertilizer—offered a pattern for managing "the problem of food production in the Orient" where "crops and conditions were similar to those existing in Mexico."[55]

This version left quite a bit out. Henry Wallace, by then a McCarthy-era pariah, earned respectful mention, but without his vision for a global consumer's century. The war, the agronomists' professional insecurities, the Depression-era crisis in U.S. agriculture, and the continuing paradox of plenty failed to make the cut. More importantly, the Mexican experience illustrated (as the official version did not) the painful trade-offs between increasing national wealth and addressing social goals. The reports were silent on the destinies of those "liberated" from the *ejidos,* even though the foundation had a fair idea of where they were going. Rockefeller grantees George I. Sanchez and Lyle Saunders were among the first to document the "wetback problem" that would burst onto front pages in the 1950s. The 1.5 million migrants who crossed the border annually, their studies found, came from a growing "oversupply of cheap, unprotected labor" in rural Mexico.[56]

Since the 1970s, analysts have revisited the consequences of the MAP's work, highlighting its role in narrowing the genetic base; supplanting indigenous, sustainable practices; and displacing small and communal farming with commercial agribusiness, pushing millions of peasants into urban slums or across the border. These correctives have strikingly little effect on how the Mexican parable is retold in congressional hearings or news accounts discussing the future of rural development. Local outcomes are scareculy visible from the global standpoint of the model. When Cynthia Hewitt de Alcántara, in a 1976 report for the United Nations, attributed the decline of the *ejido* land reform, the principal achievement of the Mexican revolution, to the foundation's emphasis on large-scale irrigated cultivation, she angered Rockefeller Foundation scientists not so much by her criticisms as by her rejection of the narrative conventions that justified their work. Borlaug found it "amazing" that she failed to weigh Mexico's loss against the potential benefits for India and Pakistan.[57]

Model building emerged in the 1950s as a foundational tool of developmental thought. As old conceptions of international order broke down under the pressure of Depression, war, and Cold War, Americans consciously sought new schematics for interpreting the world. Joseph Schumpeter's trend models of business fluctuations, Wassily Leontief's simulations of organizational systems, and the game theories devised by John Louis von Neumann and Oskar Morgenstern "mapped" complex social functions onto simplified frames. As political scientist Harold D. Lasswell noted, for policymakers "trapped in the corridors of the present," the model offered almost the only way to envision an indeterminate future. Before theories of modernization, aid officials had to improvise their own explanations of the causes of backwardness and the larger purposes of their projects. In the vocabulary of development, a model referred to a loose analogue encapsulating a country's history as a sequence of strategic moves open to imitation. "The steps which achieved dramatic changes in Mexico," Borlaug instructed the Pakistani government, "will show whether a revolution can also happen in Pakistan."[58]

In the aftermath of war, American leaders were desperate for a reassuring template to guide their actions in Asia. At the moment of Japan's surrender, Acheson reminded a Senate committee in 1946, few could have foreseen that in less than a year the United States would be contending with a civil war in China, the collapse of the British Empire, and nationalist rebellions in Southeast Asia. "Destruction is more complete, hunger more acute, exhaustion more widespread than anyone then realized. What might have become passed off as prophecies have become stark facts." Strategists surmised that the material and manpower resources of Asia would be decisive in the next global conflict, and that the Soviet Union sought to draw them into its orbit, but they had little sense of how the United States might intervene to quell the rising hostility toward the West. Just as alarming was the Asian nations' movement toward state economic planning that, if continued, would require the United States to respond in kind, "allocating foreign goods among importers and foreign markets among exporters and telling every trader what he could buy or sell, and how much, and when, and where," Truman warned. "It is not the American way. It is not the way to peace." Scarcity aggravated the trends, scarcity of dollars, machinery, and fuel, but most of all food. To Americans in

Asia, hunger was the inescapable reality. "Even at 10,000 feet you sense it," Stewart Alsop reported. "China, with its scratched and crabbed land, its scarred mountains, its endless jumble of mud villages, its brick red rivers carrying precious topsoil to the sea, looks like some vast hungry ant heap." The persistent threat of famine overshadowed all other issues in Asia, compounding the collapse of social restraints and the inexorable slide toward anarchy. It was hunger that fanned conflicts over ideology, trade, or land into elemental struggles for survival.[59]

The problem of hunger was one Americans felt uniquely qualified to address. Augmented during the war years by mechanization, artificial fertilizers, DDT, and other broad-spectrum pesticides, American agriculture produced a surplus sufficient to supply the home front and the allied armies with enough left over to feed war-ravaged Europe and Asia. This advantage, as unique as the atomic bomb, afforded one of the few levers the United States had to reverse the "mass attitudes" drifting in the enemy's direction. Communism and economic nationalism had tremendous ideological appeal, but Truman and Acheson felt the practical benefits of scientific agriculture could meet the demands of hungry people more tangibly than the promises of radical philosophies. The panel of scientists and policymakers Henry and Ethel Ford assembled in 1949 to set a direction for their new global charity reached the same conclusion. "Men submit to authoritarianism when hunger and frustration undermine their faith in the existing order," the Ford Foundation's founding document declared. "Faith in any order can survive only where that order holds more hope for the future, if not more benefit for the present, than does the totalitarian alternative." Like their colleagues at the Rockefeller Foundation, they saw hunger not as a symptom of poverty or environmental limits, but as a condition that could be relieved through organization and applied research. On the far outposts of containment, freedom and order would be armed with science. "The future guardians of the Asiatic heartlands," Robert Payne concluded in *The Revolt of Asia*, "will not be the feudal owners but the trained agricultural chemists."[60]

The MAP did not offer the only recipe for intervention in rural Asia. In the late 1940s, before there was an official foreign aid program, before modernization was theorized, engineers and agronomists were quietly working to reconstruct rural Asia. They conceptualized their projects as models. Land reform, community development, and water reclamation were contenders, each combining an analysis of the Asian crisis with a reading of the New Deal experience, each offering a solution to the mystery of economic growth. Throughout the 1950s the distinctive features of the MAP model—its post-Malthusian interpretation of the underlying instability and emphasis on increasing grain yields—were less urgent to policymakers less than models that struck at the psychological sources of peasant unrest or promised to fill the vacuum of state authority in the countryside. But nurtured by the Rockefeller and Ford foundations, it would continue to evolve, adapting its lessons and its vision of modernity to changing perspectives in Washington and fresh emergencies in Asia. In the meantime, it remained an answer in search of a riddle.

3

A CONTINENT OF PEASANTS

U.S. intelligence analysts expected communist forces to breach the Yangtze defenses in April 1949, but they were unprepared for the scale and speed of the attack. The soldiers of the People's Liberation Army (PLA), led by Lin Biao and Mao Zedong, had been derided as malnourished, illiterate, "farmers with rifles," but their coordinated assaults took the American-trained Guomindang military by surprise. Within days they captured Nanjing, bursting into the U.S. embassy and turning the startled ambassador out of bed. By the end of the month, PLA troops riding sleek Mongolian ponies or captured American trucks were pursuing Jiang Jieshi's broken armies toward the sea. Reporters called it "the Big Push." Revolutionary columns, swollen with recruits better fed and better clothed than they had ever been in civilian life, advanced southward singing as they went: "Green bean rice, with barley. Take one bite, sweet as honey. Fills the stomach, frees the mind."[1]

During the previous year, diplomats had reassured themselves that Mao's drive for power would be overwhelmed by China's immensity. The country's scale and population had frustrated Japan as well as previous conquerors, but the southern advance moved as if borne along by some invisible social undertow. Admiral Thomas Inglis, chief of U.S. naval intelligence, gasped at the "superiority and strategic direction of the Communists. . . . It just doesn't seem Chinese." In post-mortems that began even before the Guomindang collapsed on the mainland, Americans reproached themselves for underestimating the peasantry's latent power. Mao had never disguised his reliance on the peasantry or his strategy of building strength in the countryside and waiting for the cities to fall when they were "ripe." The communists "rode to victory," Secretary of State Dean Acheson told Congress, on "this great revolutionary movement which is going on throughout all Asia." Jiang had been "brushed aside not by Communist regimes but just by masses of the peasants and people in the country."[2]

U.S. officials became aware in 1949 just how urgently they needed to understand these country people. Outside of Japan and China's coastal enclaves, Asia was almost entirely agricultural, and its rurality constituted a strategic threat. Intelligence reports discerned a trackless, cityless continent thick with villagers untouched by the state or markets and prone to sudden and decisive changes of allegiance. The collapse of imperial domination left vital territories in South and Southeast Asia without effective authority, in Acheson's phrase, "an unknown world." The dominant figure in this landscape was the peasant. By most accounts the majority of Asians, more than 80 percent of whom made a living from agriculture, were peasants. The term itself had an Asiatic character, connoting a degree of rural poverty unknown in the Americas or Europe. Americans, self-consciously affluent and urban, doubted their ability to identify with this alien caste. "As a country with a dominant middle class," China expert John King Fairbank cautioned, "we have failed to grasp the dynamics of revolution in a peasant society." The Truman Doctrine cast the Cold War as a choice "between alternative ways of life," but while the Kremlin clearly had a program for mobilizing the rural masses, Washington did not. Despite the Marshall Plan's success, strategies that worked in industrial Europe had little bearing on the conditions of Asia. The vast social gulf separating urban and rural ways of life, George Kennan believed, threw the whole notion of U.S. leadership into doubt. "We are deceiving ourselves," he warned, "when we pretend to have answers to the problems which agitate many of these Asiatic peoples."[3]

Scholars assessing American identity at mid-century also perceived a dangerous divide of history, affluence, and knowledge separating the United States from its strategic frontiers. With only 11 percent of Americans living on the land, David Potter noted, the organizational and scientific values of the metropolis now shaped the national character. To David Reisman, the city-bred American was two stages of personality development removed from the "tradition-directed" peasant, making meaningful communication all but impossible.[4]

This estrangement had troubling implications for the United States' capacity to intervene, or even to imagine interventions, in the contested Eurasian heartland. "Communism has a tremendous original advantage," Reinhold Niebuhr warned. In "the dying sleeping cultures of the Orient," Western systems of belief had no foothold. "We are in danger, therefore, of facing the international 'class struggle' with an uncomprehending fury or complete dismay." Arthur Schlesinger held out hope that "American study of village sociology could help us . . . release the energies so long pent up in the villages of Asia," but the sense that Americans were marooned on the wrong side of the urban-rural divide persisted. In 1958 the authors of the best-selling policy novel *The Ugly American* still beheld "an Asia where we stand relatively mute, locked in the cities, misunderstanding the temper and the needs of the Asians."[5]

Throughout the Cold War, the temper and needs of the peasant were at the center of official and scholarly debates on development and counterinsurgency. As with other recycled stereotypes, the picture of the peasant evolved as colonial certainties gave way to less stable realities. Once stolid and impassive, he was recast as demanding, volatile, and suggestible. Experts agreed on his inherent poverty and mystical attachment to the land, but they held contrary ideas as to what impelled him to political action, whether he was motivated by ancestral tradition or modern aspirations, a desire for leisure or wealth, community or autonomy. After the trauma of China's repudiation, Harold Isaacs noted, Americans perceived Asia in "images of anathema." The peasant represented the inverse of his urban, American alter ego, but Americans disagreed on what their own distinctive qualities were. To Fairbank the peasant was intrinsically communal, a "villager" whose innate collectivism had been harnessed to Mao's mass movement. Americans in their materialism and "concern for the individual" had overlooked the strength of this group urge. But Pearl Buck, the best-known authority on rural Asia, stressed how little appeal America's group-oriented, mass consumption, mass production society held for the fiercely nonconformist peasant, "the world's great Individualist," whose material yearnings the communists exploited. These incompatible peasants were never reconciled, either in theory or policy. Instead, they inspired separate but equally ambitious nation-building schemes.[6]

The fledgling governments of "free Asia"—the Philippines, Malaya, Indonesia, India, and others—shared a common weakness inherited from the imperial regimes they supplanted, a concentration of authority in the cities that steadily diminished the farther one moved into the hinterlands. This postcolonial condition has been called "dominance without hegemony." American advisers helped their client regimes subdue the countryside by framing powerless rural majorities as bounded subjects, persons incorporated within national communities but without recognition as full citizens, in short, as peasants. U.S. officials never expected "inexpert

74

and sometimes corrupt governments" to inspire the full devotion of their publics, but with outside aid they might summon enough compliance to thwart insurgency. Part of the mission of development and theories of development was the demarcation of a domain of peasant politics apart from and subordinated to the politics of the client state, a task made more difficult by disagreements about who the peasant was and what he wanted.[7]

The debacle in China coincided with the "discovery" of mass poverty as a global strategic problem. President Harry Truman launched his global aid program, Point Four, in 1949 with only a dim idea of its scale or ultimate goals, but it raised development to the top of the national agenda and simultaneously galvanized a worldwide movement. The pledge to use American technology and "know-how" for the welfare of backward areas "hit the jackpot of the world's political emotions," *Fortune* reported. National delegations lined up to receive assistance that a few years earlier would have been seen as a colonial intrusion. Development fit social problems into a novel concept of time, asserting that all nations followed a common historical path and that those in the lead had a moral duty to aid those who followed. "We must frankly recognize," Assistant Secretary of State Henry Byroade observed, "that the hands of the clock of history are set at different hours in different parts of the world." Leaders of newly independent states, such as Jawaharlal Nehru of India, accepted these terms, merging their own governmental mandates into the stream of nations moving toward modernity. Development was not simply the best, but the only course, Nehru explained, because "there is only one-way traffic in Time."[8]

The Truman administration and its successors enlisted economists, sociologists, and psychologists to devise techniques to accelerate the pace of modernization, but even the experts knew little about the dynamics of change. "Little systematic inquiry has been made into the causes and conditions of economic progress," the *Economist* pointed out. "Nobody can claim to know the factors that must be present before the spiral can begin to revolve. Climate probably has something to do with it." Social scientists were nonetheless ready to try. At Harvard, John Kenneth Galbraith remembered, no "subject more quickly captured the attention of so many as the rescue of the people of the poor countries from their poverty." Interdisciplinary teams, funded by private foundations, the Pentagon, and the Central Intelligence Agency (CIA), developed a canon of modernization theory, a conceptual framework for planning the renovation of distant societies, to fill the informational void that perturbed policy-makers. "Unless we make an extraordinary and explicit effort to understand what is happening," the Massachusetts Institute of Technology's Center for International Studies (CENIS) warned the Senate Foreign Relations Committee, "we are in danger of losing control of our own destiny."[9]

Modernization theorists differed within a broad analytical consensus, but one firm point of agreement was that the United States already manifested the modernity toward which all other countries were moving. To Walt W. Rostow, whose voluminous writings defined the new orthodoxy, the historical lesson of the United States consisted of "two massive facts": the unbroken continuity of its development and its distinctive triumph "as a national society." The Rostovian synthesis resonated with American myths of national mission, according the United States the privilege of stepping in at the decisive moment in each nation's history to dispense the vital ingredients of progress. Rostow's enormous personal influence, and the significance of his masterwork *Stages of Growth,* may justify an impression that academic theory inspired the large-scale development schemes backed by the United States. The methods pursued in rural Asia in the 1950s, however, were more often ad hoc affairs, improvised from some of the same ideas that went into the modernization consensus, but with a few cultural ingredients of their own.[10]

For U.S. officials hoping to ride their own social movement to victory in Asia, two varieties of "rural reconstruction" appeared to offer the best chance in the 1950s: community development and land reform. Neither model originated in the academe. In common with the Mexico model and Tennessee Valley Authority (TVA)–style projects, they projected an idealized New Deal onto other societies at a time when Americans were uncertain about the meaning of the New Deal experience. In renovating the Asian countryside, designers drew from many modernist traditions. They approached fundamental issues of planning, rights, technology, and history in different ways. Unlike the Rockefeller agronomists, they concentrated on the social world of the peasant rather than on techniques of farming or issues of scarcity. They diverged from the Rostovian synthesis most strikingly on its essential tenet, the universal relevance of the U.S. example. Land reformers celebrated a yeoman culture already passing from the American scene while community developers extended a critique of the urban slum into a vision for the peasant village. Much like modernists in the creative arts, their designs contained both a vision of an ideal order and a critique of modernity's present forms. The originators sustained their critique in the face of intensifying pressure to conform to a development agenda increasingly set by social scientists, and they paid a price for their iconoclasm.

Cells of the Nation

The Indian government chose Mohandas Gandhi's birthday—October 2, 1952—to launch an ambitious plan to remold rural India "along Gandhian lines" by building more than 15,000 model villages. The project was funded by one of the largest grants yet disbursed by the Ford Foundation, the United States' newest and largest philanthropy, and by $50 million from Point Four. Community development, the *Washington Post* reported, was not altogether different from colonial-era "village uplift" programs, except that "American experts have provided the inspiration." The terminology was new in international usage. Suddenly, historian Hugh Tinker noted, "community development is a word of power" esteemed by democrats and autocrats alike. Prior to 1950 it referred to urban renewal—in the United States it was synonymous with slum clearance—but in 1956 the United Nations (UN) designated community development (CD) as the official term for initiatives aimed at rural villages, a choice that highlighted the program's significance, and inadvertently, its American derivation. Its methods and philosophy were worked out in India in a pilot project under the direction of a New York real estate developer.[11]

With India's high-profile undertaking, CD emerged as one of the leading strategies of rural modernization. Indonesia, the Philippines, and other governments created CD ministries. A decade later it became the operational methodology of the Peace Corps, and in its militarized form—the Strategic Hamlet—an instrument of pacification in Vietnam. "A hundred years from now the history books will give a paragraph or two to India's foreign policy," the *New York Times* predicted, but "a fat chapter to an experiment called the Community Development Program." It was "the key to the future of India and Asia," Ambassador Chester Bowles explained, "an administrative framework through which modern scientific knowledge could be put to work for the benefit of the hundreds of millions of people who have long lived in poverty." Among the major U.S. institutions, only the Rockefeller Foundation distanced itself from CD. After visiting India in March 1952, Warren Weaver concluded that the vast sums invested would produce only a mirage of progress. He urged the foundation to "stay away from this particular program, and pray."[12]

Community development was a procedure for improving the components of village life—sanitation, animal husbandry, crops, education—by applying specialized knowledge and motivating peasants to participate voluntarily. Its doctrine identified rural areas as vast reservoirs of idle labor that might be tapped for national development if peasants could be made to relinquish their stubbornly low material and social expectations and adopt a modern work ethic. Instilling this new rationality was the job of the village social worker, the *gram sevak,* who was assigned to catalog the village's deficiencies, refer them to experts, and generate a "desire for change," a spirit of receptivity and cooperation known as "self-help." The project aimed "to improve the people through improving the land, and to improve the land through improving the people." India's plan presupposed that after a period of "intensive" intervention, a village would undergo a collective psychological awakening, after which progress would accelerate through the peasants' own initiative. The transformed village would then become a beacon of modernity, diffusing technical and administrative innovations into the surrounding territory.[13]

The prospect of a low-cost breakthrough attracted U.S. donors, but they were also motivated by the southward shift of Cold War battle lines in the wake of the Korean War. India in 1952 was where China was in 1945, explained Paul Hoffman, president of the Ford Foundation. To complement its military areas of strength in Japan, the Philippines, and Taiwan, the United States needed to create "economic areas of strength" in India. Horace Holmes, an adviser to the program, explained that the targeted communities would provide a "foothold" in the immensity of the Indian social problem. Both governments identified the village as the crux of that problem. Nine-tenths of the population lived in villages producing all of India's exports and most of its wealth, but experts agreed that they were dangerously disconnected from the life and work of the nation. "India slumbers in her villages—550,000 of them," S. K. Dey, the new CD minister observed. "They have to be awakened to their obligation to the 'welfare state' we are pledged to build."[14]

In the postwar policy lexicon, the village represented a dangerous combination of poverty, population, and isolation that threatened the security of Asia. U.S. policymakers' fear of isolated community extended from a shared interpretation of the causes of World War II. The interruption of global trade during the depression, in this view, led to the formation of self-contained autarkies—the Soviet Union, Germany, the British Empire, the Japanese Co-Prosperity Sphere—vying for resources and manpower necessary to make their isolation complete. Animated by ideology and the quest for self-sufficiency, relatively small and undeveloped powers swiftly assembled the ingredients of a modern war machine capable of challenging the United States.[15]

The autonomous peasant village represented the early stages of this cataclysmic process, as Isidor Lubin, Harry Truman's foreign aid adviser, warned in 1952. In densely inhabited Asia "the so-called rural population is packed into what virtually constitutes an endless village . . . a breeding ground for violent revolution." China's civil war revealed the hazard of this vast sea in which Maoist fish could swim, but "even if Soviet totalitarianism came to an end," Lubin believed, the endless village could germinate "a series of ideologies that in the light of the next century might make the totalitarianisms of this century seem pale." The rural landscape was an island, cut off from mechanisms of taxation and control, an unknown terrain inhabited by Naxalites, Hukbalahaps, Viet Cong, and other violent indigenes. Asian elites shared the Americans' dread of this closed sphere. "Many of us are two generations removed from the villages," an Indian official confided to Bowles. "The villages appall me." An outpouring of research in the 1950s reinforced conceptions of an insular society lightly touched by Western colonialism. Social science constructed the village as the opponent of the state, the final bastion of habits and attitudes obstructing the smooth functioning of central power.[16]

Paradoxically, the breakdown of the village's historic seclusion intensified its dangers. Academic, journalistic, and intelligence reports depicted an Asia in social ferment, its traditional cultural bonds ruptured by the infiltration of modern ideas and technology. The "spread of industrial civilization," Truman explained, forced new nations to confront the "expectations which the modern world has aroused in their peoples." Their incomplete initiation to modern influences made peasants unpredictable. Because of the revolution of rising expectations, the CIA warned in 1949, "the region must be . . . regarded as in dispute sociologically as well as geographically." The village was presumed to be the social unit that would mediate an explosive encounter between tradition and modernity, and consequently, it was where the battle for the mind of Asia would be won. The United States would have to compete with communism, Bowles confirmed, "at the village level."[17]

While strategists and social scientists pathologized villages overseas, in the domestic setting the term carried nostalgic and utopian connotations. Federal policy encouraged the demolition of neighborhoods in the center of U.S. cities to make way for urban villages. In the lexicon of housing policy, "village" signified a restoration of intimate, participatory community that had been lost in the depersonalized modern city. The inversion of meanings was more than incidental or ironic. The "blighted" slum and rural village both represented zones of poverty and social stagnation that were alike illegible to the state. The Ford Foundation targeted urban "gray areas" with a combination of services and self-help similar to that applied in India, a strategy also called community development. The two community developments had a more direct link in the person of Albert Mayer, a designer of New Deal slum clearance projects in New York and the Indian pilot project at Etawah, Uttar Pradesh.[18]

An American architect and urban planner, Mayer came to India as an officer with the Tenth Air Force in 1943. He designed airfields at the south end of the dangerous 530-mile "hump" route from India over the Himalayas to China. Based in Assam and then New Delhi, he was never content to remain cooped up in U.S. military compounds and he traveled throughout India, sometimes accompanied by Indian builders, visiting the great monuments of Mughal and Dravidian architecture. His travels soon brought him into contact with the Indian nationalist movement. In Bombay, he witnessed the brutal suppression of the Quit India demonstrations and gained the acquaintance of a number of nationalists, eventually including Gandhi and Nehru, leaders of the pro-independence Congress Party.[19]

In 1945, shortly after his release from jail for the last time, Nehru welcomed Mayer to his home in Allahabad where conversations over several days led to an invitation to draw up plans for renovating Bombay and a scheme for village housing. Tirelessly earnest, Mayer "was the sort of person who would welcome late night, wide ranging discussions with a man like Nehru," an associate later recalled. "Nehru was looking for breathing space, a symbolic way of showing concern for the needs of the mass of the people in the Indian countryside." A preliminary report suggested physical modifications of the village's built environment, but after touring the sites of earlier village schemes in December 1946 Mayer became convinced that the social and "spiritual" basis for improvement did not exist. He withdrew his original plan and substituted a vision of a psychological transformation to make the village a "funnel" for expert guidance from outside. Awarded the title of Planning Advisor to the Government of Uttar Pradesh, he set up a small mixed staff of Indian and American experts based at Lucknow under the direction of Horace Holmes, an agronomist on leave from the U.S. Department of Agriculture (USDA), initially paying expenses out of his own pocket. Mayer returned to New York, but on annual visits to India through 1954, he elaborated on the philosophy of the project, launched in 1948 at Etawah, a green, well-watered district of about a thousand square miles along the Delhi-Kanpur railway. He aimed to formulate a wholly original approach to rural modernization that would bring progress without colonial paternalism, Soviet coercion, or American extravagance.[20]

Educated as a civil engineer at Columbia, Mayer had gone into the family business of constructing Manhattan apartment towers. His personal wealth (his mother was a Guggenheim) gave latitude to his interests; in the 1930s he joined Lewis Mumford, Henry Wright, and Clarence Stein to advocate for large-scale, planned public housing projects. The "Housing Study Guild" inspired the Wagner-Steagall Act and a national program of slum clearance and planned public housing. The guild warned that the modern city suffered from decay, overdevelopment, and suburban competition. Before the war and after, Mayer urged a design strategy blending greenbelt towns and high-density "tower in a park" urban housing to address problems of congestion and nuclear civil defense. Cities had become "unpleasant to do business in, wasteful of people's time, and a strain on their nerves," and the decline could be reversed by restoring a sense of small community in distinctive, self-contained neighborhoods. Stuyvesant Town and Knickerbocker Village in New York, Thorneycroft in Queens, and suburban villages in Pittsburgh and Los Angeles expressed these principles.[21]

As an urban planner, Mayer brought an original perspective to the problem of rural reconstruction. To social scientists the American city—especially New York—represented modernity's ultimate achievement, the model to which the village should aspire. Mayer, having spent much of his career demolishing parts of New York, held a different view. He forecast a "revalidation of rural living" and extolled the Indian village as "the small community which we in the West are now trying to create." In his New York high-rises, he sought to reconnect modernism with nature and face-to-face intimacy. His apartment block at 240 Central Park South, completed in 1941, compromised modernist austerity with curvaceous enclosures, landscaping, and rooftop conservatories to create a sense of community within the city. But his designs for Indian cities contain

Mayer's most explicit statements about the permanence of the village in the modern world. In 1949, as work on Etawah was still under way, Nehru commissioned Mayer to draw the master plan for the new Punjabi capital at Chandigarh.[22]

Along with Brasilia, Chandigarh is considered one of the preeminent manifestations of high modernism in urban design. Nehru intended it as an aesthetic expression of the new India, an administrative capital to replace Lahore, a dazzling imperial city detached by Partition. It was planned from scratch. Nehru chose a site at the foot of the Himalayas, a broad plain from which farmers had been forcibly removed allowing Mayer to "start with just a blank sheet of paper." Chandigarh is often identified with the utopian modernist Edouard Jeanneret, known as Le Corbusier, who designed its monumental structures, but as a condition of his contract, Le Corbusier accepted Mayer's master plan. His refinements enhanced its principal features, which emphasized segregation of the city's constituent functions (living, traffic, work, retail) and continuous green valleys running between walled neighborhood "superblocks" that Mayer designed to "perpetuate the Indian village community." Houses and schools within each sector turned inward toward plots of green space rather than outward toward the street.[23]

Mayer's achievements in housing policy, urban planning, and village development have been recognized separately, but what is seldom recognized is that the three projects progressed simultaneously and engaged a single theme: creating a "human scale" community. His work in Chandigarh, New York, and Etawah each reflected a belief that the village was the authentic, natural unit of human society, the building block of cities and nations. The city was conceived as a modular arrangement of superblocks, each constituting, in Le Corbusier's phrase, a "vertical village." City and village performed instructional functions. Because Chandigarh's residents were "still villagers and small community people at heart," urban design should introduce new habits and forms of interaction. Mayer encouraged "modern" nuclear families and discouraged charcoal burning, for instance, by eliminating space for extra beds and *tandoors*. He encouraged bicycle riding with dedicated paths. Three unreconciled assumptions about the essential nature of the village written into the design of Chandigarh—its authenticity, modular reproducibility, and didactic function—also informed the practices of community development.[24]

Journalists often described India as a nation of villages, but for Mayer it was more than a figurative expression. In common with American social scientists, he viewed the village as a natural system to which the individual owed "prime" loyalty akin to the bonds of family. The individual's connections to the city or the nation were contrastingly tenuous and fraught with the artificialities of bureaucracy and caste. In his urban designs, Mayer elaborated on the theme of neighborhoods as "individual organic cells" strengthening the social tissue. His plans for Bombay (1947), Chandigarh (1950), and Reston, Virginia (1957) recommended the formation of neighborhood associations, to "foster the demand for planning and interest in it." Community development likewise treated the village as an organic whole embracing all of the regenerative, creative, and ritual functions of human society. Mayer romanticized it as both socially indivisible and naturally democratic. His plans contained scant references to sectarianism, untouchability, gender, property, or other distinctions that might perpetuate inequities or disunity. The village was the smallest, most intimate social space accessible to a government worker, a place where an outsider could gain "entry into the people's minds, into their feelings, into their own expectations and needs." At this "molecular" level of society, Mayer felt, India would either progress toward an "era of great achievement" or ignite "a delayed civil explosion of vast extent and world-wide repercussions."[25]

Central to Mayer's conception of "self-help" was the idea that culture could be used instrumentally to harness the village's energy for the nation. He embraced dualisms contrasting a spiritual India against a rational, material West, but he accepted these attributes as reinforcing rather than antithetical. In his first explorations in 1946 he concluded that unless modern improvements were grafted onto a social and cultural base, they would end up like the ruins of colonial model villages that littered the Indian landscape. Custom should not be dismissed as obstinacy, but engaged creatively to accelerate change. Mayer understood culture as a potent but nonetheless transparent collective consciousness that could be accessed and even manipulated by the outsider. It included legends, sacred spaces, dates, and symbols capable of "evoking emotional allegiances." He used the term "culture" interchangeably with "values," a real estate idiom that described distinctive features and institutions (built-in bookshelves or a neighborhood park) through which occupants acquired an emotional stake. Values could arise spontaneously from within a community, or they could be built by the developer.[26]

Mayer was unusually conscious of the need to differentiate his approach and vocabulary from those of generations of modernizers who had made the village a social laboratory since the nineteenth century. In imperial India the village was constituted as the embodiment of timelessness and thus the natural target of reform. In 1830 Charles Metcalfe, governor general of India, described villages as "little republics, having nearly everything they want within themselves. . . . Dynasty after dynasty tumbles down, revolution succeeds to revolution . . . but the village communities remain the same." The authentic, unchanging village exposed the artificiality of India's unstable state, justifying British succession to a long line of alien rulers. Development projects often start from a putative baseline of pristine tradition, but Mayer recognized that the Indian village had been subject to official experiments for at least a century. In the tragic history of village reform, he identified conceptual failures that gave him an opening.[27]

Previous schemes, he recognized, had either romanticized or demonized village culture. Gandhi's autonomous *panchayat* village councils overidentified with the miseries of the villager, idealizing asceticism and weakening the motivation for improvement. But he was more disdainful of British efforts to fence, whitewash, ventilate, and sanitize villages into the twentieth century, a tradition realized in Frank L. Brayne's Gurgaon scheme in the 1920s. Brayne pressed quinine, ploughs, and convection ovens on the residents of a Punjabi district. Under his direction, Gurgaon's residents were admonished by placard, radio, and traveling guides to "stop burning dung cakes," "use mosquito nets," and that "jewelry is a wicked waste." The scheme collapsed upon Brayne's departure, and Mayer read its fate as confirmation that aid workers had to work with tradition rather than fight it.[28]

His belief in locally rooted development set Mayer at odds with other modernists. His most consequential disagreement with Le Corbusier— one Mayer decisively lost—concerned the inclusion of local and vernacular elements. Le Corbusier categorically rejected Mayer's attempts to lend the city a sense of heritage and place. Rather than facing structures with local brick and stone, he insisted on "brute concrete," and he replaced Mayer's conical "Buddhist" capitol with defiantly alien structure. While Mayer wanted modernism without "robbing the Indians of what is distinctly theirs," Le Corbusier exulted in stripping the city of history and tradition. Nehru, who sided with Le Corbusier, believed (as later modernization theorists would) in a singular, convergent, and international modernity. Mayer allowed for multiple modernities. Progress should unfold "not by destroying or Westernizing but by purifying and enriching the enduring spiritual values of India." It required sensitivity and insight, on the part of the modernizer, to discern "how far certain traditions should be respected and fostered and sublimated."[29]

To negotiate delicate trade-offs between tradition and modernity, Mayer felt, Indians could rely on empathetic outsiders, especially Americans. Coming from an advanced culture, Americans could see India's future in their own present. His job in Chandigarh was to "develop the city as modern, self-confident Indians would, if there were such a group." From his modern vantage, an American in India could see forward and backward in time. He could anticipate problems and, with an awareness of local values, deduce how Indians might address them. "We can not only do a more viable job," he suggested, "but a more Indian job than they could, because I think we can really enter into their spirit." With the advantage of foresight, Americans could also steer clear of their own developmental mistakes (such as slums and congestion) and seek outcomes that were "integrally" modern.[30]

In village development, too, Mayer placed primary importance on the sympathetic outsider—the *gram sevak* or the foreign consultant—able to see solutions beyond the time horizon of the inhabitants. With financing from the United Provinces government, the FAO, and later the Ford Foundation, he assembled a circulating "pool" of diagnosticians. Holmes directed the project from a cramped bungalow in Lucknow that doubled as an office and sleeping quarters for Eveline Holmes, their four children, and a rotating cast of experts including Eldon Collins, an agricultural engineer; Dudley Trudgett, a town planner; and Arthur Mosher, an economist. Their job was to train *gram sevaks* in specific techniques, but also to embody the problem-solving outlook they aimed to instill in villagers. As critical as it was to the program, this reliance on the outsider to see things both as they were and as they should be inevitably clashed with the program's other core principle, the respect for local values. Mayer's philosophy was riddled with such contradictions, but they were not a liability at first. They were what supporters in the Indian and U.S. governments found most appealing about community development.[31]

Mayer's strategy built momentum by helping villagers get what they wanted, but his ultimate interest was in improvements they did not yet want. The villagers' opinions—their "felt needs"—were largely of tactical value to the community developer, who could foresee aspirations two steps ahead. "The first duty of those responsible for community development programmes is to identify the felt needs of the people," a UN report explained. "They should also assist the people in making better judgments for themselves on what their needs are and how to satisfy them. Finally, they should be able to identify needs not yet perceived and make the people conscious of them." Official and philanthropic backers represented CD as a democratic, decentralized alternative to coercive communist or imperialist schemes, but they also viewed the peasant *(kisan)* as psychologically unprepared to contribute to planning. Community developers expected villagers would learn to want wells, schools, fertilizers, and roads, and that their demands would announce the beginning of their political maturation. Once the *kisan* "feels that partnership is a common task," Nehru explained, "we can get anything out of him—enthusiasm, yes, but hard work, too."[32]

Nehru valued Mayer's approach because it imposed policy through the authority of the village without conceding its political legitimacy. India's government was top heavy with national and state-level bureaucracies, but thin below the district level. Most villages went years without a visit from an official. The gap had its origins in the constitutional convention, held in 1950 while the wounds of Partition were fresh. From the beginning of the resistance struggle, Gandhi had declared the *panchayats,* the councils of village elders, to be the authentic voice of liberated India, but amid the disintegration village leaders came to be seen as inciters of violence while the "steel frame" of the bureaucracy held steady. "What is the village," Dr. B. R. Ambedkar, leader of the untouchables, asked, "but a sink of localism, a den of ignorance, narrow-mindedness and communalism?" The convention rejected plans for decentralization, and left *panchayats* out of the federal system.[33]

This deficit of democracy in the countryside—a condition shared by many postcolonial states—defined the core mission that shaped all of community development's tactics and methods: how to enlist the peasant's participation while leaving the center free to direct and plan. The peasantry had risen in support of the nationalist movement, Dey admitted, but "below the State Headquarters, the countryside is yet to wake up to the full implications of her freedom." National leaders were largely urban, but they relied on rural votes. CIA analysts described community development as "the main effort of the Congress Party to ingratiate itself with India's rural population and thereby remain in power."[34]

Museums of the Present

Although Mayer often urged patience, he expected lightning conversions. CD aimed to awaken the peasant through techniques such as "dawn processions" in which advisers paraded into a village at 5:00 A.M. with flags, placards, drums, and chants "to rouse the villagers from their slumber." Mayer also arranged trips to fairs and cities where peasants could be enthralled by machinery and monuments. Steinbeck and Redfield had imagined modernization as an epic voyage from country to city, but the Indian government made the journey real, sending peasants on a train, "the kisan express," thousands of miles through the new India to see hydroelectric dams, shipyards, and the art deco apartment towers along Bombay's seafront. Mayer encouraged participants to enshrine photographs of these "new pilgrimages" in village temples alongside "the Shivas, the Krishnas, the Ganeshas, the familiar pictures of the Hindu pantheon."[35]

Instead of invoking the authority of science, Mayer's methods of persuasion aimed to fit innovations into existing systems of knowledge and belief. Two of his principal techniques—"expanding culture" and the "dirty hands method"—were taught in the thirty-four training centers financed by the Ford Foundation. *Gram sevaks* expanded culture by appropriating symbols, festival days, and "heroes and legends" for the project. Mayer put his headquarters in a temple in Mahewa village. He encouraged trainees to study cultural anthropology and Indic faiths. Superior knowledge of tradition often allowed them to trump local opposition. As an example, Mayer pointed to a *gram sevak* in Ikari village who outdebated a Brahmin scholar on the ethics of green manure. Occasionally, the program could even manipulate tradition through official channels. In one locality a feral antelope, the *nehil gae* (blue cow), ravaged pastures until Holmes convinced the government to reclassify it as *nehil goa*, blue horse. The now unvenerated animals were promptly eradicated. "Dirty-hands" stressed the value of approaching the villager unpretentiously. *Gram sevaks* were to live among the people, dress and act like them, and labor personally in any project undertaken. Mayer himself exemplified this spirit, sleeping in village huts and eating only local fruit and vegetables. On one occasion, engine trouble forced him to borrow a pony to get to the next village. After a few miles he dismounted and insisted that its owner, who had gone along to retrieve it, take a turn in

87

the saddle. Mayer stressed that humility distinguished the CD worker from the status-conscious officials occasionally sent to superintend the countryside.[36]

While Mayer warned against anecdotal victories, he nonetheless stressed the importance of simulation and display. Etawah's peasants lived in a kind of museum among exhibits of crops, wells, injections, and schools. A year before independence, Nehru complained that the British had left only "museums of antiquity"; the new India "must have museums of the present" where peasants could go, see, and learn. Mayer arranged Chadigarh so that visitors passed through a belt of museums before entering the city. In Etawah, successful demonstrations would expand, eventually encompassing an entire community. The displays would then be aimed outward at visiting dignitaries and film crews, who would arrive to see the results. Western observers attached great importance to this dramaturgical function. If Mayer could "scatter them through India so that what he does becomes an example," Assistant Secretary of State George McGhee suggested, "you can continue to have a stable government in India."[37]

Trials of new techniques were carefully staged. In a typical procedure, Holmes introduced a wheat variety, Punjab 591, by arranging a challenge between neighboring farmers. On harvest day, judges measured and staked out comparison plots; the new and old varieties were harvested separately, threshed and poured into scales in front of an audience of villagers. Punjab 591 "was found to have produced 26 percent more than the usual seed. A bulletin board was erected in the village, proclaiming the results with appropriate pictures." Eleanor Roosevelt was enchanted by the juxtapositions: "an old-style wooden plow would be shown beside a modern steel plow, old knives beside new knives." The aim, another visitor noted, was "better personal and social living based on measurable improvement." Etawah pioneered the development of new measures of agricultural progress, including "crop equivalents" that gauged the relative "efficiency" of dissimilar crops, such as peas and cabbages. Project workers were often confused by the contradictory insistence on comparable targets and locally defined needs, but Mayer maintained that the demonstration method would make peasants calculate their interests by the numbers. Trial, proof, and mass conversion, he explained, comprised "a potent sequence for bringing conviction to rural people."[38]

Mayer and his backers wanted CD to spread across the country, but through imitation rather than pressure from the center. Paul Hoffman, president of the Ford Foundation, concluded in 1950 that there was "no reason why all 500,000 of India's villages could not make a similar advance." But it was essential for the model to self-replicate, as Senator Kingman Brewster explained, because repeating the labor put into Etawah would soon exhaust donors: "The idea, of course, must be that it will be infectious and spread," because if it did not, "25 teams or any number of teams wouldn't get around that whole thing [India], and you would have to live with them for probably a thousand years." Accordingly, Mayer valued solutions that were symbolic and adaptable, rather than definitive. He divided Etawah district—an "average area" without "outstanding problems"—into geographic "blocks" of roughly 100 villages each. The pattern, still in use today, eventually subdivided the entire nation into 5,723 blocks, without regard to population or terrain, imposing an illusory uniformity.[39]

By emphasizing replicable, universal problems, CD avoided taking on more controversial and stubborn issues. The generic euphemism "villager" disguised stark disparities of power and wealth. Property holdings and conditions of landlessness varied widely within and between villages, but the overall problem was staggering. Almost half the cultivators in India owned less than an acre or no land at all. Community development simply disregarded larger structural issues, such as land ownership, but that was the way officials in Delhi and Washington wanted it. Land-ceiling legislation, suggested in the first five-year plan, aroused intense opposition, and U.S. aid officials steered clear of the controversy. Nonetheless, some critics felt rural poverty and apathy could be addressed only through redistribution, and community development advocates were often put on the spot.[40]

Under hard questioning, Holmes admitted to the Senate in 1951 that most of the benefit from any increase in agricultural productivity would go to absentee landlords, the incentive for peasants to improve was correspondingly reduced, and improvements diminished only the chances that landlords would voluntarily give up their land. Still, he argued, community development addressed the peasant's main problem, which was scarcity: "Even though the actual bushels of wheat that they pay as rent are greater," he testified, "the actual bushels of wheat they themselves have are likewise greater, and they are quite happy." Once the struggle for resources had abated, he suggested, advisers would be able to experiment with model redistribution schemes. "I do not understand your argument," admitted Senator Theodore Green. "The more profitable that land becomes for the owner, the less likely he is to agree to any change." But blunt logic could not shake the presupposition that solutions would take the form of models rather than laws.[41]

Mayer predicted modernization would steadily eradicate historic inequities such as landlessness and female seclusion by creating a climate in which new social opportunities could emerge. His solution to other structural injustices, such as racial segregation in the United States, likewise stressed the catalytic effect of model solutions. Although he opposed racial preferences in housing long before it was fashionable, he never reflected on how his conception of "organic" neighborhoods as anchors of identity might complicate the process of desegregation. Across the country, high-rise public housing projects were often sites of bitter struggles, but Mayer clung to his original beliefs. He claimed in 1967, shortly before the Harlem riots, that residential segregation was disappearing in New York owing to the influence of modern housing projects. Community development contained a similar degree of wishful thinking, but its evasions actually appealed to the prevailing sense of urgency among policymakers. The global crisis afforded little time for prolonged, inconclusive reform drives. CD concentrated on immediate technical fixes and fed hopes that small changes would produce an effortless transformation. It was the disappointment of these hopes that ultimately doomed the program.[42]

Ford and Point Four funded a massive and abrupt expansion from pilot project to national program. Beginning with 25,000 villages in 1952, it reached 123,000 villages with 80 million inhabitants by the end of the first plan period in 1956. On this scale, the anecdotal victories that drew attention to Etawah disappeared into a mass of statistics showing unremarkable gains. Mayer later blamed Point Four for placing material achievements above the essential "spiritual and internal" prerequisites of change, but the Congress government, too, needed to show results. The second five-year plan relied on a steep increase in village productivity, both in cottage industries and farm production, to balance industrial investment. The initial publicity provoked an enthusiastic response from villages, a rapid accumulation of statistical victories, and a sudden influx of national and international resources. It then tailed off into a series of increasingly critical government investigations.[43]

The 1957 Balvantray Report signaled the end of the honeymoon for CD in India. It compared the cost of the program to the meager gains in living standards and food production, but it also exposed the gap between conditions in the villages and Mayer's assumptions. Based on extensive interviews in villages inside and outside the project, it found a striking contrast between pronouncements about local culture and self-help and the actual practice of community development. The program seldom allowed villagers to instigate projects; instead, headquarters handed down plans to overworked *gram sevaks* who dragooned untouchables to work without pay. Rather than a supple decentralized strategy, community development turned out to be a traditional, ineffective, and massively expensive public jobs program. Even more surprisingly, a set of control villages untouched by CD had adapted to changes in the national economy faster than those in the program. Purportedly "stagnant" villages reported substantial gains in productivity using techniques local residents developed on their own. The reconsideration of CD had been prompted by shortfalls in farm production that had derailed the second five-year plan. The realization that agriculture was critical to industry cast tenants and smallholders in an entirely new light. No longer isolated or passive, the report hailed them as entrepreneurs who needed no outside help to build a resilient and evolving community.[44]

Nehru's government curtailed funding and replaced the community development agency with a decentralized scheme run by *panchayat* village councils. The Ford Foundation also pulled the plug. After eight years and $10 million, Indian farms had made no gains in productivity. It may not have been coincidence that Mayer's style of urban development also came under attack in the late 1950s, for many of the same reasons. William Whyte and Jane Jacobs documented the vibrant complexity of supposedly blighted city neighborhoods and the sterility of towers and standardized superblocks. Planning, once the urban poor's best chance for decent, hospitable living spaces, came to be derided as heavy-handed social engineering. Jacobs's epic battle with New York's infrastructure czar Robert Moses for the future of lower Manhattan turned in her favor by 1959, confirming that a village could not be created by planners, but only saved from them.[45]

At the low point in 1960, even as Mayer reflected that his program's fallen reputation was "to a great extent deserved," community development was about to acquire a second life as a counterinsurgency strategy. Forced to accept a flimsy neutrality in Laos and alarmed by the deterioration in Vietnam, the Kennedy administration appointed a high-level task force on the "internal defense of the less developed world." The special group, headed by White House military adviser Maxwell Taylor, concluded that the most critical national security threat, present and future, would come from peasant-based "subversive insurgency." Years of experience had given the communists a "tested doctrine for conquest from within," but the United States had no effective counterstrategy and needed to find one "on an urgent basis." Insurrections were aggravated by the strains of the development process and by governments estranged from the people, the group determined, but the solution could only be found "within the local population." National Security Action Memo 182, the action plan that remained in force for the remainder of the decade, interpreted security as an aspect of community building. "In loosely constructed countries where the government has not gained the support of the peasantry, an apathetic rural population is a vulnerable target." Consequently, "the battle must be joined in the villages," which stood at "the critical social and political organizational level."[46]

The administration adopted CD as a "vital" nation-building tool for taking "government to the countryside." It equipped allied militaries for "civic action" projects in which soldiers, acting as *gram sevaks*, provided clinics, sanitation, and agricultural advice. Community development merged with counterinsurgency in the belt of fortified "agri-metro" villages defending the northern frontiers of Thailand and Burma and in Vietnam's strategic hamlets. The list of felt needs expanded to include bamboo-stake barriers and small arms training for village militias. Pacification specialist Edward G. Lansdale told departing Green Berets in 1962 that with small improvements, a pump or a generator, a village "finds itself becoming linked up closely to the nation, a real part of something bigger. As it does so, the political life of the community grows also, demanding more meaning in answer to the question: What is worth risking a man's life to defend?"[47]

Kennedy's advisers tried to bring Mayer in as a consultant, but he declined. The new practitioners, he felt, had lost sight of the values that originally inspired his approach. Institutional and covert agendas took their place. The CIA deployed CD to reduce the influence of rural oligarchs and cultivate their own cadre of young leaders. A dummy foundation put workers in 7,000 villages in the Philippines, according to one case officer, "in order to take complete control of these basic units of Filipino society without the peasants or the old-style political bosses realizing what was happening." The Peace Corps adopted CD because the job was vague enough for untrained college graduates to take on. Aid agencies treated the village as the end of the pipeline, sending out whatever materiel came to hand. Community development, Mayer believed, was ultimately a test of character; success would depend on whether Americans could set aside the "dominant impulses" of their culture and engage Asians in an equal exchange. "If we can freely learn, dispassionately evaluate, and organically absorb," he argued, "maybe we are a great people and ours is a great generation."[48]

Flawed as his analysis was, Mayer was among the first to grapple with what Henry Stimson called "the fundamental problem of the peasant." Although many of his ideas would be abandoned, their rejection shaped the ambitions of the rural reconstruction schemes to follow. A dozen years after China's revolution, the peasant's motivations and temper were still a mystery, but CD paradoxically persuaded many that tackling issues of psychology and culture directly was an ill-defined exercise unlikely to lead anywhere. Henry Heald, the Ford Foundation's new director, determined that peasants could be motivated only by visible structural changes in their landscape and economy. "After you give a lot of young Indians a six months course in village development," he complained, "you really haven't got much." Mayer's stress on gradual, autochthonous development was rejected in favor of a new emphasis on engineering and dramatic technical breakthroughs. The growing strategic stakes demanded bolder action. Despite fresh weaponry and advisers, reports from Vietnam remained discouraging and the surviving dominoes looked shakier than ever. Asians were "fighting today for a bigger bowl of rice and a better home in which to live," Vice President Lyndon Johnson explained. "Either we convince them that these things are quickly attainable through the institutions of freedom" or "pull back our defenses to San Francisco and a 'Fortress America' concept." Although CD remained in the pacification repertoire, it was pushed to the margins as the Viet Cong gathered strength and U.S. officials searched for faster, more dramatic remedies.[49]

Community development returned to the United States in a variety of forms. Lyndon Johnson's community action programs, aimed at the inner city, and Richard Nixon's Community Development Block Grant program each used its concepts and methods. Mayer, who continued to plan cities in the United States and around the world, incorporated its lessons in his urban designs, most notably in Reston, Virginia (1957), a much-imitated "master planned community" in which suburban "villages" were constructed around cultural focal points: a bandshell, a lake, or a golf course. Mayer's last work in New York, a community center and playground at East Harlem Plaza (1960), contained a "dell" surrounded by low walls resembling those at Rajpura village in Etawah. The design, he said, would "give everyone in East Harlem a feeling that this is our part of town."[50]

Community development represented a modernism as different from land reform or the Mexico model as Cubism was from Art Noveau. Walt W. Rostow believed development carried humanity toward a stage of higher mass consumption; for Le Corbusier, modern man's highest ambition was to join into a harmonious order. At the heart of Mayer's modernism was a search for home. In 1951 the Armed Services committee tried to discern the symbolism of Etawah: "What do you represent to them?" a senator asked. "Do you represent America?" Holmes paused a moment before replying. "As we have worked with them and they have come to accept us," he explained, "well, they take us to the innermost sanctum sanctorum of the temple, and there is nothing but friendship and cooperation that we get."[51]

Land Reform on Trial

In November 1954 the agricultural attaché to the U.S. embassy in Tokyo, Wolf Ladejinsky, was attending a trade conference in Washington when he was summoned to the office of Assistant Agriculture Secretary Earl Butz. Ladejinsky was nationally recognized as the architect of Japan's highly successful land reform, a measure credited by General Douglas MacArthur, Senator Walter Judd, and others with sparing Japan from the peasant uprisings that plagued the rest of Asia. After some fidgety preliminaries, Butz informed him that his appointment was being revoked, that being foreign born he lacked the "American farm background required to represent American agriculture abroad." Ladejinsky read in the newspapers the following day that he had been fired for security reasons, a move that seemed preposterous even then, at the height of the red scare, because he was not only staunchly anti-communist, but famously so. It was, James Michener wrote, as if Richard Nixon had been charged with subversion.[52]

The "Ladejinsky affair" that unfolded over the following year provoked editorial outrage, high-level resignations, and an overhaul of the security system. The case reprised all the McCarthy-era controversies—privacy, anti-Semitism, xenophobia, the widening rift between internationalists and isolationists—but the underlying issue was land reform. Editorialists alternately described Ladejinsky's creation as "the only successful anti-communist step we have taken in Asia" and "inherently wrong and un-American." Ladejinsky himself was either a "commissar" or "a symbol of the American interest in helping farmers in backward countries obtain a fair stake." Land reform was debated as symbol and strategy, as a representation of American values, and as a forecast of agriculture's destiny.[53]

Development policy is notably driven by changes in theoretical fashion. Analysts and practitioners variously attribute its fleeting paradigms to trial and error, the counterclaims of donors and recipients, or academic sparring. Perhaps understandably, a field preoccupied with change lacked fixed certitudes. Development was a heterodox movement; each model propagated its own catechism, its claim to the authentic path, and its distinct answers to the mysteries of modernization. Ladejinsky himself had observed that to be successful, planners often had to ignore facts and rely on a "reform mystique" that resembled faith: "Reforms cannot be 'researched' or 'studied' into existence. Of far greater importance is the acceptance of the reform idea, to begin with, in such a manner that technical problems are not an excuse for inaction, but something to be resolved."[54]

The Ladejinsky case revealed the nature of sectarian conflict in the early days of the development project. An authority on Asian agriculture from 1935 to 1975, Ladejinsky was a transitional figure. His early writings analyzed imperial and socialist experiments in plantation and collectivized agriculture. In the years in which he formulated his ideas on land reform, between 1948 and 1954, modernization theory in its Rostovian form had not yet matured, although many of the constituent ideas floated in official discourse. He was thus able to assemble an original conception of the motivations of the peasant and the instrumental functions of land and rights. The criticisms that coalesced in the security case likewise constituted an attempt to fashion a counternarrative of Asia's agricultural future out of unorganized materials, principally critiques of the New Deal, a defense of property rights and land-grant research, and idealizations of the American farmer. The controversy revolved around a fundamental disagreement among experts over what attributes marked *American* agriculture as modern and, consequently, how Asia's modernization would likely unfold.

Forecasting the future of the countryside presented an unsolvable puzzle for social scientists who conceived of progress as a process of urbanization. Redfield's folk/urban model, Emile Durkheim's organic/mechanic binary, and Talcott Parsons's pattern variables each imagined modernity and rurality as poles on a cultural scale, spatially and temperamentally opposed. Only in the 1960s did sociologists begin to challenge the assumption that attitudes toward family structure, authority, work, and leisure could be fixed along a "rural-urban continuum." Until then, the countryside could be infinitely improved, but by definition it could never be modern. Visions of the rural future relied therefore on a limited stock of inapt, indeed antagonistic, analogies. From the 1920s on, proponents of agricultural improvement in the United States envisioned an industrial destiny for the countryside, with farming evolving toward factory-like efficiency, mechanization, and reliance on managerial (rather than artisanal) expertise. But industrial analogies could be applied in different ways. For example, was the farm a corporation or a subsidiary within a larger corporate system? Did the farmer act as an entrepreneur, a worker, a technician, or a stockholder?[55]

The language of business contained room for many rural futures, and modernizers explored variations on this theme in the 1950s and 1960s. Michael Harrington later identified Ladejinsky as the first of the "new physiocrats" who placed the land and its gifts at the foundations of economic and political progress. Ladejinsky conceived and defended land reform as a comprehensive psychological, political, and economic strategy for defeating the communist advance, democratizing Asia, instilling Western values and habits of thought, and rationalizing production and consumption. And land reform would be criticized in the same manner, not as a technique but as a worldview.[56]

During World War II, military planners had anticipated that land redistribution could be a tool for achieving postwar objectives in both Japan and Germany where propertied elites had thrown their support behind militarist dictatorships. The division of Germany and the East-West confrontation that erupted in 1948 in the Berlin blockade put a stop to the breakup of Jünker estates called for by the Morganthau Plan, but the intensifying Cold War had the opposite effect in Asia. The American occupation instigated land reform to undercut the power of a "feudal" class that had supplied the officer corps of the Imperial army. When MacArthur's staff arrived, 70 percent of Japan's farm families were sharecroppers, surrendering half or more of their crop to landowners. "We walked on the land and we talked to the people, the peasants as well as the landlords, the money-lenders, and the Japanese agricultural experts," Ladejinsky recalled. The agronomists "had been struggling for years with the chronic crisis of Japanese agriculture, but had been kept from accomplishing any significant reforms by the entrenched opposition of the landlord class." The occupation administration purchased 5 million acres, roughly 80 percent of the rented land, and transferred it to tenant cultivators. Ladejinsky presented reforms as a democratic revolution from above, awakening a conservative, entrepreneurial peasantry naturally allied to the occupation's aims.[57]

Meanwhile, in Korea, General John R. Hodge authorized reforms of tenancy and ownership as part of an attempt to create a "middle-of-the-road coalition" to isolate the communists politically. U.S. aid financed redistributions of land in China's Yangtze Valley in an attempt to forestall the Nationalist collapse. In 1950 Acheson submitted a land reform resolution to the UN, and the departments of state and agriculture agreed that Point Four should make "a world-wide land reform" a primary strategy for "strengthening the system of free enterprise by diffusion of private property and re-inforcing the economic foundation of the State."[58]

Commentators across the political spectrum endorsed land reform as an answer to the communist ideological offensive. "The economic misery and social backwardness of the Middle and Far East constitute an open invitation to Soviet penetration," columnists Stewart and Joseph Alsop explained. The answer was "a sort of Oriental new deal . . . based on thorough agrarian reform." *Fortune* championed it as a "dynamic alternative to Communism." U.S. military observers attributed the rapidity of the collapse in China to the communists' use of land reform to win peasant loyalty, but it was a weapon available to either side. "There is no reason why Communism should be left with its hand on this lever of social change," Barbara Ward declared. As architect of the first successful postwar reform, Ladejinsky was its foremost authority, appearing regularly as author and subject of articles in magazines and newspapers. Presidents and dictators sought his advice. He was so closely identified with the cause that Ambassador John M. Allison dubbed him "Mr. Land Reform."[59]

In interpreting these programs for policymakers and the public, Ladejinsky stressed connections between land and power in Asia. The son of a wealthy landowner in the Ukraine's Jewish Pale, he had experienced the violence of revolution. His native shtetl, Ekaterinopol on the outskirts of Kiev, had been overrun alternately by white, red, and Ukrainian nationalist armies and sacked by anti-Semitic pogroms before the Bolsheviks consolidated control and confiscated his family's properties. He said afterward that he never resented the soldiers and tenants who took the land, only the regime's increasing hostility to peasants and the wastefulness of collective farming. He emigrated to Hoboken and worked briefly in a shirt factory. He learned English selling magazines at a stand on Sixth Avenue in Manhattan, then at the heart of the midtown speakeasy belt. He applied for a scholarship to Columbia and studied economics under brain-truster Rexford Tugwell. A blend of anti-communism and New Deal activism characterized his writing from the beginning. His M.A. thesis, which received unusual attention from the *New York Times,* diverged from the celebratory treatment of collectivization often heard even from intellectuals critical of the Soviet experiment. Calling attention to the famine and declining productivity on modernized farms, he observed that the Soviets had misapplied machine metaphors to agriculture. Farms, unlike factories, could not be managed by rules. Unless variations in climate, land quality, population and other "imponderables" were factored in, the catastrophe would continue. Soviet attempts to standardize human nature would also fail. *Agrotekhnika* shouldered "the task of de-peasantizing the peasant" when it might instead harness his nascent entrepreneurship and "acquisitive ideas." Stalin, he concluded, had "overestimated the importance of the tractor and underestimated the importance of the human."[60]

As a correspondent for the Agriculture Department, he developed a reputation as an Asia expert, reporting from Manchukuo, the Dutch Indies, and China on agriculture's emergence from feudalism and colonialism. He ratified the postwar consensus that Asia was on the cusp of a sweeping social revolt. Popular works by Edgar Snow and Wendell Willkie pictured a continent gripped by a restless expectancy. To Secretary of State James F. Byrnes, Asia was a "great smoldering fire" in which "a huge mass of humanity, the majority of the people on this earth" were spontaneously combusting "from the Middle Ages into the era of atomic energy." Ladejinsky brought the situation in the countryside into sharper focus. Industry, he argued, "has made but a small dent in the character of Asia." Consequently, "Asia's problem is the problem of land," and the state's most powerful tool for shaping the political consciousness of the peasant lay in its capacity to regulate relationships between land and people. The communists exploited this realization, but Ladejinsky stressed that land reform was ideologically neutral, a weapon available to any government that chose to use it. Anticipating Rostovian theorists, he characterized communists as scavengers, seizing on aspirations for land and independence that they would ultimately betray. The West had an opportunity to inoculate the peasant against communism by offering him a stake in a capitalist future, but it would be peasants—not urban elites or national governments—who would ultimately choose between the two systems.[61]

This was fitting, he believed, because peasants were the only sizeable population in Asia equipped with a modern sensibility. Political economists from List to Marx and Schumpeter cast the peasant as a stubborn enemy of progress, but proponents of land reform depicted an entrepreneurial peasant, obstinate only in his demand for respect and obedient only to the laws of the market. The peasant got bad publicity, Michener noted. "True, he's conservative and suspicious, but if I can demonstrate a principle, and if it works and saves him money, he'll adopt it right away." Pakistani sharecroppers refused to buy fertilizer or new tools, Ladejinsky explained, because they recognized that 70 percent of the return would go to the landlord. Subscribing to Herbert Norman's characterization of the "Janus-faced" peasant, alternately conservative or radical depending on self-interested calculations, Ladejinsky nominated "the common man of Asia" as a reliable champion of American values "simply because his own interest lay in the same direction."[62]

The urban, educated landlord, by contrast, was a relic of feudalism, an "uneconomic man" capriciously aiding any empire or ideology that preserved his privilege. "The landlord has a pre-modern mind," explained Owen Lattimore, a China specialist and State Department consultant. His "feudal conception of the nature of property" was not the same as capitalism. Feudalism, "government of the landlords and by the landlords and for the landlords," Justice William O. Douglas agreed, was "feeding the fires of communism in the Middle East and Asia." Advocates transposed the social strata of medieval Europe onto Asia, complete with ancestral fiefs and vassals. Even "molecular" proprietors owning less than an acre apiece purportedly controlled Japanese society by subordinating "the town mayors and its money lenders, the county officials, the village cops." Ladejinsky depicted a parasitic city where self-indulgent, educated elites ("all dressed up and no place to go") swelled "the ranks of the Communist chorus out of sheer frustration induced by lack of suitable occupations." Only a few allies might be found among urban professionals, scientists, and industrialists, who possessed what Lattimore called "a modern cost-accounting mind."[63]

Updating orientalist distinctions between pretentious, town-dwelling *effendi* and authentic, virile natives, land reform advocates typecast peasants as sturdy yeomen in a frontier drama. Although he spoke no Asian languages, Ladejinsky, in his articles, placed himself in conversation with straight-talking peasants whose demands could be understood by any American with a connection to the land. Liberated from the apathy of tenancy, "owner-cultivators" valued Western expertise but they viewed political and scientific innovations with an alert and calculating eye. Like Mayer, he posed his methods as a reproach to the presumption of diplomatic officialdom. Ambassadors and bureaucrats must learn "to feel and act in terms of the common man." He insisted that development respect "their logical framework," their stores of local knowledge and history. Plans could not be advanced by recommendation or fiat but only through "indirection," a pattern of incentives structured so ideas gained acceptance through the free play of choice. Land reform was a modernization of order and plan, but not mastery. It relied on cultivating mutualities of interest between peasants, elites, and U.S. foreign policy.[64]

For this reason, agrarian modernization required social rather than technical transformations. The TVA and Soviet tractorization left marks on the land, Ladejinsky explained, but "a traveler passing through Japan's countryside would never know that here a momentous economic and social change is being effected." Reforms addressed underlying structures of taxation, control, and prestige, bringing about an altered "mental outlook," a new awareness of rights and obligations. The adjustment of property simply initiated the process. Cooperatives, loans, price supports, subsidies, and political mobilization—Wallace's whole New Deal farm program—would deepen patterns of reciprocity between the farmer and the state. Other development models envisioned the transformed peasant in economic terms, as a supplier or consumer; Ladejinsky imagined him as a citizen.[65]

The Truman and Eisenhower administrations both regarded tenure reforms as a potent counterinsurgency tool. Vietnamese and Chinese communists realized its "powerful propaganda value," John Foster Dulles warned. "Something should be done on our side, with our help [to] put this emotional and basic element to work for us." Between 1945 and 1959 the United States urged or implemented land reforms in nearly every nation along its defensive perimeter from Japan to Pakistan. President Ramon Magsaysay's offer of "a house and a title" to rebel peasants, Admiral Arthur Radford told Congress, "had as much to do with breaking the back of the Huk movement in the Philippines as any other one thing." The liquidation of the imperial system provided the historical rupture necessary for sweeping revisions of rights and property in Japan and its former colonies, but in newly independent states in south and southeast Asia, propertied classes retained enough residual power to frustrate reforms. U.S. experts drafted meticulous plans largely vitiated by the Philippines and South Vietnam. Provincial officials and landlords ignored Thailand's modest reform—a reduction in rents—conferred by royal decree in 1951. Although India's Congress Party spoke forcefully of abolishing *zamindars* and radically restructuring land rights, it came to power with a civil service committed to colonial legalisms and a constitution that ceded agricultural policy to the states. The resulting fragmentary redistributions abetted a cycle of agrarian unrest and emergency interventions that increasingly disturbed U.S. observers. "Nowhere in Asia," Bowles complained, "have sweeping land reforms been enacted by a free and democratically-elected legislature."[66]

It was easier to dictate land reform than to legislate it. A martial law edict redistributed parcels to 200,000 Pakistani farmers in 1959. The U.S. military government in Korea reduced rents and seized Japanese-owned property, but its land reform statute stalled in the landlord-dominated legislature. Occupation governor Maj. Gen. William Dean used his powers of fiat to distribute Japanese lands to 502,460 farmers in 1948. Expropriation could be difficult, even where civil society offered no resistance. A Taiwanese peasant told presidential hopeful Thomas Dewey that prying property from the landholding class was like "negotiating with a tiger for his fur." U.S. officials were never comfortable with the coercion required, and much of the artistry of designing a reform went into the incentives and compensation packages that made the process of condemnation appear legitimate to outside observers. Taiwan's 1954 act recompensed 106,490 owners with shares in state-owned industries that held their value just long enough for the transfer to take place. On maturity, the certificates were nearly worthless.[67]

A successful reform required proficiency in law, economics, and dozens of technical specializations, as well as fortuitous timing. Defining targeted lands, identifying recipients, setting valuations, assembling mechanisms for titling and compensation each involved a special set of problems. Japan's ten major laws, thirty-one ordinances, fifty-one ministerial regulations, and 120 explanatory circulars still had to be supplemented by a dense network of national, provincial, and local committees to carry the transfer to completion. Within the Foreign Agricultural Service (FAS), Ladejinsky led a cadre of activists committed to Wallace's vision of democratic planning. Acolytes including Arthur Raper, Robert Hardie, and John Cooper carried techniques honed in Japan to New Delhi, Tehran, Manila, Saigon, and Taipei.[68]

Ladejinsky's preoccupation with the social precursors of change was more attuned to the uneasiness of the immediate post-war years than to the self-assurance of the emerging modernization synthesis. Sharing misgivings about a "cultural lag" between scientific and human progress, he agreed with the 1950 Gaither Report—the Ford Foundation's inaugural document—that the global crisis arose "out of man's relation to man rather than his relations to the physical world." Land reform rested on appeals to justice and the dignity of labor instead of the material achievements associated with development. Truman administration officials recognized a pressing need for an inspirational message to counter communism's call to historic destiny. It was patronizing to peddle the U.S. "standard of living" in the wake of China's revolution and the North Korean attack, wrote Barbara Ward, one of the most vocal champions of foreign aid. "These are days for poetry," she declared, "not statistics."[69]

Ladejinsky also doubted that numbers or technology could inspire. While Point Four offered scientific know-how to the world, land reforms placed a premium on persuasion and legal and administrative proficiency. He acknowledged that his own training was in history and economics and that his only specialization was in gaining "the confidence of the people who make the decisions." Like Mayer, he measured results in attitudes. Although he expected reform to improve yields, productivity was not the standard by which it should be judged. The rationale for technology on American farms—increasing labor productivity—simply did not apply to Asia, where land was the scarce ingredient. In yields per acre, Japan already doubled American farmers' production in rice and wheat using hand cultivation. Technology would only throw farmers out of work and set back the social and political objectives of reform.[70]

His unconcern with productivity set him at odds with growing apprehensions about overpopulation sparked by Vogt and Osborn. The Foreign Policy Association suggested in 1951 that land reform might be inappropriate for overpopulated countries where plots were already uneconomically small. "The problem," as Senator Walter Judd posed it, "is more food, not more dirt." Ladejinsky suggested trade might overcome shortages, but he never envisaged more than a "partial escape" from the population trap. The growing salience of the population issue meant that Ladejinsky's project came to be evaluated on grounds he considered unrelated to its true aims. As modernization theory gained currency, land reform no longer seemed the only answer to peasant unrest.[71]

Perhaps land reform's greatest handicap was that it sat uneasily alongside the myths out of which ideas of modernization were fashioned. Development's most difficult task, Ward explained, was "the discovery of the version of our society which is appreciable to the backward peoples of Asia." Recognizing that his program had to appeal to Des Moines as well as Rangoon, Ladejinsky cultivated a "reform mystique" by associating it with familiar versions of the American past. To describe the desired outcome, he evoked Jeffersonian or Turnerian images of a land of independent homesteaders. He cited Thomas Hart Benton's admonition that "it should be the policy of republics to multiply their freeholders, as it is the policy of monarchies to multiply tenants." But to explain the actual process of expropriation and suspension of property rights, Ladejinsky struggled with allusions to Henry George and General Sherman's dispensation of "40 acres and a mule" to freed slaves. The initiative's direct antecedents—in Mexico and Puerto Rico—highlighted the paradox: Americans approved of land reforms for others, not for themselves. Drawing parallels in the present tense was nearly as difficult. The large-scale, mechanized American commodity operation of the 1940s bore little resemblance to the "family-sized" farms the United States was encouraging in Taiwan, Korea, and Japan. The State Department urged caution in modeling Asian agriculture on the American experience; the "motives and methods" of U.S. agriculture could be duplicated, but not its "form and structure."[72]

This discrepancy between the family farm idealized in New Deal rhetoric and the growing emphasis on scale, mechanization, and science in American agriculture set the stage for Ladejinsky's troubles. Between 1939 and 1959 the number of farms in the United States fell by 40 percent while the size of the average operation grew by two acres a year. Moreover, the earnings of the largest 6 percent grew to equal that of all the remaining 94 percent combined. An internal debate over the meaning of these trends for foreign agricultural policy surfaced in the controversy over Ladejinsky's security clearance. The FAS, where Ladejinsky had worked since the 1930s, had been transferred during the war to the Department of State. New legislation shifted it back to USDA, but citing "security and technical requirements," Agriculture officials declined to rehire Mr. Land Reform.[73]

The explosion over Ladejinsky's clearance occurred amid controversy over a redirection of U.S. farm programs proposed shortly after Dwight

D. Eisenhower's inauguration. "Our nation is moving swiftly into an entirely new balance between our population and our food supply," Eisenhower had told campaign audiences. "The time is coming when all the scientific knowledge we can muster will be needed to keep production equal to its task." Agriculture secretary Ezra Taft Benson proposed a radical break with the New Deal structure of production limits, price supports, and "parity" subsidies that held the ratio of farm and industrial incomes near a benchmark set in the 1910 to 1914 crop years. Benson argued that parity was a stopgap to meet the emergency of the Depression and mobilize surpluses for war, but no action had been taken to reconvert agriculture to fit peacetime needs. Subsidies encouraged huge surpluses of "basic" commodities: corn, wheat, rice, sugar, and tobacco. His "freedom to farm" program aimed to phase out controls and "handouts," changing patterns of production and restoring competition.[74]

Critics called it a throwback, but Benson presented his plan as an overdue renovation that would place farmers in the mainstream of technological and economic change. For the first time since the Populists, John Kenneth Galbraith reported, "farm policy is being viewed in Washington as a matter of conflicting ideologies—the radical price fixing policies of the Democrats versus the conservative alternative of the free market." Benson's challenge was the last time the USDA seriously questioned the advantages of a permanent policy of farm price supports. His ultimate defeat would have implications for the development of corporate farming and trade, global grain markets, and the eating habits of the American public. More immediately, it produced an uproar within the influential bloc of rural voters by pitting the vested powerful farm interests against cherished images of rural independence.[75]

In speeches and testimony, Benson argued that parity embedded farmers in a tragic narrative. By applying subsidies to re-create an imagined "golden age of agriculture," the USDA froze agriculture into an imagined past rather than leading it toward an open future. Acreage controls, he argued, paid farmers not to use their genius and technology to wring the most from the earth. Benson worried about the moral decline of the farmer, once the "strongest bulwark of our free way of life," now penned in and fed through the bars by government. Mechanization, electrification, and scientific methods should give farmers confidence in the future, but "instead they were disturbed and worried."[76]

Benson's future envisaged high-tech farms linked to sophisticated distribution networks responsive to changes in a global food market. He proposed a "modern parity" that would cushion transitory market shocks (such as weather) while aligning prices with broad trends in demand. Scientific and market research would increase consumption by lowering costs, devising new packaging, diversifying diets, and finding industrial uses for crops. USDA agents would aggressively seek overseas markets. Farm organizations denounced it as a plan to liquidate the "traditional" family farm in favor of corporate agribusiness, a characterization Benson partly accepted. Farms, small or large, would survive through efficiency and adaptability, not tradition. He explicitly questioned the continued viability of the independent small farmer, at one point suggesting that owners of unprofitable farms should consider taking factory jobs. The 1954 farm bill pitted the "farm vote" against an unusual coalition old-guard Republicans and urban liberals, such as Senator John F. Kennedy, who supported the aim of lowering consumer food prices. It ended in an almost total defeat for Benson, but for a moment—a crucial moment in the development of modernization theory—policymakers put forward a new ideal of the modern farm, its scale, its virtues, and its relationship to science and the city.[77]

Observers on both sides regarded the 1955 Ladejinsky case as a renewal of the farm bill debate in a new guise. Senator Hubert Humphrey, an opponent of Freedom to Farm, stated that Ladejinsky's firing indicated a repudiation of land reform world-wide. The National Farmers' Union regarded parity at home and land reform abroad as inseparable parts of a global strategy for rural prosperity. It attacked Benson for showing "the same favoritism to landlord-dominated agriculture in U.S. foreign policy that he is pushing in U.S. domestic policy." While some criticized attempts to export Bensonism to Asia, the *Chicago Tribune* warned that "social levelers . . . might want to see the pilot experiment introduced in Japan extended here if conditions could be rendered favorable."[78]

Attacks on Ladejinsky played up his New York education, Russian and Jewish origins and, implicitly, his urbanity. Republicans challenged his suitability as an adviser on rural affairs. "Why can't the State Department get a real agricultural expert from one of our agricultural colleges?" Rep. Carl Curtis (R-Neb.) wanted to know. Benson maintained that the issue was technical expertise: Ladejinsky "didn't know enough about U.S. agriculture" and "it was agriculture we were interested in not land reform." Attaches needed proficiency in agronomy, genetics, plant pathology, as well as marketing—skills taught by land-grant schools—to function as the "eyes and ears" of U.S. agriculture abroad. Humphrey unwittingly reinforced the stereotype by defending Ladejinsky's "intelligent anti-communism" at odds with Benson's rustic Americanism.[79]

Ladejinsky's opponents argued that land reform placed the wrong farmers on the wrong farms. The dispossessed "landlords" were a politically reliable educated class, according to Eugene Dooman, one of the principal accusers, reform was chiefly a means of "effectively pauperizing an element that could be counted on to resist the communists." USDA officials asserted that the occupation had done peasants no favor by burdening them with taxes, marketing, and "all the paperwork that goes with running a farm." The characterization of the peasant as employee and landowner as manager mirrored Benson's modern farmer, "in truth a business man" responsible for "using capital wisely [and] maintaining a skilled labor force." Benson and his allies substituted a talented gentry in place of Ladejinsky's freeholder as the bulwark of the state. They doubted family-sized operations were suited for mechanization and higher productivity. A commentator for the *Los Angeles Times* argued that redistribution had led to the "un-economic atomization of farms" in Japan, while "its contribution toward stopping Communism . . . is at least debatable."[80]

Within this critique lay a vision of a way forward for Asian agriculture, a path toward large consolidated operations guided by science and the market. The Ladejinsky case marked a turning point for rural development, a moment when the image of a modernized countryside changed. Both community development and land reform envisioned progress as the renovation of the peasant, the enhancement of the status, health, productivity, and allegiance of villagers and tenants. After 1955, the goals of rural development would increasingly be expressed in terms of yields, resources, and revenues. Rostow and other development economists regarded agriculture as external to the "modern sector" they sought to build; it could enlarge (or shrink) the pool of available capital, but land rights or equity had little effect on development as they understood it.[81]

The Ladejinsky controversy sputtered on for two more years. Benson, still on the ropes from his farm bill defeat, eventually deescalated, allowing Dulles to dispatch Ladejinsky to the safe distance of Saigon, where despite a close personal relationship to Ngo Dinh Diem, he was unable to coax more than token concessions from the regime. Rostow later urged President Kennedy to keep him in place because Ladejinsky was "a wise old boy on Asia as a whole," but by 1961 strategic hamlets had taken the central role in pacification. Diplomats were on notice that advocating land reforms too stridently could hurt a career. No development remedy is ever entirely discredited—the World Bank and U.S. agencies still employ community development and land reform as tools in postsocialist and postconflict reconstruction—but in the 1960s these methods were subordinated to an all-out drive for increased outputs of grain. The Development Decade would be marked by days of statistics, not poetry.[82]

4

WE SHALL RELEASE THE WATERS

In May 1960 the historian Arnold Toynbee left Kandahar and drove ninety miles on freshly paved roads to Lashkar Gah, a modern planned city known locally as Little America. At the confluence of the Helmand and Arghandab rivers, close against the ancient ruins of Qala Bist, Lashkar Gah's 8,000 residents lived in suburban-style tract homes surrounded by broad lawns. The city boasted an alabaster mosque, one of Afghanistan's best hospitals, the country's only coeducational high school, and the headquarters of the Helmand Valley Authority (HVA), a multipurpose dam project funded by the United States. This unexpected proliferation of modernity led Toynbee to reflect on the warning of Sophocles: "the craft of his engines surpasseth his dreams." In the area around Kandahar, traditional Afghanistan had vanished. "The domain of the Helmand Valley Authority," he reported, "has become a piece of America inserted into the Afghan landscape. . . . The new world they are conjuring up out of the desert at the Helmand River's expense is to be an America-in-Asia."[1]

In the heroic age of development, river valley projects constituted the most majestic and lasting efforts to remold rural Asia. Dams and systems of dams lit new cities, "reclaimed" arcadias from swamps and deserts, inundated whole regions, and built enclaves of modernity whose acronyms indicated their derivation from the Tennessee Valley Authority (TVA), the New Deal agency that built twenty-six dams that tamed the upper South's turbulent rivers and politics. A "multipurpose" project, managing industries, research, agricultural extension, forestry, navigation and recreation throughout a vast watershed, the TVA, according to its wartime director, David E. Lilienthal, represented a unique compromise of technocratic planning and public participation, a "democracy on the march."[2]

Although the United States never duplicated the TVA within its own borders, Democratic and Republican administrations saw it as an indispensable remedy for underdevelopment. Truman envisioned "a TVA in the Yangtze Valley and the Danube." "These things can be done and don't let anybody tell you different," he told Lilienthal. "When they happen, when millions and millions of people are no longer hungry and pushed and harassed, then the causes of war will be less by that much." Eisenhower warned that the TVA represented a form of creeping socialism and he restricted federal dam construction, but his administration promoted projects "on the pattern of the TVA" for the Nile, Tigris, Jordan, Indus, Mekong, Irawaddy, and Ganges valleys. Domestic opposition to river control—from property owners and corporate interests—grew during the 1950s, but rather than dispelling the romantic allure of large dams, it simply shifted it offshore. Kennedy could disparage the actual TVA as an overgrown public utility while extolling the model TVA's "tremendous international implications." Interests and ideologies encumbered the politics of older, industrialized countries, but according to Walter Lippmann, the "underlying question of Asia" was a straightforward "question of land and food and rivers." The discrepancy reflected assumptions about Asia's "hydraulic" civilizations and an American mission to tame landscapes through technological mastery of water. Toynbee was mistaken; the engines had barely started, but the dreams raced on ahead.[3]

Where community development and land reform attacked longstanding problems of human relations, dam builders classified poverty, feudalism, and even international tensions as by-products of an overriding "resource constraint," the supply of water. Planners expected a variety of favorable consequences to flow from efforts to unchain the waters, but they seldom distinguished between immediate and secondary effects or between material and symbolic goals. Lilienthal, who personified the "TVA idea" as roving diplomat, best-selling author, and director of the Development and Resources Corporation, a full-service international development consultancy, saw no distinction between hydraulic and social engineering. A "great dam," he emphasized, "will produce more than electricity and irrigation. . . . It will produce a change in spirit, a release of creative energies and self-confidence which are the indispensable factors in the future of that country." Despite, or perhaps because of its mechanical aspect, water infrastructure development came to be invested with iconic functions in an expanding portfolio of national, professional, and strategic narratives. In the sheer variety of their symbolic uses, dams provided an indispensable resource for American and Asian nation-builders.[4]

Nothing becomes antiquated faster than emblems of the future, and it is difficult, after only fifty years, to envision the hold concrete dams once had on the global imagination. In the mid-twentieth century, the austere lines of the Hoover Dam and its radiating spans of high-tension wire inscribed federal power on the American landscape. Vladimir Lenin famously remarked that communism was Soviet power plus electrification, an equation captured by the David Lean film *Dr. Zhivago* in the image of water surging, as a kind of redemption, from the spillway of an immense Soviet dam. In 1954, standing at the Bhakra-Nangal canal, Nehru described dams as the temples of modern India. "Which place can be greater than this," he declared, "this Bhakra-Nangal, where thousands of men have worked, have shed their blood, and sweat and laid down their lives as well? . . . When we see big works, our stature grows with them, and our minds open out a little." For Truman, Eisenhower, and Kennedy, as much as for Nehru, Ayub Khan of Pakistan, and Zahir Shah of Afghanistan, the panoramic wall of a dam was a screen on which they would project the future.[5]

Dams symbolized the sacrifice of the individual to the greater good of the state. A dam project allows, even requires, a state to appropriate and redistribute land, plan factories and economies, tell people what to make and grow, and design and build new housing, roads, schools, and centers of commerce. Tour guides are fond of telling about the worker (or workers) accidentally entombed in dams, and construction of these vast works customarily requires huge, unnamed sacrifices. While land reformers sought to solidify the peasant's connection to community and the soil, dam builders felt fully justified in bulldozing graveyards and mosques and displacing thousands from ancestral homes. Julian Huxley, the British humanist, noted that "the planner placed in charge of the destinies of a region finds himself in a position not unlike that of Jesus" tempted by the lure of absolute power. Nor did all planners exercise forbearance. India's interior minister, Morarji Desai, told a public gathering beneath the Pong Dam in 1961 that "we will request you to move from your houses after the dam comes up. If you move, it will be good. Otherwise we shall release the waters and drown you all."[6]

River valley projects proliferated across Asia in combination with national economic planning and planning ideology. By the end of the 1950s,

Afghanistan, Pakistan, India, Sri Lanka, the Philippines, Burma, Thailand, Indonesia, and Malaya each had a multiyear economic plan and a river development project under way. Applications for multilateral financing required detailed projections, but dams and plans went together in other ways, too. Both offered technocratic management as a replacement for colonial paternalism and lent international sanction to the new state's stewardship of the public welfare. Reviewing India's designs for the Damodar, the United Nations (UN) affirmed "the destiny of the people of the valley and their future is the obligation of the government." Dams occupied a special place in planning documents. Asian economies were overwhelmingly agrarian and artisanal, but plan commissions nonetheless displayed an "urban bias," preferring to funnel scarce material and administrative resources into large industrial projects rather than dispersing them into the countryside. India's chief planner, Prasanta C. Mahalanobis, explained that such "concentrated" endeavors allowed decisions to work through a small committee while initiatives benefiting the "unorganized" rural sector relied on cooperation from a distressingly "large number, maybe hundreds of millions of persons." Dam projects were the exception: an incursion into the hinterland, a domain in which the peasantry could be made accountable to schedules, targets, and oversight. In the United States and Asia, the TVA model circumscribed an "inner citadel" of the economy where central direction could operate without the social friction that plagued the larger national realm.[7]

Lilienthal, Huxley, and other promoters equivocally maintained that valley development would consolidate the authority of the state while also "undercutting and transcending nationalist sovereignties." The resource constraint offered a basis for a postcolonial alliance founded on technical competence and a shared struggle to bring natural forces under human control. Official publicity characterized rivers as fearsome and capricious destroyers of civilizations. The Helmand had buried Hellenic, Persian, and Ghaznavid cities in turn, according to HVA's mandate, but modern Afghanistan in league with American technicians would fight back. India's Damodar Valley Corporation underscored the river's "immense power to spread ruin and desolation." Against this adversary, engineers-errant joined forces with Asian peasants on terms that affirmed their common purpose while demonstrating the superiority of American methods. Above the Nangal cofferdam, Lilienthal was moved "beyond belief" by the sight of parallel columns, human and machine, shifting crushed stone up the slope, on one side Punjabi women "in flowing garments" bearing their loads in head baskets, and on the other a line of twenty-ton Euclid trucks.[8]

Martial analogies conferred on dam builders the status of a technocratic warrior elite. Harvey Slocum, chief designer of the Bhakra Nangal, placed himself in the company of "Napoleon, Eisenhower, Alexander the Great, all the great generals." In the mystique cultivated by an enthusiastic press, an unsentimental realism masked the engineers' idealistic intent; they were in Lilienthal's phrase, "dreamers with shovels." Dams were "schools" for transferring the profession's pragmatic, can-do ethic to a cadre of native apprentices, who could then tackle other complex technical problems. The extraterritorial amenities Toynbee glimpsed at Lashkar Gah, and the legendary salaries Slocum and his brigade of fifty engineers personally negotiated with Nehru, signaled a mutual agreement to dispense with the soft courtesies of benevolence and assign talent its true worth. Disdaining community developers who wanted to "crawl into mud huts and make themselves loved," dam builders modernized not by coaxing peasants out of old habits but by frontal assault on the physical impediments to progress.[9]

On the opening page of *Democracy on the March,* Lilienthal urges the reader to look beyond the fog of words surrounding political questions and see "reality in the world as it actually is." Engineers operated in this objective realm, a sphere of physical action and straight talk that hovered above politics and social conflict. The TVA's claim to nonpolitical status dated from the fierce Senate battle over the Douglas Dam in 1941 when Lilienthal rallied voters to "keep TVA out of politics," and it subsequently grew from institutional myth into a broader generalization about scientific- and technology-based development. The United States put "too much emphasis," Rostow and fellow Massachusetts Institute of Technology economist Max Millikan noted, "on pacts, treaties, negotiation, and international diplomacy" while failing to deal with "the nature of forces at work in the world."[10]

Because conflict theoretically stemmed from demands for the material ingredients of power, it followed that solutions could be achieved by manipulating these tangible factors. Lilienthal, alert for international disputes amenable to "common sense and engineering," proposed in 1951 that India and Pakistan could resolve their differences by jointly developing the Indus Valley, which bisected their contested border. "Artificial" issues, such as massacres, abductions, and the symbolism of Kashmir enflamed political discourse, he admitted, but "partition did not repeal engineering or professional principles." The World Bank followed through, negotiating in 1960 a ten-year, $1.3 billion plan that was hailed as a diplomatic breakthrough until the Indo-Pakistan War of 1965. Only a month prior to that disappointment, Lyndon Johnson had proposed a massive scheme to dam and irrigate the Mekong Valley as a solution to the Vietnam War.[11]

The themes of the TVA idea were themes of state-building: the legitimacy of rulers, the reach of central authority, the tending of borders and populations, and the training of elites. From this perspective, rather than from a purely engineering standpoint, several generations of nation builders regarded it as an ideal method for developing Afghanistan, with its porous frontiers, feeble monarchy, and critical position on the Soviet Union's southern flank. This chapter examines how the Helmand venture's representational ambitions supplanted the "practical" goals of increasing productivity, income, and the welfare of its purported beneficiaries. Because of its scale and longevity, the project assumed roles in a succession of modernizing myths. The New Deal, the New Look, and the New Frontier each revised the stakes and symbolism of development, and these figurative strands entwined with meanings Afghans wove around the project. Within Afghanistan's government, the impulse to modernize went back into the early twentieth century when tribal and ethnic loyalties were reformed as a national identity. Planting a modern city next to the colossal ruins of Qala Bist was a calculated gesture asserting an imagined line of succession from the Ghaznavid dynasty to the royal family presiding in Kabul. The Helmand project symbolized the transformation of the nation, representing the legitimacy of the monarchy, the expansion of state power, and the fulfillment of the Pashtun destiny.

The Accidental Nation

Afghanistan, at its origin, was an empty space on the map that was not Persian, not Russian, not British, "a purely accidental geographic unit," according to Lord George Curzon, who put the finishing touches on its silhouette. Both the monarchy and the nation emerged from strategies Britain used to pacify the Pashtun peoples along India's Northwest frontier in the last half of the nineteenth century. Consisting of nomadic, seminomadic, and settled communities with no common language or ancestry, Pashtuns comprised for colonial officials a single racial grouping. They occupied a strategically vital region stretching from the southern slopes of the Hindu Kush range through the northern Indus Valley into Kashmir.[12]

To prevent tribal feuds from inviting Russian influence, colonial officials devised a double-pronged strategy to bring the Pashtun belt under British control. First, they split it in half by surveying the Durand Line, the 1,200-mile boundary that today separates Afghanistan and Pakistan. Plotted in 1893, the "scientific frontier" followed a topographic ridge line that could be held at strongpoints blocking key mountain passes. By disrupting tribal homelands and the seasonal migration of three million pastoralists following herds of Persian fat-tailed sheep between lowland and upland grazing areas, the Durand Line restricted Pashtun autonomy and facilitated new forms of indirect influence over peoples on both sides of it.[13]

Rather than demarcating the spatial limit of British sovereignty, the Durand Line marked a division between types of imperial control. On the India side, a smaller Pashtun population, the "assured clans," could be co-opted and deployed as proxy armies against Pashtuns on the Afghan side, precluding the emergence of a regime in Kabul hostile to British interests. The Mohammadzai—the clan of Zahir Shah, ruler of Afghanistan from 1933 to 1973—was such a subaltern force, benefiting from British power without being fully constrained by it. Straddling the Khyber Pass, they used subsidies and arms to overwhelm their rivals on the Afghan side. This variety of indirect rule, known as the "Forward Policy," kept Afghanistan firmly under British influence for the first half of the twentieth century.[14]

The Line complemented a cultural strategy of pacification known as the Pathan (Pashtun) Renaissance, through which colonial agents aligned their own interests with those of their tribal allies. Cultivating a Pashtun identity as a unitary "pure" race in contrast with the "mixed" Tajiks, Baluchis, Hazaras, and others with whom they were mingled, colonial officials invented the reputation of the Pashtuns as a warrior caste. They were "our chaps," natural rulers, the equals of the British. "You're white people, sons of Alexander, and not like common, black Mohammedans," the title character of Rudyard Kipling's *The Man Who Would Be King* explained to the Afghans. Pashtuns were entitled to subsidies, to rank in the Indian Army, and to a direct relationship to the crown. Schooling internalized the racial taxonomy, supplanting allegiances to village, family, and clan, while linking Pashtun identity with modernization. Edwardes and Islamia colleges, founded in Peshawar in the early twentieth century, inculcated a consciousness of Pashtun nationhood and suggested "the place which the Pathan might fill in the development of a subcontinent." An awareness of race distinguished the literate few from the vast majority of uneducated Afghans unable to discriminate between ethnographic types.[15]

As it was meant to, the sublimation of the Pashtuns reconfigured politics on both sides of the frontier. When Nadir Shah crossed the Durand Line and seized Kabul from the Tajiks in 1929, he established a monarchy based on Pashtun nationalism with overtones of scientific racism. Comprising less than half the Afghan population, Pashtuns claimed an entitlement based on their status as an advanced race, the bearers of modernity and progress. Punitive expeditions against Tajiks in the north and Hazaras in the south and west, in which German-made aircraft supported mounted troops, broke the autonomous power of these regions, opening them to Pashtun settlement. Nadir Shah built a professional army—new in Afghan tradition—of 40,000 troops, linked by kinship and personal loyalty to the monarchy and trained by French and German advisers. The monarchy economically disfranchised Kabul's vibrant Jewish and Hindu communities, placing private trading and banking businesses in the hands of state cartels. Its order for the expulsion of the Jews, thwarted temporarily by British diplomacy, was effected only after Indian independence. A system of secularized schools and a change of the national language from Dari, a Persian dialect, to Pashto, demonstrated the new regime's determination to bring all of Afghanistan's ethnicities, including the ungoverned tribes, under the control of a rationalized, central state.[16]

For Nadir Shah and his son Zahir, who assumed the throne after his father's assassination in 1933, political survival depended on enlarging and deepening the authority of the state. To its new rulers, Afghanistan was an unknown and dangerous country. It had few roads, only six miles of rail (all of it in Kabul), and few internal telegraph or phone lines. For most of the 10 or 12 million Afghans (Afghanistan has never completed a census), encounters of any kind with the central government were rare and unpleasant. Laws were made and enforced in accordance with local custom and without reference to the state; internal taxes existed only on paper. Evidence of royal authority—easily visible on Kabul streets patrolled by Prussian-helmeted palace guards—disappeared as rapidly as the pavement underneath a traveler leaving the city in any direction. There were no cadastral maps, city plans, or housing registries, an absence that made Afghanistan less *legible* and therefore less governable than countries that had been formally colonized. Modern states are able to govern through manipulation of abstractions—unemployment, public opinion, literacy rates, and so on—but in Afghanistan interventions of any kind, and the reactions to them, were brutally concrete. The prime minister, on his infrequent inspection tours of the countryside, traveled under heavy guard.[17]

Zahir Shah sought help from Japanese, Italian, and German advisers, who laid plans for a modern network of communications and roads. A German-built radio tower in Kabul allowed instant links to remote villages and the outside world for the first time. Through a national bank and state cartels, the government supervised a cautious and tightly controlled economic modernization. German engineers built textile mills, power plants, and carpet and furniture factories to be run by monopolies under royal license. Tax codes and state trading firms began to bring ungoverned sectors, such as stock raising and trading, within reach of accountants and assessors in Kabul. These efforts met with sporadic—and occasionally bloody—resistance, but the regime persisted in slowly and firmly laying the politics of abstraction and principle over the hot-blooded politics of bazaars and clans.[18]

During World War II the United States replaced Germany as the external partner in the young king's plans. The Holocaust and submarine warfare caused Afghanistan's external trade to undergo a sudden and advantageous reorientation. One of the country's chief exports was karakul, the pelt of the Persian fat-tailed sheep converted in the hands of skilled furriers into the glossy black fur known as astrakhan, karacul, or Persian lamb. The former centers of fur making—Leipzig, London, and Paris—closed down during the war years and the industry moved in its entirety to New York. From 1942 through the 1970s, New York furriers consumed nearly the entire Afghan export, 2.5 million skins a year, which resold as lustrous black coats and hats ranging in price from $400 to $3,500. A tiny fraction of the retail revenue went back to Afghanistan, but the fractions added up. The government employed exchange rate manipulations to exact an effective tax rate of more than 50 percent on karakul, making it the country's most lucrative source of exchange as well as revenue. Afghanistan ended World War II with $100 million in reserves, and in the midst of the postwar "dollar gap" crisis in international liquidity, Afghanistan was favored with a small but steady source of dollar earnings.[19]

The collapse of the British Empire created a chance for Pashtun reunification and lent new significance to the modernization project. From the vantage of Kabul, the Partition of India in 1947 invalidated whatever justification the Durand Line once had. A Pashtun separatist movement emerged in Peshawar and Kashmir, and with the encouragement of India, Zahir Shah proposed the creation of an ethnic state—Pushtunistan—consisting of most of northern Pakistan, which would give the assured clans an option to merge with Kabul at some future date. It was a hopeless proposal—the frontier was internationally recognized—but the king stuck to it rather than allow Pakistan to inherit the decisive instruments and influence of the Forward Policy. The assured clans represented a continuing threat to the Afghan state. After 1947, members of the royal family spoke of building in Afghanistan a secure, prosperous base for the recovery of Pashtun lands.[20]

Over the next two decades the Pushtunistan controversy drew Afghanistan into the Cold War. U.S. diplomats dismissed it as fantasy, but to the monarchy Pushtunistan was as solid as France. A visitor in 1954 found government offices in Kabul hung with maps on which the "narrow, wriggly object" plainly appeared, "wedged in between Afghanistan on one flank, and the remains of West Pakistan on the other." The dispute periodically turned hot, with reciprocal sacking of embassies and border incidents that gradually converted the Durand Line into the kind of politico-geographic feature that typified the Cold War, an impassable boundary. The movement of goods across the frontier was tightly restricted, and in 1962 Pakistan closed the passes to migration, terminating the seasonal movement of the herds. From the mid-1950s until the end of the Soviet occupation, Afghanistan's legal exports and imports moved almost exclusively through the Soviet Union, which discounted freight rates to encourage the dependency.[21]

In the immediate aftermath of World War II, however, the Soviet Union was preoccupied with internal reconstruction, and Afghanistan looked to the United States for help in consolidating a centralized state that could assume responsibility for the public welfare. Through its development programs, the monarchy assumed a relationship of trusteeship over the nation, presenting the king as retaining custody of the state during a dangerous transitional period but ready to relinquish power once modernity was achieved. Official terminology coupled underdevelopment and Afghan identity. "Afghanistan is a backward country," insisted

Mohammed Daoud, the king's brother-in-law, cousin, and prime minister, in 1959. "We must do something about it or die as a nation." Large-scale development projects, visible signs of national energy, would stake the Pashtuns' claim to the future and the royal family's claim to the present. One such scheme particularly appealed to the king; he wanted to build a dam.[22]

A TVA for the Hindu Kush

A dam-building project would vastly expand and intensify the authority that could be exercised by the central government at Kabul. Remaking and regulating the physical environment of an entire region would, for the first time, render Afghanistan into a legible inventory of material and human resources in the manner of modern states. Using its karakul revenue, the Afghan government hired the largest American heavy engineering firm, Morrison Knudsen, Inc. of Boise, Idaho, to construct a dam. Harry W. Morrison, builder of the Hoover Dam, the San Francisco Bay Bridge, and soon the launch complex at Cape Canaveral, had a legendary reputation in the world of heavy construction. *Time* ranked him first among America's "ambassadors with bulldozers." His firm operated all over the world, boring tunnels through the Andes and laying airfields in Turkey. Its engineers, who called themselves Emkayans, were drawing up specs for a complex of dams in the gorges of the Yangtze River in 1949 when Mao's People's Liberation Army drove them out. Afghanistan hired Morrison Knudsen in 1946. Quartered in a crumbling Moghul Palace outside Kandahar, the firm began surveying the Helmand Valley.[23]

The Helmand and Arghandab rivers constitute Afghanistan's largest river system, draining a watershed covering half the country. Originating in the Hindu Kush a few miles from Kabul, the Helmand travels through upland dells thick with orchards and vineyards before merging with the Arghandab twenty-five miles from Kandahar, turning west across the arid plain of Registan and emptying into the Sistan marshes of Iran. The valley was reputedly the site of a vast irrigation works destroyed by Genghis Khan in the thirteenth century. The entire area is dry, catching only two to three inches of rain per year. Consequently, river flows fluctuate unpredictably within a wide range, varying between 2,000 and 60,000 cubic feet per second. Before beginning, Morrison Knudsen had to build an infrastructure of roads and bridges to allow movement of equipment. Typically, it would also conduct extensive studies on soils and drainage, but

118

the company and the Afghan government convinced themselves that in this case it was not necessary, that "even a 20 percent margin of error . . . could not detract from the project's intrinsic value."[24]

The Emkayans measured intrinsic value against a baseline drawn from the common stock of cultural assumptions about Eastern societies. Postwar Americans pictured Asia as a continent of natural and human extremes—a landscape, according to Harold Isaacs, of vast "open spaces, mountains, river valleys, villages, primitive farming, bright hot deserts, wet paddy fields, [and] smells." The sheer wealth of unused potential defined it as a frontier. Brimming with mineral resources, a "large pool of underemployed or unemployed labor," and stagnant agriculture, Asia could generate "quite large" returns, according to the State Department, from "relatively small inputs" of capital. Hydraulic terminology accentuated the assurance that latent energies awaited release by knowing hands. "How do you feel about the untapped resources of the underdeveloped nations?" Cary Grant tantalized in *That Touch of Mink.* "I think," Doris Day responded, "they ought to be tapped." Americans knew from Karl Wittfogel that Oriental peoples inhabited "hydraulic societies" with customs, family structure, forms of economy and governance organized around the struggle for mastery of water, a difference that reduced the problems of Asia to well-understood proportions. Morrison Knudsen engineers could take confidence in the knowledge that they were engaged in a familiar, even ancestral, American mission: the domestication of an unspoiled land through the control of rivers.[25]

The promise of dams is that they are a renewable resource, furnishing power and water indefinitely with little effort once the project is complete, but dam projects are subject to ecological constraints often more severe outside of the temperate zone. Siltation, which now threatens many New Deal–era dams, advances more quickly in arid and tropical climates. Canal irrigation involves a special set of hazards. Arundhati Roy, the voice of India's anti-dam movement, explains that "perennial irrigation does to soil roughly what anabolic steroids do to the human body," stimulating ordinary earth to produce multiple crops in the first years while slowly rendering the soil infertile. Large reservoirs raise the water table in the surrounding area, a problem worsened by extensive irrigation. Waterlogging can destroy harvests, but it produces more permanent damage, too. In waterlogged soils, capillary action pulls soluble salts and alkalis to the surface, leading to desertification. Early reports warned that the Helmand Valley was vulnerable because it had gravelly subsoils and salt deposits. The Emkayans knew Middle Eastern rivers were often unsuited to extensive irrigation schemes. But these apprehensions' "impact was minimized by one or both parties." From the start, the Helmand project was primarily about national prestige, and only secondarily about the social benefits of increasing agricultural productivity.[26]

Signs of trouble appeared almost immediately. Even when half-completed, the first dam, a small diversion barrage at the mouth of the Boghra canal, raised the water table to within a few inches of the surface. A glittering crust of salt could be seen on the ground along the shore of the reservoir. Government officials openly questioned the company's competence. "The Afghans had been taken for somewhat of a ride," concluded John Hlavacek, one of the few reporters to visit the site in the early years. "It smacked pretty much of a mistake on the part of the Americans. At least it looked that way to me." In 1949 the engineers and the government faced a decision. Tearing down the dam would mean a loss of face for the monarchy and Morrison Knudsen, but from an engineering standpoint the project was a bust. The necessary reconsideration never took place, however, because it was at this moment that the unlucky Boghra works was overtaken by the global project of development.[27]

Under the new logic of foreign aid inaugurated by President Truman in January 1949, Afghanistan became an "underdeveloped" country, and owing to its position neighboring the Soviet Union and China, the likely recipient of substantial assistance. Point Four's technical aid could take many forms—clinics, schools, new livestock breeds, assays for minerals and petroleum—but Boghra was an invitation to something grander, a reproduction of an American developmental triumph. The TVA had totemic significance for American liberals, but in the diplomatic setting it had the additional function of redefining political conflict as a technical problem. Britain's solution to Afghanistan's tribal wars had been to script feuds of blood, honor, and faith within the linear logic of boundary commissions, containing conflict within two-dimensional space. The United States set aside the maps and replotted tribal enmities on hydrologic charts. Resolution became a matter of apportioning cubic yards of water and kilowatt hours of energy. Assurances of inevitable progress further displaced conflict into the future; if all sides could be convinced that resource flows would increase, problems would vanish, in bureaucratic parlance, downstream.

Afghanistan applied for and received a $12 million Ex-Im Bank loan for the Helmand Valley, the first of more than $80 million received over the next fifteen years. Afghanistan's loan request contained a line for soil surveys, but the bank rejected it as an unnecessary expense. In 1952 the national government created the Helmand Valley Authority—later the Helmand and Arghandab Valley Authority (HAVA)—removing 1,800 square miles of river valley from local control and placing it under the jurisdiction of expert commissions in Kabul. The monarchy poured money into the project; one-fifth of the central government's total expenditures in the 1950s and early 1960s. From 1946 on, the salaries of Morrison Knudsen's advisers and technicians absorbed an amount equivalent to Afghanistan's total exports. Without adequate mechanisms for tax collection, the royal treasury passed costs on to agricultural producers through inflation and the diversion of export revenue, offsetting any income gains from irrigation. Although it pulled in millions in international funding, HAVA soaked up the small reserves of individual farmers and may well have reduced the total national investment in agriculture.[28]

HAVA supplemented the initial dam with a vast complex of dams. Two large dams for storage and hydropower—the 200-foot high Arghandab dam and the 320-foot Kajakai dam—were supplemented by diversion dams, drainage works, and irrigation canals. Reaching out from the reservoirs were 300 miles of concrete-lined canals. Three of the longest (the Tarnak, the Darweshan, and the Shamalan) fed riparian lands already intensively cultivated and irrigated by an elaborate system of tunnels, flumes, and canals known as *juis*. The new wider canals furnished a more ample and purportedly more reliable water source. The Zahir Shah canal supplied Kandahar with water from the Arghandab reservoir, and two long-distance canals stretched out into the desert to polders of reclaimed desert: Marja and Nad-i-Ali. Each extension of the project required more land acquisitions and more displaced people. To remain flexible, the royal government and Morrison Knudsen kept the question of who actually owned the land in abeyance. No system of titles was instituted, and the bulk of the reclaimed land was farmed by tenants of Morrison-Knudsen, the government, or contractors hired by the government.[29]

The new systems magnified the problems encountered at the Boghra works and added new ones: waterlogging created a persistent weed problem. Storage dams removed silt that once rejuvenated fields downstream. Deposits of salt or gypsum would erupt into long-distance canals and be carried off to deaden the soil of distant fields. The Emkayans had to contend with unpredictable flows triggered by snowmelt in the distant

Hindu Kush. In 1957 floods nearly breached dams in two places and water tables rose, salinating soils throughout the region. The reservoirs and large canals also lowered the water temperature, making plots that once held vineyards and orchards suitable only for growing grain. After a decade of work, HAVA could not set a schedule for completion. As engineering failures mounted, HAVA's symbolic weight in the Cold War and Afghanistan's ethnic politics steadily grew.[30]

Engines and Dreams

Like the TVA, HAVA was a multipurpose river authority. U.S. officials described it as "a major social engineering project," responsible for river development but also for education, housing, health care, roads, communications, agricultural research and extension, and industrial development in the valley. U.S. ambassador Henry A. Byroade noted in 1962 that if successful, HAVA could boost Kabul's "earnings of foreign exchange and, if properly devised, could foster the growth of a strata of small holders which would give the country more stability." This billiard-ball alignment of capital accumulation, class formation, and political evolution was a core proposition of the social science approach to modernization that was just making the leap from university think tanks to centers of policymaking.[31]

Following behavioral explanations of development, U.S. aid officials sought to ally themselves with tutelary elites possessing the transitional personalities that could generate nonviolent, evolutionary change. At first glance, the king and his retinue appeared almost ideally suited. Educated in Europe and the United States, royal government officials spoke in familiar terms of ways to engineer progress. Daoud presided as supreme technocrat. Educated in France and at English schools in Kabul, he became prime minister in 1953. "We members of the royal family," he told anthropologist Louis Dupree, "were all trained in the West and have adopted Western ideas as our own." Since coming to power in 1953, Daoud had accelerated the economic tempo, believing that without rapid growth, Afghanistan would dissolve into factionalism and be divided among its neighbors. He was sure U.S. and Soviet generosity sprang from temporary conditions and that his government had only a short time in which to take all it could. To American officials, Afghan modernizers appeared too eager, too ready to jump ahead without the necessary planning and information-gathering steps, and too ready to take aid from any source. Daoud's receptiveness to Soviet and Chinese aid was particularly troubling. As Dupree put it, "A nation does not accept technology without ideology. A machine or a dam is a product of a culture."[32]

Daoud's regime made no effort to disguise its chauvinism. Controlling positions in the government, army, police, and educational system were held by Pashtuns to such a degree that the name "Afghan" commonly referred only to Pashtuns, not to the minorities who collectively comprised the majority. A U.S. diplomat described the kingdom as a Soviet-style "police state, where there is no free press, no political parties, and where ruthless suppression of minorities is the established pattern." But despite their favored status, Pashtuns revolted against the Mohammedzai eight times between 1930 and 1960. Open violence between ethnicities was less common than conflict that pitted clan autonomy against central authority. In 1956 Daoud welcomed Soviet military aid and advisers. His security forces kept order with a heavy hand, and in 1959, when mullahs in Kandahar again led a movement against the government, the army used tanks and MiGs to crush the rebellion. Daoud brought the Cold War to Afghanistan.[33]

To the Eisenhower administration, Morrison Knudsen's outpost in Kandahar was the scientific frontier of American power in Central Asia, guarding the high passes between risk and credibility. The company was "one of the chief influences which maintain Afghan connections with the West," Secretary of State John Foster Dulles believed. "Its departure would create a vacuum which the Soviets would be anxious to fill." He wanted to preserve Afghanistan's buffer role, but the perennial provocations along the Durand Line conjured scenarios in Dulles's mind in which a Soviet-backed Afghan army attacked U.S.-allied Pakistan—another Korea, this time beyond the reach of U.S. air and naval power. Daoud's Pashtun extremism led his government to welcome Soviet arms while instigating mob attacks on Pakistani consulates and border posts. In 1955, Dulles dissuaded Pakistan from a plan to overthrow the royal family, while his brother Allen, head of the Central Intelligence Agency, suggested using the same methods against Daoud that had recently worked to depose Mossadeq in Iran. The United States wanted to separate the dual ambitions of Pashtun nationalism, preserving Daoud's modernization drive while disposing of the Pashtunistan issue.[34]

The Helmand project offered a way to counter Soviet influence by giving Daoud what he wanted: a Pashtun homeland. As originally envisioned, HAVA would irrigate enough new fertile land to settle 18,000–20,000 families on fifteen-acre farms. Together with Afghan officials, U.S. advisers launched a program to sedentarize the nomadic Pashtuns whose migrations were a source of friction with Pakistan. Settling Pashtuns in a belt from Kabul to Kandahar would secure the area for the government and bring reformed drovers within reach of modernization programs. Diminishing transborder flows would eliminate smuggling and the periodic incidents that enflamed the Pashtunistan issue. The complementary development project in the Indus Valley, also funded by the United States, settled nomads on the other side, making the Durand Line a modern boundary, a division between isolated economic spheres.[35]

Nomadism is a scarce and valuable expertise, largely unrecorded but refined over many generations. Skilled selection of the size and composition of the herd and the effective rotation of livestock between high and low pastures are critical for maintaining fragile rangelands. The ability of Pashtun herdsmen to extract wealth from marginal terrains where settled agriculture was either unprofitable or unsustainable was a heroic achievement, but to Americans and royal officials the nomadic population and its disregard for laws, taxes, and borders, symbolized the country's backwardness. Ann Morrison, whose monthly travel column was required reading for Emkayans, was unsettled by the "moth-eaten" caravans of "camels, goats, sheep, dogs, men, women, and children" that clogged company roads and mounted occasional raids on work sites. Pastoralists generated the bulk of the nation's income, but their wandering made revenue difficult to capture. Rural modernization, in Afghanistan and elsewhere in Asia, seldom meant increasing income or productivity for farmers. More often, it was a process of discouraging thriving lucrative practices and promoting politically acceptable ones in their place. Border hostilities required Afghanistan to create a territorialized economy and a measurable, geographically fixed tax base in place of the seasonal migrations that furnished the livelihoods of the nation's people. To build a state, Afghans would have to be made into peasants.[36]

The program of sedentarization (some have called it *peasantization*) expanded HAVA's mandate for the social reconstruction of the region. Those seeking land and families already occupying ancestral plots were required to apply to HAVA for housing, water, and implements. In the late 1950s HAVA began constructing whole communities for transplanted pastoralists in Marja, the Shamalan, and Nad-i-Ali while simultaneously trying to break the authority of leaders of nomadic clans, known as *maliks*. Maliks led their people "Moses-like, to the promised land" according to a report, as they had led them in years past over the Khojak Pass and into the orchards and valleys of Quetta. HAVA "always informed the new settlers that they could choose new village leaders, to be called *wakil,* if they so desired. None did." Resettled families would receive a pair of oxen, a grant of 2,000 Afghanis, and enough seed for the first year. To replace the need for winter pastures, the UN brought in Swiss experts to teach nomads to use long-handled scythes to cut forage for sheep from high plateaus. But even with the closing of the border and the attraction of subsidies and well-watered homesteads, it proved difficult to entice Ghilzai Pashtun to live within fences. Freer and richer than the peasants whose lands they crossed, the nomads regarded their new Tajik and Hazara neighbors with contempt. This may have served Kabul's purposes, too. The government, according to Hafizullah Emadi, planned to "use these new settlers as a death squad to crush the uprisings of the non-Pashtun people of the west, southwest, and central part of the country."[37]

The Helmand project symbolized Pashtun power, and the royal government resisted efforts to attach alternate meanings to it. U.S. advisers made several attempts to imitate the "grass roots" inclusivity of the TVA. Aiming to dispel tribal feuds and foster a common professional identity among farmers, they established local co-ops and 4-H clubs, but Daoud's security forces broke them up. Courting the Muslim clergy was also forbidden. Agricultural experts found the mullahs to be a progressive force, "constantly look[ing] for things to improve their communities, better seed, new plants, improved livestock." Regarding religion as an inoculation against communism, policymakers wanted to associate the Helmand project with Islam. In 1956 the U.S. Information Agency produced "a 45-minute full color motion picture, which featured economic development, particularly the Helmand Valley Project, and the religious heritage of Afghanistan." Daoud, however, regarded the mullahs as a subversive element. He discouraged their contact with foreign advisers and resented, according to U.S. intelligence, "any reference made in his presence to Islam as a bulwark against communism or as a unifying force."[38]

In 1955 Afghanistan became the first target of Premier Nikita Khrushchev's "economic offensive," the Soviet Union's first venture in foreign aid. More than $100 million in credits—the largest Soviet overseas loan—financed a fleet of taxis and buses and 500 Soviet engineers to construct airports, a cement factory, a mechanized bakery, a five-lane highway from their own border to Kabul, and, of course, dams. The Soviets constructed the Jalalabad Dam and canal and organized a joint river development scheme for the Amu Darya River. Soviet competition substantially elevated the stakes for U.S. aid. The scale of the credit—triple the size of the U.S. loan for the Helmand, on terms the Afghans could not conceivably repay—created a dangerous dependency, but the U.S. response was to counter with more aid and loans and to encourage European allies to do the same.[39]

By the 1960s Afghanistan had Soviet, Chinese, and West German dam projects under way and was engrossing one of the highest levels of development aid per capita of any nation in the world. It was a testing ground, according to Henry Kissinger, for a type of economic warfare the United States could pursue in the "gray areas," countries on the Asian periphery (including Iran, Burma, and Indochina) too remote for the deployment of U.S. troops. *U.S. News and World Report* took note of this "strange kind of cold war" fought with money and technicians, instead of spies and bombs. Publicly, U.S. officials declared it was the kind of competition they wanted, just a chance to show what the different systems could do in a fair match, but privately, they worried the rules were jiggered in favor of the other side. The Soviets could win by losing, by deepening the disruptive effects of development. Unless the United States could open "a vista of hope," Dulles told the Senate, Kabul would "almost inevitably turn toward the terrible and cruel experiment of communism." Afghanistan had become a new kind of buffer, an arena for a tournament of modernization.[40]

James A. Michener, the popular novelist, visited in 1955 and assessed the stakes of the developmental contest in terms that echoed frontier myths in which white Americans won over "hostiles" with demonstrations of personal honor and skill. The turbulent Helmand "symbolize[d] the wild freedom of Afghanistan" that regrettably had to be "brought under control." In his 1962 novel of Afghanistan Michener captured the dilemmas of progress in two characters: Nur Muhammad, religious, proud, suspicious of change, and Nazrullah, a foreign-educated expert, impatient, outspoken, and eager for help from the Americans if possible, the Soviets if necessary. Nazrullah was an engineer, damming the Helmand with boulders blasted from a nearby mountain. "Each day we must throw similar rocks into the human river of Afghanistan," he tells the American narrator. "Here a school, there a road, down in the gorge a dam. So far, our human river isn't aware that it's been touched. But we shall never halt until we've modified it completely."[41]

Competition altered the significance, but not the fortunes, of the Helmand project in the 1960s. Launching the "Development Decade," John F. Kennedy determined not only to surpass Soviet initiatives but also to demonstrate the superiority of American methods of development. Presidential emissary Averill Harriman, sent to Kabul in 1965, coupled food as a measure of progress with a vision of autonomous selfhood. The Soviets could not produce a good harvest, he explained, because of the "character of farm work which requires hardworking individuals with personal stake in operation, rather than hourly paid factory hands paced by machine."[42]

Evidence for the efficiency of American techniques was scarce in the Helmand Valley. The burden of American loans for the project, and the absence of tangible returns created, according to the *New York Times,* "a dangerous strain on the both the Afghan economy and the nation's morale" which "may have unwittingly and indirectly contributed to driving Afghanistan into Russian arms." Waterlogging had advanced in the Shamalan to the point that structural foundations were giving way; mosques and houses were crumbling into the growing bog. In the artificial oases, the problem was worse. An impermeable crust of conglomerate underlay the Marja and Nad-i-Ali tracts, intensifying both waterlogging and salinization. The remedy—a system of discharge channels leading to deep-bore drains—would remove ten percent of the reclaimed land from cultivation. A 1965 study revealed that crop yields per acre had actually dropped since the dams were built, sharply in areas already cultivated but declines were evident even in areas reclaimed from the desert. Withdrawing support from HAVA was impossible. "With this project," the U.S. ambassador noted, "the American reputation in Afghanistan is completely linked." For reasons of credibility alone, the United States kept pouring money in, even though by 1965 it was clear the project was failing. Diplomats complained about having the United States' reputation hang on "a strip of concrete," but there was no going back. Helmand was an economic Vietnam, a quagmire that consumed money and resources without the possibility of success, all to avoid making failure obvious.[43]

Revisions in modernization theory reinforced the urgency of changing strategy in the Helmand. Dual economy theory, which conceptually divided each economy into a self-propelling industrial sector and a retrograde but vitally important rural sector, gained the attention of policymakers in the early 1960s. "Agricultural development is vastly more important in modernizing a society than we used to think," Rostow noted. Agriculture was "a system" like industry, and modernizing it required "that the skills of organization developed in the modern urban sectors of the society be brought systematically into play around the life of a farmer." Development was still fundamentally a problem of scarcity, but while the Emkayans had filled voids with water and power, the U.S. Agency for International Development (USAID) sought to build reservoirs of organization, talent, and mentality. Rejuvenating Afghan agriculture, aid officials believed, would require "a revolution in mental concepts."[44]

The Kennedy and Johnson administrations renewed the U.S. commitment to HAVA with a fresh infusion of funds and initiatives, raising the annual aid disbursement from $16 million to $40 million annually. The approach pioneered by the Rockefeller Foundation in Mexico would bring a new organizational system into play around the farmer. In 1967, USAID and the royal government imported 170 tons of the experimental dwarf wheats developed in Mexico. The high-yield seed, together with chemical fertilizers and tightly controlled irrigation, were expected to produce grain surpluses that would be distributed through new marketing and credit arrangements. Resettlement subsidies had paid off by the mid-1960s, and the Helmand Valley was beginning to have a lived-in look. The large corporate and state farms had vanished, and nearly all of the land that could successfully be farmed was privately held, much of it by smallholders. Legal titles were still clouded by HAVA's inattention to land surveys, but the settlers had nonetheless sculpted wide tracts of empty land into irregular fifteen-acre parcels divided by meandering *juis,* tree-lined canals that served as boundary, water source, and orchard for each farm.[45]

Unfortunately, the *juis* system proved incompatible with the new plans. The small, hilly, picturesquely misshapen fields contributed to runoff and drainage problems and prevented the regular, measured applications of water, chemicals, and machine cultivation necessary for the Mexico model. It would require, in effect, a land reform in reverse: merging small holdings into large level fields divided at regular intervals by laterals running from control gates on the main canals. As the wheat improvement program got under way, a team of U.S. Department of Agriculture advisers proposed that HAVA remove all of the resettled families, "level the whole area with bulldozers," and then redistribute property "in large, uniform, smooth land plots." HAVA adopted the land-preparation scheme, but implementation proved difficult. Farmers objected to the removal of trees, which had economic value and prevented wind erosion, but they objected chiefly to vagueness of HAVA's assurances. HAVA acknowledged, as bulldozing proceeded, that questions of what to do with the population while the land was being prepared, how to redistribute the land after completion, and whether to charge landowners for improvements were "yet to be worked out." When farmers "met the bulldozers with rifles," according to a USAID report, it presented a "very real constraint" that "consumed most of the time of the American and Afghan staffs in the Valley throughout the 1960s."[46]

The valley's unrest coincided with Afghanistan's brief experiment with political liberalization. Daoud stepped down in 1963 and the monarchy issued a constitution permitting an independent legislature and government ministries. The economy remained under central guidance. Political parties were banned, and the king continued to control the army and maintain a paternal supervision over government, but high ministerial posts went for the first time to persons outside the royal family. Laws requiring women to wear the burka were lifted (although custom maintained the practice in much of the country), and restrictions on speech and assembly were eased. In Kabul an energetic student and café politics emerged, with daily street demonstrations by socialist, Maoist, and liberal factions, while outside of the capital dissent coalesced around Islamic mullahs who articulated, according to U.S. embassy officials, "latent dissatisfaction with the low level of economic development and progress in the Afghan hinterland." In the partyless parliament, ethnic politics took precedence as minority representatives attacked Pashtun privileges while the majority defended them. Legislative deadlock, the stalling modernization drive, and the growing burden of external debt fed perceptions of official ineptitude. The government of Prime Minister Mohammad Maiwandwal, which initiated the wheat improvement effort, needed modernization to produce tangible results.[47]

By 1969 the new grains had spread to a modest 300,000 acres, leading to expectations of an approaching "yield takeoff," but the 1971 El Niño drought destroyed much of the crop. Monsoon rains failed through 1973, reducing the Helmand to a rivulet. In 1971 the Arghandab reservoir dried up completely, a possibility not foreseen by planners. With the coming of détente in 1970, levels of aid from both the United States and the Soviet Union dropped sharply. The vision of prosperous, irrigation-fed farms luring nomads into their green embrace proved beyond HAVA's

129

grasp. Wheat yields were among the lowest in the world: four bushels per acre (Iowa farms produced 180), farm incomes in the valley were below average for Afghanistan and declining, and the karakul economy had been wiped out. State Department officials found it difficult to measure the magnitude of the economic crisis "in Afghanistan where there are no statistics," but student strikes and the suspension of parliament pointed to a "creeping crisis" in mid-1972. "The food crisis," the embassy reported, "seems to have been the real clincher for which neither the king nor his government were prepared."[48]

In July 1973, military units loyal to Daoud deposed the king, who was vacationing in Europe, and terminated both the monarchy and the constitution. U.S. involvement in HAVA was scheduled to end in July 1974, and USAID officials strenuously opposed suggestions that it be renewed. Nonetheless, when Kissinger visited Kabul in February, Daoud described the Helmand Valley as an "unfinished symphony" and urged the United States not to abandon it. The Nixon administration relented. Land reclamation officers remained with the project, making little progress against its persistent problems until the pro-Soviet Khalq party seized power in 1978.[49]

Official and unofficial postmortems identified misperceptions at the root of the project's failures. Lloyd Baron, an economist given access to the U.S. aid mission's records in the 1970s, noted a "development myopia" that identified water scarcity as the sole obstacle to agricultural abundance. Planners subordinated complex social and political problems within the more manageable engineering problem of overcoming the water constraint. The goals and effects of the project were never viewed outside the distorting mirror of modernization theory. Pastoralists produced the country's primary export and most of its foreign exchange revenue, and yet HAVA's plan to convert them into wheat farmers was never seriously questioned. "Any anthropologist could have predicted," Arnold Fletcher observed in 1965, "that the happy notion of settling Afghan nomads on the reclaimed lands would not work out." But if illusions doomed the project, they also created and sustained it. HAVA's evolutionary advantage was an ability to take on the protective coloration of a succession of modernizing myths. The disastrous effects of dam-building were visible in 1949 and only became more obvious as the project grew. But camouflaged by dreams of Pashtun ascendancy and American influence, HAVA was as resilient as development theory itself, able to survive repeated debunkings while shedding the blame and the memory of failure.[50]

Soviet economic development also failed to create a stable, modernizing social class. The Khalq was not broadly based enough to hold onto authority unaided. Against the threat of takeover by an Islamic party, the Soviet Union launched the invasion of 1979. During the Soviet war, both sides found ways to make use of the Helmand Valley's infrastructure. In early 1980, according to M. Hasan Kakar, "about a hundred prisoners" of the Khalq "were thrown out of airplanes into the Arghandab reservoir." The project's concrete water channels provided cover for Mujaheddin fighters, and its broken terrain was the site of intense fighting between the resistance and Soviet forces as well as among ethnic factions. Soviet troops felled trees to smash the irrigation canals and extensively mined the fields and orchards, driving the population into refugee camps in Pakistan.[51]

International and U.S. aid agencies rushed to fill the void left by the collapse of the pro-Soviet regime by rehabilitating the Helmand-Arghandab system. Surveys using satellite imagery and global-positioning technology revealed that, amazingly, the irrigation works had functioned without interruption throughout the twelve years of war even though the agricultural economy had nearly collapsed. One-fifth of the irrigated land was idle and unoccupied, large tracts were uselessly salinated, and much of the remaining land was planted in poppies. Opium grows well in dry climates and alkaline and saline soils. In 2008, according to the UN Office of Drugs and Crime, the Helmand Valley produced two-thirds of Afghanistan's opium, more than half of the global supply. "If Helmand were a country," the survey concluded. "It would be the world's biggest producer of illicit drugs." The Taliban movement, which began in the valley, used opium revenue to finance its rise. Once in power, the Taliban invested in the dams and finished one project begun but not completed by the Americans in the 1960s: linking the Kajakai Dam's hydroelectric plant to the city of Kandahar. Work was finished in early 2001, just a few months before American bombers destroyed the plant.[52]

In the wake of the American invasion, dam construction again topped the list of developmental priorities. In 2003 U.S. Ambassador Zalmay Khalilzad announced that agriculture would be the centerpiece of postconflict reconstruction and outlined plans to invest $20 million in repairing the Helmand's turbines and irrigation canals. The FAO joined the effort with projects to encourage cultivation of raisins and nuts. Once again, the effort aimed to displace a lucrative cross-border trade in agricultural goods, this time in opium, to create a centrally directed, geographically bounded market. This goal, the irreducible minimum requirement of modernization, keeps drawing aid dollars back to the Helmand. In 2009 President Barack Obama announced a "civilian surge" of agriculture specialists to wean farmers away from the poppy with credit and subsidies, and in February 2010 15,000 NATO troops drove the Taliban out of Marja in an operation intended to "make or break" the war effort. Fifty years after they started, American technicians are still trying to turn Afghans into safely mortgaged farmers. Afghanistan cannot be a stable modern state unless it can isolate and control its internal economy, and dams "improve" agriculture not by increasing income or value but by enclosing and regulating it. Throughout recorded history, Afghanistan has been a caravansary, a place for people and goods to pass through, but to its misfortune, development requires it to be enclosed.[53]

Other major dam schemes fared better than the Helmand, but also fell short of expectations. Pakistan's Indus Valley project suffered from persistent salination problems. Two of the four dams planned for India's Damodar Valley were never completed owing to funding shortfalls and growing popular resistance. Political disappointments attended the most ambitions projects. Kennedy's support for Ghana's Volta Redonda project provided insufficient motivation to draw Kwame Nkrumah into the Western camp, just as Egypt's Gamel Abdel Nasser proved unfaithful to Moscow despite the Aswan High Dam, the most visible triumph of Soviet overseas development. Lilienthal was deeply shocked by the collapse of the Shah's regime in the 1970s after three decades of hydroelectric modernization in Iran. But as in Afghanistan, setbacks never entirely dispelled confidence in the model. A 1998 study criticized the World Bank for steering more than half its lending into environmentally destabilizing infrastructure projects such as large dams, roads, and power plants, but at the announcement of a loan for the $1.25 billion Nam Theun dam in Laos in 2005, the bank insisted that it had learned from earlier mistakes.[54]

Even at the height of its influence in the 1950s and 1960s, the TVA model never offered universal solutions to the problems of rural Asia. Indeed, part of its appeal lay in the spatial and political specificity of its intervention; it reinforced borders and established "inner citadels" of state authority. As concerns about population assumed prominence in development planning, however, modernizers looked for technological levers with a capacity to diffuse transformations across whole nations and regions. In India, already the most irrigated nation on earth, new dams raised local productivity substantially, but had an imperceptible effect on poverty, which Indian leaders identified, at the moment of independence, as their most urgent problem. The U.S. administration took longer to recognize poverty as a strategic threat, but when it did, the scale of India's need made it the country to watch.

5

A VERY BIG, VERY POOR COUNTRY

Harry S Truman could imagine India, but he couldn't imagine why "anyone thought it was important." He pictured a country "jammed with poor people and cows wandering around streets, witch doctors, and people sitting on hot coals and bathing in the Ganges." He was far from alone in this impression. The National Security Council (NSC), in its first assessment of India's strategic value in 1949, concluded that an alliance with 300 million Indians living near the "margins of subsistence" would encumber rather than bolster U.S. defenses. It was essential, the council emphasized, not to give the new nation any firm assurances, and to "scrupulously avoid responsibility for raising Asiatic living standards."[1]

Only a decade later, Senator John F. Kennedy put forward a radically different appraisal of the value of India and the strategic meaning of poverty. The sheer scale of India's deprivation, he argued, made it the decisive ideological battleground and "a world power with a world audience" in its own right. Walter Lippmann agreed. To win over "the submerged masses in the old imperial lands" the West needed a proxy, "a very big and very poor country" in which to demonstrate a "take-off from the ancient stagnant poverty of Asia toward a progressive, independent, modern economy." India was not just an ally, but a surrogate in the Cold War's most decisive encounter.[2]

The story of how India became strategically important illustrates a further step in the evolution of poverty from a domestic social problem into an international crisis. The debates over aid to India coincided with the emergence of economics as a policy language. As the Cold War shifted from Europe to Asia, the terminology of alliances, iron curtains, and armaments gave way to a language of takeoffs, five-year plans, and growth rates. In the minds of American planners, India's position at the center of a line of containment, as well as its stance as a nonaligned nation, were superseded by its more crucial function as an "answer to the Communist argument," a living example of development without revolution. But for India to represent a democratic alternative, its development had to be packaged in a way that differentiated it from the Soviet or Chinese experience. This ambition—to mark off India as a developmental model that was both attractive and distinctly Western—inspired aid officials, economists, and the press first to create the "problem" of hunger and then make solving it an international goal.

Prior to the Korean War India did not measure up, as an ally or a supplicant, in Washington's calculus of Cold War strategy. In its original version the containment concept centered on holding defensible lines and strategic bases, ports, and industries, none of which could be found in India. The problem of what to do with large populations caught between the defended perimeters and the communist advance troubled military officials, but tight postwar budgets precluded alternatives. Although the first two U.S. ambassadors to India, Henry Grady and Loy Henderson, cabled persistent and imaginative appeals for aid, the Truman administration demurred.[3]

Aid officials concluded that the immensity of South Asia's poverty would rapidly exhaust the limited sums available. Despite the public attention given to Point Four, the 1949 aid budget amounted to less than $40 million. While Prime Minister Jawaharlal Nehru complained of American plans to "buy up countries and continents," Washington was sure India was one it could not afford. The term most frequently applied to India's condition was "chronic." Its economy was characterized, according to intelligence officials, by "the predominance of an underdeveloped agriculture" with an unbroken record of "chronic stagnation." Government economists warned that aid to India would become a "chronic affair in view of the frequent recurrence of famines."[4]

If the sheer scale of India's needs justified dodging a commitment prior to 1950, the Chinese revolution and the North Korean attack on the South reversed Washington's calculations. Reformulating containment in the wake of these setbacks, the NSC realized that pervasive poverty offered communists a "springboard for further incursions" in Asia. The power of the peasantry—demonstrated by Mao's "Big Push" offensive—confirmed the danger of allowing large, ideologically vulnerable populations to slip. The notion of a linear defense running through a chain of islands along Asia's coast gave way to a strategic concept emphasizing control over populations and resources. Intelligence officials foresaw a struggle in which each superpower gathered "those elements of human and material power in the Far East which will ultimately help weigh a world balance in their favor."[5]

The new doctrine attached greater strategic value to both South Asia and foreign aid. State Department officials presented India and Pakistan as front-line states, reservoirs of military manpower and raw materials that could be won over by showcase development programs that produced "early and obvious results." In a picture essay in *Life* magazine, former diplomat William Bullitt conjured an image of India as half treasure house, half slum, "an immense country" with "enormous natural resources and superb fighting men" where millions survived on "fewer calories and vitamins a day than even the Chinese." Its tiny but able corps of British-trained civil servants were engaged in a unique experiment to transform an illiterate peasantry, one-fifth of humanity, into citizens of a new Asia. In the spring of 1951 Truman authorized the first wheat loan to cover shortages caused by droughts in Madras and Bihar, and went to Capitol Hill to lobby in person for an additional $8.5 billion in aid, including $50 million for India's community development scheme. It was vital, he argued, to prevent "more of the peaceful millions of the East" from turning "into armies to be used as pawns of the Kremlin."[6]

Despite strongly favorable public opinion, aid to India remained a tough sell in Congress owing to Nehru's legendary truculence. Legislators took notice of his unflattering remarks on the American character, but his disdain for Washington's efforts to defend his continent provoked a more acute reaction. After initially supporting the counterattack in Korea, the Indian prime minister denounced MacArthur's decision to carry the war past the 38th parallel and went on to condemn U.S. actions in Taiwan, Indochina, and the United Nations (UN). His statements nearly derailed the aid program as congressional leaders lashed out at India's betrayal. Editorials branded him a fellow traveler who lent "aid and comfort to the enemy" while "playing us for suckers." The prime minister shot back that naturally sympathy for exploited nations would meet disapproval from "great powers who directly or indirectly share in that exploitation." He made a deal for Soviet and Chinese grain, increasing the pressure for a U.S. counteroffer while raising the temperature on Capitol Hill another notch.[7]

The effrontery of Nehru's neutrality was aggravated by his admiration for Soviet economic methods. The new government's plans to exclude foreign investment and launch an industrialization drive modeled on Stalin's five-year plans drew fire from the business press and a Republican congressional majority bent on rolling back the New Deal at home and communism abroad. Convinced that only planned development would reverse the distortions of the colonial economy, Nehru and his chief planner Prasanta Mahalanobis set their sights on a rapid buildup of heavy industries: machine tools, steel, electricity, chemicals, and mining. Food aid would underwrite the growth of the state sector; government warehouses would sell American wheat and deposit the earnings in rupees into a "counterpart" fund for development. The Truman administration opposed the industrial focus chiefly on strategic grounds. An industrial drive would eat into India's agricultural surplus, which fed the British army in the last conflict. War planners envisioned the Indian economy as an "Asiatic production and supply base in the event of general war" with food and agricultural products as its primary contributions. Indian planners were happy to steer U.S. aid toward agriculture while diverting other resources into manufacturing, but disagreement over means and ends built a tension into the aid relationship. When ships containing 2 million tons of American wheat berthed in Bombay in August 1951, both nations toasted a new era of friendship, but U.S. officials had already begun to lean toward Pakistan as a more tractable partner.[8]

The fiscally orthodox Eisenhower administration assumed a still more skeptical stance toward aid and India. The president's "New Look" policies merged Point Four into the military aid program and categorically rejected public disbursements as a cure for "chronic" underdevelopment. A formal alliance with Pakistan, sealed in 1954, and Congress's determination to deny assistance to neutrals "not clearly aligned with the free world" left Secretary of State John Foster Dulles with his hands tied. Extending the program would be difficult, but terminating it would place him in "the rather untenable position of believing [the] increased stability of India as very much to our interest but not being able to do anything about it." He managed to keep official aid at current levels while passing more under the table, in the form of food shipments and secret trade in atomic materials. Democrats, including senators Hubert Humphrey and John F. Kennedy, condemned the administration's neglect of India as proof of a flawed Asia policy.[9]

The Fateful Race

In the 1950s debate on foreign aid, images of a grateful, dependent India clashed with perceptions of a defiant socialistic state personified by

Nehru. In a flurry of travel accounts, James Michener, Norman Cousins, Chester Bowles, and other writers accounted for India's nonconformity in developmental terms, as the brashness of an immature society yearning for the trappings of success. "No one likes a rich uncle who flaunts his wealth in the face of your poverty," Eleanor Roosevelt explained. Supreme Court Justice William O. Douglas likened India's leaders to America's founding fathers, equally sensitive to the fragility of their hard-won independence. Nehru, according to Margaret Bourke-White, "represents a maturing Asia, growing out of feudalism and entering into modern industrial civilization, learning to dispense with European masters and teachers." Liberal academics, politicians, and journalists organized an informal "India lobby" to push these themes, arguing that India was emerging as a natural ally. A partnership in modernization could dispel communism's ideological pretensions, Henry Steele Commager observed, but only if the United States could sustain the commitment despite the invective issuing from Delhi and Capitol Hill. This would be an "acid test for the American character."[10]

The lobby recast India as the free world's contender against China in a fateful race to set the course of the developing world. In an influential 1951 feature in the *New York Times,* Barbara Ward sketched an image of South America, Africa, and Asia watching the emergence of two giants. India and China had launched their five-year plans simultaneously, juxtaposing systems so similar "in tradition, in structure, in problems, and in resources that the contrast in their methods takes on an almost clinical accuracy." Two methods of modernization, one democratic, the other totalitarian, would "in the next decade be pursued side by side." Editorials and congressional testimony embellished the picture. "The future of Asia, and eventually the world balance of power," Bowles asserted, hinged on "the competition between democratic India" and China. "With more than half the world's people now deciding between China and India," Senator Millard Tydings agreed, "we must do what we have to, we must spend what we need to, to help India." USIA asked readers to imagine "a beam-scale set across the Himalayas" with its vast pans balancing "two ancient peoples hard at work transforming their economically underdeveloped countries into industrialized nations." Symbolism soon morphed into political reality. Washington closely tracked the rivalry, according to development theorist Walt W. Rostow, regarding it as "a kind of pure ideological test of great significance." Until then, India had played its own game, outside the superpower sandbox, but now it was on track, running a development race—alongside the arms race and the space race—the deciding heat in a Cold War triple crown.[11]

The race was a wholly Western construction. India refused to be drawn, even rhetorically, into a new version of the Great Game. When the suggestion began appearing in foreign papers, Nehru addressed it directly. There was no race, he argued, firstly because India and China, "these great chunks of humanity," had more in common with each other than with either bloc. The slogan of the moment was *Hindi Chini bhai bhai,* India and China are brothers, a kinship sealed by warm exchanges between Mao and Nehru and a 1954 treaty of friendship known as the *Panchsheel.* The agreement only vaguely promised peaceful co-existence, but for Nehru it signified a new post-imperial order in Asia and a vision of national progress without rivalry. This spirit refuted the assumption of a singular modernity, which Nehru himself had once endorsed; development followed no one track, and neither India nor China could stand in for a system. *"Panchsheel* means that there may be different ways of progress" he assured the Lok Sabha. "Truth is not confined to one country or one people; . . . Each country and each people if they are true to themselves, have to find out their path themselves."[12]

Congress was also skeptical. North Dakota Republican Usher Burdick allowed that "Red China and India under Nehru are the same breed of cats." But the concept of a race captured the Eisenhower administration's ambivalence, allowing it to acknowledge the urgency of India's need, while continuing to disown Nehru and neutralism. Ambassador George V. Allen answered a chorus of congressional objections by pointing out that "a lot of attention is being paid to whether China is going to make progress faster than India" and cutting aid would "assume the attitude that India is finished."[13]

The race allegory marked a further evolution of India's position in U.S. strategic thinking: its conversion into symbol. From 1954 through the 1960s, every NSC position paper on the region echoed warnings that "the outcome of the competition" would produce a "profound effect throughout Asia." India's "war potential" remained negligible next to its real significance as an answer to the "Communist argument." The Federal Reserve Board, which oversaw U.S. and World Bank loans, dropped its categorical objections to India's five-year plan in light of "the inevitable comparison" to China "which is bound to be drawn throughout the world." The parable enabled security planners to regain a sense of movement, to bypass the deadlock of containment and nuclear standoff. "For several years," Henry Kissinger wrote in 1956, "we have been groping for a concept to deal with the transformation of the Cold War from an effort to build defensive barriers into a contest for the allegiance of humanity." The race for modernization furnished the longer arc onto which India's crises and struggles were scripted.[14]

It remained for social scientists to stake out a course, set rules, and calculate the odds. Specialists handicapping the duel agreed that rapid industrialization offered the only route to a demographic transition, higher incomes, urbanization, and other developmental milestones. Starting with equally dense populations and low incomes, the players followed an inevitably similar path, according to Ward: "Its chief planks are rural reorganization and the capital formation needed for expanding industry." Both moves, however, put severe strains on the countryside, a large but delicate mechanism supplying both capital and labor. John Kenneth Galbraith explained that the rural sector was a kind of gyroscope within the economy holding a steady equilibrium at a subsistence level. Industry could grow by capturing the rural surplus, but squeezing the peasantry could easily backfire and tip the country into revolution. It was in the two countries' responses to this dilemma, commentators suggested, that their values were most clearly revealed. While China brutalized peasant labor, Bowles testified, Indian villagers participated in "a completely free economy." The only question was how far India's amateur tactics would set it back.[15]

Experts harbored two grave doubts about India's chances. The first was a recurring fear that techniques originating in the metropolitan West had no bearing in the alien environment of the Asian countryside. The Marshall Plan and Japan's postwar revival relied on a skilled workforce and an existing, if damaged, social infrastructure. In India and Southeast Asia, Point Four technicians found extensive regions devoid of machinery, engineers, banks, or teachers. Moreover, cultural impediments would prevent effective use of the few resources available. Economists agreed that even in modern economies, farmers responded feebly to market forces, and the Asian village represented a further degree of market irrationality. Analysts sketched "backward-rising" and inverted curves to illustrate the leisure-addicted peasant's "perverse" response to cash incentives. Western doctrines were of little use, Galbraith warned, in a setting where "technical progress as we understand it is abnormal, and in some sense unwanted."[16]

Second, U.S. officials worried that "slave economies" were better equipped to engineer the overnight industrial revolution the race required. A command system directed resources for maximum effect, intelligence analysts noted, but "in a representative system like India's, where issues are put up for debate," planning was hampered by public demands. Administration officials supported knockoffs of Soviet or Chinese methods, such as land reform, price controls, and state-run steel mills and dams, but they desperately wanted a technique that was uniquely Western. "These Communist countries [can] achieve certain economic results by means which are cruel," Dulles conceded. "You force them to do it. They may die in the process. . . . There finally emerges, however, something you can show to starry-eyed visitors." Developing democracies had yet to find a distinct, humane, and voluntary approach that could match this advantage.[17]

In February 1955 Rostow published an article intended to set these fears to rest. Pointing to reports of crop failures in both China and Russia, he challenged the assumption that communism could mobilize agriculture more effectively. "Bitter struggle" tactics had not produced the growth surge China had hoped for. Instead, terror undermined modernization by impoverishing "the village gentry and other middle class elements" and leaving a "smoldering, unproductive peasantry." Turning prevailing assumptions on their head, he argued that communists, not capitalists, suffered from urban bias. "Marx was a city boy," he declared, and his successors did not understand the peasant, either. Land was less important to the farmer than consumer goods, which could be acquired only by growing and selling more food. The West's opportunity lay in the countryside. Rostow confidently predicted victory while redrawing the course of the race. The finish would not be marked by the rise of factories or office towers in Bangalore, but when China's "chronic starvation" dispelled the notion that "Communism holds the key to rapid economic growth."[18]

Rostow's argument appealed to Harold Stassen, director of the foreign aid program. In 1955 India's overflowing granaries gave it a clear lead in the developmental contest. As China imposed rationing, New Delhi announced harvests two million tons over target. After three successive years of self-sufficiency, the *Far Eastern Economic Review* concluded, "the fear of famine became a thing of the past." Collectivized farming, Stassen told Congress, was "proving to be a weakness" in the communist argument; if peasants recognized that China had an "evil agricultural system" it would turn the ideological tables. He appealed to the Indian planning commission to differentiate its voluntary, noncoercive principles from communist methods by placing "primary emphasis" on agriculture. But Indian planners had another option, made possible by abundant harvests half a world away in the American Midwest.[19]

India's request for food aid helped the Eisenhower administration alleviate a difficult domestic problem: the mounting grain surplus caused by farm price supports. As export markets shrank after the war, federal granaries amassed enormous stockpiles of subsidized crops. Storage alone was costing the government an estimated $1 million per day, and the overhang grew larger with each harvest. The Army doubled rations in Korea to help ease the strain. Agriculture Secretary Ezra Taft Benson wanted to reduce the surplus by "modernizing" price supports, selectively reducing them to discourage overproduction, but farm state Democrats preferred to keep the subsidies and dispose of the surplus in Asia. Backed by farm groups representing 20 million Midwestern votes, senators Hubert Humphrey and J. William Fulbright linked the surplus problem to foreign policy in Public Law (P.L.) 480, the Food for Peace program, passed in 1954. When Benson's farm bill failed the same year, Eisenhower embraced the scheme and P.L. 480 rapidly grew into the principal mechanism of nonmilitary aid, expanding by 1958 to more than $6 billion with the largest shipments, principally wheat and cotton, going to India.[20]

Despite (and possibly because of) P.L. 480, grain stockpiles kept growing. Wheat farmers reacted predictably by stepping up production, and rice growers lobbied for a P.L. 480 quota so they, too, could expand. Storage costs soon reached one-half billion dollars per year, placing the State Department under pressure to dispose of ever-larger stocks of grain. Still, P.L. 480's supporters touted it as the only long-range solution, framing their arguments in a developmental dichotomy. Agricultural excess was an inescapable consequence of American technical proficiency, Humphrey maintained, just as Asia's traditional agriculture inevitably entailed shortage. "We are going to have an abundance of food and fiber for the foreseeable future," but rather than suppressing or concealing it out of "a feeling of shame," the United States should use it systematically to win allies. Farm groups urged the administration to employ this "windfall" to finance in Asia "such a vast upsurge of economic development and growth that poverty would become obsolete." Against this consensus, a few witnesses pointed out the potential downside of unloading the U.S. farm glut on markets struggling to adjust to postcolonial conditions. The UN Food and Agriculture Organization (FAO) and some State Department officials warned that dumping food in poor countries would unsettle prices and production. The United States was putting its "surplus on the market now at just about as great a clip as we can," Undersecretary of State Thomas Mann cautioned; increasing the flow would only hurt the very people it was meant to help.[21]

Those most closely associated with South Asia, however, recognized they could use P.L. 480 to bypass congressional scrutiny and put aid to India on a secure multiyear footing. After failing to get approval for long-term grants, John Sherman Cooper, the U.S. ambassador to New Delhi, negotiated a three-year agreement, signed in 1956, to quadruple U.S. aid and integrate the flow of commodities and counterpart funds into India's planning process. Eisenhower renewed the agreement in 1960 for another three years, this time for 16 million tons of wheat and 1 million tons of rice, the largest contract ever signed. Beginning in 1954, carloads of hard red winter wheat shuttled from the Salina depot by rail and barge to New Orleans, and thence by grain tanker through the Panama Canal, arriving at Bombay or Calcutta after a six-week journey. The Commodity Credit Corporation (CCC), an independent agency insulated from congressional oversight, arranged storage and shipments. P.L. 480 thus constituted an autonomous aid budget, separate from the foreign aid bills that took a beating each year on Capitol Hill. CCC representatives assured Indian officials that they could expect to receive a share of the surpluses for as long as they wanted.[22]

India's Planning Commission had particular reasons to welcome these assurances. It had set the goal of achieving a "socialistic pattern of society" with rising per capita incomes and an acceleration of industrial growth "to the maximum possible extent." The first phase, emphasizing steel, chemicals, and machine tools, presented a problem. Heavy industries would generate additional wages, but no consumer goods. As the plan pumped money into the economy, it would trigger inflation, shortages, and a backlash at the polls. Initial drafts called for village industries to supply the consumer sector, but planners were losing confidence that the community development scheme would deliver. To make matters worse, dry weather in 1955 and 1956 raised the cost of food and cotton cloth, fuelling a spike in the overall price index. P.L. 480 gave Indian regulators a tool for managing prices and public opinion just at the moment they needed it most.[23]

P.L. 480 soon became the basis for India's food policy. The Food Min-istry set up a network of 50,000 fair-price shops offering discounted flour. Price controls on other goods largely failed, leaving wheat the prin-cipal instrument for holding down inflation. Nehru continued to urge the states to grow more, reminding his ministers that "we cannot create money out of nothing," but with free food arriving every day, they actu-ally could. The deflationary effect allowed the Reserve Bank of India to finance steel plants at Rourkela and Bhilai simply by printing money. American wheat had other advantages, too. "From the point of view of food administration, import has a certain advantage over procurement," a Food Ministry panel noted. While markets dictated the quantity and price of home-grown grain, "all the imported grain comes into the hands of the authorities." Cheap food created an atmosphere of confidence and softened resistance to central planning, and the commission came to value the "psychology of abundance" created by P.L. 480. The fair-price shops, intended for the poor, soon appeared in affluent suburbs. Mechanized bakeries turned out inexpensive, plastic-wrapped loaves with a brand that captured the national mood: Modern Bread.[24]

India's imports of American wheat grew from 200,000 tons in 1954 to more than 4 million in 1960. Economists watched the increase and debated the ultimate effects of P.L. 480, but one conclusion was clear from the start: cheap grain influenced consumption and production in ways that deepened the dependence on imports. Artificially low wheat prices, in combination with rising prices for other goods, adversely affected pri-vate investment in the farm sector. Community development and irriga-tion increased wheat acreage, but yield per acre declined by 12 percent from 1952 to 1958 and then stagnated. Mahalanobis anticipated this trade-off and was able to keep overall wheat production growing by 2 percent per year, but planners were alarmed by unexpected effects on other crops. The diet of the rural poor and urban laborers, supposedly rooted in immutable customs, proved unexpectedly responsive to price changes. Now that they could afford it, Indians began to eat more. Over-all consumption grew sharply, while demand for coarse cereals—maize, millet, lentils, and barley—fell off. Going along with the trend, the Food Ministry declined offers of P.L. 480 corn and insisted on "superior" grains as the quickest and most popular way to increase per capita ca-loric intake. The shift in diet hit growers of traditional staples hard, and total food production dropped triggering spot shortages and price fluctuations.[25]

Despite the rapidly evolving food picture, Indian planners could manage with the help of P.L. 480. Because agriculture could not match the industrial advance called for in the Second Plan (1956–1961), the commission anticipated a food gap that only imports could fill. Congress Party officials evinced a growing concern about the effects of dependency. At a press conference in 1955, reporters asked if wheat discounts were causing hardship in the countryside. Nehru responded testily that "lower prices are much better than higher prices; they make it much easier for us" to manage wages and supplies. But by early 1957 the government had to revise its grain procurement targets down by 40 percent. The food minister, B. B. Ghosh, noted that even the new figures failed to account for demand, now rising much faster than supply was falling. "We will have to rely on imports at present," he advised, citing forecasts of large grain surpluses in the United States. In 1957 a special Foodgrains Enquiry tallied the damage, but recommended maintaining the program as a calculated move to meet plan goals. "The assurance of continued imports," it concluded, "will constitute the very basis of a successful food policy for some years to come." The reciprocal dependency lasted into the next decade. In 1961 a Kennedy administration official asked facetiously about India's food reserves. "Oh," a junior minister replied brightly, "they're in Kansas."[26]

While planners and CCC experts could write off P.L. 480 as a necessary evil, a 4-million-ton food deficit abruptly redrew the odds on the developmental race. If Beijing's statistics could be believed, China was registering 7 percent annual gains in grain production between 1952 and 1958 and plowing the surplus into industry. India's harvests, by contrast, fell behind population growth after 1956, and observers read the disparity as an indicator of critical weaknesses. Food shortages, speculative runs, and bread riots across North India, the *New York Times* reported, were "part of the price the country is paying for the use of democratic methods in her national build-up." Concern turned to alarm in May 1957 when Finance Minister T. T. Krishnamachari cancelled the most ambitious targets owing to an unexpected drop in India's exchange reserves and urgently appealed to donor nations to rescue the "hard core" of the plan. U.S. analysts attributed the disastrous shortfall—equal to the total amount of foreign aid then coming in—to overruns on capital projects, but public concern fastened stubbornly on food and population. Indians of all classes were better fed during this period, as measured in both quantity and variety. Gains in food consumption paralleled rates of urbanization and rising incomes, not population growth, but Western eyes, fixed on the supply side, saw scarcity in India as identical to hunger. Commentators brushed aside the subtleties of consumer behavior and pricing and concentrated instead on a presumptively binary relationship between population and food supply.[27]

The "food gap" provided a common agenda for an emerging community of American and international agencies, research institutes, and philanthropies vested in India's development. The UN, under the secretary-generalship of economist Dag Hammarskjöld, claimed international development as a primary function, and the FAO evolved from a custodian of trade statistics into an "operational" agency assigned to orchestrate a global increase in food supply. Growing fear of Soviet competition spurred the Eisenhower administration to redouble its aid effort. At the urging of high-ranking State, Central Intelligence Agency (CIA), and World Bank officials, the Ford Foundation took on India as a special charge, investing in community development and an economic advisory mission led by Max Millikan of the Massachusetts Institute of Technology (MIT).[28]

Even the CIA measured the strategic threat to India by the benchmarks in the Second Plan. The collapse of the plan, the 1958 National Intelligence Estimate warned, "would result in India's becoming increasingly vulnerable to extremist, and especially Communist, influences." With the entire uncommitted world watching, the plan would be, Millikan believed, the "crucial determinant of world history over the next decade." Success depended on the untried techniques of development economics. For all its journals and research institutes, the field had no theoretical consensus. Differences widened on the subject of rural economics. Modernizers held conflicting views on how—or even if—the rural sector could contribute to an industrial drive, and in India almost 90 percent of the wealth and labor were in the countryside.[29]

Big Push or Takeoff

The earliest theories of development outside the Marxist tradition came from émigré economists working in the United States and British investigations of "tropical" economies. Both schools located the root of backwardness in a defective linkage between an industrial, "modern" sector and an extrinsic rural sphere that sequestered essential manpower and resources. An economist at the University of Vienna before the war, Paul

146

N. Rosenstein-Rodan counseled the U.S. government on postwar reconstruction before heading the economic advisory staff at the World Bank. He was part of an influx of social scientific talent from Eastern Europe that included Ragnar Nurkse, an Estonian, and Hans Singer, a Holocaust refugee who studied under Keynes at Cambridge, and Albert O. Hirschman, who fled Germany and ended up at the Federal Reserve Board. Their models shared a "structuralist" emphasis on the need for top-down interventions to overcome built-in bottlenecks, "equilibrium traps," and "vicious cycles," impediments they associated with rurality.[30]

Postwar economists identified the countryside paradoxically as both the source of poverty and as a reservoir of wealth waiting to be tapped. Their analysis started from a carefully wrought distinction between a modern or "progressive" sector that responded to theoretical expectations and the "special situation" of agrarian areas. The blank space of the Asian interior lacked the standard Keynesian and neoclassical landmarks. Income, savings, and investment had no real meaning in "a country like India," Nurkse observed, because peasants sterilized their wealth by stowing it in nonpecuniary assets, such as jewelry, land, or children. Structuralist models relied heavily on national incomes accounting, a technique that equated calculability with utility, and economists were troubled to find the Asian interior rife with "disguised" forms of exchange and consumption, habits of sharing food and labor that buried wealth before it could be counted. For this reason, overpopulation represented the most damaging special condition. High birth rates sustained habits of exchange and "make work" that locked surplus labor and food in the countryside, starving the modern sector of capital.[31]

Structuralists counseled against spending foreign aid on peasants, and concentrating it instead in capital investments that could lure assets away from agriculture. Development was a process of relieving the agrarian sphere of counterproductive surpluses, primarily of labor. Rural areas teemed with unoccupied relations, "sons, cousins, uncles and aunts, who live on a farm and pretend to do something since they are there," Rosenstein-Rodan explained. "All the agrarian economists of the world agree that if those people were removed from the land agricultural output, far from falling, would increase." In fact, structuralists calculated the utility of rural labor at zero; in other words, their models assumed that value came from farms but not from farmers, who added nothing no matter how hard they worked. Theodore Schultz, a dissenter at the University of Chicago, observed that globetrotting economists were especially fond of the doctrine of zero labor value. Carrying an image of Western efficiency in their minds, they saw peasants "producing unbelievably little when they work, and many of them appear to be idle much of the time." Nonetheless, this view had few challengers except among population economists, who assigned peasant labor a negative value.[32]

Zero-value labor was the starting point for W. Arthur Lewis's Nobel Prize–winning prescription for "development with unlimited supplies of labor." Lewis shared the European economists' experience of exile, a background that deepened his antiruralism. Escaping the racism and provincialism of his native St. Lucia, he earned acclaim at the London School of Economics where he developed his theory of the "dual" character of tropical economies. He was on a street in Bangkok in August 1952, he later recalled, when it occurred to him that the primary function of the rural sector was as "a reservoir of cheap labor for the other" modern part of the economy. Significantly, this model treated population growth as a neutral variable. With enough factory employment, high fertility could actually accelerate growth, allowing cities to grow by drawing labor—not food—from the countryside. By 1980, he predicted, India would import one-fifth of its food, paying with returns from manufactured exports. Mahalanobis was particularly swayed by Lewis's view of India as an industrial hub for rural Southeast Asia. At the 1956 Bandung Conference he proposed a regional common market to give the nonaligned movement an economic bloc of its own.[33]

Expressed as an overall plan, the structuralist formula called for simultaneous investments across a wide range of industries and sectors to trigger a revolutionary burst of developmental momentum. Adopting the name of Mao's southern offensive, Nurkse called it "the Big Push." Exports, manufacturing, agriculture, education, and administrative capacity would advance together, along a continuous front, to prevent flank attacks from remnants of the traditional order. Economists devised algorithms for calculating the intake of investment (the "absorptive capacity") needed to stimulate the Push. Agriculture, like foreign aid, would act as an exogenous source of capital for the modern sector, so the timing and nature of rural improvements were critical. Levels of technical proficiency and production had to be carefully calibrated to achieve three goals: the smooth evacuation of redundant labor, a sharp increase in available food and fiber, and most importantly, the commoditization of food crops. Peasants had to be prevented from hoarding the surplus or

148

"leaking" it into consumption. Aggregate increase was less important than quantification and control.[34]

From a policy perspective, the Big Push looked like a big gamble: massive, scattershot investments in every sector with no guarantees. Structuralists hedged, insisting that "non-resource" factors of motivation, culture, and politics affect capital accumulation to such a degree that growth could not be predicted or assured. They offered a methodology for studying development, not a technique for making it happen. But there was another emerging paradigm for India's development better tailored to the needs of legislators and diplomats. Multidisciplinary collaborations of social scientists created a "practical" set of conceptual tools and priorities useful to planners. Among the major institutes studying modernization, MIT's Center for International Studies (CENIS) generated some of the earliest and most influential insights about food and population. The group fielded an impressive roster of academic talent, including Clifford Geertz, Daniel Lerner, and Lucian Pye, but its leading lights were the entrepreneur, Max Millikan, and Walt Rostow in his customary role as publicist and visionary.[35]

From its inception, CENIS framed food as a tool of "political warfare." The center began as Project Troy, a joint effort by Harvard, MIT, and the Department of State to develop sociopsychological strategies for use against the Soviet bloc. In 1952 the Ford Foundation urged Troy's participants to expand the target area to include noncommitted nations and to investigate how efforts to "expand their productivity and standards of living" could be used as a psychological weapon. Following visits to India by Millikan and propaganda theorist Ithiel de Sola Pool in 1953, the group set about assembling a framework that cast technology, military action, and economic aid as aspects of strategic communication. Food, CENIS suggested, constituted a particularly strong transmitter of developmental messages. The United States' stock of surplus wheat had enormous potential to "create bitterness among hungry peoples" or to "raise their hopes."[36]

In a set of draft recommendations prepared for the NSC in 1954, Millikan and Rostow argued that due to the peculiar psychology of transitional societies, surpluses and shortages of food affected development less straightforwardly than generally supposed. Challenging the "serious misconception" that hunger intensified revolutionary impulses, they compared the sleepy fatalism of low-calorie subsistence communities with the

149

aroused militancy of the slightly better off. The early stages of economic development kindled aspirations for consumer goods, mobility, and status. This dawning awareness, if combined with the "energy-stimulating effects of better nutrition," could stoke explosive pressures for change. Rather than a precondition for modernization, food availability was an indicator, a gauge of the pitch and roll of popular attitudes as the economy accelerated toward "the take-off into sustained growth."[37]

Rostow's concept of "takeoff" called for a concentration of effort similar to Nurkse's Big Push, but it identified more precisely when and where aid investments should go, and to whom. Extrapolating patterns from the eighteenth century onward, Rostow narrowed the opportunity for takeoff to a window of two to three decades, during which economies either went into a sustained climb or stalled. India and China, "the two outstanding contemporary cases," began the decisive initial sequence in 1952. Rostow stipulated that only manufacturing, engineering, power generation, and mass communications could attain growth rates fast enough to outstrip rising populations. Derivative sectors, such as agriculture, would be carried along behind. He also singled out modernizing elites whose "appropriate value system" encouraged receptivity to new methods. Military officers and urban merchant-entrepreneurs were the best bets. Groups with connections to the land—whether as large landowners or peasants—comprised the likely opposition. In Rostow's jet-age metaphor, agriculture figured as a coefficient of drag. Although improvements in cultivation often followed, the takeoff itself, he insisted, could not be stimulated by "new agricultural tricks."[38]

Rostow's interpretation of human motivation set him apart from other development practitioners and from economics as a discipline. Taking the profit-maximizing "rational man" as normative, structuralists saw modernization as a cure for the pathological, leisure-oriented peasant. At a psychological level, the Big Push was a process of constructing urban showpieces—factories, schools, administrative centers—to entice the more intrepid peasants across the mental divide between country and town. Rostow, by contrast, characterized his developmental subject, rural or urban, as fundamentally ambivalent, torn between conflicting appetites for consumer goods, status, reproduction, and leisure. Communist propaganda, he warned, played on these temptations. The fact that agriculture contained so little economic potential only enhanced its role in shaping the psychology of the transition. Restive rural populations needed visible signs of movement, indicators that changes afoot in distant cities were affecting their own prospects and material circumstances. It was more important for rural development to be spectacular than effective.[39]

CENIS expected agricultural modernization would make a negligible contribution to growth, perhaps 1 percent, but this small amount would have a catalytic effect on the attitudes and latent abilities of villagers. "A little extra food in the stomach can hardly be expected to insure stable and harmonious political development," the institute explained to the Senate Foreign Relations Committee, but showpiece projects could instill a "healthy focus," and "a sense of community in which seeds of class struggle and violence tend to die." Without conceding the singularity different cultures, Rostow's formula accepted this part of the analysis of Geertz, Robert Bellah, and Karl Wittfogel, who advocated rural reorganization as an anthropological fix for "involuted" peasant societies without a Protestant ethic. An infusion of scientific methods could overhaul basic values, habits, and relationships, cultural modernists believed, and usher in "new ways of handling food that involve new ways of handling men."[40]

India's exchange crisis presented a classic example of the hazards of transition, Rostow told the Senate Foreign Relations Committee: "To use my takeoff analogy, India is really gathering momentum down the runway, but there is sputtering in one motor." A steady flow of foreign aid, coupled with a positive outlook, would allow it to throttle up and reach escape velocity. Diplomat Louis Halle later complained that Rostow's images reduced "this great, multifarious, fluid, and largely unknown world of ours [to] a child's plaything," but the senators clearly appreciated his vividness and urgency, as well as his readiness to whittle social theory down to clear priorities. Aid dollars could be maximized, he specified, by using them to create "social overhead capital (roads, railways, electric power, etc.)" with a smaller budget going to cosmetic "impact" programs designed to create psychic reverberations in the countryside.[41]

India's economic crisis, the communist aid offensive, and public alarm over the launch of two Soviet Sputnik orbiters in the fall of 1957 caught the Eisenhower administration flat-footed. Lyndon Johnson, leader of the Democratic majority newly installed in the Senate, sensed that after Sputnik Washington had the mentality "of the manic depressive—high points of elation when 'we' make an important advance; low points of despair when 'they' outstrip us." The setback in the space race gave the "Rostow-Millikan doctrine" new urgency. In March 1958 Kennedy proposed a radical increase in aid, giving India first priority "in light of the decisive nature of the competition" with China. His legislation, the

Kennedy-Cooper resolution, became the centerpiece of a liberal critique of the New Look. Underscoring the symbolic realities behind the mirage of military power, he argued that arms and alliances left no trace on the "fluid pattern of events in the uncommitted world." The vital challenge was to dispel the "glamour" of communism's "answer to the overwhelming problems of economic mobilization and takeoff." Quoting Rostow and Barbara Ward, Kennedy exhorted Congress to shake off self-doubt and join India in the "shared adventure" of modernization.[42]

A New Frontier in Asia

Only rarely does a bill land in the legislative hopper just as the public mood inclines decisively in its favor. Kennedy-Cooper initially garnered the routine skepticism accorded to aid handouts, but in October as it languished in committee, the *Saturday Evening Post* began serializing William J. Lederer and Eugene Burdick's interpretation of the dynamics of communist subversion. Three weeks later *The Ugly American* hit the top of the best-seller list where it remained for the next eighteen months. Lederer, a Navy publicist, and Burdick, a political scientist, sketched a scenario set in a fictional Southeast Asian country resembling Vietnam. Part editorial, part espionage thriller, it dramatically revised the narrative of the Cold War encounter, and with it the terms of debate. The United States was wasting time worrying about Sputnik and the arms race, the authors argued; the Soviets were already winning a more decisive contest "in the rice fields of Asia."[43]

Dispelling the image of an Asian interior untouched by Western hands, *The Ugly American* portrayed a continent thick with foreign projects and personnel. The United States, claimed the authors, supported "a horde of 1,500,000 Americans" engaged in a quiet war for Asia's hearts and minds. Based in comfortable enclaves, they were constructing "huge technical complexes" designed to win friends among the nationalist elite, but in the process alienating the ordinary people whose livelihoods were disrupted. While Americans built roads, dams, and stadiums as monuments to their own engineering prowess, communist propagandists cunningly pitched their appeals around the rustic concerns of average Asians. "Powdered milk and cattle are part of politics, and therefore part of history," a Maoist insurgent explains. "America had its chance and it missed." The plot consisted of a series of vignettes contrasting stock careerists—striped-pants diplomats, slick admen, and gold-digging secretaries—against a dedicated minority of "ugly" Americans, dirty-handed mechanics, priests, and agronomists, willing to "get into the countryside" and meet Asians on their own terms. These pioneers join forces with native counterparts, steeped in tradition but practical enough to respect the white strangers' competence with chickens and irrigation pumps.[44]

Despite their urgency, Lederer and Burdick offered a reassuring lesson. Just as Rostow had, the authors separated the disruptive necessity of "big economic development" from the essentially symbolic work of rural modernization. In the countryside, development was communication. Americans could win hearts and minds by remembering their own rural past, working with their hands, and rallying allies with a program that could be understood in "farmyard English."

Kennedy pitched aid to India in the same vein, as a chance to restore U.S. ascendancy in Asia and Europe. Together with Rostow, Eugene Black, and the India Lobby, he sought to leverage U.S. loans by rallying a consortium of European donor nations. Even if the sums involved were small, joint action would revitalize the Atlantic alliance, Barbara Ward explained, and "enable the Western powers to recover their own confidence and effectiveness" after years of inertia. A partnership for development would reinstate the West (or, as Kennedy preferred it, the North) in a position of heroic responsibility for the postcolonial nations. The United States had found in India "the opportunity—indeed we may call it a privilege," wrote Walter Lippmann, "of playing a leading part in a noble and fascinating and decisive human adventure."[45]

Recast as a summons to join in a mythic enterprise, foreign aid experienced a groundswell of public support. A bare majority of Americans approved of continuing aid in February 1958, but by the end of the year more than 60 percent wanted to expand the program. The changed mood affected Eisenhower. After reading *The Ugly American* the president dismissed talk of "giveaways" and informed the NSC that aid was vastly more important than "another new missile program or another aircraft program." He pushed forward with plans for an India consortium and appointed a special commission loaded with Establishment heavyweights—current and former chairs of the Joint Chiefs of Staff; überbankers William H. Draper, John McCloy, and Joseph Dodge; and undersecretaries of Defense and State—charged with revamping the aid effort.[46]

The Draper Committee ratified a growing consensus that economic development represented the primary defense against an evolving communist strategy of subversion and economic penetration. The stabilization of Japan and Formosa in the Ear East and Europe on the western flank meant that "the *schwerpunkt* of Soviet-Chinese strategy will be directed at the middle area" of South and Southeast Asia. India was the prime target. The committee recommended doubling aid resources, unifying the development effort under a single agency, and preparing for a prolonged test of will and ingenuity. Its boldest recommendation, however, was that the United States should plan and finance an effort to "deal with the problem of rapid population growth" worldwide.[47]

The Draper Report marked the emergence of the "population issue" in aid policy, but the consensus had been growing for several months. Recent investigations by the Ford Foundation and the World Bank detailed a demographic threat to India's economy. A "Food Crisis Report" prepared by the Ford Foundation for the Indian government in April 1959 forecast an impending gap of 28 million tons of grain by 1965. Ignoring disruptions caused by P.L. 480, a team of American and Indian experts identified "the crux of the problem" as a gap between food supply and "a rapidly increasing population." It recommended a crash program of irrigation, fertilization, and mechanization to feed the extra 80 million Indians who would be born before the end of the Third Plan. The World Bank commissioned a joint investigation by an economist, Edgar M. Hoover, and a demographer, Ansley Coale, that swung academic opinion behind family planning. It quantified, with ostensible precision, the economic advantage of contraception by plotting a "high" population trajectory based on continuation of current patterns, and a "low" figure assuming a 50 percent decline in fertility, along with calculations of India's national income, welfare spending, and investment for each trend. The difference was dramatic. With birth limitation, Indians could expect a demographic bonus of almost 40 percent more income by 1986.[48]

These studies effectively reversed an academic and policy consensus that regarded free trade and rising populations as engines of growth. Keynes himself associated high fertility with economic vigor, and for years economists had applauded the demand-side effects of "dynamic" populations. This reasoning now struck World Bank director Eugene Black as backward because "the more dependents in a poor society—the more children to be fed, clothed, and educated—the less savings are available for investment." Eisenhower advocated trade as the primary driver of development and, until 1959, aid missions actually discouraged recipients from boosting production of wheat, because it was an internationally traded commodity. In July the administration changed course, redirecting funds toward the goal of self-sufficiency. If underdeveloped economies could not withstand "free enterprise in the forms we understand," Vice President Richard Nixon conceded, the United States might have to accept or even promote trade restrictions.[49]

Analysts of the 1960 presidential elections forecast major changes in foreign aid regardless of who won. Both Kennedy and Nixon pledged to encourage birth control and push Congress for more aid. Kennedy came into office with a bold commitment "to those peoples in the huts and villages across the globe struggling to break the bonds of mass misery." In the 1960s, he told Congress, the United States had a "historic opportunity" to move two-thirds of the world to the takeoff point. His appointment of academic specialists in key positions—Rostow on the NSC, David Bell to head the new U.S. Agency for International Development (USAID), Galbraith as ambassador to India—and the prominence of India hands Dean Rusk and Chester Bowles at the State Department—signaled a new emphasis on modernization in the "key area" of Asia. "In 1961 development economics was at the height of its vogue," George Ball later recalled. "The professors swarming into Washington talked tendentiously of 'self-sustaining growth,' 'social development,' [and] 'the search for nationhood.'" After a disastrous initiation at the Bay of Pigs, Kennedy embraced development, in place of covert action, as his primary weapon for fighting the Cold War.[50]

The new team knew that winning the uncommitted nations depended on mastery of the rural sphere. "The peasants who control the food supply constitute a substantial majority of all underdeveloped countries and are in a crucially important political position," Bowles advised in an early policy memo. Rural poverty would be the "focal point" of communist pressure, and although "Stalinists never understood the peasantry . . . Mao Tse-tung does." Military adviser Maxwell Taylor explained that the Cold War had moved into a phase of "indirect aggression" characterized by insurgency, subversion, and revolutionary populism targeting isolated populations. India's size and symbolic weight made it the "key nation" in this struggle, and the administration scrambled to devise programs and concepts to accelerate transition in the Indian countryside.[51]

Reports of famine in China spotlighted agriculture as the vital ingredient of developmental success. Serious food shortages began in 1959, but to outside observers the picture remained unclear until refugees began pouring into Hong Kong in early 1961. The utopian features of the Great Leap Forward—the closing of markets, confiscation of private plots, and grossly unrealistic crop targets—ravaged the rural provinces and led to tens of millions of deaths. Intelligence officials could measure the suffering only by China's own admissions—missed industrial targets and a $300 million Canadian grain deal—but the damage appeared huge. China's craving for factories had "landed it in the soup," psywar wizard Edward Lansdale crowed. Now was the time for "a strong psychological campaign." In a press conference in April, Kennedy contrasted China's difficulties with the technical achievements of American agriculture, "one of the most extraordinary and admirable facets of our national life." The famine exposed the flaw in coercive methods, the Policy Planning Staff noted. Agriculture was "the weakest link in communist economies everywhere." Most gratified of all was Rostow, who saw history unfolding according to plan. China's tragedy would dispel the charisma and inexorability of the communist appeal and allow the West to regain the lead in the development race. "This may be the hinge." he told the president, "on which your administration will turn."[52]

In May Kennedy presented the Foreign Assistance Act to Congress and launched a campaign to make India's modernization the mainspring of his Asia policy. In September he urged the UN General Assembly to designate the 1960s a Decade of Development. He pressed Congress and the India Consortium to raise more than $1 billion for the Third Plan, and urged Rostow, Bowles, and South Asia adviser Robert Komer to devise a style of assistance that would set his new initiatives apart from those of the Eisenhower administration or the Soviets. An emphasis on four features—central planning, human resources (education, health, and family planning), "disinterested" aid without political strings, and scientific agriculture—characterized the "new look." Agriculture Secretary Orville Freeman saw possibilities for "a real agricultural foreign aid program" tied "closely to agriculture, where we have the know-how, the technicians, and can, in a sense, plan national production."[53]

Political and economic limitations motivated Kennedy to deemphasize industry. Economic recovery in Europe, coupled with a stagnant domestic economy, had stimulated a "gold crisis" in 1960 as foreign creditors began to exchange dollars for gold at a rate of $2 billion per year.

Unchecked, the outflow of currency might weaken the dollar, and administration officials recognized that foreign aid, even disguised in the form of P.L. 480 wheat, contributed to the leakage. For the time being, a "Big Push" was politically unrealistic. Kennedy held a slender majority in Congress thanks to conservative Southern Democrats who had little affection for foreign aid or for India. Nehru, as usual, made matters difficult. His annexation of Goa and purchase of Soviet MIG fighters provoked howls from Capitol Hill. Under the circumstances, additional funds for the plan would have to come by augmenting internal resources, boosting agricultural exports, and containing imports. USAID's best move in India, according to Galbraith, was to concentrate "on a few subjects concerned with bread-grain production."[54]

Administration officials believed their emphasis on agriculture clearly distinguished "Free World" methods of development from socialist alternatives. At a speech at Punta del Este in January 1962, Rusk diagnosed Cuba, North Vietnam, and the Soviet Union with the same ailment that gripped China. These "areas with remarkable natural resources have failed to provide even the elementary needs of food," he argued; "wherever Communism goes, hunger follows." The pattern of famines confirmed that Western methods of modernization were not simply more humane, they were "technically the efficient way." Ward, with characteristic poignancy, argued that agriculture was where "the winds of change blow most fitfully, that men are most firmly attached to the ways of their forefathers, that all the encrusted customs, traditions, and superstitions . . . survive most tenaciously." India's ability to make headway against these obstacles would determine "whether the open society has any future in Asia at all."[55]

China's October 1962 attack along India's northern border only confirmed the storyline already built into Kennedy's policy and rhetoric. Agriculture held the key to winning the developmental race and the answer to a long list of strategic, political, and economic problems. But consensus on this broad point masked conflicting opinions on what "agriculture" was for, and what a modernized agriculture would look like. Officials and economists linked it to diverse goals—financing industrial takeoff, offsetting population growth, instilling a psychology of abundance, creating an Indian alternative—without agreeing on which took precedence. In the abstract, the mission seemed to call only for ingenuity and will, the kind of challenge the new president relished. With characteristic audacity, Kennedy forecast "a scientific revolution" in agriculture to "rival in its social consequences the industrial revolution." It would "involve the whole economic and social structure of each nation" entailing "the building of new institutions, the training of a new generation of young people, . . . the energies and talents and the creative abilities of half of mankind."[56]

Polish children queue up for American food relief in 1919. For President Herbert Hoover, hunger was the root cause of revolution and war. Herbert Hoover Presidential Library.

Norman Borlaug shows the test plots at Chapingo to Elvin Stakman (left) and Henry Wallace (right) in 1946. Rockefeller Archive Center.

Borlaug's breeding strategy was better adapted to the large-scale irrigated farms in the Yaqui Valley than to the village *ejidos* of central Mexico. An *agrónomo* in training in 1950, Ignacio Narvaez (right) later received a PhD from Purdue and headed the Rockefeller initiative in Pakistan. Rockefeller Archive Center.

Horace Holmes demonstrates a steel plow in Etawah District in 1950. The "dirty hands" ethic stressed the importance of humility and physical labor to community building. Special Collections Research Center, University of Chicago Library.

Morrison-Knudsen project manager Ted Johnston (left) tours the Kajaki Dam with Afghan dignitaries in 1957. Modernization meant creating ordered landscapes in which resources were controlled, but Afghanistan's wealth came from the wild highlands, seen here in the distance, where nomadic herders fiercely guarded their autonomy. Lyman Wilbur Collection, Albertsons Library, Boise State University.

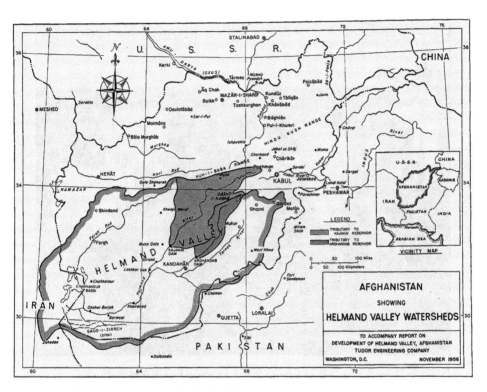

Stretching across the southern half of Afghanistan, the Helmand Valley development was designed to act as an economic buffer, shielding the United States' "northern tier" allies, Pakistan and Iran, from Soviet influence. International Cooperation Administration, Report on Development of Helmand Valley, 1956.

President John F. Kennedy welcomes Prime Minister Jawaharlal Nehru to Washington in 1961 as John Kenneth Galbraith, Dean Rusk, Vice President Lyndon Johnson, and B. K. Nehru look on. India was the "very big, very poor country" the administration needed to demonstrate the benefits of growth and democracy. John F. Kennedy Library.

Walt W. Rostow, architect of modernization as theory and policy, saw agriculture as a drag on growth. Only industry could accelerate the pace of change to the desired "takeoff" point. Lyndon Baines Johnson Library.

Robert Chandler introduces Presidents Lyndon Johnson and Ferdinand Marcos to IR-8 at Los Baños in 1966. "The war on hunger," Johnson explained, "is the only war we seek to escalate." IRRI.

IRRI displayed the contrast it wanted to create throughout Asia. Modern glass and aluminum laboratories faced an experimental farm where rice was grown in "traditional" ways. Scientists were expected to "wade right in." IRRI.

6

A PARABLE OF SEEDS

Waving his hand toward a patch of willowy, pale green rice stalks, Benigno Aquino showed an American reporter what scientific agriculture meant to the Philippines in the fall of 1966. "Here is the bullock cart. Here is the nineteenth century," he said. Then, pointing across the road to a paddy of stubby, dark shoots planted in orderly rows, "here is the jumbo jet! The twentieth century." Fertilizer-dependent plant varieties developed in the 1960s sharply increased yields of rice and wheat and brought the entire commodity chain under state control, but what most impressed Aquino, the *New York Times,* the scientists at the International Rice Research Institute (IRRI), and the institute's patrons in Washington and New York was how the rice looked. "It's something you can see," Ford Foundation vice president Forrest Hill explained, "You can say, 'well, go out and look at it.' It did happen."[1]

What made "miracle rice" a success even before the first crops were harvested was its unique capacity to display the arrival of modernity. The new rice partitioned the landscape, drawing a boundary between traditional and modern agriculture clear enough to be seen through the chin bubbles of helicopter gunships. To diplomats, transnational scientists, and Southeast Asian technocrats, grain became a living symbol of abundance, an apparition capable of inducing mass conversions. In the development discourse, "technology transfer" denotes a moment when gifts of science change hands and economies are forever transfigured. IRRI's "modern varieties" plotted this moment spatially, marking the ground with a line separating the bullock cart from the jumbo jet. The dark green rice stopped where consumerism, allegiance, and order left off and subsistence, insurgency, and isolation began: at the edge of the free world.[2]

Technology, as the second of its Greek roots implies, is a type of rhetoric, an argument in the form of an object. The technologies that affected

159

foreign policy the most, nuclear weapons and petroleum, were not simply—or even principally—tools, but markers of status and restraints on behavior. The political influence of a technology comes less from the motivations behind its invention than from the way the artifact affects thought, revealing or limiting the range of priorities and possibilities, an effect that has been called "technicity." IRRI self-consciously practiced technicity, using technologies—such as architecture, the training of scientists, and especially rice—to project visible boundaries between tradition and modernity. In the late 1960s the dwarf rice known as IR-8 was deployed throughout Southeast Asia as a symbolic divider marking the onset of a new political and economic dispensation.[3]

The Philippines and Vietnam were the first countries to cultivate IR-8 extensively, and they illustrate how rice technology could be employed for pacification and to consolidate client regimes, but more importantly they exemplify the element of spectacle that made the introduction of dwarf rice and wheat a pivotal event in Indonesia, Sri Lanka, and India as well. "Here is an opportunity where irrigation, fertilizer, and peasant education can produce miracles in the sight of the beholder," Robert McNamara observed. IR-8's power to make modernity visible was what excited wealthy landlords, postcolonial politicians, aid officials, and foundation grantslingers. The new seeds had "an element of drama, an element of excitement—some sex appeal, if you will," William Gaud, director of the U.S. Agency for International Development (USAID) explained. "Development . . . suddenly came down to a very simple proposition: one man seeing his neighbor doing better than he was doing."[4]

Development experts in the 1960s recognized a connection between sight, technology, and the modern state. Foreign assistance, as Daniel Lerner explained in 1968, was in essence a process of creating and consuming images: "Every nation that regards itself as more developed now transmits pictures of itself to those less developed societies that figure in its own policy planning," while the nation receiving the images "decides, as a matter of high priority for its own policy planning, which of them constitutes the preferred picture of its own future." Scientists, military officials, and modernizing regimes valued IR-8 because they believed it possessed an unusual capacity to induce peasants, voters, and governments to see their situation differently, and to recalculate their interests and allegiances accordingly. McNamara and other observers used religious terminology to describe such conversions, appropriately perhaps, for development has been described as a "global faith," a belief—often in the face of contrary evidence—in the redemptive power of science and economic growth. As the Viet Cong, Ferdinand Marcos, USAID, and others recognized, however, the denomination of that faith was up for grabs. While modernizers spoke of conflict between innovation and tradition, they waged a more consequential struggle for the authority to decide which slogans, war aims, or geopolitical agendas would be associated with the spectacle of the miracle harvest.[5]

Throughout the Cold War, U.S. officials considered their ability to display the fruits of modernity to be a powerful weapon against communism. Client states served as "showcases of democracy" and aircraft carriers as floating apparitions of technological power. "I want to show you this kitchen," Vice President Richard Nixon told Nikita Khrushchev at the 1959 American National Exhibition in Moscow. The refrigerators and dishwashers, Nixon explained, symbolized a freedom of choice "that's the spice of life." But placing visions of abundance before millions of Asian peasants proved difficult. In 1957 Clement Johnson, head of the U.S. Chamber of Commerce, suggested that communism might lose its appeal if "one-tenth of the People of Asia had ever seen a Sears, Roebuck catalog," and the Kennedy administration later consulted, unfruitfully, with Sears executives about putting the plan into effect. Walt Rostow, who joined the National Security Council under Kennedy, wanted to put "television sets in the thatch hutches of the world" to defeat both tradition and communism with the spectacle of consumption.[6]

Showcasing had become a standard feature of foreign aid and development projects by the mid-1950s. Rural experiment stations and model villages presented miniaturized futures for people to visit and emulate. The nature of this display changed in the 1960s as the Johnson administration escalated the war in Vietnam. Executives of the Ford and Rockefeller foundations—along with Ferdinand Marcos's "technocrats" and counterinsurgency warriors in Vietnam—used technology to draw a more visible dividing line between stagnation and progress, across which Asian peasants would "begin to sense, however dimly, what an affluent society could mean for them and their children." They wanted to sharpen the edge of the modern, to force a decision between old and new ways of life. IRRI's agricultural revolution spearheaded this effort.[7]

Good for Their Character

The Ford Foundation funded IRRI after its earlier venture, community development, failed to generate sufficiently dramatic results. Disruptions in India's second five-year plan, caused by lagging agricultural production, shifted concern from peasant unrest to the more immediate problem of raising yields. The State Department and the Central Intelligence Agency (CIA) urged the foundation to take action. The new director, Henry Heald, hired a Cornell agronomist, Forrest F. "Frosty" Hill, to reorganize the international development program. Hill had visited the Rockefeller-funded corn and wheat research stations in Mexico, and since the early 1950s he had pushed the idea of bringing the Mexico model to the rice fields of Asia. He made no predictions that a joint Ford/Rockefeller initiative would abruptly enlarge the world's food supply or avert a famine in Asia. IRRI's selling points were that it represented a new scientific approach and a new institutional arrangement. The Ford Foundation promoted "project-oriented research," a scientific work culture that originated in the Office of Scientific Research and Development during World War II and reached its fullest elaboration in James Webb's NASA. Project-oriented research had proven itself in the Rockefeller Foundation's wheat improvement program in Mexico. It was the United States' answer to the threat of totalitarian science in the shadow of Sputnik. Instead of solitary inventors or a hierarchical science establishment, scientists would work in egalitarian, interdisciplinary teams on projects determined by the national interest. Foundations also believed in "institutionalizing" change, and that foundations were an especially useful type of institution. Ford and Rockefeller pledged $7 million to create IRRI, and Hill began negotiations in 1959 to establish it as the first tax-exempt foundation in the Philippines. In line with the latest social science theories of modernization, Hill felt development required new institutions, attitudes, and technology. IRRI would bundle all three in one package. It marked a transition in the Ford Foundation's philosophy of development. Instead of incrementally improving practices and technologies already in the developing world, it would introduce something completely different, a Manhattan Project for food.[8]

Hill and Robert Chandler, the former president of the University of New Hampshire and IRRI's first director, viewed scientific research as a kind of moral instruction, a solvent for national and elite prejudice. Chandler incorporated this ethic in everything IRRI did, starting with the buildings laid out on a site adjacent to the University of the Philippines campus at Los Baños. Foundation officials selected an internationally known architect, Ralph T. Walker—a modernist famous for his designs of American military bases, suburban research campuses (Bell Labs, General Electric), and industrial pavilions at the 1939 World's Fair—to supervise a team of Filipino architects preparing plans for one of the largest construction projects ever undertaken in the Philippines. Walker's design made no concessions to either climate or local conventions. There was "no true Philippine style," he assured foundation officials; nationalistic styles had given way to the modern idiom. Constructed completely of imported materials, the sprawling one-story aluminum-and-glass structures featured modular walls to encourage an egalitarian office culture. Air conditioning, tiles, plumbing, and upholstery conveyed "the power and richness of American life," and also a sense of permanence. Walker felt his buildings emblemized "a new type of imperialism" based on "specialized knowledge generously given to backward peoples."[9]

Chandler came under attack for his extravagance, but he defended the design as necessary for IRRI's mission. Other grantees especially resented the housing compound that, they felt, failed to display a proper pioneering spirit. The ranch-style homes (4 br, 2 ba, air, W/D, tennis, pool, lake vu) cost $60,000 apiece in 1961. Each came equipped with a generator, a luxury that astonished visitors from neighboring Ford Foundation village development projects. "What this seems to say," a grantee laboring in a village in Marawi noted, "is that IRRI residents should never be without electricity and water. There are none of us in that enviable situation." Chandler replied that the homes were not for Americans, but for Asians, who would for the first time enjoy the amenities of life in the developed world. From their air-conditioned offices and living rooms, trainees from Karachi or Saigon would view the problem of underdevelopment from the vantage of modernity.[10]

Chandler was especially concerned with training scientists to negotiate the passage across the edge of the modern, and IRRI's landscape and work routines guaranteed that trainees would practice that journey daily. Facing the laboratory buildings was an eighty-hectare experimental farm laced with underground pipes to allow individual plots to replicate the rainfall and drainage patterns of any part of the tropical zone. Soil imported from Java, the Mekong Delta, and the Plain of Jars was laid out in separate national paddies, making the farm a miniature Asia, an agricultural war room where scenarios could be gamed out in virtual space.

Care was taken to ensure that scientists approached this microcosm in a spirit of humility and self-reliance. Visiting scientists were required to "take off their shoes and wade right in" and run experiments themselves. "We always start trainees behind a carabao, out in the fields," an IRRI official chuckled, "It's good for their character. About once every three days they are likely to come in and say, 'Why are we here?' but after a month or so, they get right enthusiastic." Specialists were encouraged to base their knowledge on experience rather than on published studies. Each day's routine—leaving the office to tend and inspect plantings, and then returning to write up the results—symbolically enacted science's obligations to the underdeveloped world.[11]

IRRI was founded in the salad days of development economics when "the prospect of leading the Third World into the twentieth century," according to Kennedy adviser George Ball, "offered almost unlimited scope . . . to sociologists, psychologists, city planners, agronomists, political scientists and experts in chicken diseases." The presumption that Asian scientists could learn the dignity of toil from their American mentors indicates the influence of modernization theories just then coming into vogue among policymakers and academics. In 1957, with IRRI still on the drawing board, Hill anticipated problems with the Asian "plant breeder who sits in his office and sends his untutored field hand to make crosses." His concern drew on recent behavioral theories emphasizing the importance of steering the restless energies of the "transitional personalities" on whom modernization depended. In a seminal 1956 article Zbigniew Brzezinski complained that Western-trained Third World intellectuals were "on the whole elitists, despite their protestations." Contemptuous of their countrymen and envious of the colonial powers' technology, they rejected "slow and chiefly self-directed economic development" in favor of communism's quick solutions. Lucian Pye coined the term "expectation gap" to describe the psychological chasm separating young Asians from the "peasant standards and values" that surrounded them. Frustrated young men risked becoming "victims of their own impatience" unless nation building could give them a "sense of belonging" in both the village and the modern world. Cold warriors recognized the subversive potential of these unfulfilled yearnings. An Indian student told Ambassador Chester Bowles that his generation lived "with one leg in the world of the ancients and the other in the rational scientific world of the modern, with the feeling that both of these worlds are breaking to pieces under our feet."[12]

IRRI aimed to outfit its trainees with a hybrid professional identity they could carry back into Asia's fractured culture. Removed from the debilitating atmosphere of colonial bureaucracies and caste-conscious schools, trainees found their native abilities with a suddenness that surprised Chandler. IRRI's routines banished politics and privilege. Indian and Pakistani agronomists lived and worked together. Habits formed in colonial schools were systematically discouraged, and specialists were rewarded for eschewing the comforts IRRI took pains to provide. No standing was given to academic rank; no degrees were offered. Research aimed at visible results in the field that would overwhelm the scorn of bureaucrats and peasants back home. Trainees were told to expect such resistance, but also to face it with the support of their international team. The institute's "first-class" facilities were instructional, inculcating the oppositions—modernity/tradition, practice/theory, science/politics—that defined both the institute and the agronomist.[13]

To Filipinos, the structures signified a different opposition, between luxury and poverty. In a country where *palabas,* or showiness, governs political and economic life, IRRI went over the top. The *Manila Chronicle* likened it to a hotel lounge, and Filipino officials called it "Hollywood on Los Baños." The charges actually predated IRRI's first use as a film set. In 1966 director Cornel Wilde, taking advantage of the institute's ability to furnish "Asian" and "stateside" locations, used it as backdrop for the film *Beach Red,* in which Rip Torn consoled Jean Wallace on a divan—Chandler's divan—in the IRRI lounge while marines assaulted the experimental rice fields outside. Aside from the U.S. military bases, the IRRI residential compound was the Philippines' first gated suburb. Wolf Ladejinsky toured the Philippines in 1963 and found conversations about IRRI invariably turned to the subject of the gate guard, "a symbol of exclusiveness." Chandler considered the criticism unfair because the surrounding poverty made a place as "modern and well equipped as the IRRI complex an obvious attraction to burglars." He gradually grew accustomed to having the institute's intentions misconstrued. It was easier to create contrasts than to control the meanings people gave them.[14]

Looking like an Ohio consolidated high school perched on a volcano, IRRI appears misplaced even today. In the 1960s the effect was startling. "The entire installation is so different from the ramshackle construction characteristic of much of Filipino life at home," a *New Yorker* reporter observed, that it "attracted a good many sightseers." Once IRRI was dedicated in 1962, busses from Manila brought a thousand tourists a week to

Los Baños for a glimpse of the future. IRRI opened a welcome center and conducted guided tours, offering visitors education and a sense of time-travel, much like Colonial Williamsburg, another Rockefeller-sponsored theme park. Williamsburg, according to its guidebook, was "more than a bricks and mortar reconstruction," it was a "symbol of democracy in the troubled world today." IRRI reached for the same symbolism, reassuring visitors that science would ease the passage between tradition and modernity. An eleven-minute film introduced Filipinos to themselves, as they were seen by outsiders. Beginning with a shot of peasants weeding and planting, tasks some in the audience had performed that day, it observed that these "primitive methods" of cultivation were "inefficient, wasteful of human energy," and posed the essential question: "Can modern science help these people grow more rice? Two American foundations think that it can."[15]

Los Baños was a destination for pilgrims even before IRRI. Visitors came for its healing baths and to visit Makiling National Park, which adjoined the institute's grounds. The proximity to Mount Makiling, a sacred spot since pre-Christian times, cast a spiritual aura over IRRI that the discovery of miracle rice only confirmed. The rainforest-cloaked volcano is named for Mariang Makiling, a *diwata*, a light-skinned place-goddess whose profile can be discerned in the mountain's slope. In pre-Spanish times, Makiling visited local people (as the Virgin Mary has since) in response to appeals for help. One well known legend tells of her taking pity on a poor farmer to whom she gave a basket of ginger. Disappointed, he carried the basket home and on arriving found that the coarse tubers had turned to gold. In the twentieth century the mountain's dense forests gave refuge to political utopians—Katipuneros and the Maoist New People's Army—and to syncretic sects whose Christ, the nationalist leader Jose Rizal, revealed that the mountain contained an underground paradise, "a garden of flowers and fruit trees." Chandler never invoked Makiling's legends, but an echo of these associations may be heard in the vernacular names the Philippine press attached to IRRI's first high-yielding varieties, IR-8 ("miracle rice") and IR-5 (the "more miraculous rice") and the name the Marcos administration gave IR-8: Rizal Seed No. 1. The apotheosis of rice technology, which proceeded in earnest after 1966, began in a commingling of legends, American and Filipino, placing IRRI at the source of earthly abundance and asserting its guardianship of nature's secrets.[16]

The Target

IRRI's scientists set out to "change the architecture of the rice plant"—to make it shorter, greener, with fewer leaves and more panicles—their mission dictated as much by a need for institutional distinction as by the requirements of Asian agriculture. Modernization schemes must stand by their claims to novelty, a problem Chandler felt acutely as he struggled to establish his program's preeminence in a region thick with colonial, national, and United Nations (UN) centers devoted to improving rice. Rice breeding, once an artisanal skill of farmers, became a state function in colonial Asia, and in the late 1940s the UN Food and Agriculture Organization (FAO) considered it one of the few aspects of Asian production that had been adequately modernized. The Philippines, like most countries, had national and provincial research stations, including one located in Los Baños. The FAO set up an international rice center in Bangkok in 1962. In this crowded field, Chandler needed to display the merits of his project-oriented approach with sufficient splash to justify Ford's and Rockefeller's massive investment. From the beginning, therefore, he elected to avoid incremental improvements in rice varieties and go for "the big jump."[17]

Once an international staff was assembled, Chandler asked it to produce specifications for an "ideal plant type," a variety that would most efficiently convert sunlight, water, and chemical inputs, particularly nitrogen, into food. The scientists settled on eight characteristics of this Platonist ideotype, known at IRRI as "the target": The rice would be short to avoid wasting materials on stalk; dark green, to absorb sunlight better; and rigid, to allow for machine harvesting. It should grow anywhere in tropical Asia, and have resistance to pests and diseases. Breeders rejected or modified strains that met only some of these criteria. Chandler wanted to take plant genetics to its limits, to "show the world that higher yields were possible."[18]

Philippine agronomists tried unsuccessfully to discourage the Big Jump strategy. Dioscoro Umali, dean of the University of the Philippines College of Agriculture, attended IRRI's Thursday seminars in 1963 and 1964. The target variety, he pointed out, would require expensive inputs: not just fertilizer but also herbicides to prevent shading by taller weeds. Shallow-rooted dwarf plants needed more precise hydraulic control than most peasant farmers could manage. Farmers would have to discard nearly all of their practices and adopt new techniques for planting, weeding, irrigation, harvesting, and threshing. New chemicals and equipment would require credit and distribution networks that the region did not have. If adopted, the target variety would radically disrupt the social environment in which rice was grown. His criticisms hit upon an unstated objective of the Big Jump strategy: to induce social change by displacing the culture and economy of rice cultivation. Umali was the first but not the last scientist to try to rescue the practical objective of increasing rice yields from the unrealistic expectations beginning to grow around the project.[19]

The dream of using food to reform Asia originated in the Rockefeller Foundation amid concern about the political consequences of runaway population growth. Foundation demographers believed only modernization across a broad front—involving urbanization, the spread of literacy, consumerism, and external contact—could induce a demographic transition, reducing birth rates and forestalling a crisis. The best hope lay in stimulating an "industrial revolution of agriculture, whereby agricultural personnel are taken off the land and put to work in factories." Kennedy expanded on this vision in his June 1963 call for an agricultural revolution. It would neither "begin nor end on the farm," he maintained. Instead, it would transform "the whole economic and social structure of each nation."[20]

Paradoxically, development economists expected a single technology to propel this sweeping change. A massive Ford Foundation/Social Science Research Council inquiry into the sources of economic development begun in 1955 postulated that "epochal innovations" (the steam engine, radio, electricity) drove historical and economic transformation. But Albert O. Hirschman, writing in 1958, suggested that the technological trigger could also be something as ordinary as a rice seed. Rejecting the structuralist orthodoxy that required simultaneous economic, social, and scientific advances to generate a "big push" toward growth, he argued that a disruptive technology, an "inducement mechanism," could stir unused talent and capital into activity. Like an atomic pile, underdeveloped societies would undergo a "chain of disequilibria" as energy was released from the breaking of traditional bonds. John P. Lewis, former head of the India USAID mission, told Congress in 1969 that Hirschman had written the history of the green revolution in advance. "He taught many of us to realize that this is the way you expect successful development to happen. When it succeeds, you get a thrust, one sector moves ahead, and it begins to create effective pulls on the laggards." The inducement mechanism's psychological influence was thus more important than its economic effect. "Rice planting is more than an economic activity," Bernard Fall observed, "It is a way of life, a whole Weltanschauung in itself." Social scientists still debated whether it was possible for peasant to be rational in an economic sense, but IRRI's project proceeded from an assumption that peasants were *not yet* rational. Their awakening to modernity would begin with the decision to plant IRRI's seeds.[21]

IRRI defined its target in January 1965 during the pause between the Tonkin Gulf Incident and the onset of ROLLING THUNDER, the bombing of North Vietnam. At that moment, ocean and air currents were shifting in a pattern now known as El Niño, pushing monsoon clouds away from the Asian land mass and deep into the Pacific Ocean. El Niño oscillations subsided between the 1920s and the 1970s, granting tropical Asia a reprieve from catastrophic drought, but in 1966 the monsoon never came. The break in the weather cleared skies over North Vietnamese targets and accelerated the Pathet Lao's dry season offensive, but U.S. concern focused on India. An Asian drought would severely test the U.S. administration's claim that free men ate better. Rostow noted that Johnson tracked "the fall of rain in India and Pakistan as closely as he did along the Pedernales." Typical of El Niño years, the 1965 drought coincided with a cool, wet summer, as well as a record number of tornadoes, in the U.S. Midwest and Great Plains. American meteorologists noted strange "shifts in planetary wind currents" but failed to draw the connection to the Indian drought that was obvious to Johnson's advisers on food aid. Large harvests in North America furnished the United States with both means and opportunity to rescue India. The Perkins Committee, a special presidential advisory group on foreign aid that included Gaud, Dwayne Andreas of Archer Daniels Midland, and David Rockefeller, urged that this momentary leverage should be used "to force India to increase her agricultural productivity." The force had to be subtle, however. "Any such use of our power must be done cautiously," the committee warned. "Such a policy has hazards and the powerful and rich cannot do this sort of thing too publicly."[22]

The changed climate refocused IRRI's mission from reforming institutions and attitudes to averting famine. "We have now reached a point," J. George Harrar, IRRI's board chairman, told the National Academy of Sciences, "that the combination of annual deficits in world food supplies and the onrushing population increase could spell disaster for the attainment of world peace and prosperity." IRRI took on the mood of Los

Alamos as crops withered in India and Pakistan in the fall of 1965. Scientists spoke of a "race against time" as they monitored the results of more than 570 crosses on the experimental farm. "We keep telling them what responsibility they have to produce," Chandler observed, "because of all the money that's been invested, and the whole world is looking at us, and all that." By 1966, plant breeders had narrowed the field to three: IR-8, IR-9, and IR-5, each derived by cross-breeding short-stemmed varieties with Peta, a hardy Indonesian strain. Each variety needed to be monitored for several generations more, but the Philippine government had already chosen a winner. The Nacionalista ticket headed by Ferdinand E. Marcos had won election in 1965 on the slogan "Progress is a Grain of Rice." Seasonal rice shortages, a byproduct of colonial trade patterns based on cotton, sugar, and other export crops, had grown intolerable to urban electorates in the Philippines and across South Asia. Marcos's Harvard-trained technocrats, some of whom sat on IRRI's board, determined to press the institute for a solution. In early 1966, before the scientists were ready, Chandler approved and USAID funded Project SPREAD, large-scale multiplication and field trials of IR-8. Concerned about disease susceptibility, the breeders urged caution, but before the crop could be taken in the Philippine press proclaimed a breakthrough.[23]

As the August harvest came in the Philippines was gripped by a modern tulipomania. IR-8 was sold in the lobbies of banks and fashionable department stores, and harvested grain was too costly to eat. Newspapers promised a tenfold increase in yield. "Miracle Rice—Instant Increase," proclaimed the *Philippines Free Press,* assuring readers that spectacular yields were automatic, "lodged in the grain itself—a built in productivity." That this was decidedly not true was what made IR-8 attractive to the technocrats and to the American aid officials who jumped on the miracle rice bandwagon. USAID began distributing IR-8 in a package with Atlas and Esso farm chemicals while another leading manufacturer, Caltex, built a nationwide distribution network. The foundations took criticism, then and since, for enabling U.S. multinationals to penetrate Third World agriculture, but this analysis actually understates the ambition of IR-8's modernizing project. The technocrats knew reliance on manufactured "inputs" afforded opportunities to impose a solution to the rice crisis by extending government supervision over millions of subsistence farmers living largely outside the cash economy. Marcos set up a coordinating council directed by Rafael Salas to direct the supply of seed, chemicals, loans, and machinery, enabling the government to control prices and supply at every step of cultivation. Agriculture and marketing, already en-meshed in international commercial networks, came under a new central-ized discipline. "Even if it wasn't such a spectacular producer," Salas believed, "one would advocate pushing miracle rice culture if only to train the Filipino farmer into thinking in terms of techniques, machines, fertil-izers, schedules, and experiments." An American USAID official affirmed that creating "an American time pressure culture" was essential to the program. "If people do not accept discipline," he observed, "we cannot progress."[24]

The race against time reached the wire in 1966. In January the CIA forecast "widespread starvation" in India. The pope appealed to the world for help as students rioted in Bengal and Communist unions paralyzed Calcutta with a general strike. In October President Johnson toured the Philippines and Vietnam, his only trip to the region as president. Johnson wanted to signal the permanence of America's commitment to Asia, Eric Sevareid told CBS viewers, to construct "a cause with a capital C, a new manifest destiny, a new Americanized, modernized, version of Kipling's white man's burden." IRRI served as a convenient backdrop. Striding onto the experimental rice field beside Ferdinand and Imelda Marcos, Johnson crouched and sampled the soil with his fingers. "Drawing on your experi-ments, your new rice strains, the technical training you are giving," he told IRRI's staff and a global television audience, "we can escalate the war on hunger. That is the only war in which we seek escalation."[25]

The following month, at a press conference at the Manila Hotel, IRRI formally "named" IR-8, announcing that it produced five to eight metric tons per hectare—double the average—"under careful management." The institute advertised IR-8 as a cosmopolitan rice, able to produce high yields throughout tropical Asia. "IR-8 was to tropical rices what the Model T Ford was to automobiles," a pamphlet explained, "a rugged variety that could go almost anywhere." But at the time of release the only thorough testing had been under IRRI's tightly controlled condi-tions, and it had been barely tried outside the Philippines at all. IR-8's breakthrough lay mainly in the sensation it created and its close resem-blance to the ideal architecture IRRI had set out to achieve.[26]

IR-8 appeared to solve the rice crisis, and for the Marcos administra-tion, the appearance of success was sufficient. The new variety covered 1 million acres in the Philippines in 1968 according to IRRI (750,000 ac-cording to the CIA). U.S. intelligence reports noted that the gap between production and consumption of rice was about 10 percent, roughly what it had been before miracle rice was introduced, but that the technocrats had produced a bountiful harvest through fraud. The Marcos administration, which first claimed national self-sufficiency in 1968, maintained the illusion well into the 1970s through the simple device of exporting small quantities amid great fanfare while secretly importing tons of rice from Hong Kong and faking the figures. Marcos's reputation as a modernizing, technocratic leader—as well as his victory in the 1969 election—rested on the feigned achievement of this agricultural milestone. Marcos's publicity agents wrote the early drafts of the green revolution legend: "Coming at the precise moment in history when the Philippines' growing population was forcing the country steadily and surely into a maelstrom of hunger," a spokesman elaborated, "the development of miracle rice marks a turning point which may not only arrest this possibility, but makes possible a complete reversal toward self-sufficiency."[27]

Dwarf rice and dwarf wheat furnished the flagship program for a new generation of populist leaders whose slogans emphasized developmentalist rather than redistributionist goals: Marcos ("Rice, Roads, and Schools"), Indira Gandhi of India ("Remove Poverty"), Ayub Khan of Pakistan ("Together Let Us Build"), Suharto of Indonesia ("Father of Development"), and Dudley Senanayake of Ceylon ("Grow More Food"). Development rhetoric and the promise of scientific solutions to poverty allowed these regimes to neutralize class antagonisms within their coalitions, appeal to supposedly universal demands for increased consumption and national strength, and identify the opponents of progress. The modernization idiom of American social scientists proved astonishingly successful at mobilizing Asian electorates. With the help of USAID and the J. Walter Thompson advertising agency, Marcos presented IR-8 as answering "the promise of a better life." The achievement of self-sufficiency in 1968 allowed Marcos to sweep to victory in 1969, making him the first Philippine president to win reelection. Developmental populists couched the goal of self-sufficiency in nationalist terms, as an attribute of a progressive, independent nation. Rice imports, once justified by the older economic logic of comparative advantage, were now regarded as a national embarrassment.[28]

U.S. officials favored this brand of nationalism over the chauvinistic style of the early post-independence leaders or the "radical nationalism" of a younger generation that "resent[ed] any overtones of American domination—political, economic, or cultural." The United States encouraged developmentalist regimes to assert an independent identity and strategic posture. Since the 1950s think tanks and social science journals had theorized the emergence of leaders of a new type, technocrats who would seek legitimacy "through modernizing achievement" and possess the ability to "reinterpret traditional beliefs, adapt them to modern needs and translate them into a modern idiom." The task before these leaders would be to close the "aspiration gap" between the stubbornly traditional peasantry and the impatient millions seeking a better life in the cities. Like IR-8 itself, the developmental regimes that introduced the rice appeared in fulfillment of scripture. Rostow had written in 1960 that nationalism would pass through two phases. The first generation of nationalists, "weighted too heavily with interests and attitudes from the traditional past" to achieve breakthrough, would give way to a "generation of men who were not merely anxious to assert national independence but were prepared to create an urban-based modern society." These charismatic leaders would promote "radical changes in the productivity of agriculture" as "a precondition for take-off."[29]

IRRI's press release noted that IR-8 was sometimes called "miracle rice." Chandler had mixed feelings about selling science as superstition, but although IRRI soon renounced the name it was taken up by IR-8's promoters. News accounts played on biblical metaphors and the occult uses of rice in Eastern tradition. Given scriptural images invoked by the multiplication of food, the apotheosis of IRRI's achievement was perhaps natural, but when USAID translated IR-8's miraculousness into other languages and other faiths it followed an old occidental custom of holding up modern marvels before astonished natives. Designed to instill a modern, rational outlook, IR-8 paradoxically fulfilled a yearning for magic, for the kind of psychological stunt not even the communists could match.[30]

As Important as Bullets

In the early stages of the Vietnam conflict, American policymakers and journalists often explained the war as a struggle for the control of rice, the food supply of Asia. Other issues eclipsed that claim by 1967, but rice remained significant as an indicator of progress (or deterioration) in the vaguely defined but critical mission of pacification. Military and civilian advisers agreed that progress on the military and diplomatic fronts hinged on Saigon's ability to demonstrate confidence and extend its authority in rural Vietnam. They envisioned pacification as a process of rural modernization: civil programs in health, agriculture, education, and security would win the allegiance of distant villages and expand the influence and presence of the central government. Even as bombing and ground combat escalated, the dwindling supply of rice in urban markets revealed Saigon's weakening hold on the countryside. In 1965 Prime Minister Nguyen Cao Ky threatened to shoot one merchant per day until the rice shortage disappeared, but by the following year the capital, isolated within one of the largest rice growing areas in Asia, lived on grain imported from the United States.[31]

At war summits at Honolulu, Manila, and Guam in 1966 and 1967, Johnson directed resources into pacification and assigned it the same priority as combat operations. Robert Komer, the chief of Civil Operations and Revolutionary Development Support (CORDS) the pacification command, advertised the new policy with the slogan "rice is as important as bullets." In weekly progress reports, known as Komergrams, a summary of rice prices and supply served as pacification's stock ticker. The pressure for measurable results steadily increased. Only visible demonstration of Saigon's viability, Johnson believed, would bring Hanoi to the table and sustain domestic support for the war. Johnson pressed Komer to "search urgently for occasions to present sound evidence of progress in Vietnam." Rather than new programs or techniques, Komer's "new model" pacification program, initiated in mid-1967, emphasized "a series of new measurement systems," including a computerized Hamlet Evaluation System (HES) that tracked government influence over villages by security and developmental criteria, a CORDS Evaluation Branch to document progress, and provincial tracking polls to monitor attitudes among the rural population. Komer put the main effort into villages in the middle range of the HES scale, to consolidate rather than enlarge the government's zone of influence and allow the pacified area to appear clearly marked on briefing maps sent to Washington.[32]

IR-8 arrived in Vietnam as pacifiers were searching for methods to mark the separation between enemy and friendly areas on the landscape. Until 1967, pacification had proceeded on the principle that the benefits of modernization, generally distributed, would win hearts and minds and ease rural disaffection, creating conditions for expanded government influence. Modernization was thus a temporal shift; villagers proceeded through developmental stages to reach a level where they were no longer susceptible to persuasion by the Viet Cong. Dissenting counterinsurgency theorists, however, argued for a more focused rural pacification effort in which "material benefits should be so distributed as to create a marked difference in the quality of life between the areas controlled by the GVN [Saigon] and those contested with the VC." The boundaries of modernization could be drawn by increasing rice production "in GVN controlled areas only, by subsidizing provision of inputs such as fertilizers and credit." In a series of seminars in McLean, Virginia, in 1966, U.S. Army planners endorsed this spatial reorientation. Pacification should seek to bring "tradition bound village dwellers into more frequent and more intimate contact with modern elements of the society through the matrix of a town-village economic complex" by stimulating "a farm surplus to be traded by the peasant for a higher level of consumer and investment goods." By the time Jose Ona, a Philippine rice specialist, brought the first seeds from IRRI, planning on both policy and theoretical levels anticipated the introduction of an ingredient that would dramatically increase crop yields and depend on continual inputs of fertilizer and credit. IR-8 arrived right on schedule.[33]

Branding it Thân Nông, after the agriculture god and divine progenitor of the Vietnamese, the U.S. aid mission launched a "Madison Avenue-style campaign" to sell Vietnamese farmers "on the glories of IR-8." Gene Roberts was conducting a round of interviews in Washington before taking over the New York Times Saigon bureau. "Forget the war," a White House official told him. "The war is over. Now we have to win the peace. The thing to keep your eye on is IR-8 rice." He arrived in country in October 1967, just in time for the unveiling. With the speed and efficiency of a military operation, USAID dispatched fifty tons of IR-8 to Vo Dat, sixty miles northeast of Saigon, an area thought to be secure. Army units escorted the seed bags from IRRI to the Manila docks. On arrival in Saigon, it was airlifted by Army Chinook helicopters to a landing zone where it was offloaded by fifteen chieu hoi (Viet Cong defectors) and parceled out to villagers arranged on bleachers surrounding a test plot. Roberts listened to the speeches for a while, and then spotted a knot of men squatting near the edge of the crowd, chewing on blades of grass. When he asked through a translator what they thought of the proceedings they all began talking at once. "Basically," the translator explained, "they said fuck IR-8 rice." That morning ARVN troops had put the farmers on a bus at gunpoint and driven them forty miles to Vo Dat. They only wanted to be allowed to go home.[34]

The initial experiment called for twelve hectares to be cultivated by professional American and Philippine agronomists and another 778 by nearly 1,000 Vietnamese families who were given free seed, chemicals, and water pumps but "told nothing authoritatively" about the nature of the rice or the project they were involved in. U.S. agricultural adviser C. F. van Haeften expected to produce test data and enough seed to plant 20,000 hectares the following spring when it would be deployed throughout South Vietnam. As the project geared up, one pacification expert tried unsuccessfully to separate IR-8's proven value from the hype. George L. McColm, director of the strategic hamlet program, had been a military adviser on agrarian reform in occupied Japan, Korea, and now Vietnam. Echoing Umali's arguments, he observed that IR-8 would require "an entirely new approach to rice production" and might open a one-time opportunity to push subsistence farmers into commercial agriculture. In two widely distributed memos in late 1967 he cautioned against "wild and irresponsible promotion of IR8" and urged that distribution and trials take place only "under strict technical supervision" to avoid building expectations that could not be met.[35]

McColm aimed to salvage some economic benefit from what was becoming a psywar operation, a "high impact" program to penetrate the closed world of the Vietnamese village. He was unable in the end to dampen extravagant predictions that IR-8 would turn the tide in the countryside by inducing a kind of social catharsis. American officials blamed South Vietnamese corruption for the failure of earlier efforts to deliver a modernizing stimulus through land reform or strategic hamlets, and they were desperate for a mechanism that could work around bureaucratic interference. With its dependence on imported inputs, they believed, IR-8 would widen the arc of influence unaided by bloody or soiled hands, automatically linking remote villages to chains of supply and distribution radiating from Saigon.[36]

As combat activity tapered off in weeks before the 1968 Tet holiday, Ambassador Ellsworth Bunker announced Operation TAKEOFF, combining a stepped-up PHOENIX program (assassinations and terror directed at the Viet Cong "infrastructure") with extensive demonstrations of IR-8 to be held the following summer. The seeds were expected to stir up a generational revolution, turning young innovative peasants against their tradition-bound ancestors. Once the yields of IR-8 were demonstrated, young farmers would begin dreaming of the motorbikes, radios, and sewing machines such a harvest could buy. A visiting agribusinessman found U.S. and Vietnamese officials in Saigon "running around waving IR-8 pamphlets like Red Guards with the Mao books." Johnson had demanded "coonskins on the wall," dramatic, visible evidence that pacification was succeeding. IR-8 would soon supply the first coonskin. "Things really looked great," an agricultural adviser noted in April 1968, "until the Tet Offensive came along."[37]

The surprise attack on provincial capitals and Saigon itself in January 1968 thwarted the planned rice revolution. North Vietnamese and Viet Cong troops severed the main truck routes, cutting the experimental fields off from the vital supplies of fertilizer. For the next three months, van Haeften's team waited in Saigon, the fate of the dwarf shoots unknown. USAID Director William Gaud had planned to feature the agriculture/consumer revolution in his March Senate testimony on Vietnam aid. Instead, he had to acknowledge that "this was all before January 30. What the situation will be in the future is pretty hard to tell." When agricultural advisers returned to the countryside, they found the crop stunted by neglect but still bearing seed. The rice infrastructure fared less well; throughout Vietnam, dikes and paddies were cratered by mortars and bombs and damaged by tank tracks and defoliant. Johnson's announcement of a bombing halt in March and the initiation of the Paris peace talks undercut the rationale for Operation TAKEOFF.[38]

After Tet, IR-8 became part of a reorganized pacification effort designed to foster an image of South Vietnam as a self-supporting state capable of surviving a peace settlement. William Colby, Komer's successor, set 1969 targets for reducing Viet Cong strength by 33,000 through Phoenix activities and raising rice production by 1 million tons with IR-8. As with TAKEOFF, agricultural and military actions were coordinated so that "the spread of miracle rice," Colby noted, "would occur in the communities where new local territorial forces were assigned and self-defense groups organized." He considered it "the best organized and conceived operation since Ngo Dinh Nhu's strategic hamlet program." Miracle rice became the visible mark of a pacified landscape. "As the percentage of A, B, and C [pacified] hamlets kept rising on HES charts in staff offices," South Vietnam's pacification chief noted, "the refreshing green surface of rice seedlings gradually expanded everywhere." Fertilizer and seed subsidies allowed the Commercial Import Program to bring Saigon's consumer culture to the countryside, and IR-8 came to be known as "honda rice" after the motorbikes that were acquired with the proceeds. Advisers announced that South Vietnam would be self-sufficient in rice by 1973, but as in the Philippines, statistical yields were harvested on paper. An American official observed that Vietnamese "service chiefs were ordered, often somewhat arbitrarily, to revise yield figures, lower consumption figures, or decrease estimates of drought damage" to ensure the program's success. American planes leafletted North Vietnam with photographs of dwarf rice fields captioned "IR-8, South Vietnam's Miracle Rice. All Vietnamese can enjoy this rice when peace comes."[39]

In the waning months of the Johnson administration, U.S. negotiator W. Averell Harriman held forth IR-8 as the technological edge that might yet win the war. At Paris, Harriman and North Vietnamese representative Xuan Thuy deadlocked over the shape of the table and conditions for the cessation of bombing, but found room for agreement on IR-8. On October 17, after a difficult morning haggling over representation for South Vietnam, the two delegations adjourned for tea and plunged into conversation about miracle rice. Harriman returned to Washington convinced that IRRI's technology might provide the basis for a settlement. "Miracle rice is one of the most important things to them," he told reporters. Hanoi was anxious to break its food dependence on China. "If they could get miracle rice and the techniques of growing it from us, I think they would hope to be independent of China." Ford Foundation officials congratulated themselves and voted an increase in IRRI's funding. "It now appears that 'miracle rice' is going to play a major role in concluding the war in Vietnam," Hill observed.[40]

The Nixon administration's negotiator, Henry Kissinger, failed to pursue the IR-8 opening, but by mid-1969 it may already have closed. Viet Cong propagandists initially sought to discourage plantings of IR-8 by spreading rumors that the rice caused impotence and leprosy, but in mid-1969 the National Liberation Front reversed course, urging its members to cultivate the new seeds in liberated areas. In September 1969, when U.S. troops came upon well-tended fields of IR-8 growing deep in enemy territory beyond the reach of hondas or subsidies, it was as if they had discovered a Viet Cong helicopter factory. The story was reported around the world, and Congress expressed concern about seeds making their way to China or Cuba. North Vietnam did acquire IR-8, either via the Ho Chi Minh Trail, through trade with Pakistan or Sri Lanka, or through independent development. As early as July 1968, North Vietnamese agronomists had disseminated "Southern dwarf" seeds to farmers in the Red River delta. North Vietnam was embarking on its own agricultural revolution to divert labor from rice farming into industry and the military in preparation for the final stages of the war. In 1972 the CIA confirmed that one-fifth of North Vietnam's paddies were planted to IR-8.

The edge of the modern had advanced beyond the horizons of American power.[41]

Until a helicopter evacuated the last IRRI adviser from a Saigon rooftop, IR-8 continued to supply imaginary victories. Despite repeated ignition failures, it never lost its reputation among war managers as an engine of change. Instead, it adopted new transformative powers (cultural solvent, bargaining chip, economic stabilizer) to suit new desired futures. The sheltering discourse of modernization protected it from the imputation or the memory of failure. "Our achievements were not tremendous because the fighting interfered with our work," Chandler later remenisced. His recollection reveals that achievement was defined not by the diffusion of the innovation but by its political effects. The agricultural revolution had been designed to preclude a political revolution. It took Vietnam to show that the two could go together. Two years after the fall of Saigon, the newly merged Socialist Republic made IR-8 the centerpiece of a brutal program of rural reconstruction. Gen. Vo Nguyen Giap, architect of the military victory, argued that scientific agriculture would restore discipline and reverse "the outmoded working and thinking habits of centuries" of capitalist agriculture. Vietnam is one of the few places where IR-8 is still grown.[42]

Development is a visual language of blueprints, charts, and symbols. Miracle rice furnished a visual representation—and later a memory—of what happens when modernization comes to the countryside. In the 1960s, the idea of a rural modernity was a conceptual innovation. Rostovian theorists and Gandhian critics both envisioned rural development as the introduction of habits and forms from the outside, but the origins and content of those "pictures of the future" were as important as their effects. Increasing yields was never enough; the increase had to offer a moral lesson for those who witnessed or read about it. IR-8's real achievement, therefore, was literary. It took diffuse processes unfolding over decades—the spread of irrigation and market arrangements, new political relations between farmers and the state, and the rise and fall of developmental regimes—and contained them within a parable of seeds.

7

YOU CAN'T EAT STEEL

As the American scientific establishment geared up to combat India's food crisis, Indian agriculture was quietly experiencing an export boom. Output of tea, coffee, tobacco, cashews, dyestuffs, and shellac sold to Europe, the Soviet Union, and China exceeded targets set in the first plan, while agriculture as a whole surpassed industry in rates of growth and earnings. More than three-quarters of India's export income came from the farm, and village crafts—chiefly textiles and leather goods—comprised the bulk of its manufactured exports. Textile fibers grew on more than 20 million of India's most fertile and irrigated acres. Favorable prices and new American varieties fuelled a surge in production, and acreage under cotton and other fibers grew by more than 50 percent in the 1950s.[1]

A single crop, jute, accounted for a third of India's foreign exchange earnings, even though it was a miracle the industry survived past 1947. Partition left jute lands in Pakistan cut off from the mills across the border, but five years later Calcutta looms were processing nearly a million tons of burlap for sale abroad. Jute was the city's lifeblood, employing 300,000 workers in 115 mills clustered on the banks of the Hugli in an area known as the Bengal Ruhr. Its red brick factories, faithful replicas of the jute mills built by Scottish traders in Dundee in the 19th century, rose over a Dickensian slum. "A mere glance into an Indian jute mill or the homes of the workers would probably horrify the Western observer," an industry report advised; still, workers had "more to eat and a little higher standard of life than the average farmer."[2]

Low wages and cheap fiber gave India a lock on the world market, and jute bankrolled the rise of India's first industrial empires, Tata Group and Birla Bros., Ltd., from textiles into chemicals, shipping, insurance, automobiles, metals, and refining. Congress Party politicians admired Soviet-style socialism from a distance, but they listened closely to the private industrialists who furnished their campaign funds. "It was generally believed," Agriculture Secretary B. Sivaraman later recalled, "that the jute and the cotton trades were the milch cows for the political system." Textile interests had clout, but they could also claim that export crops meant economic independence.[3]

Jute brought in hard currency. More than half of total output went to the United States, generating $200 million a year. Americans used it for packaging, furniture, drapes, carpets, and apparel. It was woven into bucket seats in Ford Thunderbirds and sandbags for troops in Korea. Jute-wallahs bid up whatever stocks Chinese or Pakistani traders could offer, but most of the demand was met by growers in West Bengal, Orissa, and Bihar who responded to rising prices and government incentives by planting jute on more than a million acres that formerly grew grain. To Bengali peasants and national planners it made sense, so long as prices remained high, to grow jute instead of wheat. With the export profits, India could buy Argentine or Canadian flour, and machinery besides.[4]

Trade papers and U.S. and United Nations (UN) agencies monitored cotton, tea, and jute volumes and prices on international exchanges, but this picture of a dynamic, diversified, globally linked agriculture was absent from discussions among American donors and scientists. The Rockefeller Foundation launched its project in 1956 after a study mission declared Indian agriculture stagnant, a "tragic situation on a grand scale." The report discussed grain, soils, implements, livestock, and rainfall but made no mention of the fibers and nonfood crops that grew on one-fifth of India's acreage. Similarly, a 1959 Ford Foundation report calling for emergency measures to induce "an immediate and drastic increase in food production" did not recommend plowing up cotton lands to grow food. Experts defined agriculture, according to Gunnar Myrdal, "so as to exclude the plantation sector, which we consider to be essentially industrial." This tailored vocabulary to suit a particular theme: India's problem was "too many people, too little land."[5]

"Agriculture" is a category invented by city folk, a designation for a subordinate sphere within a presumptively urban-centered economy. Literate elites mold its terminology to sanction their powers over the countryside, interpreting each fresh scientific or governmental intervention as a logical reaction to environmental limitations. Each part of this vocabulary—food supply, models, irrigation, rice, the village, the peasant—framed agriculture in ways that advanced some agendas and forestalled others. In the 1950s Rockefeller agronomists were still struggling to fix a narrative frame around wheat. They would later argue for the inevitability of their program; the pressure of population impelled India to launch a drive for self-sufficiency. But so long as Public Law (P.L.) 480 aid flowed freely and birth rates aroused little alarm, other options, other futures, seemed open.

To many informed analysts in the mid-1950s, jute's success pointed the way forward. A 1956 survey by U.S. aid experts recognized India's comparative advantage in non-food and industrial crops, and urged a policy of "export promotion and export consciousness." Eminent economists, including Arthur Lewis, reached the same conclusion, arguing that India could manufacture its way out of scarcity by selling textiles and factory goods in return for food from Southeast Asia and Africa. Rostovian theory asserted that only an industrial takeoff could outpace population growth. To the Indian planning commission, the distinctive feature of Indian agriculture was its "excess of food crops over non-food crops." The predominance of industrial crops was a characteristic of modern economies. Besides generating foreign exchange, jute and other fibers, as well as cashew (a source of high-grade machine lubricants), were essential to industry; when scarce, they had to be procured from abroad with hard currency. Wheat, on the other hand, could be imported cheaply, by barter, or—through P.L. 480—for free. For Indian planners, modernizing agriculture meant integrating it into an expanding industrial sector, drawing off its surplus labor and savings, and mobilizing its export earnings, or as one planner put it, getting "more from the rural areas than we are at present getting."[6]

In the end, though, wheat won out over jute. It was not a competition for space. Wheat comprised 8 percent of India's total cropping pattern, jute less than one percent. Neither crop was more "indigenous" than the other. Both were occasional crops in North India until colonial-era irrigation works expanded production. Each had support from American and Indian specialists. The stakes, as was often the case with development, were at once symbolic and consequential. Jute and wheat represented alternative paths to modernization, alternative definitions of India's future and its past. To champions of wheat, India was an agricultural nation that had struggled for 400 years against famine, but to industrial planners the predominance of agriculture was an aberration, a vestige of British mercantilism. Precolonial India had been a manufacturing and trading power, and in independence the nation would recover its true character.[7]

Foundations cast their effort to reform rural India in the 1960s as a confrontation between expert and peasant, a struggle "to sell progress to some of the world's most skeptical customers." Observers have focused on the same polarity, interpreting modernization as a triumph of the state's domineering scientific outlook over the cumulative experience encoded in local tradition, *techne* over *metis*. But in this case, and in many others, the chief lines of division were between modernizers. Conflict could arise from disputes over means and goals, but more often from incompatible ways of envisioning and telling the story of growth. Development should be analyzed not as a process or an outcome but as a narrative strategy. The Indian state was torn between rival diagnoses of the economy's deficiencies, the requirements of progress, the constraints holding it back, and the nature of its eventual success; it could "see" more than one way forward. Resistance to the New Agricultural Strategy arose first and most significantly from modernizers committed to the story wheat displaced, the narrative contained in India's five-year plans.[8]

Two Plans, Two Futures

As Rockefeller agronomists transferred the Mexico model to India they ran square into a countermodel advanced by the Indian Planning Commission, which had its own interpretation of agriculture's place in national development. The commission held unmatched, but not unlimited, power to accelerate "the tempo of economic activity" and build a socialist society. Chaired personally by Nehru and comprised of leading intellectuals, including the brilliant statistician/physicist Prasanta Mahalanobis, it had authority to negotiate foreign aid and loans, license imports and exports, and steer investment and foreign exchange. But its deepest influence, as Swedish economist Gunnar Myrdal discerned, came from its controlling position in the discourse on planning. Exchanges between leaders, the press, opposition parties, foreign governments, and international agencies revolved around the periodic release of draft plans which set terms of reference for "all strivings for political, social, and economic reform." Planners cultivated a rationalized vocabulary as a substitute for the dangerous partisan and communal rhetoric of the political sphere. "In the course of time," commissioner Pitamber Pant foresaw, "national political parties, instead of being labeled by ideology, may begin to be identified with the rates of growth they represent."[9]

In its language and scope, the second plan (1956–1961) evoked an image of an economy subject to conscious and detailed direction. It mandated the construction of three gigantic steel mills, a doubling of electrical power; bountiful harvests; and expanded production of coal, cement, and textiles. National resources of all kinds—food, labor, gold reserves, and factory capacity—were matched to specific goals listed as numerical targets. The brass ring was the top end of the production chain—electronics, automobiles, shipbuilding, aircraft—for no country had ever become rich or powerful without industrializing. High-priced imports, such as steel and machine tools, would be replaced by local manufactures in order of priority. Economists now call this strategy import-substituting industrialization (ISI). It was "not a matter of dry statistics" for Nehru, "but rather a living, moving process affecting the lives of hundreds of millions of our countrymen." Steel, electricity, machinery, the "mother industries," under the state's paternal direction, would give birth to a New India of unlimited possibilities.[10]

The planners, however, did not have unrestricted authority. The constitution reserved fiscal and policy powers to the states, and these included jurisdiction over food and agriculture. Local variations in land taxes, property rights, subsidies, and prices made agriculture significant, the one area in which states could creatively distinguish themselves from each other and the center. The Punjab was virtually alone in investing heavily in basic research. Assam, West Bengal, and other states tightly regulated food prices and distribution, while Madras, under the leadership of Chakravarthi "Rajaji" Rajagopalachari and his youthful food minister, Chidambaram Subramaniam, went the other way, decontrolling prices and lowering rents to channel income to producers. This cumbersome federalism further predisposed the Plan Commission to invest in "concentrated" sectors—industry, transport, minerals, and power—where the center had direct authority.[11]

Agriculture was critical to the success of the industry-first strategy. Rapid expansion of heavy industries would intensify demand for cereals, textile fibers, and other essential commodities and without an equivalent rise in rural productivity, inflationary pressures would defeat the plan. As Finance Minister T. T. Krishnamachari explained, "food holds the key to the control of inflation. Our hopes of earning additional foreign exchange by exports turn largely on the prospects for agricultural production." But new investments in fertilizer, farm equipment, or seeds would also thwart industrial goals by exhausting the supply of foreign exchange. The solution to this paradox, planners believed, was being tested in China. In 1956 a study mission issued an enthusiastic report on Beijing's success in boosting agricultural yields by 30 percent through village cooperatives. It confirmed the planners' suspicions that idle rural labor could be mobilized both to feed the growing population and provide a surplus for capital formation. If China could wring an extra 30 percent from its surplus rural labor, Nehru decided, surely free Indians could achieve fifteen "without additional expenditure."[12]

In common with structuralist economists in the United States, Indian planners banked on the tremendous latent energy supposedly frozen within traditional agriculture. S. R. Sen, an economist on the planning staff, advised that farming was "a bargain sector, a sector with a large unexploited potential which can produce the requisite surplus with relatively low investment and in a comparatively short time." Investments went first into heavy industry while agrarian improvement was programmed for the longer term. In the meantime, inexpensive renovations—community development, land reform, and cooperatives—would release "waste labor" salted away in the countryside. Estimating it would take ten to fifteen years to begin making artificial fertilizers locally, Mahalanobis urged farmers to use manure instead. With these assumptions, the second plan's expectations for agriculture were even more utopian than for industry. "We had begun to believe," the food minister, A. P. Jain, later recalled, "that by the sheer utilization of the waste labor power you can achieve anything and everything."[13]

Nehru interpreted India's poor agricultural performance as a reflection, not of policy, but of the character of its peasantry. He was fascinated, according to Judith Brown, "by China and its people, who seemed disciplined, unified, organized, and hard-working" in implicit contrast with domestic disorder he faced. He hoped a similar national industrial push would remedy the communalism that was "the major disease or weakness of India" and bring his nation closer to China. Mahalanobis and other planners also nurtured the conviction that India and China were engaged in a joint project to redefine socialism in an Asian context, a common purpose enshrined in the *Panchsheel* and the doctrine of *Hindi Chini bhai bhai*. The absence of a threat along their mutual border would allow each country to divert arms spending toward industrial growth. The planners urged (but had no power to compel) state governments to raise taxes, establish Chinese-style rural cooperatives, and control the trade in food grains to reduce consumption and equalize the burden. Meanwhile, fertilizer imports and spending on agriculture were slashed to less than half the amount in the first plan, with most of the remaining budget earmarked for oilseeds, cotton, and jute.[14]

The plan stopped short of giving agriculture a purely sacrificial role in the evolution of India's economy. Land reforms would protect farmers from predatory rents, and higher earnings from export commodities would compensate for underpriced food crops. Most important, medium-sized and cottage industries—weaving, ropemaking, leatherwork, and handicrafts—would jump-start a new rural economy. Scattered throughout the countryside, rural workshops would create a characteristically Indian pattern of development free of the slums and crime endemic in the industrial West. These "khadi" industries, named for the handspun cloth that became a symbol of the freedom struggle, fulfilled a Gandhian vision of economic self-renewal, instilling technical skills and providing "a connecting ladder" of opportunity between village and city. The commission set a target of twelve million new khadi jobs, most of them in village factories.[15]

The "Mahalanobis model" provided a reassuring template for policy, prescribing the functions of trade, investment, foreign and defense policy, the obligations of citizens, and solution to unemployment and internal discord, but despite their optimism the planners knew they were gambling India's stability on a bid to industrialize in a single generation. The pressure to stray from the plan, to falter during a crisis or chase an easier alternative would require political discipline. It would mean, Krishnamachari warned, a continual "struggle for the allegiance of our people." Even so, they felt up to the challenge. The eminent British economist J. B. S. Haldane told Nehru that, even allowing for "a 15 percent chance of failure through interference by the United States, a 10 percent chance of interference by the Soviet Union and China, a 20 percent chance of . . . political obstruction, and a 5 percent chance of interference by Hindu traditionalism, that leaves a 50 percent chance for a success which will alter the whole history of the world." These odds, however, did not factor in the weather or the Rockefeller Foundation.[16]

Factory-first and food-first policy options were not necessarily exclusive; compromise allocations of fertilizer and capital goods, taxes, and incentives might have been found, but behind those choices lay incompatible answers to a crucial question: What was agriculture for? Foundation experts and their Indian allies represented wheat improvement as a comprehensive social reform, a trigger mechanism for dramatic, irreversible changes in human reproduction, attitudes, resources, and diplomacy. The Second Plan likewise cast agriculture as the resource and labor base for an industrial modernization that would overhaul India's social structure, culture, and international standing. In the high-modernist era, few solutions were ever put forward as partial or provisional measures. "Piecemeal" was a term of dismissal. Each prescription, however minor, came wrapped in assurances of far-reaching catalytic effects. These rival narratives each assigned a different meaning to agriculture.

The Rockefeller and Ford foundations were early and forceful advocates of the food-first strategy. At a time when economists struggled to discern the impediments to development, foundation experts focused on two obstacles: food and population. They defined issues quantitatively. Institutional imperatives, especially a need to concentrate funds on "practical" features of wider problems, encouraged reliance on numbers, but experts also believed material disparities were at the root of social pathology and war. Raymond Fosdick's "human ecology" doctrine persisted through the influence of his protégé, Warren Weaver, a mathematician and supervisor of the Rockefeller Foundation's ventures in agriculture. Weaver interpreted conflict as a function of quantifiable imbalances. The "ratio of resource to population," he believed, explained "the trouble which on the individual level expresses itself as want, hunger, suffering, and anxiety and on the international level as fear, distrust, political instability, and world tension."[17]

Weaver cast the population/food crisis as a scientific challenge, a threat analogous to the tropical diseases conquered by Rockefeller scientists. The postwar world faced "an unprecedented situation in which a population already outrunning its food resources is still increasing at a fabulous rate." The Ford Foundation took a darker view. Its charter identified population and food as obstacles to global welfare and peace. In 1949 at the peak of furor over the Osborn and Vogt studies, the Gaither committee found that rising birth rates could engulf the entire project of development, and that advances in medicine had opened the floodgates. Unchecked by disease, Vannevar Bush warned, population would "increase exponentially without limit, exhaust[ing] the resources of the earth, and leav[ing] a few miserable remnants crawling about in barbarism."[18]

Weaver emphatically rejected neo-Malthusian pessimism. Resources, he argued, were finite but vast, and science would find a way out. In terms of total energy, food and fuel, the earth had a total caloric surplus of 100,000 times the current usage. Additionally, demographic observations revealed that the ongoing geometric surge in birthrates was likely to be temporary. He was deeply concerned, however, about its timing. Occurring just as fragile new states made their first steps toward modernization, the population surge could smother efforts to raise living standards and leave struggling regimes vulnerable to subversion. The population crisis was not an issue of human survival, he argued, but of the survival of America's allies in noncommunist Asia.[19]

Transition theory suggested a strategy. Higher levels of consumption, particularly of food, would trigger a drop in birthrate. Advances in agriculture would also improve health, incomes, and productivity. "People who are well fed are usually more efficient, vigorous workers," he explained. "As the efficiency of agriculture is improved, more workers can be spared for making other needed improvements in transportation, manufacturing, sanitation, housing, clothing, education, etc." Scientific agriculture would accelerate the onset of the demographic transition, and thereby modernize the whole society. Given the backwardness of agriculture in Asia, Weaver predicted, quantum improvements in efficiency were not only possible, but likely, and increased food consumption "usually results in a reduced birthrate."[20]

Agriculture was the key to the entire development equation, the regulator of fertility, catalyst for breaking down social and familial customs, and stimulant for a general expansion of national wealth. Backed by the Balfour report and sympathetic trustees, including Dean Rusk, John D. Rockefeller III, and Karl Compton, president of the Massachusetts Institute of Technology, Weaver persuaded the board to shift the foundation's focus from medicine to agronomy and spin off related charities, the Population Council and the Asia Society, as part of a comprehensive effort to advance the region to a new economic and social equilibrium.[21]

Populous and precarious, India stood at the center of their concerns. Rockefeller and Ford analysts focused on food scarcity as a strategic liability, an incitement to communist expansionism. "In this struggle for the minds of men," Weaver observed, "the side that best helps satisfy man's primary needs for food, clothing, and shelter is likely to win." Fact-finding missions cataloged the problems: a "deteriorating population-land-production ratio, . . . high birth rates," and primitive farming methods that "cannot hope to keep pace." The degree of its backwardness—Weaver estimated American farm practices were 150 years ahead—magnified the potential for a dramatic change. India's overpopulation, low living standards, and strategic significance, Compton agreed, made it the ideal site for a demonstration. "Just as Mexico offers a key opportunity on the American continent, so India may offer a key opportunity from a world point of view."[22]

India's position in Cold War strategy as a showpiece of democratic development caught the attention of private donors. National security officials urged foundations to work in "difficult areas" like India, where official aid would arouse "the suspicions of the indigenous governments." Central Intelligence Agency (CIA) director Allen Dulles was "particularly interested in what could be done to produce success in the rural and agricultural fields." But foundations also guarded their separate identity and their reputation for neutrality. While U.S. diplomats often got a hard reception in New Delhi, Ford grantors could boast of coming "back from India with the Taj Mahal under one arm and Nehru under the other." They believed that by focusing on material conditions, they could remain apolitical while still producing political effects. The principal aim, according to Weaver, was to help India "attain by evolution the improvements, including those in agriculture, which otherwise may have to come from revolution."[23]

With wheat, as with rice, they sought a quantum jump in yields with attendant psychological effects on fertility, consumption, work habits, and political alignment. In 1952 Harrar, Mangelsdorf, and Weaver traveled through India in a reprise of their 1939 station-wagon survey of Mexico. They found a society mired in ignorance, caste prejudice, and stifling custom, but encouragingly fragile, ready under the right pressure to yield to a rural renaissance. Because the traditional cultural pattern had an organic base, a sudden biological shift could pull the rug out from under it. "The village system is a well-established ecological complex, centuries old, in which three elements—plants, cattle, and man—exist in a strange symbiotic relationship," they observed. "A change in any one will inevitably affect the entire system." Their goal was not to fashion a new India but to pull down the old.[24]

The thorny problem of exchange reserves did not intrude into the foundation's vision. Rockefeller officials had already grown frustrated with development formulas that demanded large, sustained investments in return for hypothetical outcomes. They instead sought more "concrete" psychological and physiological solutions that would address the fundamental components of human motivation. They were unimpressed by Albert Mayer's experiment at Etawah and skeptical of Point Four engineering projects, neither of which altered what they saw as the underlying behavioral constraint. They recommended concentrating instead on an "isolable technical problem" that touched every village and peasant household. A dramatic breakthrough on an important crop, such as wheat, could induce the kind of sweeping cultural disruption they were looking for.[25]

A Device for Educating a Country

Characteristically, Rockefeller officials put their faith in a research process rather than a specific technology. Although Borlaug was still searching for a major breakthrough in wheat production, the foundation viewed the Mexico program as its best investment. Mexican farmers eagerly adopted new rust-resistant strains developed in 1948, and positive trends in Mexico's economy and relations with the United States substantiated the program's value. Borlaug believed the next breeding goal should be nutrient absorption, and he made a collection of plants that could handle heavy fertilizer doses. Short stems particularly caught his attention. As with rice, lodging limited the amount of fertilizer wheat could safely take in. Extra nitrogen made the stalks so tall that a rainstorm or even a stiff breeze could flatten a field into a tangled, unharvestable mess. The short plants he collected invariably turned out to be aneuploids, solitary mutants unable to pass traits to the next generation. Then, in the early 1950s, he learned that Orville Vogel, a U.S. Department of Agriculture (USDA) researcher at Washington State, was experimenting with a dwarf variety called Norin 10.[26]

Vogel was already legendary among wheat researchers as both a breeder and an inventor. His seeders and threshers, designed for experimental plots, sped up the process of crop testing and earned him admirers in plant nurseries across the country. When Samuel C. Salmon, an agricultural adviser to MacArthur's occupation government in Japan, encountered an unusual dwarf strain at an experiment station in Honshu in 1946, he sent samples to Vogel. Well-fertilized and watered, it stood only twenty-three inches high, just more than half the height of average wheats, but a more striking trait was its propensity to "tiller," sending out a dozen or more stalks from a single root system. Instead of the thin rows of waving wheat, Salmon found it growing in shrub-like clumps. The origins of Norin 10 reflected global patterns of genetic exchange going back almost a century. It was derived from three "American" varieties: Fultz, a winter wheat developed in Pennsylvania probably from Mediterranean stock, and two hard red varieties—Daruma and Turkey Red—brought to Kansas in the 1870s by Mennonite immigrants from the Crimea. Japanese researchers obtained samples in the 1920s and succeeded in crossing the three strains to produce Norin 10, which after experimental plantings was released for general use in 1935. Vogel got his first look at a sample in 1946 and began crossing it with Brevor, one of his own disease-resistant strains.[27]

In 1953 Vogel sent a sample of the Norin-Brevor crosses to Borlaug, who initially had difficulty getting them to survive. They were winter wheats, unsuited to the longer, hotter Mexican days, and prone to the Yaqui Valley's stem and leaf fungi. By early 1955 Borlaug had succeeded in pairing it with native strains, and the potential of the "newer architectural design," when combined with irrigation and chemical fertilizer, was unmistakable. He noted that "for each pound of nitrogen applied, there was a proportionate increase in grain yield" up to a very high number. Other advantageous traits could be grafted onto Norin derivatives, and Borlaug found he could adjust their photosensitivity, adapting them to different climactic conditions and growing seasons. Under the right conditions, he could double the size of each seed head, from the usual three kernels to five or six per spikelet. Most surprisingly, the favorable adaptations "moved together." Rather than offering genetic trade-offs, these plants seemed to want to break free of theoretical limits.[28]

By 1959 Borlaug had enough confidence in the new dwarfs to put them into circulation. Two trial varieties, Pitic and Penjamo, performed well in trials at Chapingo and Ciudad Obregón, and a second generation of semi-dwarfs, which would include the legendary varieties Lerma Rojo, Sonora, and Super X, was in development. Since 1955 the Rockefeller Foundation's experiment stations had invited local farmers to annual "field days." Stakman thought it good policy to include *ejidatarios* as well as large landowners in these events, so as not to appear partial to either class. Initially, they drew only a few dozen onlookers but soon evolved into elaborate tours, with more than 1,500 farmers, journalists, and officials conducted through the nurseries on flatbed wagons drawn by tractors. Although guides strictly warned against taking away seeds, Borlaug considered the inevitable pilferage to be good publicity in advance of the formal release of a new variety. He staged his test plots to create an impression, setting them between rows of taller wheats, which lodged, leaving only the dwarfs standing. He was unprepared, however, for the reaction. As the first group pulled up there was a shout. Farmers jumped from the wagons and began tearing off seed heads and filling their pockets. Watching from a distance, Borlaug knew that in weeks his brainchild would be spreading across the valley.[29]

The impending success of the dwarfs helped persuade foundation officials that they now had "a device for educating a country to the needs and values of the intelligent, consistent, and efficient application of science to social welfare." Borlaug went on the road, visiting six Latin American countries in 1959 and traveling to Libya, Egypt, India, and Pakistan the following year. He left samples of the dwarf wheats at each stop. He brought "a large amount of genetic material" to Pakistan's wheat research institute near Lyallpur, where two of his Mexico-trained "apostles," Mansur Bajwa and Nur Chaudhri, began reselecting it for local conditions. Bread riots had precipitated the collapse of Pakistan's constitutional government in 1958 and in the face of an increasingly critical grain shortage, the military developmentalist regime of Ayub Khan shelved plans for industrial expansion and reinvested in agricultural modernization. Borlaug was impressed by Pakistan's official commitment to wheat improvement and its facilities, which included fertilizer plants and regional nurseries patterned on his own system in Mexico.[30]

Borlaug also stopped briefly in New Delhi, but on this first visit his efforts attracted little interest. He gained a poor impression of Indian agronomists, trained in the British tradition, each "digging his little gopher hole of security in his own discipline." There was too much emphasis on basic research, often on minor crops, and not enough fieldwork. Indian wheat hybrids had unusually large, vitreous, white kernels, having been selected for "beauty of grain . . . rather than total yield." Chemical fertilizers cost more than in Iowa, but Indian and even U.S. experts seemed unconcerned. India was favored with a large scientific establishment and a contingent of U.S. and UN Food and Agriculture Organization (FAO) advisers backed by the largest foreign aid endowment in Asia. It had all the familiar problems—overpopulation, tired soil, backward technology—but Borlaug discerned an attitude he was unable to categorize. Compared with Pakistan or Mexico, agriculture, at least as he understood it, seemed less central to the scheme of national development.[31]

Stakman and other Rockefeller envoys were equally puzzled by the Indian neglect of basic staples in favor of "ornamentals and secondary crops." Ralph Cummings, director of the New Delhi field office, set out to correct this attitude, concentrating his efforts on the Indian Agricultural Research Institute (IARI) in New Delhi. Funded by the central government, it had "surprisingly good physical plant and facilities," but in common with other Indian academies it was rigidly hierarchical and narrowly focused on crops such as cotton, jute, and tea, rather than on "the problems of Indian agriculture." Under foundation patronage, IARI's research increasingly gravitated toward wheat improvement. Grants funded the training and projects of a generation of young agronomists, including D. S. Athwal, K. B. L. Jain, S. M. Sikka, T. P. Mehta, and others, under the guidance of the internationally respected wheat geneticist Benjamin P. Pal. Shuttling between New Delhi, regional research stations, and postgraduate training in the United States, they formed a close-knit professional network, exchanging seed lines, intelligence on rust outbreaks, and the latest developments at overseas universities.[32]

Within this group, Monkombu S. Swaminathan gained prominence both because of his intellect and his political connections. As son-in-law of S. Boothalingam, secretary to the minister of finance, he enjoyed an uncommon familiarity with the planning elite and its machinations. His family had been active in the nationalist movement in Kerala, and he participated as a child in *swadeshi* (self-reliance) demonstrations in which crowds burned cotton cloth to symbolically break India's dependence on imported goods. He graduated from Coimbatore Agricultural College, and after postgraduate work at IARI, applied in 1949 for a government career, only to learn that there were few positions for specialists in agriculture. With a UNESCO (United Nations Educational, Scientific and Cultural Organization) fellowship, he took degrees in genetics at Cambridge and the University of Wisconsin, returning in 1954 to the rice institute at Cuttack and then to New Delhi. Before 1956 he worked on hybridized potatoes, but with Pal's encouragement he began experimenting with X-rays as an agent for inducing mutations in wheat. To a young agronomist in the late 1950s, wheat breeding was surrounded with a sense of patriotic urgency. Census reports tracked an ominous uptick in population growth from 1.2 to 2 percent, but population anxieties motivated Swaminathan and his peers less than the opportunity to show what agricultural science could contribute to the national cause. India increasingly depended on P.L. 480 imports from the United States, and the prime minister appealed for redoubled efforts to grow more wheat to ward off threats of inflation and dependency. The Ford Foundation's 1959 Food Crisis Report, widely publicized in India, confirmed a sense that India's economic autonomy hinged on a solution to the food question.[33]

At about the same time, research objectives at the institute began to shift. Wheat breeders formerly sought to outdo popular varieties such as Punjab C518 and C591, which had the amber color, moist texture, and "chapatti quality" customers wanted and could also tolerate drought and low-fertility soils. These genotypes—which green revolutionaries would later call "traditional" varieties—were developed in the 1950s at Punjab Agricultural University at Ludhaina with assistance from the Ford Foundation and Ohio State agronomists. Two of the outstanding wheat breeders of the day, Chaudhari Ramdhan Singh and Dhaniram Vasudeva, artfully combined qualities appealing to both consumers and farmers, fostering the "beauty of grain" that Borlaug disdained. Increasingly, however, researchers catered to different constituencies. A combination of pressure and incentives from the food ministry, planning authorities, and the Rockefeller Foundation motivated geneticists to narrow their breeding objectives to two: disease resistance and nutrient response. They were looking now for a very different type of wheat, one that could grow in dense plots and absorb larger fertilizer loads.[34]

The shift in breeding goals reflected a larger crisis in confidence as two of the main premises of the second plan began to crumble. The belief that P.L. 480 could be used to hold inflation in check suffered a setback as 1959 market deliveries fell to unexpected lows. Despite record harvests, farmers preferred to hold onto their grain rather than sell it at the artificially reduced price. In April, the food ministry began implementing state trading in grain, but without enough warehouses, cooperatives, or fair-price shops to actually control retailing, the scheme only added to the turmoil. In parts of the country, food prices rose by 50 percent. The second plan was endangered, according to a ministry analyst, by "the failure of the foodgrains market to behave in the national interest."[35]

Expectations about China's behavior were also off target. Following the outbreak of the Tibetan revolt in March, China began amassing troops in the border region and asserting claims to 40,000 square miles of territory that had been undisputedly Indian. War rumors intensified the inflation and hoarding. Nehru warned that hostilities on the northern frontier would kill his vision, "it means fashioning our five year plans, our budgets, our everything, in a different way. It means austerity and hard living and hardship." As much as these realizations disturbed planners, the algorithms governing policy remained the same. Forward momentum relied on conserving foreign exchange and increasing agricultural output without new investments. In its outline for the Third Plan (1961–1966), the commission assigned the "highest urgency" to attaining self-sufficiency in foodgrains, but it reduced spending on fertilizer and irrigation still further. "Though the outlay on agriculture will be smaller," the commission maintained, "it should be possible to reach or even exceed the targets provided there are no upsets caused by natural calamities."[36]

Misgivings in Delhi were more than offset by the energy emanating from Washington, where the new administration was orchestrating a big push for the Third Plan. In April 1961 Kennedy committed more than a billion dollars, challenging the India consortium—Canada, France, West Germany, Japan, Britain, and the World Bank—to match it. Planning was at the heart of his "new working concept" for foreign assistance. He consolidated—or in New Frontier terms, "streamlined"—aid under a new mandate, the U.S. Agency for International Development (USAID), with an emphasis on continuity, targets, systematic budgeting of national resources, and "long-range plans instead of short-run crises." Support for the Third Plan would demonstrate U.S. leadership and seize a "historic opportunity" to "move more than half of the people of the less-developed nations into self-sustained economic growth."[37]

In 1961 Indian wheat breeders began coordinated trials, distributing seeds for testing at research stations and demonstration farms across the country. USDA advisers added a number of American wheats to the mix, including Gaines, a winter wheat Vogel had bred from Norin 10, but Indian breeders took little notice. Nitrogen-hungry strains had little appeal because farmers, caught between high fertilizer prices and low wheat prices, needed varieties that could thrive without added nutrients. It was not until early 1962, when Swaminathan encountered an article on Gaines in the *American Journal of Agronomy* that dwarf wheat began to be seriously discussed. He immediately wrote Vogel and subsequently Borlaug requesting information. In the meantime, he began experimenting with Gaines at IARI and in April 1962 drafted a grant proposal for an intensive breeding program using dwarf varieties from Mexico. It got immediate action. With funding from the Rockefeller Foundation and P.L. 480 counterpart funds, Swaminathan enlisted the participation of other institutes and invited Borlaug to visit the following year. Virtually alone among Indian agronomists, he was thinking beyond the parameters of the plan, envisioning farmers responding to incentives and inputs that, under the prevailing assumptions, were unrealistic. But those assumptions were about to change.[38]

India shares two borders with Chinese Tibet, one in the east across the Chumbi Valley between Nepal and Bhutan, and a longer frontier to the west in the Himalayan region of Ladakh. China's repudiation of colonial boundaries and CIA support for Tibetan rebels destabilized the frontier after 1959. Increasingly aggressive troop movements and hostile propaganda issuing from Beijing should have been taken as warning, but Indian diplomats continued to trust in the *Panchsheel*. On October 20, 1962, Chinese forces launched attacks on military posts along both frontiers. Within days they shattered a defending force of 12,000 and advanced unopposed deep into Indian territory. As news of the disaster reached the capital on November 17, the government reacted with shock and confusion. Cabinet ministers prepared to evacuate to the south as home guard troops sandbagged offices to defend against Chinese paratroopers rumored to be on the way. Hoarding of grain and gold propelled a spike in inflation. News filtered back that the elite Fourth Division had been cut to pieces, that troops at the front lacked proper weapons and boots. "The humiliation of the Indian Army, India's especial pride, was complete," V. S. Naipaul commiserated. "Independent India was now felt to be a creation of words." When China announced a unilateral ceasefire and withdrew to its claim line on November 21, panic gave way to anger.[39]

The debacle dramatically worsened India's food and financial crises, but more fundamentally it broke the Nehruvian consensus, stripping the aura of competence and high purpose from the government, the Congress Party, and Nehru himself. A visibly enfeebled prime minister acknowledged that the government had been "out of touch with reality in the modern world" but explained that "there is such a thing as being conditioned in a certain way and, I am afraid, even now we are conditioned somewhat in that way." The pan-Asian concord evaporated, and the mother industries that were supposed to propagate national strength and prestige proved barren. Foreign exchange reserves were nil. A 10 percent war surcharge brought industrial growth, already faltering, to a standstill.[40]

Nehru tried to rally patriots and allies behind the economic program, declaring that planning, science, and national discipline were more essential than ever. This was "an attempt to destroy the Indian way of life," Ambassador B. K. Nehru told *Meet the Press*. "All that you have to do to destroy a free system in a poor society is to stop development." The government steered new investments into arms industries, reducing the allocation for agriculture still further. The prime minister's strategy, according to *The Hindu*, was to "insist that the plan was an integral part of the war effort and so the best way to consummate this effort was to fulfill the plan." He stocked his emergency cabinet with commission members—

Krishnamachari took portfolios for defense and finance—and steered revenue into arms industries while reducing the allocation for agriculture still further. But Nehru no longer had the vitality to maintain the momentum singlehandedly.[41]

He seemed demoralized; his distinctively erect frame was now stooped and his left foot dragged as he walked. Advisers and close relatives urged him to rest, but he waved them away, demanding "what for; to what end should I recover my strength?" The London *Times* concluded that "politically India will never be the same again," its decline symbolized by its broken prime minster. Decision-making authority began to shift from Nehru to a "syndicate" of regional party bosses headed by K. Kamaraj Nadar, head of the Tamil Nadu branch. But the 1963 spring by-elections revealed that the party itself was in trouble. Congress suffered significant losses to left and the right. The conservative Swatantra Party, founded by C. "Rajaji" Rajagopalachari, the dynamic chief minister of Madras, mounted a sustained attack on the regime of controls, the "permit-license-quota raj," imposed by the plan commission. Agriculture policy was the main point of criticism. The government had bungled price controls, Rajaji charged, but more fundamentally, ten years of paternalism had sapped individual initiative and cast "an all-pervading and deep sense of uncertainty, drying up all interest in land and factory alike." Together with Jan Sangh, Janata, and other parties rooted among rural landowners in North India, Swatantra resisted land reform and urged an "intensive programme of agricultural improvement" to give proprietors fertilizer, materials, and incentives to meet "the paramount need for increasing food production." These rightist splinter groups presented the first real opposition to Congress rule, and they foreshadowed an incipient fragmentation of the party along class, linguistic, and religious lines.[42]

Partly because of this threat, the Kennedy administration chose not to use the debacle to push India to change course, either in foreign or economic policy. Averill Harriman, dispatched to Delhi as a special envoy, predicted India would discard the nonalignment policy and probably Nehru as well, allowing "the rise of younger, more dynamic, generally more pragmatic leadership." The war would also cripple the economy at a time when India's internal stability was under severe strain. Food prices were up by 10 percent, taxes by 20 percent. Urging USAID not to be "penny-wise about India," Kennedy pledged $60 million in arms and $500 million in economic aid for the next fiscal year. The administration still wanted more emphasis on agriculture, but the times, Galbraith stressed, called for "stopping the talk, cooling the debate" over methods and doing what was necessary to rescue the third plan. The Rockefeller wheat initiative was ideally timed to upset this equilibrium.[43]

Bringing the Plan Down in Shambles

New Delhi was still tense in late March 1963 when Borlaug arrived with 1,000 pounds of seed. He had stopped at Lyallpur en route, and in addition to 613 different Mexican varieties, he brought new Pakistani crosses bred for the South Asian environment. He met with Pal and S. P. Kothi, head of the All India Coordinated Wheat Improvement Program, but he was particularly struck by Swaminathan, who had "one of the most brilliantly swift agricultural minds" he had encountered. Swaminathan, in turn, was intrigued by Borlaug's "child-like simplicity of behavior and expression and self-effacing temperament." They spent five weeks traveling through wheat regions in the Punjab, the Ganges Valley, Bihar, and Uttar Pradesh inspecting test plots and meeting officials and scientists.[44]

Since each state had its own farm policy, the agronomists barnstormed research stations and governor's mansions across the wheat belt like candidates in a presidential primary. Borlaug returned the next March for more campaigning, and his presence lent the wheat strategy a global context. He assured audiences that Egypt, Argentina, and other developing nations were struggling with the same worn-out soil, the same population pressure, and bureaucratic inertia. Reporters trailed the "food scientist from Mexico," who confirmed that "Mexico and India are alike in many ways" especially "in their determination to develop into modern societies." Mexico's threefold increase in wheat output was the cornerstone of its economic strategy, according to India's food ministry, and Borlaug was "the man responsible."[45]

Before a contentious gathering of agronomists at Kanpur, Borlaug predicted that if dwarf varieties were sown on a significant scale, India would double or triple wheat production within a few years, but to do so it would need fertilizer. Domestic production was pitiful, and imports were restricted; that would have to change. He recognized that this meant a reconsideration of fundamental economic assumptions. "The seeds are the catalyst," he stressed. "You have to support them with a total package of modern technology—and with strategy, with psychology, and with firm, guaranteed economic policy from the government." Before the situation in the fields could change, "there were much bigger, much greater factors to be settled at the top," starting with the price structure and its underlying logic, which forfeited to the state any income accruing to the farmer above the point of subsistence. To realize the dwarf seeds' potential. India would have to change its expectations of agriculture, what it could do, how it functioned, and whom it served.[46]

The existing system of price controls acted as a disguised tax, transferring income from the countryside to the urban factory sector. Cheap calories and P.L. 480 imports sustained the "psychology of abundance" that compensated for lower wages. Industrialists and trade unions favored cheap-food policies, and so did U.S. advisers until 1964. They now urged India to reverse course. Ford Foundation adviser Sherman Johnson pointed to the "illusory benefits" of a "consumer-oriented" price structure. He proposed a revised strategy—reduced prices for fertilizer and water, increased and standardized prices for grain—that would shift income toward growers who used the new seeds.[47]

American advisers knew fertilizer was essential, but they also knew it would break the budget. "India is not overpopulated, it is underfertilized," had been a perennial refrain of Frank Parker, an agronomist for the FAO and USAID since the early 1950s. The Ford Foundation's food crisis report declared fertilizer an urgent necessity, yet the amount applied per acre was the same in 1960 as it had been five years earlier. In part this was a consequence of India's obsession with federal equity (the plan assigned one fertilizer plant per state, even those without raw materials), but a more fundamental obstacle was money. Despite their technical aura, Galbraith noted, "these plans were, in fact, budgets for the expenditure of money." The most coveted account, and the limiting factor on all development projects, was the budget for foreign exchange. India could import machinery and raw materials only with dollars accrued through exports and aid. Because U.S. aid came in the form of grain rather than cash, exports offered the only chance for earning dollars. The plan reserved four-fifths of India's exchange reserves for machinery and equipment and the remainder for "developmental imports" of essential raw materials. Each factory, dam, and power plant was assigned a foreign exchange ranking. Fertilizer factories ranked in the double figures, well behind the high-priority steel mills and dam projects. Within the smaller developmental imports budget, fertilizer was less essential than industrial raw materials such as jute, imported to keep the Bengal mills running at capacity. While fertilizer might have an indirect effect on the plan's numerical targets, jute went through the mills and out again as high-value exports, producing an immediate, measurable increase in the exchange balance.[48]

India's national finances were so structured that an increase in fertilizer meant a decrease in jute, and industrialists and planners saw little to recommend that course. The *Eastern Economist,* voice of manufacturing interests, predicted that "a more imaginative policy with regard to imports of raw jute can bring in a spectacular rise in the export of jute goods" and consequently "a sizeable foreign exchange balance for the country" while any reduction in the allotment would injure not only the textile sector but employment and productivity across the economy. Throughout this period, Krishnamachari, the powerful finance minister and plan commissioner, guarded the jute allotment like a bullmastiff. TTK, as he was known in the press, struck Galbraith as "a man of incredible vanity" and the CIA as "a highly articulate, urbane, and flamboyant technician." His links to the Birla conglomerate fuelled corruption allegations that periodically sidelined him but never shook his commitment to an industry-centered plan. Even in the midst of the 1965 drought, he maintained that requirements for "certain raw materials, the most important of them being jute" made it "impossible to allocate any more foreign exchange for import of fertilizers without causing damage to the rest of the economy."[49]

Nationwide field tests of dwarf varieties in 1963 and 1964 thus pulled Rockefeller scientists into an ongoing feud over the future of Nehru's industrial experiment. A successful field test would stand as an indictment of the Third Plan and demonstrate a viable alternative strategy. As he traveled, Borlaug encountered impassioned support and opposition from politicians, farmers, and economists. The issue of exchange priority was the focal point, but other objections hit closer to issues of identity and the cultural costs of modernization. The most contentious concerned chapatti, the unleavened flat bread that was the main course in meals cooked over dung fires in north Indian villages, the tiffin lunches of Bombay office workers, and factory canteens in Bengal. Made of stone-ground *atta* flour, salt, oil, and water, its flavor and texture derived from the specific properties of the wheat used. Norin 10 and the Mexican dwarfs had hard red kernels that could be ground into a dark flour. Breeders and government officials regarded this coarser product as inferior to white flour made from amber Punjab grain. The chapatti's whiteness suggested purity, luxury, even modernity. At a time when the Food Ministry was cultivating a "psychology of abundance," a return to brown bread seemed a giant step backward.[50]

The quality versus quantity debate resurrected anti-modernist arguments about the deadening hand of standardization and the cultural and biological erosion of Indian identity. "Chapatti quality" flour had a particular balance of starch and gluten, but it was also an essentially subjective judgment about elasticity, taste, and smell. A number of academic and government experts worried that the mass substitution of local for exotic varieties meant the obsolescence of distinctive flavors, the end of Indian cuisine as they knew it. "Wheat" as an undifferentiated, mass-marketed commodity was unknown in actual Indian markets, where consumers chose among wheats of all colors and textures. Darker wheats sold for 15 to 20 percent below the price of white grain. Borlaug had no patience for such aesthetic considerations. He dismissed the issue as "minutia" and warned foundation executives in New York that "this whole matter of grain color and grain price is rather artificially based and only represents another unnecessary barrier to solving India's wheat production problem." When the dean of an agricultural college raised the issue again in 1964, he dismissed it as a technical problem that could be addressed "down the road a way." Meanwhile, Swaminathan scrambled to develop white Punjab/Norin crosses and chemical tests for chapatti quality.[51]

Indian officials also worried that inequities in Borlaug's strategy would lead to violence. Swaminathan and Borlaug openly advocated a "betting on the strong" approach; they preferred to test on large irrigated farms rather than in small tenant plots because cultivators who could afford risks produced better results. Planners believed "uncertainties with regard to land reform" might choke off investments in new technologies, but even more frightening was the chance that the new seeds would disproportionately enrich wealthy landholders. Class favoritism would delegitimize the planning process and intensify communal and separatist demands. Concentrating scarce fertilizer on some fields meant withholding it from others, and any plan based on wheat favored the north over the rice-growing regions in the south. If enacted, the strategy would invite a backlash from those left out. Borlaug had little to say on this score. "I wasn't worried a damn bit about equity at this point," he confessed. "I just wanted to provoke shock."[52]

Critics also warned of trade-offs that would mitigate or cancel potential gains. Shorter straw meant less feed for livestock. Mahalanobis's statistical models showed greater yields from distributing fertilizer in smaller amounts, rather than concentrating it on irrigated plots, a conclusion endorsed by a World Bank mission. USAID consultants warned that relying on a single variety was an invitation to disease. Borlaug dismissed these as foot-dragging by self-interested bureaucrats who failed to grasp the psychological potential of the new seed. "The greatest resistance to change comes from the scientists themselves, of which the economists are the worst offenders," he complained. "Their untouchable and holy shrines, the Planning Commissions, represent the ultimate in this philosophy."[53]

Recalling these debates in 1967, he stressed that he advised Indian agronomists to let the wheat make the argument for them: "I want the differences in yield to be so big that everything they've believed in comes down in shambles all around them." Convinced of the new seeds' immense potential, Swaminathan structured field tests for psychological effect rather than clinical accuracy. Instead of standard controlled experiments, he scheduled showpiece demonstrations in 150 villages, three in the Delhi suburbs, pitting dwarfs against whatever local growers had. "My control was the entire living memory of the farmer and the whole scenario in the village," he explained. If improvement could be shown, "not marginally but in a big way," then "you have broken the crust of conservatism."[54]

Lerma Rojo produced an immediate sensation. Leaf rust, to which the Mexican varieties later proved vulnerable, did not surface in 1964, and the early demonstrations were an unqualified success. "The impact on the minds of other farmers was electric," Swaminathan recorded. One could see "retired officials, ex-army men, illiterate peasants, and small farmers queueing up to get the new seeds. . . . Queues for seeds! Five years ago, the very idea would have raised a laugh." Although there was no official release, samples and rumors spread outward from the "seed villages" to neighboring communities. Government officials also took notice; the stunning reports from the test fields were about the only good news that spring.[55]

The prime minister's health steadily declined, and on May 27, after suffering a stroke, he died at his Delhi residence, a short distance from the parliament buildings. Congress leaders took only hours to name Lal Bahadur Shastri to India's top office, carefully avoiding a succession fight that might shatter the party. Nehru's opposite in demeanor and appearance, Shastri was soft-spoken and diminutive. He had been a trusted behind-the-scenes adviser, but his sudden elevation took many in Washington by surprise. "The architect is now dead," the CIA concluded. "Nehru's vaunted economic plans have, in some measure, plateau-ed and will require new thinking," but his successor seemed to lack fortitude. He "may be too weak to be wise," Secretary of State Dean Rusk predicted. But Shastri's first act was to declare the food crisis his first priority and increase budget allocations for agriculture. Moving to neutralize the Swantantra threat, he named C. Subramaniam, Rajaji's former deputy, as agriculture minister. Subramaniam sought out Swaminathan and the two began building a comprehensive program of incentives, investments, and production around the new varieties. Announcing upcoming field demonstrations over All-India Radio, Shastri urged his countrymen to let "the new crop that is to be sown mark a turning point in our country's future." The prime minister, according to Gucharan Das, had "gambled the nation on this new wheat."[56]

The gamble rearranged the nation's priorities. Wheat meant, first, a scaling back of ambitions for industry. Nehru's dream of erecting a dynamic manufacturing base in a single generation, a "brave effort to fashion our future," gave way to an anxious effort to fill basic needs. While this sacrifice is seldom associated with the green revolution in retrospect, it was clear to its proponents at the time. When asked in 1966 why India grew nonfood crops, Harrar explained the trade-off: "If they are going to try to develop national industry they are going to have to earn dollars." Without dollar earnings from jute and other commercial crops, the ISI strategy was dead. Wheat meant liberalization: dismantling (or reducing) tariff barriers, the exchange budget, the state-run industries, and opening the country to foreign investment. Under the plans, India had doubled its output of machinery, chemicals, and power, but it was now learning that "you can't eat steel."[57]

Suspending the industrial drive also meant a defeat for the plan's redistributive goals. In the countryside, interventionist strategies based on land reforms, community development, and khadi industries gave way to acceptance of existing structures of ownership and status. The "socialist pattern" had always been less evident outside the cities. Land reform and village projects were long on slogans and short on achievement, but the commitment to equity, while unfulfilled, set a standard for governmental performance. Without it, the ruling party lost its universality and much of its charisma. Congress had "a vital and seemingly successful political philosophy" until Nehru's death, the London *Times* observed, but now "the administration is strained and universally believed to be corrupt, the government and governing party have lost public confidence and belief in themselves as well." The technocratic ideal yielded to the politics of disunity, linguistic, sectional, and religious.[58]

Wheat also signified a retreat from the utopian heights of nonalignment and the *Panchsheel*. The example of a rising democratic giant blazing a "third way" gave hope to a world hemmed in by ideologies and superpowers. "The time is past, if it ever existed, when India could attempt to save the world by precept," Ronald Segal repined, "She must now try to save herself by her own efforts." Because the plan relied on peaceful coexistence, war overturned developmental and diplomatic dogmas together. An increase in defense spending by an amount equal to half the plan budget killed fiscal discipline and touched off an inflationary surge that P.L. 480 could not hold back. The Plan Commission's influence would not have declined as far or as fast without the Chinese attack, which ultimately did as much as the Rockefeller Foundation to revise the economic rules and bring about the green revolution. The planning process had allowed Indians to accept aid on their own terms, even while dependence on external support increased drastically. Kennedy refrained from wielding aid as a lever, but Lyndon Johnson would not shrink from using whatever tools he could find to alter India's positions on neutrality, Vietnam, and agriculture.[59]

8

THE MEANING OF FAMINE

The architects of India's wheat revolution gathered one last time in March 1990 for a reunion in the city they knew in former times as Madras. Norman Borlaug joined M. S. Swaminathan at the rostrum to welcome the guests, many in their seventies and eighties, to Chennai and urge them to record their collective wisdom for the benefit of future generations. Chidambaram Subramaniam recalled his epic battles in the legislature and cabinet against opponents of the "new strategy," and he saluted B. Sivaraman, who orchestrated the massive imports of fertilizer that made it possible. Over the next two days, much of the discussion concerned policies and techniques that could be used again in other countries, but Borlaug, at age seventy-five still active in promoting high-yield technology in Africa, observed that timing and luck had mattered in India's case. The 1966–1967 famine provided an "opportune moment indeed. Had government policy not been changed at that time, it might have been very difficult to change it later when, perhaps with better rains, the situation would not have been quite so grave." Subramaniam agreed, noting that he had first learned about India's famine when he traveled to Washington in December 1965. The crisis had been propitious. He believed, in fact, that "the problem itself would not have arisen unless there was a corresponding solution."[1]

In green revolution lore, famine is the seminal event, the fulfillment of years of warnings and the nadir from which India's agricultural resurgence is measured. But at the time, the characterization of the episode as a famine was more doubtful. The Indian government preferred to call it a "scarcity situation." Although forecasters expected thousands to starve, official reports claimed no deaths occurred. Western observers maintained that famine had been averted. Bihar, according to a headline in *The Economist*, was "the disaster that never was." This may indicate a singular success, or something else, depending on whether famine is a natural or a political calamity. Like Borlaug and Subramaniam, Lyndon Johnson remembered it as an opening. "If we went about it in the right way," he wrote in his memoirs, "I thought we could encourage increasingly far-reaching changes in India's farm economy and in the supporting actions of other nations." Famine is a subjective condition, but it is *politically* subjective. The capacity to declare an emergency confers substantial power, and for that reason states, politicians, and factions vie for the authority to predict, define, and explain famine. The green revolution's "opportune moment," and the historical memory of it, emerged from just such a struggle.[2]

The Package

To many in the new Shastri cabinet, Subramaniam's transfer from the steel ministry to food and agriculture in June 1964 looked like a demotion. He had served the party faithfully since independence, always in the shadow of more illustrious men. A protégé of Rajaji, the brilliant, uncompromising chief minister of Madras who defected to found the Swatantra Party, Subramaniam chose to remain with Congress. He gained a reputation as a fixer of all trades, managing education, health, industry, and parliamentary affairs at state and national levels. He joined Nehru's inner circle in its final troubled months, and it was he who went from the prime minister's deathbed to announce the news to the stunned Lok Sabha. Now, at fifty-four, he was thrust into prominence for the first time in a role that would demand all his insider skills. The two previous food ministers had each promised to make the country self-sufficient, and both had failed. Rice riots and rationing catapulted agriculture to the top of the national agenda, but the impasse remained; India's modernization drive was designed to divert rural resources toward industry, with the result that growers were lowballed, mortgaged, and taxed to the point of resignation. A rural Brahmin, he disliked the rigidity and urban bias of the plan regime. To shift the terms of exchange in agriculture's favor, he would have to untie India from Public Law (P.L.) 480, win over the World Bank, and overcome opposition from the cabinet and the states. But most of all he needed to give the debate "a new ideological orientation," to break free of the constraints of the Mahalanobis model.[3]

The dazzling success of the wheat trials caught his attention. Ralph Cummings drove over from the Rockefeller field office in the Ashoka

Hotel to brief the new minister on the latest results. Twenty scientists under the direction of R. Glenn Anderson, a Canadian plant pathologist, were running pilot studies at Delhi, Ludhaina, Pusa, and Kanpur. On Borlaug's advice, they used an off-season nursery in the Nilgiri Hills for shuttle breeding, which allowed them to take a new variety through three generations in one year. One hundred kilograms of seed, air-freighted in from Mexico, would be planted in on-farm demonstrations in the fall of 1964. Meanwhile, Swaminathan ran tests through the Intensive Agricultural Districts Program (IADP), a Ford Foundation project that grew out of the community development scheme of the 1950s. It operated in fifteen of the 320 CD districts, providing irrigation, credit, fertilizer, improved seeds, and technical advice, but unlike Etawah it was staged to display gains in productivity rather than welfare. Yields were 10 percent above average, but because credit and inputs were tied to procurement, the fifteen IADP districts supplied one-third of the grain that came on the market nationwide. Cummings underscored the lesson: for getting food from field to table, legal and economic tools were as crucial as technology. He had suggestions for credit and price policies and a draft law against seed counterfeiters, but it was up to Subramaniam to repackage the experiments as a legislative agenda.[4]

The fundamental problem, as he saw it, was the "uneconomic price" of food. Prices at the retail end had jumped 50 percent since 1963, but with wholesale ceilings in force the profits went entirely to black marketers. Farmers had scant incentive to grow more or bring their surplus to market. Despite good weather and a record harvest, grain deliveries in 1964 were one-third below the previous year. Subramaniam pushed the Lok Sabha for a policy of "remunerative and incentivized" pricing to transfer income to the farmer, and in January 1965, it created two new agencies: an independent agricultural pricing board to remove price decisions from industry-dominated ministries and a national food corporation to buy grain at the fixed rates. Legislators expected that without sufficient storage it would take years to implement, but an unexpected dry spell in the wheat district that summer emptied granaries and enabled the agency to procure 1,252,000 tons for current consumption and set a floor price of 75 rupees per *quintal* (100 kg). The credit problem was less easily solved. Less than one-fifth of Indian farmers had access to government or commercial credit, and although loans were typically small—less than $200 per year at today's values—most came from local bosses who demanded either crippling interest or political fealty in return.

Private lenders steered farmers toward high-value export crops, such as jute, cotton, or sugar. A functioning national credit system would require funding on a scale only international aid could provide as well as a network of lending agencies capable of reaching more than 100 million cultivators.[5]

Fertilizer presented another bottleneck. Overcoming the scarcity would require a sixfold increase in domestic output, but the public sector monopoly, coupled with foreign exchange constraint, offered almost no room for growth. Subramaniam's deputy, B. Sivaraman, led an investigation that determined that India's fertilizer prices—higher than in any other country—were the principal impediment. India could not finance enough additional capacity on its own even if it wanted to, and existing factories faced "severe shortages of experienced technical and managerial personnel." Sivaraman also discovered that India's coal-fired plants produced a lower-grade product at higher cost than petroleum-fuelled plants. The San Francisco-based Bechtel Corporation offered to construct five large factories, each turning out 750 tons of nitrogen per day, but insisted on company control over prices, distribution, and credit arrangements. A further condition was that India buy oil from Bechtel's partners, Gulf and Texaco, instead of from the Soviet Union, which had supplied oil on concessional terms since the 1950s. Knowing full well the kind of opposition this would stir up, Subramaniam put forward the proposal anyway.[6]

Seeds, prices, credit, and fertilizer comprised a "package" Subramaniam wanted the cabinet to adopt in whole. The package included a final ingredient: population control. Unless family planning accompanied the agricultural revolution, foundation advisers explained, galloping birth rates would cancel out gains in food output. World Bank, United Nations (UN), and U.S. advisers all pushed for a more forceful program, but mass contraception had never been attempted anywhere, and most of India lacked even rudimentary health facilities. Nonetheless, the Ford Foundation urged India to deploy "tried, technical means for checking the alarming rise in yearly births" such as "the intra-uterine contraceptive device for women" and "sterilization, especially for men." Economic officials agreed, and Subramaniam formed a coalition with Krishnamachari and planner Ashoka Mehta to push a "massive" program based on the IUD and cash incentives for sterilization. Only Health Minister Sushila Nayar disapproved, and her objections were brushed aside.[7]

It is tempting to see in Subramaniam's strategy a radical break with developmental orthodoxy, a recognition that traditional peasants and modern industrialists respond to prices in similar ways, or that rural and urban sectors deserve like treatment. But American and Indian advocates of high-yield agriculture, no less than other modernizers, targeted the rural sphere for top-down social and psychological renovation. Rather than relying exclusively on Tennessee Valley Authority–style technical solutions or institutional changes, such as land reforms or community development, the package offered a mix of scientific and administrative innovations. Like earlier interventions, it was designed to induce a mental awakening. Subramaniam hoped for a "shock" that would instill a modern outlook on family planning, education, and the market. The price-credit-fertilizer-contraceptive combination would, according to Rockefeller advisers, "overcome the lethargy associated with traditional farming." Tellingly, proponents did not defend farmers' entitlement to fair prices or technology; instead, they presented these as motivational tools. The package would galvanize peasants to work harder to fill industry's needs.[8]

The package drew objections from all sides. Communists, trade unions, and industrial interests united in opposition to higher prices, reinforced by dire warnings from the Finance Ministry. "Food holds the key to the control of inflation," Krishnamachari protested. Savings, internal resources, and foreign exchange all depended on holding the line. The plan commission insisted community development was still the only affordable way to increase food production. The Bombay tabloid Blitz, the impudent voice of urban labor, denounced this "bogus self-sufficiency plan" designed to "turn the clock back, muzzle industrial progress, and reconvert this land of ours into an agrarian appendage of the industrial United States." By April 1965 the Lok Sabha had rejected the Bechtel deal and slapped restrictions on foreign investment in fuel and fertilizer. But to some extent the struggle at the center was irrelevant because the states had no desire to relinquish authority over agriculture. Three conferences of chief ministers failed to shake their resolve. Maharashtra, Kerala, and other states, who obeyed earlier directives favoring non-food crops, bitterly complained that Delhi's shifting moods would now deny them their "justifiable rewards." The confrontations took place against a backdrop of increasing unrest, as Bombay and Calcutta imposed rationing, and hunger marchers clashed with police. But instead of dispelling

209

the crisis atmosphere, Subramaniam heightened it, using his proposals to underscore the stark choices facing the government.[9]

He aimed to expose the highly charged issues of prestige and control that lay behind the food question. Nationalists suspected foreign capital and science carried an invisible threat to India's sovereignty. During the Bechtel debate, V. K. Krishna Menon, the former foreign minister, characterized American expertise as a subtle tool of infiltration. He wryly asked the assembly to excuse his "obsession about empires," explaining that he knew something of their habits. "They come in by the front door; they come in by the back door; they come in by the side door; they come in as our guests and do not depart." But for many, P.L. 480 represented a more humiliating vulnerability. Officials expressed nostalgia for the days when "people starved to death, but at least India was free from foreign gifts." Subramaniam urged legislators to decide which endangered the national integrity more. He conceded that price increases threatened to upset planning in the short run, but argued that forced deflation might set off a cycle of scarcity. Only by breaking through to surplus production would agriculture return to its role as the "hand maiden of industry." Above all, he insisted on an all-India policy; the states would have to cede control. On this point the press agreed. "The conflict among the States is no longer a covert struggle," the *Times of India* declared. "What is alarming is that hardly anything is being done by those in authority to reverse the current dangerous trends."[10]

Observers in offices along the Potomac were similarly alarmed. "America's war on poverty is a mild skirmish compared to this," James Reston observed, "and not only the well-being of the Indian people but the balance of power in South Asia may depend on it." As Lyndon Johnson committed his administration to war in the wake of the Tonkin Gulf incident, the White House kept a wary eye on the largest domino. Advisers worried India might fall to pieces without the gravitational pull of Nehru's personality, and setbacks in the food debate seemed to confirm Shastri's diminished power. State Department observers diagnosed a variety of problems—border conflicts, nuclear ambitions, and India's criticism of Vietnam policy—as symptoms of a dangerous weakness at the center. Their pessimism was amplified by Selig Harrison, an influential *Washington Post* correspondent who predicted India would break apart on linguistic lines within the decade, with communists taking control of the larger fragments. Massive U.S. aid might prevent "the uglier

210

forms of totalitarianism," but the real issue was "whether any Indian state can survive at all."[11]

The Central Intelligence Agency (CIA) discerned a triple threat to party, state, and central control. In the provinces, frustrations left by the incomplete land reforms of the 1950s were eroding Congress's support just as the party began to lose its urban base to Hindu nationalist parties. At the state level, separatist movements were gaining strength. Finally, a "bitter factionalism" paralyzed the center as powerful ministers and a syndicate of party bosses challenged Shastri's authority. Johnson and at least one of his advisers recognized that the food crisis could be a key test on all three fronts. Although unsure of many in the Kennedy circle, the president trusted Orville Freeman, a former governor of Minnesota who served as secretary of agriculture. In early 1964 Johnson sent him to India. Freeman visited the IADP experiments and met with planning and cabinet officials and Rockefeller and Ford scientists, and came away convinced that "a successful national food policy would further one of our political objectives for India—binding together the states with new ties of interdependence and strengthening the national government." Even amid critical decisions on Vietnam and civil rights, Johnson paid close attention to intelligence reports on India. Many identified Subramaniam with a rising generation of capable and pragmatic leaders who could revitalize the party and pull the country back from the brink. The Indian ambassador was surprised at how much the president seemed to know about the activities of the food minister. "That Subber Mainyam of yours," Johnson confided, "he's a good feller."[12]

As much as Johnson disdained the intellectual theorizing that surrounded development policy, he was powerfully drawn to its visionary ambition. Having worked during his thirty-year career to electrify and irrigate rural Texas, he equated politics with the delivery of government projects to "backward" regions. He has been described as "unencumbered by philosophy or ideology," but schemes for economic and social betterment filled his worldview. Flying over Asia in October 1965, he stood at a window and told his staff of America's destiny in the continent below. "This is the way of the future . . . unlimited resources untapped . . . two thirds of the people." He found the clearest expression of his goals in the writing of Barbara Ward, whose books, he once admitted, were the only ones he read. Her commentary in *The Economist* and the *New York Times* and frequent appearances on television made her perhaps

211

the best-known expert on the problems of the Third World, but she was also a confidante and occasional speechwriter to the president. She had a unique facility for casting economic planning as high moral drama. Her best sellers, *India and the West* and *The Rich Nations and the Poor Nations,* put the rescue of India alongside the conquest of space among the "stirring adventures of the human spirit."[13]

While other theorists spoke of dangers to poor countries, Ward cast global poverty as a test of survival for the rich. Throughout history, from "Belshazzar down to the latest ducking of Hollywood starlets in swimming pools full of champagne," luxury had sapped great nations of energy and conscience. The declining economic performance of the industrial countries and their indifference to India's plight were both symptoms of moral decay. The United States was pulling its weight, but Britain, Canada, Australia, and Western Europe, absorbed in their own welfare-state experiments, had lost a sense of global responsibility. Only by leading them in a vast "world-building" effort, starting with India, could the United States revitalize the Atlantic community. Ward coined the term "Great Society" for Johnson's domestic war on poverty, and her themes of interdependence and the duties of wealth were at the heart of his effort to "internationalize" the Great Society.[14]

The scale of Johnson's ambition was matched by his frustration with the aid establishment. The World Bank, Congress, and aid agencies were pulling in different directions on India. European donors were ready to back away after watching the Third Plan come crashing down. Meanwhile, the World Bank prepared to underwrite still more heavy industrial projects. John Lewis, an economics professor newly installed as director of the U.S. Agency for International Development (USAID) in New Delhi, argued that the time had come for a Big Push. A "quantum increase" in aid of 40 percent or more, he estimated, would achieve self-sufficiency in food in five years and industrial takeoff in ten. But Lewis's memos drew only skepticism from a State Department struggling to fund existing programs. India's share, roughly half a billion dollars, was already the largest on the list. Johnson's own advisers hoped for little more than to hold the line at current levels. "Our basic philosophy," explained Robert Komer, the White House's point man on South Asia, was that India was "a long term investment, and one in which we should not be concerned about the limited short-run returns."[15]

Congress had less patience. The honeymoon that followed Kennedy's death did not include the aid bill. Three weeks after the assassination, the

House shaved $800 million from a budget of less than $4 billion. Legislators challenged the development consensus that had prevailed since Point Four: they doubted that state planning would foster either entrepreneurship or democracy, and they believed dependency would provoke more resentment than cooperation. Economists testified that the outflow of aid worsened an already critical balance of payments deficit, threatening the stability of the dollar and the whole global economy. "It's gonna break us if we don't bring it under control," warned Otto Passman, chair of Ways and Means, "We have only one foreign policy, the checkbook." Moreover, Congress had the public on its side. Johnson noted the poll numbers—88 percent wanted a substantial reduction—were "just frightening." He had a delicate balance of guns and butter to protect. With Vietnam, civil rights, voting rights, Medicare, and Medicaid on the agenda for spring, he worried that foreign aid would drive a wedge through the entire program.[16]

For Johnson, politics was process; seemingly unrelated issues were linked through personalities and timing. He was already anticipating difficulty with the foreign aid bill when, on April 13, 1965, war broke out between India and Pakistan in a marshy border region known as the Rann of Kutch. The conflict provoked what Secretary of State Dean Rusk called a "volcanic reaction in Congress." Senator Wayne Morse demanded to know "how you expect that you can maintain public support for aid if we yield to Pakistan and India." On June 5, with the battle still under way, Passman began making cuts in the India aid budget. A week earlier, Johnson's allies in the Senate had narrowly defeated a Southern filibuster of the Voting Rights bill, now on the floor of the House. The farm bill, a tax stimulus, and investigations of war spending and the monetary crisis were all before committees. General William Westmoreland was requesting an additional forty-four battalions for Vietnam, and at the end of the month, India's P.L. 480 contract was up for renewal. Johnson grasped the connections: India's food crisis, its internal stability, the weakening dollar, America's global leadership, and his domestic agenda were all part of a package.[17]

Subramaniam and the IADP teams agreed that speed would be critical in the next stage. Cultivators and cabinet ministers paid polite attention to incremental improvements, but only sudden doubling or tripling would show that "tradition [had] its price." To move from experimentation to general release, the ministry asked the Rockefeller Foundation to arrange

213

delivery of 200 tons of Sonora 64 and fifty tons of Lerma Rojo seeds. These would be multiplied at state seed farms for mass release in early 1966. Borlaug doubted whether state farms had the capacity to multiply dwarfs on that scale, and at his urging some 5,000 cooperatives and private seed dealers also took part. Logistics were a problem. The seed had to be procured and disinfected in Mexico, trucked across the border to Los Angeles, and shipped to India. If the transfer took more than a few months, the seed would germinate in the bags and arrive useless for planting.[18]

Borlaug chose seed from Sinaloa because he thought its desert climate resembled Rajasthan. The Mexican national seed agency arranged packing and transport, and the trucks crossed the border headed for Long Beach on August 13. Two days earlier a scuffle between white police officers and a motorist triggered rioting in the nearby Watts district. Fed up with police brutality, unemployment, and segregation, the largely African American neighborhood erupted. Crowds chanting "burn, baby, burn!" roamed the streets looting and torching some 600 homes and businesses. Highways closed as rioters pelted passing vehicles with bricks and Molotov cocktails. The governor declared a round-the-clock curfew and 2,000 National Guard troops staged at the Long Beach Armory before moving into the riot area. For six days the city was a battleground. The global press analyzed Southern California in terms once reserved for Third World trouble spots. The riots were caused by "deep sociological and economic factors," the Bombay-based *Times of India* explained. "Los Angeles [is] an overcrowded and poverty-ridden area."[19]

Belatedly learning that the seed had not arrived at the port, Borlaug worked the telephone for hours before finding the trucks parked alongside a closed freeway. When the curfew lifted, the shipment made the last few miles to the docks in time to sail for Bombay aboard the *President Garfield* on August 17. Borlaug breathed a sigh of relief, only to become aware that the cargo was heading into another battle zone. Within days fighting had broken out between India and Pakistan on the Kashmir border, this time involving heavy armor and air strikes on both sides. On September 6 India turned the tables by launching an invasion of West Pakistan, and in the ensuing days the two armies clashed on the outskirts of Lahore in the largest tank battle since World War II. Johnson cut off fuel and supplies to both sides, and the offensive ground to a halt. When the *President Garfield* docked in Bombay, a blackout was still in force. The city, however, was jubilant. Local papers expressed "exhilaration that we were not caught napping this time and that our armed forces are giving an excellent account of themselves."[20]

To some observers, India's victory vindicated Nehru's industrial vision. Pakistan's American-made Saberjets and Patton tanks proved unequal to India's homemade Gnat fighters and recoilless guns. Shastri, however, explicitly framed the war as a two-front struggle for Kashmir and self-reliance in the slogan *Jai Jawan! Jai Kisan!* (Hail soldiers! Hail farmers!). In a national radio address on October 10 he urged Indians to "consider self-sufficiency in food to be no less important than an impregnable defense system for the preservation of our freedom and independence." Agronomists from the Pusa institute met Borlaug's seeds at the Bombay docks and with relief found them ready to germinate. After their perilous journey, they had arrived at a moment when their catalytic powers would have a telling effect. The crisis had consolidated Shastri's control of the cabinet, and instilled a momentum, Subramaniam observed, an eagerness for "new initiatives to sweep away the cobwebs of delay, obstruction, and reaction."[21]

"The Kind of India We Want"

In Washington the Indo-Pakistan War triggered a searching reappraisal of policies on aid, India, and agriculture. On June 9 Johnson ordered an interdepartmental review with an emphasis on "how to achieve more leverage for our money." He told Freeman to hold off on new P.L. 480 contracts and begin doling out food on a month-to-month basis. He also put aid to Egypt, Ghana, Colombia, Brazil, and other countries on short-term rollovers with political and economic strings. This "short-tether" policy would remain in effect for the next three years. It mystified Indian officials, who believed Johnson was trying to bully dependent countries into supporting him on Vietnam. Bowles insisted that the United States only wanted to be sure that India was doing all it "could to raise foodgrain output." Neither theory captured more than a fraction of what was on the president's mind. The review, which Komer dubbed the "quiet new look," grew during the summer to encompass the total foreign aid budget, relations with European allies, domestic farm policy, and the future of the Democratic Party.[22]

Johnson's immediate goal was to halt the fighting, and despite advice to the contrary, he was sure that "an army fights on its belly" and that a food cutoff would stop the war. He aimed secondarily to forge a consensus among his own advisers and the international donor community. The chorus of opposition to using food as leverage confirmed his suspicion that Bowles, Komer, Defense Secretary Robert McNamara, and others comprised a cabal of "India lovers" within his administration. The Kennedy-era consensus that aid ought to be an apolitical long-term investment in India's future irritated him. "When I put my wheat down here, and it costs me a few hundred million," he explained, "I want to see what you're putting on the other side." European nations' reluctance to increase their donations, and the World Bank's "double or nothing" strategy bothered him just as much. The balance of payments crisis ruled out any major increase in aid and made it imperative for donors to unite behind a single agenda if the Development Decade were to achieve anything. U.S. leadership on India might also restrain French and German criticism on Vietnam. But in addition to the diplomatic contingencies, the "quiet new look" also considered a new challenge to the power of the domestic farm lobby.[23]

A series of voting rights cases beginning with *Baker v. Carr* (1962) mandated a monumental shift of legislative power from country to city. Since Reconstruction, states had drawn district lines that disproportionately favored rural voters. Twenty votes cast in Nashville prior to 1964 counted only as much a single vote from a rural Tennessee county. A secure rural base enabled Southern committee chairs—Passman on Foreign Affairs, Howard "Judge" Smith on Rules, and Jamie Whitten on Public Works—to dominate the House and preserve the New Deal farm subsidies from the growing power of urban and consumer interests. The 1964 farm bill passed only after rural representatives agreed to support labor legislation in return. Whitten now estimated that court decisions would cost the farm bloc fifty-four votes in the House. With the Democratic Party's base shifting toward urban and suburban voters, the era of big subsidies and big surpluses was coming to an end. Johnson needed to adapt policy to new realities.[24]

Although Komer had a surer grasp of Indian politics, Freeman's proposals came closer to covering the total spectrum of the president's concerns. Early in the discussions he produced studies showing that the crop limitation and subsidy policies underpinning P.L. 480 were no longer economically or politically sustainable. One of his innovations at Agriculture was a long-range forecasting unit, the Economic Research Service (ERS), which monitored domestic and global trends. Freeman asked the ERS to investigate the effects on the U.S. farm economy under the optimistic assumption that Asian countries could become self-sufficient in grain. P.L. 480 had been designed to create markets for U.S. commodities, but the results suggested that cutting food donations might actually increase commercial demand for U.S. food products overseas. Higher standards of living and consumption generated by an agricultural takeoff would "spill out" into demand for imported oils, meats, and processed foods that would be paid for in dollars. Freeman suggested that a strategy based on increasing food output in underdeveloped countries would invigorate the U.S. economy, strengthen the dollar, lower consumer prices, win over Congressional opponents, and "project the Great Society world-wide."[25]

The final report, prepared by Rusk, Komer, Freeman, and David Bell, director of USAID, stressed India's internal weaknesses. "The real threat to India is not invasion through the Himalayas," the advisers concluded, but "disintegration and fragmentation of the as yet fragile Indian state." A collapse of the Congress government, a situation comparable to China in 1948, would most likely arise from a failure to meet rising expectations. "Economic growth has become the test of political success," it continued, and by that standard India "hasn't done well enough." Sharply restricting aid would provide a "new impulse toward unity" and turn "swords into plowshares" by channeling India's energies away from border conflicts and industry and toward agriculture. Even if the effort fell short, the push to achieve greater production in food would discipline India's internal politics and create "the kind of India we want."[26]

Johnson warmed to the idea of linking India aid to his farm policy. In July, he commiserated with Ambassador Nehru about his congressional difficulties. Voting rights, Medicare, and the Vietnam deployments had about exhausted his mandate and he guessed he would "probably get licked" on the farm bill. He wanted Nehru's help in communicating a "food for famine" message to Congress and the public. The ambassador was taken aback. A few cities were still on wartime rations, but there was no famine. P.L. 480 provided food for industry. It was a reciprocal deal; India helped the United States dispose of a "burdensome surplus" and in the process accumulated the capital it needed for the Third Plan. Senators saw it differently, Johnson explained; they did not understand why India should be making steel instead of fertilizer. He "didn't want people to starve but he wanted the Congress to be in partnership on whatever we did."[27]

Johnson needed to appear to be driving a hard bargain. He instructed Freeman to get an agreement from Subramaniam committing him to benchmarks on fertilizer output, subsidies, price incentives, birth control, and aid from other countries. Freeman cornered his counterpart at the November Food and Agriculture Organization (FAO) meeting and made him sign a one-page list of goals. The "Treaty of Rome" was purely cosmetic. According to Subramaniam, it summarized only "those steps we had already taken and that we proposed to take," but the illusion of coercion was critical to Johnson's plans. As Freeman confided in his diary, it was "politically impossible for [Subramaniam] to be subject to harsh demands," but to sway Congress "I've got to carry back a posture of having demanded and succeeded." In the end, though, the political worlds of Delhi and Washington were not isolated enough to carry off this double game. To Subramaniam's dismay, *Blitz* obtained a copy and published it under the headline "Text of Yankee Moghul's Fatwa." It would not be the last gaffe, but in the course of the crisis, each side would learn to calibrate its messages for audiences on different sides of the globe.[28]

To save P.L. 480, Johnson needed to repackage it as an emergency measure, "just as if we were in a war." Through the fall of 1965 he developed the theme of a world food crisis brought on by runaway population growth. Fortuitously, the November monsoon failed and a severe drought scorched large areas of Maharashtra, Madhya Pradesh, and Rajasthan. At a televised cabinet meeting on November 19, he declared a "world war against hunger" requiring a reorientation of global and domestic food policy. "Our strategy," he explained, "is to encourage rapid increase in food production in the underdeveloped countries themselves." Two weeks later, as Johnson prepared to present the new policy to Congress, the Department of Agriculture produced its first famine forecasts. On December 17, before the extent (or even the existence) of a crop failure could be confirmed, Johnson declared the onset of "near famine conditions ... which may require a dramatic rescue operation." A *Washington Post* article the previous week explained the domestic link: "A series of famines, such as that threatening India, may speed the evolutionary movement of U.S. farm policy."[29]

The Meaning of Famine

It is not altogether surprising that Johnson and Nehru attached different meanings to the word "famine." Famine had rhetorical connotations in the contexts of both the Cold War and postcolonial Indian politics. From the Ukrainian Holdomor of 1921 to the Great Leap Forward, the United

218

States identified mass starvation as proof of communism's failure. Likewise, the famines of 1899 and 1943 framed the Indian nationalist movement, graphically disproving Britain's claims to imperial benevolence. Because famine constituted a breakdown of modern systems of distribution and production, its definition changed as those processes evolved. British economist Alexander Loveday noted in 1914 that "the history of famines in India is largely the story of how the meaning of that word has been modified through the force of economic transition and the perfection of administrative organization." India inherited from the British an administrative mechanism for locating and declaring famines. In the 1960s the United States devised its own scheme for forecasting famines worldwide. Each procedure encoded a narrative explaining the causes of famine, the duties of governments, and the limits on those obligations. The Bihar Famine of 1966–1967, the pivotal event of India's agricultural transition, resulted from a clash between these two fables.

The 1966 famine existed initially as a forecast based on estimates of food consumption and harvests. Since February 1961, ERS economists Sherman Johnson, Wilhelm Anderson, and Lester R. Brown had been perfecting a statistical model for anticipating global food needs. Working from demographic projections and the FAO's country balance sheets, they constructed a "world food budget" indicating total supply and requirements five years into the future. Reliable inventories of most foods were hard to come by, so they concentrated on key staples such as rice and wheat. They adapted techniques used by the CIA to gauge dietary levels in the Soviet Union and China, translating data for bulk crops into calories and multiplying population projections against national standards (2,000 per day for Pakistanis, 3,220 for Americans) to estimate per capita availability. The budget documented a sinking trend in which the number of calories per Asian was falling and would soon drop into negative figures. The ERS estimated that in the inevitable crisis food exports would have to fill the gap, making American aid and technology strategically vital. Although the reports never used the word "famine," a statistical deficit came to be seen as the same thing. Johnson's December 1965 famine warning described a national food deficit, the same deficit that had been growing alarmingly since India enrolled in the P.L. 480 program.[30]

This model represented a significant change in the way famine was understood. India continued to use the imperial "famine codes," credited by many (and still defended by some) with banishing catastrophic

famines from India for much of the twentieth century. By driving peasants closer to subsistence, the second and third plans made the codes
even more essential, and they continued to be refined into the 1960s.
Imposed at the turn of the century, they provided a system for measuring
and mitigating situations of scarcity, but they were designed less to prevent crises than to represent them in a politically acceptable way. Recurring hunger in a colony that exported food to Britain embarrassed imperial officials. Cornelius Walford, who concluded the first historical survey
of famines in 1879, found that famines resulted not from natural forces
or overpopulation but "from the failure of human means and foresight."
Their sudden increase in number and severity just at the moment when
Britain assumed control provided proof of mismanagement. Colonial
officials sought to minimize their own culpability without deferring to
private charities, which were all too ready to jump into famine relief.
"Nothing did more harm in times of famine," Governor George Hamilton believed, "than ill-regulated, unorganized, and gratuitous relief."[31]

The codes constructed famines as spatially and temporally delimited
events, rather than as symptoms of chronic deficit. A sudden rise in food
prices triggered "a period of observation and test" during which district
officers took note of signs: property sales, epidemics, crime, rail traffic, or
migrating flocks or people. A determination of famine did not incur a
greater obligation, but only more detailed reporting. Relief works were
designed to gauge the degree of distress through a series of self-actuating
tests. Victims were made to demonstrate their need by submitting to
labor, sharing quarters with other castes, or working on holy days. Al-
lowances were reduced to the very minimum required to sustain life, the
infamous "temple ration" based on Sir Richard Temple's starvation experiments during the 1877 Madras famine. The end result was a hard
count of those in absolute extremity; officers were to expel anyone
"found not to be at the end of their resources." Reports moved up the
civil service hierarchy, allowing officials in New Delhi (and eventually
London) to map the outbreak and schedule relief efforts. Famines were
to be viewed as routine occurrence accounted for in the regular budget,
instead of an emergency requiring special appropriations.[32]

American statistical models changed the nature of knowledge about
famine in four ways. First, the flow of information was reversed. Under
the codes, awareness of a crisis moved from locality to the center. In the
1943 Bengal famine, local officials appealed to New Delhi for weeks before the emergency was recognized. By contrast, the 1965 forecasts origi-

nated at USDA headquarters in Washington. Johnson needed to persuade Indian officials that a crisis existed, and they in turn confronted denials from local officials. Second, statistical forecasts were vague as to time and place. While the codes mapped and scheduled famines as precisely as a railway timetable, the ERS model forecast a shortfall for the whole of India in annualized terms. It was up to government officials to guess where and when the crisis would hit. Third, the codes avoided the issue of causation by casting famine as a recurring natural calamity. The ERS assumed causal relationships between population growth, technical competence, and food availability while implicitly discounting causes such as land tenure, wages, conflict, and trade relations. Moreover, these assumptions were then built into the policy response. Freeman's benchmarks consisted of steps to improve the statistical indicators: population limitation, grain yields, transport, and storage.[33]

Finally, statistical projections gave American forecasters much more latitude in estimating, or overestimating, the gravity of famine. The ERS arrived at its forecasts by triangulating harvests, population, and nutritional needs, but in all three columns the numbers only loosely corresponded with the realities they supposedly described. An uncertainty principle, according to Ivan Bennett, Johnson's science adviser, precluded reliable calculations: the more officials needed to know about the food inventory, the more peasants and merchants were motivated to mislead them. Population and caloric projections threw in a further margin of error of several hundred percent. As *The Economist* observed, "estimates of [India's] food gap represent, in these circumstances, a piece of political rather than economic arithmetic." Moreover, famine modeling soon spread to other agencies, giving Johnson a range of assessments, none more credible than the others. He chose the most frightening. Brown's 18-million-ton deficit was countered by CIA estimates of a "minimal" requirement of only 3.5 million tons. The CIA and the State Department characterized India's food problem as a chronic dependency, while Agriculture predicted a disaster larger than "the Bengal famine of 1943 by several fold."[34]

The drought and uncertainty about Washington's plans finally broke the remaining opposition within Shastri's cabinet. The wheat scheme's detractors kept up a stiff fight. Social scientists predicted violent evictions of tenants and mass unrest if the plan were implemented. The Statistical Institute of India investigated the field trials and dismissed claims of double and triple yields as "fanciful." Subramaniam considered the report "devastating" but Krishnamachari was his principal concern. The finance minister refused to increase allocations for fertilizer, insisting the funds should come from taxes on the rural areas where there was still "a large amount of money in the hands of many, particularly agriculturalists." On December 15 the cabinet met to discuss fertilizer imports for the next year. Krishnamachari listed the foreign exchange needs for defense, petroleum, textiles, and atomic energy before concluding: "If the cabinet approves a scheme of this nature and I am not able to find the money, what is to become of it?" Several ministers advised against adding to the uncertainty in a drought year, but when the vote was tallied, the budget passed. Sivaraman immediately ordered 2 million rupees' worth of fertilizer from the United States. Krishnamachari promptly resigned, but his departure settled the matter only at the national level. "Neither you nor I can have the final say," he warned Subramaniam, "the [state] chief ministers can wreck any central policy."[35]

On January 10, 1966, just hours after signing a peace accord with Pakistan, Shastri died of a heart attack, throwing policy once again into confusion. The inauguration of Nehru's daughter, Indira Gandhi, revived anxieties in Washington. The CIA regarded her as a placeholder for state party bosses rather than as the steady hand India needed. She had a name but no political base and seemingly no appetite for power. She broke down on the podium at one of her first appearances in the Lok Sabha and fled from the chamber. Within its first weeks, the new administration faced a wave of separatist agitation. A general strike paralyzed Kerala, and rebels clashed with army troops in Nagaland and the Mizo Hills. Once again, India prefigured a threat to all developing countries. Rostow, soon to be anointed national security adviser, warned of a "factional tendency" in modernizing states whose overburdened regimes were vulnerable to "multiple, shallowly rooted, but highly assertive parties." A strong, one-party state, such as Mexico's, offered the only chance for "a relatively hopeful evolution." Gandhi soon regained her footing. Her early moves to create a separate state for the Sikhs and retain Shastri's inner cabinet earned Komer's approval. She completed the dismantling of the plan regime, declaring a "plan holiday" and throwing her support behind Subramaniam's agenda. Still, Johnson kept up the pressure.[36]

With the aid bill before Congress, Johnson declared India's famine a prelude to a global "race between food supplies and population." Mobilizing the crisis management machinery, he set up fourteen scientific and administrative task forces to generate proposals on food supply, population, emergency logistics, and aid. He wanted to send a message, he told Freeman, "that there were people dying, that people were being hauled away dead in trucks, and that they needed food." In Independence, Missouri, on January 20, he stood next to Harry Truman and pledged a billion dollars to help nations achieve "balance between the numbers of their people and the food they have to eat." The press took up the call, declaring that only chemical fertilizer and birth control could keep mankind off a "treadmill to starvation." A panel of Nobel scientists spelled out a *Soylent Green* scenario for the Senate. Famines might bring on "a new dark age." Any delay, physicist Polycarp Kusch cautioned, would "make necessary nearly unthinkable action later on—such as feeding on each other." The congressional hearings dramatized a hair-raising prognosis Paul Ehrlich would popularize in his 1968 best seller *The Population Bomb,* a catastrophic food deficit that would force the United States to choose which among the starving nations would survive. Such lurid prophecies were a measure of just how far Johnson needed to shift the national mood. The public's generosity was stretched thin, and not just on foreign aid. In addition to Asia's problems he "had a poverty problem, a Negro problem, an urban problem, and a health problem," he told Subramaniam, and he "was trying to do something about all of them."[37]

Inconveniently, Indian officials declared the famine a sham. Despite the drought's severity, food stocks remained adequate and the codes were not invoked. "There is no famine," a ministry statement confirmed. Planning Commissioners pointed out that hunger was more prevalent in the cities, and that the problem was not food supply but unemployment. After Johnson again referred to famine at his February press conference, Subramaniam issued a denial and accused the press, and indirectly the United States, of "scaremongering." Krishna Menon and other legislators on the left denounced Johnson's "gross exaggeration." The scare stories, *Blitz* explained, were an "American trap" designed to open the country to U.S. investment. Could the Americans "have a better idea of the extent of the food shortage," the communist newsweekly *Link* wondered, "than even the best informed of the Food Ministry's statisticians?" Foreign correspondents also had doubts. Bowles grew frustrated by reporters wanting to see actual starving Indians, which he could not produce. British correspondents wondered if famine-mongers "hadn't been bleating

unnecessarily." A London *Times* headline announced: "Food Ships Streaming into Famine-Free India."[38]

But Johnson's statements had an effect. In February Pope Paul VI appealed for aid to India where, he said, "people are literally dying of starvation." UN Secretary General U Thant urged member states to help avert
a crisis "already assuming famine proportions." Dutch schoolchildren
fasted, and Italian workers set aside union dues for India. Expert demographers told Congress that "millions will starve" even if aid arrived in
time. Gandhi's advisers grumbled that the Pope's appeal made it sound
like "there were dead bodies in the streets," but in a charged political atmosphere, appearances quickly turned into realities. As Kerala, Calcutta,
and the Punjab imposed preemptive rationing, Communist-led food riots
erupted. The *Eastern Economist* blamed the United States for fostering a
deadly "psychology of scarcity." Freeman warned Johnson that "loud
international alarm about famine" could ignite violence, and Ambassador Nehru urged the president to moderate his statements to prevent
chaos. Instead, having arranged the backdrop, he urged Gandhi to come
to Washington and lay her case before Congress in person.[39]

Johnson had a flair for political dramatics. "He seems to feel a need,"
according to one aide, "for circuses, sideshows, Roman candles, klieg
lights to get his point across." The state visit, the first by a female prime
minister, captivated Washington and cast Gandhi in a heroic role. James
Reston described her as "cool, precise, and unemotional in her gleam-
ing saris." "She's lovely," Governor Nelson Rockefeller gushed, "She's
unique. She's dedicated." Speaking at the National Press Club on March
29, Gandhi presented India as a challenge to the West—destined within
the decade for either takeoff or disintegration—and herself as a sacrificial figure, patiently awaiting the rich nations' choice. Betty Friedan,
who covered the visit for *Ladies' Home Journal,* noted that the Johnson
administration's emphasis on basic needs distinctly and consciously gen-
dered modernization. "We say to them, 'Raising your own food is all you
should worry about. We will produce the industry or nuclear energy'."
The female leaders of the Third World came to Washington as nurtur-
ers or supplicants. Imelda Marcos of the Philippines and Princess Ashraf
Pahlavi, the Shah of Iran's twin sister, similarly embodied the developmental partnership. During the week-long visit, Gandhi lent her charisma
to the more troubled aspects of U.S. policy, describing Johnson as "one of
the restraining influences" in Southeast Asia. The president seized every

opportunity to place himself at her side. At the Indian Embassy he invited himself to stay for dinner and announced that he would see to it that "no harm comes to this girl." His aides saw her as "a cross between Lady Bird and Barbara Ward."[40]

Meanwhile Johnson, Freeman, and Rusk mobilized a "rescue operation." Imploring Congress not to "stand by and watch children starve," Johnson requested 3.5 million tons of grain and a billion dollars in aid before the Easter recess. Fiscal conservatives fought back ("New Indian Leader Comes Begging," ran one headline) but the mood had shifted. The passage of the India Aid Bill required coordinating the official versions of the famine, and on March 29 Rusk sat down with Gandhi and her advisers to talk about how to spin the disaster. He began by framing "the dilemma concerning the public presentation on food. It shouldn't be such as to frighten people in India, but on the other hand the need must be seen to be real in the United States." Taking up the point, Nehru stressed that "to get a response, the need must be somewhat overplayed." L. K. Jha, the prime minister's secretary, suggested that the crisis could appear to be "a natural calamity" that was "averted." Gandhi had denied up to this point that a famine existed, but she conceded that heightened alarm would serve a purpose, especially if it could "be treated as a localized matter." When she was asked the following day on *Meet the Press* if claims of famine were exaggerated, she replied that lexicon of hunger had evolved. "Today when we talk of famine it is not in the sense in which we knew these words before independence," she explained. "There is an acute shortage of food in our country in specific scarcity areas. There are no people dying of starvation." State ministers disputed both points, contending that people *were* dying and that it was a national, rather than a local problem. Language itself became a point of contention; legislators denounced the whole "starvation controversy" as "part of the cold war between the Government and the Opposition."[41]

In the ensuing months, Gandhi initiated a barrage of liberalizing reforms—a 37 percent devaluation of the rupee, shifting cotton acreage to wheat (thereby boosting imports of U.S. cotton), relaxed controls on the private sector, and opening state industries, including fertilizer, to foreign investors—moves that aligned her with her party's right wing and satisfied requirements laid down by Rusk. Devaluation pushed consumer prices up by more than 15 percent and unleashed a wave of industrial strikes. It meant, *Thought* magazine concluded, "the end of giganticism in our efforts to develop the nation's economy." The food emergency allowed

Gandhi to exert increasing authority over the states, and by appointing Subramaniam to the Plan Commission, silenced another center of dissent. As her moderate left allies deserted her she adopted a populist political style, casting herself as mother of the nation's poor. "My family members are poverty stricken," she told a crowd in Uttar Pradesh, "I have to look after them." She bypassed state and party organizations and claimed an unmediated relationship with the masses. She leaned heavily on U.S. aid to make her promises good, and Johnson volunteered to help her bid in the February 1967 elections. "You tell me what to do," he told Nehru. "Send her food? Attack her? I'll do whatever you say."[42]

Meanwhile, Johnson moved to internationalize India's crisis in two ways: first by redistributing burdens among donor countries, and secondly by promoting India as a model of a new style of economic development. Discarding the concept of a development race between rival systems, he challenged communist nations to join Europe and Japan in a global response. Unlike the turf wars over steel mills, U.S. and Soviet agronomists generally agreed on India's farm problems. Soviet aid equipped 20 of the seed farms that multiplied the Mexican wheat, and Soviet advisers backed Subramaniam's reform package. Johnson encouraged this trend. "I'm not in the slightest concerned about your getting help from Russia," he wanted Indian officials to know, "Get every damn dime of it you can." Secondly, he revoked the universal entitlement implicit in Point Four. The "inexhaustible" resources once available as a birthright of peace-loving peoples would now be reserved for those who demonstrated a capacity to help themselves. This was doubly humiliating for India, not only made to beg but to be exhibited as a model of a deserving beggar. The administration pushed the World Bank to make Subramaniam's program a template for "the national economy of every developing country." American "food power" would be "the decisive factor in shaping the policies of countries in question."[43]

The seed multiplication drive went forward despite the drought. "Seed villages" across the Punjab and the Ganges Valley produced 5,000 tons by the end of the 1966 *kharif* (July–October) growing season. Subramaniam plowed up the front yard of his Delhi bungalow to plant Sonora 64. Meanwhile, IRRI scientists conducted field tests of IR-8 and another dwarf, Taichung Native I, in southern districts. With fertilizer coming in from the U.S. and the massive Trombay fertilizer plant, Swaminathan planned to put 2.4 million hectares—all irrigated—under dwarf wheat in the next season. He dispatched two assistants to Mexico to buy 18,000 tons of Lerma Rojo, enough seed for an "agricultural takeoff" the next year. Borlaug anticipated "tremendous yield increases" that would generate "a complete change in the psychology of wheat production."[44]

A second consecutive drought deepened the distress, but as usual conflicting reports made it difficult to gauge the severity. Despite front-page images of emaciated refugees, the media consensus that thousands or millions "faced starvation" was dramatically at odds with official casualty and crop estimates. Bihar, the most severely affected state, reported food yields above 96 percent of normal; however, jute, sugar cane, and other commercial crops were heavily hit, leading to mass unemployment among landless laborers. Oxfam's field director, James Howard, visited individual villages in Bihar where nearly the entire rice crop had been wiped out (due to flooding rather than drought). He found "groups of people . . . already prostrate with starvation." "Barren fields provide mute counterpoint to statistics," Senator Gale McGee cabled from the scene in December. "It would be difficult to exaggerate the magnitude." An Indian legislator told an American researcher that the anecdotal and statistical versions could both be right: many were starving, but this was a "normal condition. The landless and the poor suffer like this normally." More than 2 million persons sought employment at relief works in Bihar, Rajastan, and Madhya Pradesh, but no famine had been declared and no deaths recorded. Freeman regarded it as a problem of distribution rather than scarcity. "They haven't had a goddamn big failure," Johnson admitted. "They've just produced 11 million more tons than they had last year. But . . . they want ten million free tons, and we want it for our farmers and so nobody here is stopping."[45]

Johnson certainly wasn't. Short-tether sustained a crisis atmosphere and kept up the pressure on Europe, Congress, and Gandhi's domestic opponents. He personally supervised the dispatch of grain—an average of three ships per day—moving just enough to prevent a cut in official rations, but not so much as to boost wheat futures on the Chicago market. "We stand here this afternoon in Omaha, at the end of a very important lifeline," he told supporters gathered beneath a towering grain terminal on the Missouri River. "At the other end of that lifeline, 8000 miles out yonder, is India." The lifeline also connected two elections. Amid uncertainty about Vietnam, urban riots, and the economy, the Democrats lost seats—especially in the rural Midwest and South—in the November 1966 midterms, leaving an even slimmer margin of support for the foreign aid bill, set for debate in February, just before a general election that would test Gandhi's control of her party and government. Hindering the flow of aid after India had complied was a "cruel performance," Bowles felt, but Johnson was able to cast it as a rescue. On December 20, 1966, following the television premiere of *How the Grinch Stole Christmas,* CBS aired a special report called "Harvest of Hope." Charles Kuralt followed the "bridge of ships" from Nebraska's mechanized farms to the tradition-bound villages where American wheat "saved an estimated 70 million Indians from starvation."[46]

Both the aid bill and Gandhi would survive, but barely. Johnson optioned the supertanker *Manhattan,* the largest commercial ship afloat, to arrive in India with 102,000 tons on February 6, the day the U.S. Congress would take up the annual aid bill, and one week before voting in India. But voters had grown tired of having their diets and attitudes managed. Senior Indian leaders, including many of the power brokers who had put Gandhi in power, lost their seats to previously unknown local and linguistic parties. The casualties included Subramaniam, who lost by more than 70,000 votes to a party called the Dravida Munnetra Kazhagam, which rallied Tamil voters to "eliminate linguistic imperialism, regional imbalance, and over-centralization." Gandhi, however, secured reelection handily, and as the last one standing, she now controlled a party that was indisputably her own.[47]

An official declaration of famine, politically impossible before the election, now became politically convenient. The famine codes superseded state authority, and Bihar had been a thorn in Delhi's side even before the drought struck. Although predominantly rural, the state had a distinctly modern economy in the Mahalanobis sense; industry and export-based, non-food agriculture—jute, tobacco, sugarcane—provided a large share of income. Unemployment was rife, particularly in the squatter colonies of Partition refugees surrounding Patna, the capital city. Consequently, the state relied heavily on P.L. 480 imports, consuming 1.3 million tons of American wheat in normal years. Large landholders (who had earlier stymied Nehru's land reforms) stubbornly resisted Subramaniam's innovations in agricultural policy. Congress decisively lost control of the state in February, defeated by a coalition of six splinter groups led by Mahamaya Prasad Sinha. Gandhi had authority to dissolve the state government and install her own minister, but as sympathetic editorials pointed out, acting so soon would appear unseemly. When famine was declared on April 20, Gandhi insisted humanitarian concerns

were paramount—"Center or state, we have one problem, poverty"—
but the central government was able to use the famine declaration to
discredit and sideline Sinha. The codes were invoked for nearly the entire
state, and the famine unfolded according to script. It was treated as a
"localized matter," a natural calamity that was averted. The province
was isolated, subjected to rationing, and fed with supplies directly from
the United States.[48]

The massive and highly publicized relief effort was a triumph for
both Johnson and Gandhi. Bihar demonstrated, according to *The Economist,* that "with the right mix of national and international cooperation, even the most backward and hopeless rural areas can be brought
to life." Special trains, seven per day, carried 20 million tons of food
from the ports into the drought area. Sacks of powdered milk, lysine-
treated flour, and protein biscuits formulated for malnutrition victims
were doled out at 700,000 relief stations all reporting to a "central control room" where an international staff tracked supplies, refugees, and
disease. UN officials were impressed, but analysts have subsequently
been less celebratory. While total mortality was probably low, losses to
livestock, property, and long-term health were ruinous. Relief programs
did little to cushion the shock in the hardest-hit areas, in large part
because the peak of the disaster occurred in late 1966, several months
before large-scale aid operations began. Politically, however, the news
was all good. George Verghese, Gandhi's press secretary, noted that
1967 would be "remembered as a bonus year when millions of people,
especially children, probably for the first time, were assured of a decent
meal a day." World Bank officials noted a startling "change in attitude,
morale, and activity" both in the Indian government and the countryside. Rostow congratulated Johnson on "a remarkable exercise" that
brought Europe, Japan, Canada, Australia, and the World Bank into
"the food aid business" for the first time.[49]

Bihar set a pattern for future "humanitarian crises." Illuminated by
Johnson's klieg lights, famine gained a new significance in international
affairs. Cataclysms unleashed by drought or the market formerly challenged local authorities but aroused little or no high-level diplomatic response. Johnson turned them into rituals of global leadership, a substitute for the periodic superpower showdowns that once offered the only
demonstration of allied and domestic solidarity. As the National Security
Council observed, a "fully visible international sharing of the burden was

necessary to maintain America's will in the field of aid and to help offset dangerous isolationist pressures in other areas of foreign policy."[50]

Vietnam was the source of the "dangerous isolationist pressures" that took the form of growing skepticism in Congress and the public. The saga of Bihar was Johnson's antidote for the credibility gap. Although his script cast the scarcity as a natural disaster, American and Indian officials both knew it was a calculated outcome of policy choices. Counseled by MIT economists and encouraged by U.S. aid, India's government dumped cheap grain on its domestic markets and squeezed its rural sector to divert as much revenue as possible into steel mills, refineries, and aircraft plants. "We had taken the deliberate decision to put whatever investment we could afford into the industrial sector rather than into agriculture," B. K. Nehru acknowledged, but while U.S. advisers promised "we could safely count on wheat continuing in 'burdensome surplus' in the United States for quite some time," the political consensus for U.S. farm subsidies weakened in the 1960s, with disastrous consequences for Bihar. Johnson similarly cast India's rescue as a victory for American technology, while privately acknowledging that it was really a matter of political pressure. India adopted the system of domestic price supports that was no longer politically sustainable in the United States. Subsidized fertilizer, irrigation, and prices made dwarf wheat a good bet for farmers. As USAID director William Gaud explained to Congress, the "new seeds and fertilizer" were just an inducement to "make sure that these countries have their eye on the producer and rather than the consumer . . . to allocate more of their resources to agricultural development than to industrial development."[51]

In the 1970s, social scientists and official commissions produced enough studies of Asia's agricultural transformation to fill a medium-sized public library. Taken together, they added up to a mixed verdict on what they called HYVs, or high-yielding varieties of wheat and rice. HYVs put more calories in Asian diets but contained fewer vitamins. Yields doubled in the first years, but diminished thereafter. Incomes increased, but so did unemployment. In good years harvests could be colossal, but in years of drought or blight the HYVs wilted faster. While this picture of complex trade-offs developed in the specialized literature, a more consequential narrative took root in the press and public memory. The green revolution legend, embellished after 1970, owes much to Johnson's imagineering. In this version the late 1960s witnessed a historic turnaround in Asia's food supply. The new seeds allowed food production in India and Pakistan to rise faster than population growth, preventing an imminent famine, and saving "literally millions of lives." This simpler and more satisfying account rests on a claim—Johnson's claim—that India actually had a close brush with its Malthusian limit in 1966. It has become the basis for a growing consensus that India's experience should be repeated.[52]

9

THE CONQUEST OF HUNGER

By February 1968 all indicators pointed to a record year. With mild weather and good rains across much of the country, India's food ministry expected all crops to come in sharply above the previous year and modestly above the 1964–1965 high. Prime Minister Indira Gandhi assured legislators there was "no doubt that a substantial breakthrough has been achieved in the field of agricultural production by the use of improved techniques." Rural incomes were expected to recover to predrought levels, and a small surplus might relieve price inflation in the cities. When April and May figures for the Ganges regions were posted the ministry upped its forecast, predicting a final tally to exceed the record by 6 million tons. But no one was prepared in early June for the tidal wave of wheat that surged out of the Punjab.[1]

In Washington, State Department officers read the India wires with growing disbelief. "Unprecedentedly large 1968 wheat crop moving rapidly to market is straining facilities," the embassy cabled. In several areas quantities were "five times level previous year." Railways ran out of freight cars, and the government began filling school buildings, sugar mills, and theaters with grain. Headlines in the Calcutta newspapers proclaimed a "Wheat Deluge." Laborers at government granaries went on strike, leaving tens of thousands of bags on railway platforms and roadsides at the mercy of rain and rats. The turnaround was even more dramatic across the border in Pakistan. Two million acres of dwarf "Mexi-Pak" wheat generated a 47 percent yield increase in West Pakistan, while IR-8 produced a rice surplus worth $35 million. The regime had scrapped its industrial plans after the 1965 war and staked its development on the new grain technologies. Mohammad Ayub Khan, a Sandhurst-trained officer who overthrew the elected government with Washington's support, invited Norman Borlaug to Pakistan to share in the triumph. "The Pakistani

232

farmers are discarding their traditional ways and accepting the new," Borlaug wrote from Lahore. "Abundance has displaced hunger and enthusiasm is banishing despair."[2]

Turkey and the Philippines also reported phenomenal increases. The very scale of the triumph aroused doubt. Yields of nearly every crop—cotton, tea, jute—were at record levels, and not just in countries where the United States had been pushing for change. Plentiful harvests were coming in everywhere, from communist China to Canada, pushing world grain prices to the lowest level in a generation. Experts who had been warning of inevitable famine now spoke of an epoch-making change. The 6 percent increase in food production throughout the developing world would generate savings and employment, breathing room for reform, and perhaps enable India to leap into the first rank of industrial powers. The Food and Agriculture Organization (FAO) reported the "world food and agriculture situation is now in a stage of transition and hope."[3]

William S. Gaud, director of the U.S. Agency for International Development (USAID), gave the milestone its name. Speaking on March 8 before the Society for International Development, he hailed a "green revolution" sweeping across Asia. The label lent an artificial coherence to two decades of fragmented and often conflicting efforts to improve agriculture in the non-Western world. "It is an assertive expression," noted British economist T. J. Byres, "It carries with it implications that there has been a major breakthrough . . . that this has been achieved by peaceful and 'democratic' means; and that a 'red revolution' has been unnecessary or has been averted." This was exactly the message the Johnson administration wanted Congress and American allies abroad to hear. In Saigon, Freeman congratulated South Vietnamese leaders on the sudden abundance winning hearts and minds in the countryside. The alterations in the world food picture were "almost beyond belief," Lester Brown acknowledged, but the political and cultural ramifications were vastly more important. Rural Asia was on the verge of a powerful and "essentially irreversible" transformation.[4]

The harvest of 1968 provided a necessary moment of culmination, a juncture at which the forward-looking project of rationalizing and planning rural development gave way to the retrospective work of analyzing and reducing it to lessons. Within the next two years, the controversies, setbacks, and conflicting ambitions of three decades would be reduced in memory to a single event: the green revolution. Pronounced a success, it came to exemplify the triumph of science over environmental limits. The green revolution became a model, a formula, and fifteen years later when a food crisis arose in Africa, it would emblemize a preference for technological solutions. Meanwhile, the struggles and political maneuvers that had led to the transformation in Asia, and which might have contained valuable lessons, would largely be forgotten.

The Basic Needs Paradigm

Foundation officials felt the payoff for a half century of effort had finally arrived. A Rockefeller symposium marking "the conquest of hunger" concluded that recent events had "finally provided vivid proof" of a workable strategy. High-yielding varieties had altered expectations across Asia. There was an evident shift "of political initiative from urban elites to rural spokesmen" who would sustain the revolution's momentum. When Congress held its first hearings on the green revolution the following year the mood was triumphant. A packed audience sporting green ties and ribbons listened to Rep. Clement Zablocki praise "the greatest success story of foreign aid since the Marshall Plan." The room was then darkened for a film, *A Future for Ram,* depicting an Indian boy whose family overcame cultural and bureaucratic obstacles to reap a harvest of dwarf wheat. "This phenomenon—the green revolution—has opened a new era," Harrar announced. "What the green revolution has done that is so important is to change attitudes, to provide hope, to point the way for even more rewarding advances in the future."[5]

To American observers, the miracle harvest appeared to alter the moral climate of the developing countries. Aid officials noted signs of new prosperity: motorbikes and sewing machines for sale in village markets, dowries of fertilizer exchanged at weddings. "The real revolution," the Rockefeller Foundation explained, "is one that has happened, not to farming, but to farmers." The dwarf varieties themselves, many studies found, generated less of the increase than new price structures, credit, rural institutions, and energy subsidies, but the seeds created a psychology that sustained these inputs. Just as Borlaug had predicted, the seeds were a catalyst for government action. Price policies deserved "primary credit" for the transformation, Gaud agreed. They not only created new incentives to produce but also shifted wealth and political power from city to country, giving peasants a sense of empowerment. "As the mold of tradition is broken, farmers become more susceptible to change in other areas," Brown explained. New innovations drew them into the mainstream of modern life, making them "more interested in education, more receptive to family planning. The economic and political relationship between farmers and the rest of the economy begins to change fundamentally." The metamorphosis would percolate upward, Gaud told Congress, affecting politics at the national and even international level: "you just can't tell what's going to happen."[6]

In India the turnaround was less apparent. Sudden abundance created as much anxiety as scarcity had. Fearing a price collapse, farmers had rushed their stocks to market but the government, resisting temptation to lower support prices, gathered the entire surplus into government warehouses. The portions of rice and chappati in the tiffins of hungry workers stayed the same. Industrial employment remained stagnant; railway and jute mill workers struck for higher wages. Even the benefits to farmers seemed unclear. Despite high procurement prices, the *Times of India* estimated that after subtracting the cost of fertilizer, pesticide, seed, and higher rents, Uttar Pradesh farmers earned 11 rupees per quintal less with Mexican wheat. In July Gandhi unveiled a postage stamp commemorating the "Wheat Revolution of 1968." It featured a graph illustrating the dramatic 38 percent increase superimposed over an image of the Pusa institute where the dwarf seeds were introduced. But the press remained skeptical. A cartoonist for the *Hindustan Times* proposed an alternate stamp showing a rat feasting on a government grain stockpile. The watershed so obvious at the global level, where food supplies were measured in tonnages and gross national product (GNP), was nearly invisible in the markets of Bombay or Calcutta or on the charcoal stoves where most Indians prepared their meals. The Central Intelligence Agency (CIA) observed that more wheat and fewer lentils and other vegetables might have "actually reduced the quality of the Indian diet."[7]

The news that India would still import millions of tons of Public Law (P.L.) 480 wheat despite the breakthrough confirmed the sense that not much had changed. Even with a 15 percent reduction in wheat acreage, U.S. farm subsidies generated a 400 million bushel surplus that Johnson needed to unload to hold domestic prices above $1.50 a bushel. It fell to Freeman to find a market. Although he knew dumping would undo much of what short-tether had accomplished, he knew "the only place to sell additional supplies is India." After some arm-twisting, New Delhi agreed to accept it. Exposing as it did the real motives behind P.L. 480, *Blitz* scoffed, this gift "must provoke laughter." Still, India now had a buffer stock to manage for the first time since 1955, and the ministry was building granaries to store the rising surplus. With the food crisis over, Gandhi restored the planning regime, reinstating controls on private and foreign business and introducing a new five-year plan. The 1966 liberalization, she maintained, had been a detour. "Those who have been opposed to planning saw their opportunity in this crisis to attack the very existence of planning." Now, "one of our basic tasks is to tap the resources accruing in the rural sector."[8]

The green revolution reinvigorated an international aid community paralyzed by donor fatigue. When Gunnar Myrdal's long-awaited study *Asian Drama* appeared in 1968, it expressed a pervasive frustration with the results of the development effort thus far. Plans had been put into place, GNP targets had been met, but poverty was just as prevalent as ever. The certainty that Western economics held the answers had been shaken. He urged a return to fundamentals, especially agriculture, "the main determinant of national levels of income and living." U.S. officials seemed particularly glad to leave behind the abstractions of takeoff and savings ratios and talk finally about tools and results. "It is no longer just a theory," Dean Rusk told the Senate, "we know that food production can be rapidly increased through the use of new seeds and more fertilizer." USAID increased funding for agriculture by 40 percent. In October 1968 the World Bank announced that it would double its loan outlays. "The splendid harvests in India and Pakistan," the bank's new president Robert McNamara declared, had dispelled an institutionalized confusion "in which it was difficult to see what had gone wrong in the past (though something clearly had) or what was the right path ahead of us." The "task now is to help the peasant make the most of this opportunity."[9]

Experts felt they were witnessing a tectonic realignment of economic forces, a "pronounced shift" the State Department's intelligence unit called it, in "Asia's food/population ratio." The problem of scarcity, the central preoccupation of development economists for more than a decade, had simply vanished leaving aid organizations to adjust to a new reality. A gathering at Oxford of leading experts, including Colin Clark, Lester Brown, and Robert Chandler, concluded that the Third World had entered a phase of surplus production analogous to the situation of the United States in the 1920s, with a possible depression and the associated upheavals immediately ahead. "We have been forced to redefine the population problem; now we worry more about idle arms than hungry mouths," an FAO official observed. Modernizers now had to move "beyond sheer physical food production to income distribution and jobs. It could be an agricultural revolution of the same magnitude as transformed Europe at the end of the eighteenth century, but the social disorganization could be so large scale as to make it impossible to realize the new production possibilities." Led by the World Bank, multilateral agencies reoriented development strategy toward social, rather than structural deficits. Under an emerging paradigm, "basic needs," including education, health care, and food, took the place of planning and industry at the head of the list of aid priorities.[10]

Despite their enthusiasm, national and multilateral agencies still had made no long-term commitment to wheat or rice research, and their attention seemed to be drifting toward other agendas. Ford and Rockefeller field offices reported that visiting delegations were sending back reports exaggerating the breakthrough. New seeds still accounted for only about 20 tons of the Asian surplus, they worried "rhetorical overkill" might lead big donors to conclude that the food problem had been solved. Seizing their moment, foundation officials convened an international summit at the Rockefeller villa at Bellagio, Italy.[11]

On the shores of Lake Como on the last weekend in April 1969, green revolution veterans, including Harrar and Chandler, who had been with the project since the 1940s, sat across the table from the heads of the richest donor organizations: McNamara from the World Bank; Addeke Boerma of the FAO; John Hannah, director of USAID; and aid ministers from a dozen countries. Following their long-standing practice of gestating ideas and then passing them to governments, the foundations wanted to get out of the business of scientific agriculture and shift permanent budget responsibility for the International Rice Research Institute (IRRI), the Mexico program, and other research ventures—more than $2 million per year—onto the ample accounts of national and multilateral donors. Frosty Hill explained that in India new wheat varieties were in such demand that laboratories had to post guards around their experimental plots. Rising farm incomes were creating demand for industrial and consumer goods, spurring record rates of growth in all sectors of the poorest economies. Over dinner and on walks in the lakeside gardens, the donors heard stories of the early days in Mexico and the stunning discovery of the dwarf varieties. They were eager to own a piece of success. Hannah promised to match any contributions that came forward from other agencies. Canada offered to underwrite continuing costs. After two days, the outlines of a plan for institutionalizing the green revolution emerged. The World Bank would administer three existing research stations in Mexico, the Philippines, and Colombia, and a new one in Nigeria, through an umbrella organization, later called the Consultative Group on International Agricultural Research (CGIAR). The Rockefeller Foundation proposed a fifth institute, for population control, but it found no support.[12]

The arrangement made the green revolution a going concern, but it also changed the way multilateral donors did business. Up to this point the World Bank had been lender of last resort to national treasuries. "Basic needs" gave it a more expansive mandate, giving it guardianship over the 40 percent of the developing world living in "absolute poverty." The assertion that all people were entitled to minimum requirements of safe drinking water, clothing, living space, and calories justified interventions that bypassed local and national authorities. Its budget and staff grew accordingly. McNamara doubled the volume of lending, with the share going to agriculture increasing fourfold. An augmented professional staff supervised programs for subsistence farmers. Formerly, multilateral aid had increased the power of central governments, which disbursed funds and set priorities. The bank and other donors now began to establish parallel infrastructures within recipient countries, directly administering aid to schools, researchers, and farm organizations, and weakening the dirigiste state. This was a significant revision of the developmental bargain, but the shocks of the previous few years, from famine to glut, sapped the confidence of national planners while raising international experts to new heights of prestige.[13]

The sudden reprieve from an Asian famine even inspired visions of a comprehensive, global solution to the problems of hunger and underdevelopment. To the FAO, the second largest multilateral donor in 1969, the turnaround provided a momentary opportunity for radically restructuring the global food market, a scheme elaborated in an eight-volume study grandly titled the *Indicative World Plan* (IWP). It called for industrial countries to phase out farm subsidies, inducing a wholesale shift in food production from the developed to the underdeveloped world. Africa, Asia, and Latin America would regain their prewar role as the world's breadbaskets, and an export-led agricultural boom would permanently redress the food/population imbalance. Reaction was positive in the developing countries, but in Europe and the United States, where key rural constituencies relied on subsidies, it hit a stone wall. The Nixon administration, alarmed by a growing U.S. trade imbalance and eager to add to Republican gains in the farm states, buried the IWP and encouraged American farmers to plant "fencerow to fencerow."[14]

Richard Nixon perceived the green revolution as a geopolitical rather than a developmental victory. He praised the "miracle seeds" in one of his first addresses to Congress, using them to justify a sharp reduction in the scale and ambitions of foreign aid. The "dramatic breakthrough in food production" had shown what could happen when "private investment and domestic resources in developing countries join together." Steering aid away from planning commissions and governments, he pushed U.S. corporations to take the lead with the help of a new agency, the Overseas Private Investment Corporation. The bumper harvests confirmed a growing sense in Washington that despite the continuing agony of Vietnam, Asia as a whole had turned a corner. Under the firm hand of developmental populists—Suharto, Ferdinand Marcos, Indira Gandhi, and Ayub Khan—the region was stable and prospering. India's central government was firmly in control. Indonesia and the Philippines had quelled their rural uprisings, and with China preoccupied by internal troubles the United States could turn its attention to other continents and other crises. "Not many years ago, it seemed all too likely that a militant, aggressive totalitarianism might well be the wave of the future in East Asia," Secretary of State William Rogers told reporters, "Yet that seemingly irresistible tide turned out to be resistible, and a quite different future is now in prospect."[15]

Pandora's Box

The first indication that the green revolution might ignite the kind of class warfare that accompanied other revolutions came in a December 1968 *New York Times* report from a model village outside of Madras, where a mob burned twenty-eight women to death. It was a small item, less than an inch of type, but at the IRRI compound in Los Baños it was read as a disturbing portent. In the course of a feud over proceeds from a crop of IR-8, landlords had taken up weapons, surrounded a hamlet, and set it afire. The scientists' forebodings became more tangible in March 1969 when Pakistan's government collapsed amid a wave of rioting. Just a year earlier, when Ayub Khan turned a golden spigot at the Indus River dams, the largest irrigation scheme in the world, he had seemed unshakable. The international aid community hailed him as a visionary who led Pakistan into a new era of prosperity and self-confidence. Now, in the wake of the first irrigated harvests, tenant farmers declared jihad. Food price hikes enflamed the cities. Students and striking workers unfurled red banners and battled with police. Barely escaping assassination, Ayub yielded power. "Pakistan's fate will certainly have a numbing effect on the world's general approach to development," the *Washington Post* predicted. In Lahore, Borlaug watched as a mob surrounded and then burned a clinic that dispensed smallpox vaccinations and birth control. When Ford Foundation officials urged him to calm the situation by endorsing a reduction in the official price of wheat, he refused. Betraying the farmers, he said, would "blow the lid off" of the countryside.[16]

Experts realized they could no longer control the social catalyst they had worked for decades to create. USAID reported that the dwarf varieties were altering the rhythms of village life in the Punjab, stimulating an exodus of landless laborers into Indian cities. There was little that could be done to stop it, the report concluded, because "these technical changes are 'beyond' public policy in so far as policy is able to exercise a veto, or even much of a brake, upon their spread." The Agriculture Department noted that the "uneven impact of technological change" could have "disastrous" consequences. If early adopters, already the more privileged segment of rural society, squeezed out marginal and subsistence producers, there would be "massive problems of welfare and equity," warned Clifton Wharton, a Rockefeller economist. The green revolution had opened a "pandora's box."[17]

Within weeks of Bellagio, World Bank and FAO officials voiced concerns about growing civil unrest. Pakistan's crisis would worsen if record harvests in West Pakistan alienated the undernourished East and accelerated the breakup of the country. Writing in *The Statesman,* Inder Malhotra urged India to take "a second look at the new agricultural strategy which tends to favor the rich and adds to the social tensions in the village." In the Philippines, a Maoist insurgency spread through the paddy fields freshly planted with IR-8. Rebels calling themselves the New People's Army met just twenty miles from IRRI in March 1969 and declared war on the government. They proclaimed their intention to capitalize on rural resentments to "develop the revolutionary forces in the countryside" before encircling the cities. To gauge what seemed to be a mounting danger, the World Bank sent Wolf Ladejinsky to the Punjab. Meanwhile, USAID commissioned Francine Frankel, a young University of Chicago political scientist to investigate the links between the high-yield varieties and the growing disturbances. The two reports, appearing nearly simultaneously in the Indian newspapers in late 1969, shifted the debate from food to equity.[18]

The studies agreed that the new technologies intensified class tensions. Income for a fortunate few with large, irrigated tracts grew substantially, but the overwhelming majority who tilled less than two acres—75 to 80 percent of peasants—watched their situation deteriorate in relative or absolute terms. Moreover, the new technologies disrupted the social cohesion of the village, breaking bonds of obligation and kinship that acted as a steam valve in difficult times. This "politically explosive situation," explained the *Times of India,* was ripe for demagogues hoping "to transform the economic polarization into open confrontation between the minority of prosperous landowners and the great majority of sharecroppers and landless labour." In the aid community, the early optimism gave way to anxiety that the revolution was turning red. FAO Secretary Addeke Boerma warned the 1970 World Food Conference against the risks of transferring technology without extensive social preparation. Unless carefully managed, the green revolution would unleash "a conflagration of violence that would sweep through millions of lives."[19]

Urgent and impressionistic reports circulated through government, foundation, and academic offices highlighted three "second generation effects": class conflict, urbanization, and political backlash. Although some studies indicated that even the landless gained from the new arrangements, they stressed that perceptions of inequity coupled with a growing consciousness of rural power fueled the violence. Early reports highlighted the emergence of a class of gentleman farmers—transplanted urbanites, military veterans, and civil servants—sinking their savings into the newly profitable wheat and rice sectors. Systematic surveys estimated these "bullock capitalists" comprised less than 3 percent of proprietors, but they symbolized a change in ownership patterns unfolding across the wheat districts. The influx of cash allowed fortunate farmers to consolidate small plots into larger holdings, producing what some observers called a land reform in reverse. They aggressively exploited ground water, forcing their neighbors to dig deeper wells to keep up. Land values jumped to triple pre-1968 levels, and landlords were charging up to 70 percent of the crop in rent. This kulak class embraced technology, employing the latest seeds and chemicals and even buying equity shares in fertilizer firms. They introduced brazenly acquisitive values to rural life and work, demanding tractors and tubewells as marriage dowries and enforcing strictly contractual relations with tenants. "With us," a novice farmer in Gujarat told Daniel Thorner, "agriculture is an industry." Divisions of caste and faction widened as the marginalized voiced their grievances through peasant unions and splinter parties. Swaminathan hoped that farmers' agitation over "politics and their place in society" would make government more attentive, but the U.S. embassy noted that the stirrings in the countryside made the technologies seem "economically sensible but politically dangerous."[20]

A more pressing danger seemed to be multiplying in Asian cities. The "liberation" of surplus rural labor had been an explicit goal of rural development from the outset. In the 1940s, Rockefeller Foundation officials set their sights on an "industrial revolution of agriculture, whereby agricultural personnel are taken off the land and put to work in factories to make farm machinery, as presently occurring in America." Economists, both structuralist and Rostovian, used urbanization as a rough index of modernization. As late as 1968, Samuel Huntington could admire the "urban slum [as] a gateway to a new and better way of life." But the annual pattern of urban explosions after Watts led the foundations to reconsider the city's place at the top end of the developmental ladder. The Ford Foundation initiated a "gray areas program" to bring Indian-style community development to inner-city neighborhoods. Shortly after the Washington riots in 1968, Rockefeller staffers in New Delhi learned that the home office, "concerned with the growing national disorder in the U.S.," was seeking ideas for "improving the attractiveness of rural areas so as to siphon some of the population away" from American cities.[21]

The green revolution drew attention to the magnitude of the migration from the Asian countryside. The International Labor Office warned that even the fastest-growing economies could not absorb more than a fraction of the refugees. McNamara expressed alarm at "the scale of social displacement and the general uprootedness of populations which are exploding not only in numbers but in movement as well." By 1970 Mexico City, Bombay, Calcutta, and Saigon were surpassing the largest U.S. cities in size, with Bangkok and Manila close behind, achieving densities that seemed to risk social breakdown. Henry Kissinger's national security aides warned that "the great influx into large cities is aggravating the natural obstacles to individual advancement" and heightening social conflict. A United Nations (UN) report noted that, by 1970, the development community had come to regard "cities as the symbol of failure."[22]

The political costs of these dislocations fell hardest on regimes that fostered development. Ayub Khan, who cultivated dwarf wheat in the presidential gardens, was replaced by the ruthless and unimaginative Yahya Kahn, "a brutal bastard," in Borlaug's estimation. Domestic opponents of Marcos and Gandhi stoked resentment among peasants and urban consumers. The crushing defeat of Prime Minister Dudley Senanayake in Ceylon's May 1970 elections revealed what kind of gamble the green revolution's promoters had made. Senanayake had staked his political future on a plan for self-sufficiency in rice. More than half the country's supply came from abroad, much of it from China, and the foreign exchange fund was exhausted by subsistence allotments provided to each citizen. In 1968 IRRI and Ford Foundation experts advised "drastic action"—IR-8, irrigation, and higher market prices—to close the food gap. Senanayake responded boldly, pouring money into rice breeding and cash incentives, and mobilizing a "land army" of unemployed youth to work idle fields. Oxfam distributed IR-8 across the country. Claiming a "modest success story" in Ceylon would have positive effects in Congress and the region, USAID pledged to provide the necessary fertilizer and the pesticide DDT. The World Bank and the UN Development Program bankrolled dams that diverted the country's largest river, the Mahaveli, to irrigate half a million acres.[23]

Weather and disease turned the tables, and advisers were soon scrambling to salvage the program from public scandal. Leaf blight ravaged IR-8 across the equatorial lowlands, and local scientists criticized IRRI experts for ignoring clear warnings. "Rice is a sensitive issue in Ceylon," a Ford official reported. "I was astonished to find varieties critically discussed in from page articles of the English papers." By March 1969 the foundation recognized that it had "clearly got problems in Ceylon." Substituting local short-strawed varieties, the agronomists got back on schedule, confidently predicting a 1970 harvest of 70 million bushels. But in January, torrential rains hit the rice-growing provinces, washing out the unfinished irrigation works and submerging the dwarf plants. Ten weeks before the elections, the entire plan was in ruins.[24]

The United States did what it could to rescue Senanayake. Anxious to prevent a return to power by Srimavo Bandaranaike, who had courted China and nationalized American-owned refineries in the early 1960s, Nixon poured in emergency aid. High-profile visits by the U.S. hospital ship *Hope* and Apollo astronauts fresh from moon orbit burnished Senanayake's technocratic image, but Bandaranaike kept the focus on the disaster of self-sufficiency. "We will give you two measures of rice," she promised enthusiastic crowds, "we will bring it even from the moon." The State Department predicted on May 25 that Senanayake would hold on to a bare majority, but the outcome, announced three days later, left his party with just 10 percent of the seats. It was, the *New York Times* estimated, "as staggering a repudiation as any political party in any democratic country has suffered in recent years." A defeat, too, for the green revolution. As Bandaranaike observed derisively after her victory, "rice must be grown in paddy fields and not on paper."[25]

Green revolution regimes that did survive did so through repression. Citing the "spreading lawlessness and anarchy throughout the land," Marcos arrested legislators and journalists and declared martial law in September 1972. The following May he launched Masagana 99, a nationwide system of rural cooperatives that encouraged high-yield techniques while monitoring peasant activities. Gandhi imposed a state of emergency in June 1975 in response to "the deep and widespread conspiracy which as been brewing ever since I began to introduce certain progressive measures of benefit to the common man and woman of India." An estimated 36,000 people suffered imprisonment without trial. Autocratic states used food production drives—often organized by the army and given operational names—to mobilize populations and regiment rural economies. At each link on the commodity chain, officials and their cronies skimmed a share of the profits; in Thailand the officer corps owned the fertilizer concession. In Indonesia, generals ran a state trading firm that acted as middleman, steering earnings into army coffers. Suharto's New Order food drive employed a form of armed propaganda, "mass guidance," which disseminated and enforced the new techniques. Throughout South and Southeast Asia, the green revolution would be linked in memory with dictatorship and military corruption.[26]

The legacies of the new strategy were still being debated when Norway's parliament announced that it would award Borlaug the Nobel Peace Prize for creating "a new world situation with regard to nutrition." In much of the world, the choice of Aleksandr Solzhenitsyn for the literature award captured more headlines. On October 20, 1970, Indian newspapers were preoccupied with exposés linking the Ford and Rockefeller foundations to the CIA, and Mexico was in mourning over the death of Lázaro Cárdenas. But the aid community and small-town newspapers across the United States paid tribute to the first peace laureate from Iowa. "We're witnessing an historic change," noted the Syracuse *Herald-Journal*. "The miracle grains . . . promise the gradual elimination of chronic hunger." Many editorials acknowledged the risks of social dislocation and unrest. "We're not sure what it has to do with peace," the LaCrosse *Tribune* admitted, but "an unfamous man has been recognized

244

for helping his fellow man, and we're glad to see him get the honor." The news was received with satisfaction at Rockefeller Center and World Bank headquarters. In Rome the FAO hailed the man who "pushed back the frontiers of hunger."[27]

The call from Oslo came though at seven in the morning, and Margaret Borlaug went to find Norman already at work in a test field at Chapingo. He finished out the afternoon's experiments before driving to his office to take congratulatory phone calls. McGeorge Bundy, president of the Ford Foundation, told him it showed "what a first rate man of science can do for the rest of the species." Foundation officials knew they would never have another breakthrough like 1968. The combination of the near brush with famine and the arrival of the miracle seeds captivated the world, but there were no more "big jump" innovations awaiting release. Advances from now on would come at a measured, less theatrical pace. The peace prize offered a rare chance to shape the historical meaning of what they had achieved, and Borlaug seized it. He was quick to acknowledge that he was only one of "an army of hunger fighters," but he nonetheless became the face of the movement and its principal spokesman. In his characteristic voice, impatient and overwrought, he framed a parable that had profound and ultimately damaging consequences for the green revolution.[28]

Rural development had been fraught with political conflict and violence for the previous thirty years, but in his acceptance address in Oslo, Borlaug portrayed a steady, single-minded movement of organizations, officials, "thousands of scientists and millions of farmers." Taking his listeners from the Neolithic revolution to the present, he posed the history of civilization as an unbroken struggle between "two opposing forces, the scientific power of food production and the biologic power of human reproduction." Neither the Cold War nor the arms race posed a comparable threat. Dwarf varieties stimulated a dramatic increase in agricultural productivity throughout the developing world, but their real achievement was in refocusing the attention of a distracted world on this precarious balance. Few understood "the magnitude and the menace of the population monster," Borlaug continued. If left unchecked, world population would reach 6.5 billion by 2000, leading to "the grotesque concentration of human beings into the poisoned and clangorous environment of pathologically hypertrophied metropoles." The green revolution offered only a temporary respite, a "breathing space" of thirty years in which to mobilize a global campaign to curb human fertility.[29]

245

Population control had gained respectability over the previous decade, but it remained a flash point for controversy. Borlaug's remarks were soon deployed against Pope Paul VI and others who raised moral or health objections to artificial fertility control on a mass scale. The disastrous rate of female mortality and morbidity in the developing world from sterilization using intrauterine devices and the contraceptive injection Depo Provera was beginning to become apparent, but Borlaug's urgency sanctioned even coercive measures. The association between dwarf seeds and population control was so explicit that in country after country rumors alleged that the new rice and wheat induced infertility. "If only that were true," Borlaug responded. "We would really merit the Nobel Peace Prize."[30]

Less than a year later, he took on a second hot-button issue by denouncing the international effort to ban DDT. In the decade since Rachel Carson's exposé *Silent Spring,* harmful effects of residual pesticides had galvanized a global environmental movement. Scientists had linked chemical compounds to the near extinction of bald eagles. DDT was found in human milk. Mosquitoes and locusts developed resistance, while bees and other pollinating insects vital to plant and human health were decimated. An estimated 10 million Americans turned out on Earth Day, April 22, 1970, to protest against air and water pollution and DDT. The Nixon administration supported total prohibition. Legislation was before the Senate, and a European commission was also contemplating a ban.[31]

Isolated from public affairs for three decades in his Mexican field station, Borlaug badly misjudged both how firmly established the ecology movement had become and the extent of its demands. He believed American and European action would be a prelude to a worldwide ban not just on DDT but on all agricultural chemicals, including fungicides and fertilizers essential to high-yield agriculture. Choosing the prestigious McDougall Lecture before representatives of 160 FAO member nations in Rome, he opened an attack on the global environmental movement. He denounced opponents of DDT as "the shrill, demanding, disharmonious, tri-tonal voices of the privileged." They were "social drop outs, social parasites in reality," who cherished natural scenery viewed mainly from car windows. Offering no analysis of the scientific case against DDT, he argued that risks to animals were morally insignificant next to the needs of hungry humans. His claims aroused an immediate reaction from the head of the European Community's agriculture commission. "I am one of those hysterical environmentalists Dr. Borlaug talked about," Sicco Mansholt replied. "I am very concerned . . . about building up our food supplies in the world on the basis of such huge quantities of poison."[32]

Undeterred, Borlaug continued his attack in hearings at the Environmental Protection Agency and at a press conference organized by Montrose Chemical, the world's largest manufacturer of DDT. "If most DDT uses are cancelled," he told reporters, "I have wasted my life's work." His alliance with the chemical lobby and the tone of his remarks led the editors of the *New York Times* to conclude that "this sadly misinformed Nobel laureate" had lost credibility. "Notwithstanding his prominence in other fields, his views on this subject must now be seriously discounted." Ford and Rockefeller officials, who had until this point largely succeeded in dispelling any appearance of corporate self-interest, could only shake their heads. The green revolution had been admired as a victory for international science and humanitarianism, but Borlaug was explicitly tying it to chemical toxins and corporate profits. He substantiated the suspicions of critics who viewed the miracle seeds as a Trojan horse. Chilean economist Andre Gunder Frank noted that the hand of U.S. petroleum interests was visible in India's food crisis as well as the Ceylon election. The Nobel, he added, was "the bourgeoisie's reward to Borlaug" for his efforts "to contain revolution through 'peace'."[33]

Despite his apocalyptic warnings about an onrushing demographic crisis, Borlaug won little backing from advocates of population control. In fact, the most visible critics of the green revolution in the early 1970s were those who shared his Malthusian outlook but not his technological optimism. An ecological worldview had motivated Rockefeller ventures in the life sciences—including the Mexico program—since the 1930s, and Borlaug's life's work was conceived around balancing resources and consumption within closed natural systems. A widening gap between this brand of "human ecology" and a newer environmental consciousness had become apparent even before the wheat breakthrough. Rejecting an anthropocentric conservationism, "deep" ecologists accorded other species a claim to survival as valid as humanity's. They foresaw imminent crises resulting from resource exhaustion and believed that any breathing room that could be gained through technology would only make things worse. In 1968, Subramaniam gave a talk at Stanford before an audience that included a young entomologist, Paul Ehrlich, who stood in the back aghast at what he was hearing. "This man is trying to tell us that in the next eight years India is going to find a way to produce enough food to support some 12 million more people than they can feed today," he thought. "Millions of Indians will die because of government attitudes exemplified by Subramaniam."[34]

Europe produced the first spokesmen for this new sensibility. Translations of Georg Borgstrom's *Gränser för vår Tillvaro (The Limits of Our Lives)* and René Dumont's *Nous Allons à la Famine (We Go to the Famine)* appeared in the United States in the mid-1960s, before William Paddock's alarmist *Famine 1975!* and Garrett Hardin's somber postscript for humanity, "The Tragedy of the Commons." Ehrlich's *Population Bomb* drew little attention when published at the height of the 1968 harvest, but after he appeared on *The Tonight Show* with Johnny Carson in April 1970 it hit the top of the best-seller list, soon to be followed by *The Closing Circle* by Barry Commoner and *Diet for a Small Planet*, Francis Moore Lappé's appeal (with recipes) for the amelioration of scarcity through "high-protein meatless cooking." The release of the 1972 manifesto *Limits to Growth* stole front page space from Richard Nixon's visit to the Great Wall of China. The level of ecological anxiety, even among international business leaders, was apparent in the roster of the study's backers. The Volkswagen Foundation, the Japanese industrial federation, and Italian financier Aurelio Peccei joined forces in 1968 as the "Club of Rome." It funded the Massachusetts Institute of Technology (MIT) System Dynamics Group and its computer simulation, "World 3," which forecast consumption and resource trajectories for dozens of commodities. The model predicted escalating resource depletions leading to a catastrophic collapse of the global economy in the near term. Even with a doubling of food output per acre and "perfect birth control," the outer limit of survival would be reached by 2050. Green revolutions, Ehrlich emphasized, would only "delay the day of reckoning."[35]

India was at the center of each of these polemics, its recent crisis cast as a harbinger of the global future. Leaving out alternate explanations—such as the disruptive effect of P.L. 480 or the shift to export crops—they portrayed the food deficit as a Malthusian denouement, the inevitable collision between exponentially rising populations and arithmetically limited food output. A failed monsoon and two consecutive lean years in South Asia appeared to substantiate the equation. In 1972 and 1973 the energy crisis and higher petroleum prices idled India's oil-fired fertilizer plants and diesel irrigation pumps. The sudden reversal, noted the Delhi embassy, had a "great psychological impact" leading to "questioning of both the reality and future of the green revolution." The CIA passed on reports of "famine-like conditions, including price rises, local scarcities and widespread unrest" and added its own doubts, suggesting that the so-called breakthrough in 1968 had only been a lucky turn in the weather. Dire press reports rolled Soviet crop failures, the southward drift of the Sahara desert, the U.S. corn blight, and the "sputtering green revolution" into a single global calamity.[36]

Indian officials objected to being cast, once again, as exhibit A for the Malthusian case. To Gandhi's economic advisers, the drought proved that India now had a stockpile large enough to withstand even multiple crop failures. "Doubts and doubters," they maintained, should not distract the country from strengthening and spreading the green revolution. Ambassador L. K. Jha took aim at the Club of Rome's "totally non-viable" prescriptions. To developmental regimes, ecology looked like a ploy by industrial nations to kick away the ladder of growth. Brazil's ambassador to UNESCO denounced "pseudo-scientific extrapolation of a terroristic or brainwashing kind" aimed at imposing "a ceiling on the development of under-developed countries." But particularly after the oil price spikes of the late 1970s, computer extrapolations were taken seriously. Using the *Limits* methodology, President Jimmy Carter's *Global 2000* report found the green revolution left long-term trends in food output unchanged while making future gains more dependent on petroleum. Forecasting an oil peak in the 1990s, it predicted a doubling of food prices by 2000 and declining caloric intake across Asia, Africa, and the Middle East. The UN General Assembly debated whether (or even if) growth could be achieved in a world of diminishing resources. The ensuing deadlock led to the formation of the Brundtland Commission charged with finding a way forward that was "sustainable."[37]

Keynesians recognized that deep ecology questioned the inevitability of growth, a previously unspoken axiom on which the entire project of global development rested. Robert Solow wondered how his MIT colleagues could reasonably "expect billions of Asians and Africans to live forever at roughly their standard of living while we go on forever at ours." Momentarily thrown by the intensity of the environmental critique, growthists soon rallied. At the 1974 World Population Conference in Budapest, Simon Kuznets boldly questioned the notion of a trade-off between expanding populations and the supply of goods, pointing to a longstanding historical link between fertility and economic expansion. Economists were particularly incensed by the technocratic pretension of World 3 and its definitive dot-matrix graphs. Architects of systems models for national economic planning took the lead in denouncing the doomsday models, which applied the same techniques but on a global scale. Henry Wallich, adviser to the Dominican Republic and Puerto Rico and soon to be governor of the Federal Reserve, called the scenarios "irresponsible nonsense" made plausible only by fetishizing statistics and the computer.[38]

The most strident counterattack came from Julian Simon, a University of Illinois economist whose previous work supported population control by modeling family size in rural societies. After seeing Ehrlich on television, he constructed a simulation of the effects of fertility variation on productivity, diet, wealth distribution, irrigation, road building, and other variables. In a bluntly worded 1974 article in *Science,* he argued that the only limits to growth were the limits of ingenuity. Food supply had increased per capita over the previous twenty-five years; the crisis in world markets arose from surplus, not scarcity. Land, energy, and raw materials were all becoming more plentiful, and increased fertility stimulated demand, inventiveness, and ultimately, economic growth. Ecologists responded with outrage, accusing Simon of "disastrous naivete." The ensuing war of words evolved from a dispute about data to one about methods, and finally to attacks on each other's rhetoric. Finally, in 1981 Simon offered to wager that resource prices would drop over time. Ehrlich and two other ecologists wrote up a contract to formalize the bet "before other greedy people jump in." They agreed to pay a thousand dollars if natural resources actually became scarcer by 1990. The price of five metals—chromium, copper, nickel, tin, and tungsten—would serve as an index of whether the earth's resources were running out. It was possibly the only wager ever tendered on the pages of a major social science quarterly. At stake was the reputation of two disciplines and, in the participants' eyes, the destiny of humanity. They were, according to the *New York Times,* "betting the planet."[39]

Although the parlay was widely seen as a test of irreconcilable worldviews, Ehrlich recognized that ecologists and economists both represented reality as a set of universal rules and closed systems. "Economic models, like ecological models," he admitted, "are often based on utterly untenable assumptions and endowed with false precision." Experts differed only in the "themes" they chose to emphasize: growth or limits. Predicated on this common outlook, the wager reduced the political and social complexities of scarcity to a number. A wider universe of concerns—

communist expansionism, governmental weakness, peasant unrest—mobilized the campaigns against hunger in the 1950s and 1960s, but Borlaug's Nobel speech memorialized the green revolution in exclusively Malthusian terms. Since the 1970s the debate about its lessons has been carried on within the confines of this narrow and ultimately irreconcilable argument.[40]

While the bet lay on the table, other analysts were beginning to challenge its core premise, the presumed relationship between population and scarcity. Investigating recent famines in India, Biafra, and Bangladesh, economists Amartya Sen, Jean Drèze, and Rolando V. Garcia discovered that food crises were not caused by shortages of food, either within a region or in immediate localities. Starvation deaths and chronic malnutrition resulted instead from societal breakdowns—war, unemployment, repression, or gender inequality—that denied people access to food. The theory accounted for the peculiarities of the Bihar crisis, the discrepancies between aggregate forecasts and the reports from the field. Famine studies revealed that arguments based on future projections of population growth, environmental damage, growth or limits had little bearing on the very real problem of hunger in the present, which was a problem not of food supply, but of food demand. Consequently, remedies had to deal with the "economic, political, social, and—ultimately—legal arrangements that affect people's entitlement to food." While these findings ought to have stimulated a searching reconsideration of the food supply paradigm, it instead produced only a parallel interpretation limited mainly to academic studies of food crises. Sen received a Nobel economics award for discovering "the economic mechanisms underlying famines," but the century-old discourse that defined food and population as opposing variables in a global equation continued undisturbed. In 1990 Simon claimed his winnings, which Ehrlich was able to pay out of his MacArthur "genius" grant, awarded for promoting greater public understanding of environmental problems.[41]

By the mid-1970s commentators had pronounced the green revolution dead. India and the Philippines were once again relying on imported grain. Despite or perhaps because of the basic needs consensus, the CGIAR institutions lost their leading role in generating new initiatives. "We got up on a high mountain," Frosty Hill observed. "We knew we were coming down, and we did in terms of reality." Borlaug blamed "the environmental community" for killing donor enthusiasm, but the resistance

251

came more from farmers and governments unable to afford the higher cost of fuel, fertilizer, irrigation, and other inputs amid the global downturn of the 1970s. High-yielding varieties spread over 35 percent of Asia's total wheat area and 20 percent of its rice area, but then came to a halt with the 1973 energy crisis. "It's said that if build a better mousetrap people will beat a path to your doorstep," Harrar complained. "We built a better mousetrap but people didn't come."[42]

The aid community followed through on the Bellagio pledge. In 1972 the newest research institute, the International Institute for Tropical Agriculture (IITA), opened on a sprawling campus in Ibadan, seventy miles from the Nigerian capital. Larger and better funded than IRRI, it boasted a $3 million starting budget and a suburb of ranch-style homes "that would resemble an upper-class Connecticut town were it not for the palm trees." It soon introduced new varieties of cowpeas, cassava, and sorghum. African countries joined the global trend toward state-supported intensification. In the early 1970s Rhodesia introduced short-photoperiod maize hybrids to replace tobacco, an export crop that was losing value in world markets, and following the change of government, Zimbabwe reoriented rural credit, research, and extension services to serve majority farmers. By the mid-1980s the country's granaries were unable to handle the surplus. In 1979 Ahmadou Ahidjo's government launched a "green revolution" to break Cameroon's reliance on low-value coffee and cocoa exports by shifting to cotton, tea, and rubber. Kenyan smallholders rushed to adopt tube wells and new high-yielding Kitale maize. Aid agencies financed imports of chemical fertilizer. IITA's high-yield fungus resistant variety transformed cassava into Africa's second most important food crop with Nigeria as the principal producer. Under McNamara, the World Bank supported agricultural intensification. The Brundtland formula left enough ambiguity to reconcile environmental and pro-growth agendas. "Sustainable" and "technologically appropriate" became the new watchwords. Governments responded by launching their own rural revitalization drives.[43]

But a combination of détente and disillusionment drained the energy from the movement. The battle against hunger shared in a more fundamental crisis affecting the entire project of global development: the slow dissolving of a political worldview in which the destiny of superpowers would be decided in the rice paddies of Asia. Then, in the 1980s, a new crisis and a new developmental ideology pinched back Africa's budding green revolution.[44]

Is It Development?

The domestic consensus behind development had always rested on a jury-rigged alliance of self-interest, strategic anxiety, and faith in the unique capacity of the United States to engineer progress. The faith gave way first. Slow defeat in Vietnam and a depreciated dollar strained confidence in America's role as torchbearer. In 1969 the Cuyahoga, an oily brown river flowing through Cleveland to Lake Erie, caught fire, incinerating two railroad bridges. American rivers, including the Merrimack and Concord beloved of Thoreau, foamed with industrial and pesticide wastes. Contaminated landscapes silently posed the question of whether development was worth the cost. The U.S. standard of living, whose uninterrupted rise once validated Washington's mastery of the arts of growth, staggered and then fell back under the pressure of war-induced inflation and unemployment, while the annual festival of urban rioting offered a recurring disproof of America's claim to social advancement. Harrar acknowledged in 1968 that interference in primitive societies could no longer be justified "in terms of what we have done to ourselves." Startling revelations of the severity of domestic poverty even discredited U.S. claims to competence in the area of basic needs. Leading a delegation to Mississippi in early 1968 to investigate segregation, Senator Robert Kennedy found himself instead answering appeals for food. Witnesses, who had come to testify on rights violations, admitted they were living on a diet of turnips. A subsequent nationwide investigation uncovered the extent of "acute hunger and malnutrition" in the world's best-fed country. The Senate heard testimony that between 4 and 10 million Americans might be malnourished, and investigators found children suffering from distended bellies, emaciation, and symptoms of kwashiorkor and other "tropical" deficiency diseases in the Bronx, Des Moines, and the Mississippi Delta. There was no need to go to Asia to find disturbing images of starvation, one report observed; "if you will go look, you will find America is a shocking place."[45]

It was a truism for Kennedy and Johnson advisers that development and security went hand in hand, but the link seemed less tenable in 1968 as police battled rioters on the shopping boulevards of Paris, Berlin, and Chicago. The incoming administration was openly skeptical of the strategic argument for modernization. Henry Kissinger opened his first position paper for the Nixon campaign with an attack on core Rostovian assumptions: that stability would follow prosperity, that communism's

253

appeal lay in its guarantee of material progress, and that modern systems and habits could be transferred at all. The social forms of the West, Kissinger argued, arose from a unique history from the ancient Greeks to the Enlightenment, an initiation "which cannot be duplicated elsewhere." The very attempt to transplant technologies, he argued, was fraught with danger, introducing disruptive elements into settings without stabilizing institutions or codes of behavior. But even if the United States had the ability to transform societies, it would make no difference to the Cold War. Communism remained a potent source of identity and authority even though its economic formula had patently failed. It was a mistake, he concluded, to compete on an economic plane, pitting aid handouts against utopian fantasies. Development was a hollow strategy, offering "a procedure for change but little content for it."[46]

Despite, or perhaps because of recent victories, even graver doubts plagued the corps of specialists who called themselves the "development community." The stated goal for the United Nations Development Decade had been a 5 percent rise in GNP by the end of 1969. India's last-minute rally put it over the mark, and the developing countries as a group also beat it by a slim margin. Even so, the Third World passed this milestone without the anticipated momentum, the "takeoff" into self-generating growth. Despite statistical gains, poverty, illiteracy, infant mortality, and social strife remained just as prevalent. India claimed self-sufficiency in food, but 80 percent of the pupils in Bombay's public schools had symptoms of chronic malnutrition. "So our horse has won, and it may well win again," Hans Singer ruefully observed. "Magnificent—but is it development?" The numerical targets were relics of an expert consensus that had all but fallen apart. At the eighteenth annual international development conference held at Washington's Mayflower Hotel in February 1970, delegates heckled speakers from the Ford Foundation and World Bank. Angry Peace Corps volunteers drove Barbara Ward off the stage, deriding her as an "imperialist." With Johnson's advisers now filling the top offices, the development establishment was firmly implicated in the Vietnam debacle. Dissenting specialists fled into the academy, discarding Rostovianism for critical theories of dependency and post-structuralism.[47]

The financial shocks of the early 1970s eliminated what was left of the constituency for foreign aid. The postwar boom ground to a halt in August 1971 with the devaluation of the dollar and imposition of wage and price controls. The Nixon Doctrine had already notified the world that American generosity had run out: The United States "cannot—and will not—conceive all the plans" for development, Nixon announced shortly after taking office. "We will help when it makes a real difference and is considered in our interest." Reductions in tariff barriers and foreign direct investment would be the principal tools. From 1969 to 1980 Congress subjected USAID to biennial budget reviews, exercising a line veto over even small expenditures. Total spending crept from $1.4 billion to only $1.8 billion. This amounted to a drastic cut in years of double-digit inflation and sinking dollar values, and an equal contraction of national idealism. "Having lost a degree of faith in our style of progress, we are no longer willing to offer other countries heavy aid to adopt it," columnist Jack Anderson observed. "Aid constitutes cultural imperialism, we have decided, and anyway it costs too much." In the overall development picture, public funds, and even multilateral aid, were increasingly shouldered aside by Middle Eastern petrodollars funneled through U.S. banks. Compared with the $400 billion lent by private bankers to Third World governments in the 1970s, the *Washington Post* observed, "aid amounts, relatively, to peanuts." Donors had once engaged with recipients in a planning process, but now they ran parallel operations. Debtor nations spent their own temporarily bloated accounts, while U.S. initiatives limped along on meager stipends.[48]

Nixon and Kissinger designed a policy architecture with the explicit aim of reducing commitments to the developing nations, and especially Asia. Nine years of war had left the United States without will or resources for foreign ventures. In any case, Kissinger asserted, "the Third World has not proved to be a decisive arena of great power conflict." The anticipated dangers, from falling dominoes or a polarization of the poor against the rich, had never materialized. The area, he argued, was "simply too heterogenous" to achieve any consequential realignment. A temporary retreat from globalism, Nixon realized, would afford an opportunity to refocus on other regions. It was imperative, he told reporters, to avoid "that kind of policy that will make countries in Asia so dependent upon us that we are dragged into conflicts such as the one we have in Vietnam." His strategy would link the interests of "northern tier" powers—China, Japan, the Soviet Union, Europe—similarly beset by internal strains and the demands of lesser powers. This "pentagonal" approach relegated the global South to a secondary place among U.S. concerns while also minimizing the role of economic policy. Nixon largely ignored economic considerations, handling subordinate nations instead through relations with a regional proxy. The reconfiguration altered the aesthetics of power, replacing the theatrics of crisis management with the pageantry of summit meetings.[49]

Repudiating symbolic partnerships the United States had carefully nurtured during the previous decade, the Nixon Doctrine cast India in a profoundly different light. Nixon took little interest in its plans or internal struggles, and certainly never saw it as embodying the aspirations of "uncommitted nations." He distrusted Indira Gandhi, viewing her regime as a Soviet surrogate hostile to U.S. strategic influence in Pakistan. The spell cast by the Asian drama had been broken. "At one time," Lucian Pye observed, "the United States did think it was helping India in a race with China which would test the relative merits of democracy and communism. With China no longer a threat, it was possible to ask in much more realistic terms what had been accomplished in India as a result of nearly $10 billion of American assistance." Attention fixed on other regions, particularly the Middle East. The Arab-Israeli confrontation was far more unpredictable than anything in Asia, Kissinger noted. Asian politics had a "liturgical quality," repetitive and dogmatic, but the Mideast rivalries engaged "intense emotions" in a high-stakes struggle for land and oil. In July 1970 Nixon told reporters the region was "terribly dangerous" a tinderbox like "the Balkans before World War I." Aid and overseas food distribution soon reflected the new pattern of concern.[50]

For decades, the goal of untying development aid from diplomatic goals had been a refrain of presidential task forces, but lacking other leverage, Nixon relaxed needs-based criteria and used it for more explicitly strategic ends. He had no interest in pouring "money down ratholes," he told his aid team. While it should "appear publicly as aid without strings" it should "bore in where it really counts" to reinforce policy goals and the workings of the self-regulating market and not frittered on humanitarian or developmental goals. The list of top recipients tallied closely with the administration's strategic map. Beginning with $140 million in food credits following the Yom Kippur War, aid to the Middle East began an upward trend that continued through the 1980s. Food aid accounted for almost a quarter of the aid total, and Kissinger used it to reward cooperation from Arab states (Jordan, Syria, and Egypt), or to make up for reductions in military aid (South Korea, Indonesia, and the Philippines). "Food is a weapon," Agriculture Secretary Earl Butz explained. "It is now one of the principal tools in our negotiating kit."[51]

But ammunition supplies soon ran low. Nixon used megaton-sized food sales as "linkage" to enmesh the Soviets in a web of dependency and self-restraint, but it was the United States that grew dependent. The Soviet purchase of 19 million metric tons of American grain in 1972 took virtually all the stocks available for food relief to West Africa and Bangladesh. While the Soviets refused even to share information on their harvests, Butz urged farmers to plant "wall to wall" to build up stocks for large-scale grain deals. Private grain dealers, Cargill and Archer Daniels Midland (both later implicated in the Watergate investigations), handled the deals, returning (or "tithing" in ADM chairman Dwayne Andreas's phrase) a share of the profits as campaign contributions. But the dependency ran deeper than political corruption. Until the 1980s the United States would need agricultural exports to offset a severe imbalance of payments aggravated by high energy prices and Asian competition. It was a highly flexible bargaining instrument. South Korea received a $22 million rice credit in return for curtailing textile exports to the United States, and Reagan used food loans to sustain Iraq's war against Iran in the mid-1980s. Even after the drop in oil prices, grain and soybeans exported to Asia financed imports of manufactured goods. A significant but unnoticed milestone was passed in the mid-1990s when China's trade in soybeans reversed direction. Formerly an exporter, China soon became the world's largest soy importer, with most of the deficit coming from Midwestern farms. After 2001 China held the largest share of the U.S. national debt, with interest paid in soybeans.[52]

Political capacity to mobilize large-scale relief dissolved just as famines in Africa awakened a public outcry. The Reagan administration channeled a larger share of food aid though Title II of P.L. 480 to "private voluntary organizations" (PVOs), such as Save the Children, CARE, and Catholic Relief Services rather than through Title III to recipient governments. While there was much talk encouraging the growth of international civil society, the surpluses available for disposal were irregular, and only 10 percent went to countries where malnutrition was critical. PVOs used food as project aid and set up relief camps sometimes in areas where food was available, disrupting indigenous systems of supply and increasing Africa's vulnerability. Perhaps the most important change, however, was that food channeled through Title II did not generate a counterpart fund for capital projects as grants under titles I and III did. In Asia, food aid under these titles had been a crucial source of state investment in the industrial sector—generating in India up to $400 million per year for employment and technology imports—but in Africa it provided only emergency relief.[53]

In the early 1980s a smoldering, decade-long drought across the eastern Sahel exploded into a full-scale famine. From the arid plains of Somalia, Kenya, the Sudan, and Ethiopia millions fled to squalid relief camps, engulfing the UN and private groups struggling to stem the death toll. Investigators from the Economic Research Service found the drought was only symptomatic of a wider crisis. Seventeen nations untouched by the Sahelian drought were nonetheless suffering critical shortages or famines owing to debt, declining export revenues, and policy failures. The problem was Africa-wide and rooted in the continent's structural relationship to the global economy. James Speth of the National Resources Defense Council explained to Congress that debt was as damaging to fragile ecosystems as it was to Africa's fledgling rural institutions. "Let's look at what countries do to try to meet the debt crisis. They increase exports. This means more cash crops more forestry exports," he said. Austerity measures raise unemployment and force people back to the land. "They also cut back on new resource and environmental management agencies that have just been put into place." Governments straining to boost agricultural exports plowed up marginal lands and curtailed imports of fuel and fertilizer forcing farmers to "take too much for their environment, putting too little back."[54]

African nations had foreseen the impending crisis, and in 1980 the Organization for African Unity approved the Lagos Plan of Action, a bold scheme to break colonial trade patterns by integrating the continent into an African Common Market. Following the import-substituting approach used in Asia and Latin America, the members would make self-sufficiency in food, textiles, and basic consumer goods the basis for a continental economic revival. Nigeria committed $16 billion to achieving food self-sufficiency in five years. The World Bank, however, had other ideas. Under a new director, A. W. Clausen, the bank dovetailed its policies with the Reagan administration's "supply-side foreign policy," an emphasis on market-based solutions, private investment, and export-led growth on the Taiwan-South Korea model. Aid from the United States and the World Bank, leveraged by the rising value of the dollar, was conditioned on acceptance of a 1981 blueprint by conservative economist Elliot Berg. The Berg Report identified government as the chief obstacle to growth. Rather than debt or declining terms of trade, it argued, corruption and ineffectual interventions in the rural sector held African economies to less than 1 percent annual growth after 1960. The solution was to dismantle bureaucratic machinery and allow markets to "get the prices right" for chemicals, credit, and other farm inputs. More fundamentally, Berg rejected the equation of development with industrialization, an assumption on which all schools of thought had agreed since the 1940s. Instead of using agriculture as a stepping stone to manufacturing, African countries should stay with what they already did best. The report dismissed "the notion that only a rapid transition to mechanized high-productivity schemes as practiced in the industrialized world, would overcome the stagnation."[55]

The Berg Report reflected a global economic and strategic configuration that had radically changed since the 1960s when the United States had been the leading creditor nation, the source of international liquidity. In the 1980s it was the chief borrower, driving up interest rates around the world. The communist threat galvanized a military and financial response in Asia, but Congress specifically prohibited interventions in Africa's civil wars to prevent another Vietnam. Asian economies diversified in a postwar era of cheap oil and global expansion, while African nations achieved independence in a period of slackening demand for commodities and minerals and dwindling aid budgets.

Consequently, while Asia experienced a decade in which strategic and market pressures favored the accumulation of capital and the expansion of industry, Africa lost that chance. Borlaug and other green revolutionaries criticized Asian nations' fetish for industry, but they recognized a complementarity between sectors; fertilizer, machinery, and irrigation infrastructure, consumer markets, and urban demand all enabled the yield takeoff. Development investments went first into industry, generating the imbalance and crisis of the 1960s, then into agriculture, and then back again. There was a "rough justice" to this pattern, Rostow explained, "because the modernization of agriculture does require a prior industrial base." The spread of HYVs in Asia, disappointingly slow through the 1970s, accelerated from 1978 to 1988 as urban employment and higher per capita incomes drove up domestic prices. In Asia hunger remained a critical problem, as it does to this day, but the gains that have occurred in nutrition did not follow on introductions of new technology or increases in food supply, but occurred instead in periods when growth in jobs and income sustained market demand for food staples.[56]

In Africa, by contrast, a flood of petrodollar loans in the 1970s deepened reliance on the plantation sector and frustrated efforts to adjust prices or change the farming pattern. In the 1980s the loans dried up. High interest rates and declining exports overwhelmed many sub-Saharan governments. "We cannot go on like this," Zaire's president Mobutu Sese Seko reminded Secretary of State George Schultz. "No country can go on paying 45 percent of its export revenues and 55 percent of its government receipts to satisfy its creditors." Imported seeds, fertilizer, and pesticides were too expensive, and U.S. aid officials found that African countries lacked the means to pay for the public investments—the co-ops, subsidies, irrigation, roads, and credit—needed to make commercial farming viable. While many nations tried to repeal the cheap-food policies squeezing the rural sector, they soon found that step could be politically fatal. Food riots in the Sudan, Zambia, and Nigeria thwarted attempts at price reform. When Liberia's William Tolbert allowed the cost of locally produced rice to increase in 1979, street riots and a military revolt culminated with the firing squad execution of Tolbert and his entire cabinet. A 1983 report by the UN Secretary General identified the lack of proper price controls as a "major factor" in food scarcity, but noted that in view of the economic difficulties facing the continent, change was unlikely. The drought brought the human cost of this political impasse into the glare of the new satellite-fed global media.[57]

Television images of emaciated refugees introduced a new post–Cold War generation to the politics of hunger. The British charity Oxfam opened an American franchise with shops and rice and water "hunger banquets" on college campuses. Bread for the World and Food First lobbied Washington to resurrect P.L. 480. The disaster galvanized an anti-hunger campaign under new institutional leadership. Bob Geldof, front man for the Boomtown Rats, an Irish new wave band, was gripped by a BBC report from a camp in Korem, Ethiopia, overwhelmed by 800,000 famine victims. The idea that "in a world of modern technology something like this could be allowed to happen as if the ability of mankind to influence and control the environment had not altered one jot" horrified him. With a transatlantic combo of rockers, including George Michael, Sting, Phil Collins, and Bono, he recorded a single "Do They Know It's Christmas?" which topped international charts in December 1984 and sold 1.5 million copies in the United States. In July 1985 the first Live Aid event, with performances in Philadelphia's JFK Stadium and London's Wembley Arena televised around the world, raised $58 million for famine relief.[58]

The rockers broke furniture on their way into the aid establishment, but the old tenants cleared space and they settled in. Geldof rejected suggestions that he take his crusade to Africa. "The last thing they need," he snapped, "is whitey coming out to take another meal off them." After the concert, he met with UN and USAID to discuss partnership. Live Aid and USA for Africa incorporated tax-exempt foundations and accepted grant proposals through "established channels." David Rockefeller donated offices in New York. Bono, U2's urbane lead singer, emerged as spokesman in the 1990s, joining forces with digital-age entrepreneurs Bill Gates and George Soros and development economist Jeffrey Sachs to form a parvenu faction in international philanthropy. The newcomers barely disturbed the prevailing "Washington consensus" that favored privatization, deregulation, and trade expansion. Their principal contribution was to rejuvenate the optimism and even the language of development's golden age and adapting it to the prevailing development-without-industry agenda. Sachs talked about a big push led by hundreds of model villages. Gates and Soros stressed just how easily Africa could be transformed if the West simply put the will and the resources into the task. Bono supplied a strategic rationale straight from Rostow's playbook. With "potentially another 10 Afghanistans in Africa," he calculated, it was "cheaper by a factor of 100 to prevent the fires from happening than to put them out." Veteran modernizers like William Easterly of the World Bank thought they had heard this all before. The rookies "didn't seem to realize aid workers had been trying for years to end poverty."[59]

By putting Africa's massive foreign debt—amounting to $207 billion—at the top of the agenda Bono reinforced the Berg Report's rationale. The G8 countries and the World Bank agreed to write off debts in return for structural adjustments including dismantling national food schemes and systems of credit, import quotas, price controls, and reserve stocks. Encouraged to "get the prices right," national governments pushed farmers to shift prime irrigated lands to production for export. Grain yields stagnated while the output of citrus fruit, cotton, coffee, and cut flowers increased. Food imports and food aid made up the difference. Just as in India in the early 1960s, declines in food production resulted not from limits of tradition or environment but from policy choices that valued national solvency over social welfare. Structural reforms methodically undid much of what aid and technical assistance had accomplished in the 1960s, with predictable results. Developing countries, which as a group had been net food exporters in the 1970s, accrued steadily larger food deficits, reaching $11 billion by 2001. The ranks of the hungry (estimated by the World Bank) increased from 536 to 800 million people.

This new food crisis, hitting at the peak of the fin de siècle globalist euphoria, evoked grand commitments of the kind not heard since the 1960s. At the United Nations Millennium Summit on September 6, 2000, Bill Clinton, Vladimir Putin, and other world leaders resolved to "halve," by 2015, "the proportion of people who suffer from hunger." The goal's algebraic precision made it sound modest, achievable, while ensuing events made it imperative. Shortly after the 9/11 attacks, President George W. Bush located hunger in the new strategic environment, backing his words with a $1.5 billion Millennium Challenge Account. "When governments fail to meet the most basic needs of their people," he warned, "these failed states can become havens for terror." The millennium initiatives combined established remedies—hybrid seeds, tube wells, fertilizer, village councils, nomad resettlement (but no dams, land reform or steel mills)—with expectations greater than experience might warrant. "For every problem you have," Sachs assured Ugandan villagers, "there is a solution." The World Bank and USAID saw the goals as a mandate for more structural adjustment, freer trade, and improved (i.e., reduced) governance. The extremity of the gap between rich and poor—all Africa could eat for "*less than 1 percent* of the income of the rich"—was taken as proof that resources could be brought to bear. Development's past failures, Tony Blair's Commission for Africa stressed, meant that the old mistakes would not be repeated.[60]

10

PRESENT AT THE RE-CREATION

Observers at Barack Obama's inaugural remarked on the similarity in tone and cadence of his address to the one that summoned the nation to a twilight struggle forty-eight years earlier. One passage in particular self-consciously renewed a forgotten American mission. Echoing Kennedy's pledge to "those people in the huts and villages of half the globe," Obama addressed "the people of poor nations," vowing "to work along-side you to make your farms flourish and let clean waters flow; to nour-ish starved bodies and feed hungry minds." The passage opened up a broad variety of possibilities drawing on long and carefully evaluated experience, but by the time the administration had fully settled in the field had been narrowed to just one. Beginning a trip to Ghana in July, the president expressed his frustration "over the fact that the green revo-lution that we introduced into India in the '60s, we haven't yet intro-duced into Africa in 2009."[1]

This may be only the latest official expression of Jay Gatsby's plain-tive protest against lost opportunity—"Can't repeat the past? Why of course you can."—or it may be an echo of the optimism of the mid-twentieth century, when history itself seemed malleable. "To an Ameri-can," *Life* magazine explained in 1953, "time is an infinite dimension to be taken like any raw material for whatever project is before us." But the plan to rewind the green revolution, which the new administration now embraced, was initially slow to develop. Through the 1980s and 1990s Norman Borlaug worked in Ghana on a pilot project called Global 2000 with the support of former president Jimmy Carter. From a small office in Accra he offered free advice, seeds, and fertilizer to villagers willing to set aside an acre for a test plot. It was lonely work. "We need desperately for the World Bank to join us," Carter complained, but the project aroused little donor interest until 2006 when a new crisis hit the headlines.

A disastrous spike in food prices, driven by energy shortages and rising consumer demand, sparked protests in Mexico and India. It hit Africa especially hard. For Tanzania, Zambia, Ethiopia, and Madagascar, beset by droughts and war refugees, it was the final straw; they broke with the Washington consensus and began restricting food exports.[2]

Borlaug's idea suddenly seemed long overdue. The Gates and Rockefeller foundations pledged $300 million to an Alliance for a Green Revolution in Africa (AGRA), headed by former United Nations secretary Kofi Annan. "The original green revolution was a huge success," affirmed Judith Rodin, president of the Rockefeller Foundation, "Now it's Africa's turn." The World Bank endorsed the idea in its 2008 report, and Democratic Party challengers set it at the top of their agenda for revitalizing foreign aid. "What the world needs," Senator Joe Biden confirmed, "is a second green revolution." The Chicago Initiative, a bipartisan commission of legislators, academics, and diplomats led by former agriculture secretary Dan Glickman, drafted plans for a $3 billion program of agricultural research and development in sub-Saharan Africa. Senators Richard Lugar and Robert Casey put the Chicago Initiative before Congress in the form of legislation. The U.S. Agency for International Development doubled food aid and put emphasis on farm technology and crop productivity. Bringing the lost arts of Keynesianism and counterinsurgency back to Washington, the Obama administration reclaimed America's role as the world's hunger fighter.[3]

Many of the claims made for a second green revolution, called "GR2.0" by some, are familiar. Hunger is characterized as a discrete problem divorced from politics, an independent variable than can be managed through technical means. A breakthrough in productivity will, nonetheless, generate political benefits. It will be a "transformative step," reshaping social structures, attitudes, alliances and securing "America's diplomatic, economic, cultural, and security interests." Echoing the expansive ambitions of Atwater, Fosdick, and Wallace, the Lugar-Casey Act pushes the starter on "an engine of economic growth . . . equity, and social justice." Technological idealism is back in style. Bill Gates describes seeds as "the coolest thing" and rhapsodizes about computerized trading floors in the bush. Once again, a battle of experts is shaping up, with proponents of genetically modified organisms (GMOs) and organic farming projecting their domestic dispute into a largely conjectural African setting.[4]

GR2.0 emits a faint echo of Cold War anti-poverty slogans. Resuming the fight against hunger, the Chicago panel observes, is essential to "renewing American leadership" in the wake of financial collapse and military missteps that cost the nation its "moral standing." Military operations echo an earlier era of pacification. The surge in Afghanistan began with operations to recapture the shores of the Helmand reservoirs and restore irrigation, all part of an effort, according to the provincial warlord, "to win the hearts and minds of the people." In Iraq, rural development units, known as Team Borlaug, are bringing seeds and livestock vaccines to farmers in the Sunni Triangle. The Chicago group notes that global economic revival, the stability of Africa, and security against failed states and terror havens all hinge on food scarcity, and that only the United States is capable of stimulating a new green revolution.[5]

It is not yet clear what a second green revolution means in practical terms. The Lugar-Casey act authorizes $2.5 billion by 2014 for agricultural aid and directs research on the "full range" of biotechnological alternatives. At a summit in July 2009, the G8 leaders pledged an additional $3 billion, but without setting any targets. Free marketers are nonetheless worried. *The Economist* sees signs of an insidious "turn away from trade, markets, and efficiency" in the rhetorical "move from 'food security' towards 'food self-sufficiency' as a goal of national policy." But another barometer indicates there may be less cause for concern. The groundwork for the second green revolution began with a careful rewriting of the history of the first. In constructing a model to conform to their still-unstated plans, proponents followed the well-worn expository conventions, emptying the past of local and geopolitical context and reducing events to formula. The result bears little resemblance to William Gaud's green revolution, but it may offer a fair picture of what is intended for Africa.[6]

The abbreviated overviews of the "original" green revolution in position papers and "frequently asked questions" sheets remind stakeholders of a forgotten triumph of compassion and technology. Ehrlich's darker forecasts are cited as a baseline reality against which the scale of the victory can be measured. Painful trade-offs, the legacies of conflict and dictatorship, and the lost alternatives of land reform and industrial planning are covered by admissions that growth often accentuates "inequities," a hazard specialists need to be mindful of. Little is said of past justifications for either encouraging or neglecting rural development. Africa, the reports agree, was "bypassed" because the aid community grew complacent and let down its guard. No mention is made of the role of the Berg Report or structural adjustment in disbanding intensification efforts in the 1980s and 1990s. Likewise, the reasons why aid, science, and diplomatic pressure came to bear so disproportionately on South and Southeast Asia during the 1960s—and what it would take to mobilize the same level of political will a second time—are left unexamined.[7]

Revisionists have been particularly eager to strip the "original" green revolution of ironies and bring it into line with free-market prescriptions. The most obvious omission is the discomfiting contrast between the production miracle and the persistence of chronic starvation and rural poverty. The green revolution epicenters—Pakistan, India, Sri Lanka, Bangladesh, Mexico, the Philippines, and Indonesia—are all among the most undernourished nations, each with higher rates of adult and child malnutrition and deficiency diseases (except for iodine deficiency) than most sub-Saharan countries. For its 2009 meeting, the Food and Agriculture Organization issued a booklet of case studies of agricultural transformation, *Pathways to Success,* which made no mention of India. With its 20-million-ton buffer stock of grain to preserve self-sufficiency, India has more undernourished citizens than any other nation, some 213 million without enough to eat. The paradox of plenty continues to underscore the fallacy of addressing hunger exclusively as a supply-side problem.[8]

Even as the AGRA and Chicago initiatives hit the press, news accounts painted a bleak picture of rural life in the former green revolution showcases. In the Punjab, India's breadbasket, aggressive exploitation of ground water has caused aquifers to sink 300 feet. In the same region, chronic indebtedness has become endemic; by some accounts it has driven some 200,000 farmers to suicide since 1997. Reacting to the crisis, the World Bank and the Indian government are funding projects to *reverse* the green revolution by retrobreeding cultivars that can be grown without chemical fertilizers or pesticides. In neighboring Pakistan the situation was even more grim. The Taliban were gaining control, according to the *New York Times,* because the countryside "remains largely feudal" and "avenues for advancement for the vast majority of rural poor do not exist." But planning for Africa does not profit from a balanced evaluation of the Asian experience. Bill Gates, speaking in October 2009, urged African countries to draw inspiration from the agricultural transformation of Asia that "averted famine, saved hundreds of millions of lives, and fueled widespread economic development."[9]

The historical record has to be trimmed even more to obscure the role of the state. While all accounts pay homage to Borlaug, they cast him as a technologist rather than as a scientific ambassador who counted prime ministers and dictators among his personal friends. He was once asked if he saw himself as a technician, a kind of county agent to the world. "No," he replied. "We move governments." Until he died in 2009, Borlaug continued to maintain that technology acted only as a catalyst for the state interventions that did the real work of energizing production. The genius of the dwarf seeds was to create a cultivar that was at once so spectacularly productive and so needy of the kind of inputs only government could provide. Only a few days after he gave the green revolution its name, William Gaud noted that it was "generally agreed" that seed technology was secondary to price policies skewed "in favor of the farmer, the producer, rather than the consumer." "All observers," he testified, "gave this change primary credit for providing the incentive" to grow more. AGRA tells a different story, maintaining that South Asia owed its successes to a policy mix that "sought to rein in public deficits, improve national balances of payments, liberalize markets, and encourage private investment." Subsidies and price incentives, the centerpiece of the 1965 Treaty of Rome reforms, are explicitly written out. While the Chicago initiative acknowledges some role for "targeted" incentives, the World Bank concludes that subsidies have only "been negative, and in some cases, disastrous."[10]

Development once meant helping rural countries industrialize, but today's efforts are designed to keep Africa out of the industrial club. The Obama administration sees agriculture as "the primary means of driving economic growth and reducing poverty," and the G8 insist on tariff reductions in return for an end to farm subsidies, in effect requiring Africa to dismantle its infant industries in return for access to Europe's markets. In theory, African economies should seek efficiency in those areas where they already have a comparative advantage, rather than gaining new competencies or transforming the productive sphere. That was never the ambition in Asia. Even Subramaniam, the most die-hard foe of urban bias, saw agriculture as a "hand maiden of industry" intended to liberate capital and labor to build shipyards and rolling mills. The purpose of the green revolution, and indeed all development, was to turn peasant societies into manufacturing centers. Africa may one day produce a stable, growing, and equitable economy based purely on export agriculture, but if it does it will be the first time in history that anything like it has happened.[11]

One might even wonder why, at the risk of inviting comparisons, the green revolution is invoked at all. The clear divergence between old and new versions hints at a number of implicit designs, the first of which is to furnish a down-at-the-heels market fundamentalism with a more imposing lineage. The past is framed in favor of prescriptions more closely resembling the export-oriented approach of the 1950s or the structural reform ideal of the 1990s than the Keynesian, import-substituting policies of the 1960s. AGRA emphasizes high-value crops for export, in some cases encouraging reprocessing staple foods into trade goods such as starch, animal feed, or biofuels. Agronomists of the 1960s would have characterized such policies as a restoration of "traditional" pattern of agriculture. GR2.0 proponents urge more production for Europe and China, more reliance on outside investment and gene technology, in short, more dependency. While concentration of land ownership was seen as a necessary but damaging side effect of rural modernization in Asia, it is part of the plan for Africa. The World Bank notes the "rising economies of scale in linking to value chains, particularly supermarkets and high-value export markets." Whatever their merits, these approaches explicitly reject the goals and methods of the "original" model they ostensibly follow.[12]

The refurbished green revolution legend also serves as a convenient deflection. In his efforts to revive an exhausted debate between agronomists and environmentalists from the 1970s, Bill Gates appears occasionally to pick fights. He told an audience in Des Moines in October 2009 that "environmentalists are standing in the way of feeding humanity through their opposition to biotechnology, farm chemicals and nitrogen fertilizer." Richard Paarlberg's recent book *Starved for Science* accuses "rich country" environmentalists of foisting an anti-science, pro-organic agenda, but he acknowledges that GMO-based solutions for Africa, such as drought-tolerant cultivars, are years and possibly decades off. No drought-tolerant GMO varieties tailored for the African environment have yet been released, or even tested, largely because companies involved in research see little profit in it. There are a few promising experiments with organic farming, such as the Mount Kenya Organic Farm, but no one is proposing a national or continent-wide program. Although the stakes of the GMO versus organic controversy remain largely hypothetical in Africa, they are both immediate and central in the World Trade Organization, where the United States is leading a campaign to dismantle European Union restrictions and open the way for unregulated U.S. commodity exports.[13]

By projecting this controversy onto Africa, advocates are following the established practice of displacing domestic disputes over resources, land, and consumption into foreign settings, but they are also evading harder questions. GR2.0 proposals give only vague explanations for how expanding farm productivity will translate into increased health, welfare, or growth. As India was in 1950, Africa today is a major food exporter. No French market would be complete without cut flowers, coffee, lobster, citrus fruits, and salad greens from across the Mediterranean. The total value of food aid coming in is less than the value of one of the smaller export segments—fresh vegetables—going out. If Amartya Sen's analysis still applies, Africans are hungry not because there is no food, but because they have no entitlement to food. The position papers do not say how Africa will defy the paradox of plenty and translate greater agricultural production into enough per capita income and employment to sustain entitlements to food. They even hint at dislocations that may have the opposite effect. Paul Collier, who advocates large-scale agribusiness on the Brazilian pattern, suggests displaced smallholders would "head to the cities" and find "local wage jobs." They likely would, but any government concerned for its own survival would have to consider what they might do if they got there and were disappointed.[14]

The eagerness to adopt a strategy linked to a legendary success in name only also reveals the extent of the failure of imagination gripping the development community. The Washington consensus disintegrated amid the financial crisis of 2008, but its demise was foreshadowed by a pervasive feeling that aid institutions had run out of ideas. In 2004 Paul Krugman, Joseph Stiglitz, and other leading economists prefaced their Barcelona Development Agenda with an admission that "there is no single set of policies that can be guaranteed to ignite sustained growth." More recently, William Easterly and Robert Solow concluded that 50 years of research and experience proved only how little is known about the mechanisms of development. Zambian economist Dambisa Moyo earned overnight celebrity in 2009 with her best seller *Dead Aid,* which claimed "aid has been, and continues to be, an unmitigated political, economic, and humanitarian disaster for most parts of the developing world." In a strange reversal, the aid community has shaken off thirty years of donor fatigue only to be immobilized by theory fatigue.[15]

269

This creeping policy nihilism is at least partly a consequence of the discourse of modeling and its recipe-box view of history, which feeds expectations for proven formulas. In the 1970s, Ford and Rockefeller officials warned against believing media "fairy tales" and they had a better grasp of the drawbacks, the second-generation effects—energy dependency, joblessness, debt, urbanization, lost biodiversity, thwarted land reform, and crop vulnerability—than their successors do today. History serves not only as an antidote to the fallacy of the model but it also cautions against both utopian expectations and neo-realist defeatism. It contains no breakthroughs, only trade-offs, but it also throws up fewer obstacles. Theorists often cite corruption and conflict as impediments that must be addressed before Africa can advance, but if we look at how U.S. policymakers weighed the same consideration in an earlier era, the far more serious corruption of Suharto or Marcos and wars in Vietnam and the subcontinent were all reasons for action rather than inaction.

Hunger—along with terrorism, migration, climate, and narcotics—belongs to an ever-larger category of international issues for which a search for technical fixes serves as a substitute for serious engagement. Political structures attuned to the twenty-four-hour news cycle are impatient with problems that require sacrifices and investments over an indefinite but undoubtedly long term. Such problems may never be solved definitively, but they can be managed with a persistent, improvisational approach. Agriculture in the United States has gained a high state of proficiency, but it is not now and has never been a completed project; policy requires continual correction in response to unforeseeable shifts in markets, values, and political alignments. In such contexts, tantalizing one-time solutions distract from the inequities of power that perpetuate poverty and hunger, as well as from the work of adaptation and compromise required to ameliorate the worst effects.

During the Cold War, humanitarian efforts were hamstrung by many conceptual limitations. The calorie mobilized action against hunger, but also misinterpreted it as an isolable, technical issue. Community development substituted technical advice for democratic accountability. The sanctity of domestic subsidies blinded Americans to the damage the resulting surpluses did to other economies. Agricultural science joined an unprofitable alliance with population control, trapping reform within a Malthusian discourse that led nowhere. Money could be thrown at engineering fiascos for decades so long as they held their strategic value, but political settlements, such as land reform, quickly fell from favor when their success did not affirm the policy trend of the moment. The persistent note throughout was the propensity to employ technology as an avoidance mechanism, as a way to escape historical responsibility and the obligation to allow people to choose, through their own governments, the future that was best for them. A new campaign against hunger should not occasion nostalgia for a golden age of development but a reflection on how, freed of these preconceptions, we might find a new way forward.

ABBREVIATIONS

AAA   *Annals of the American Academy of Political and Social Science*

AHR   *American Historical Review*

ASI   *Agricultural Situation in India*

BP   Norman Borlaug Papers, University of Minnesota Library, Minneapolis, MN

CENIS   Center for International Studies, Massachusetts Institute of Technology

CREST   CIA Records Search Tool, U.S. National Archives, College Park, MD

CT   *Chicago Tribune* and *Chicago Daily Tribune*

DDRS   *Declassified Documents Reference System,* Gale Cengage Learning, Farmington Hills, MI

DOSB   *Department of State Bulletin*

FFA   Ford Foundation Archives, New York, NY

FRBA   Federal Reserve Board Archives, Washington, DC

FRUS   *Foreign Relations of the United States*

HSTL   Harry S Truman Library, Independence, MO

IRRILA   International Rice Research Institute Library and Archive, Los Baños, Philippines

JAH   *Journal of American History*

LAT   *Los Angeles Times*

LBJL   Lyndon Baines Johnson Library, Austin, TX

NAI   National Archives of India, New Delhi, India

NARA   National Archives and Records Administration, College Park, MD

NDFO   New Delhi Field Office Papers, Rockefeller Foundation Archive Center, Tarrytown, NY

NMML   Nehru Memorial Museum and Library, Teen Murthi House, New Delhi, India

NSC	National Security Council
NSF	National Security Files
NYT	*New York Times*
RFAC	Rockefeller Foundation Archive Center, Tarrytown, NY
RG	Record Group
TL	*The Times* (of London)
TNR	*The New Republic*
WP	*Washington Post*
WSJ	*Wall Street Journal*

NOTES

1. Lyndon Johnson, *The Vantage Point* (New York, 1971), 222; Dwight D. Eisenhower, *Waging Peace, 1956–1961* (New York, 1965), 503–504; Marvin Arrowsmith, "Noble War on Hunger Asked by Eisenhower," *WP*, December 12, 1959, A6.

2. "Partial Text of Acheson's Letter to Truman on U.S. Relations with China," *WP*, August 6, 1949, 2.

3. James Michener, "Blunt Truths about Asia," *Life*, June 4, 1951, 96–114.

4. "US Aid to Others Called Essential," *NYT*, June 10, 1955, 23.

5. Alfred Thayer Mahan, *The Problem of Asia and Its Effect upon International Policies* (Boston, 1900), 91; Halford MacKinder, *Democratic Ideals and Reality: A Study of the Politics of Reconstruction* (New York, 1919), 110–112; Henry L. Stimson Diary, March 26, 1936 (New Haven, microfilm, 1983).

6. Josiah Strong, *Our Country* (New York, 1891), 28.

7. Walt W. Rostow, *The Process of Economic Growth* (New York, 1952), 104; J. K. Galbraith, "Conditions for Economic Change in Underdeveloped Countries," *Journal of Farm Economics* 33(4) (1951): 690.

8. Dean Acheson, "Crisis in Asia," *DOSB*, January 23, 1950, 112.

9. Amanda McVety, "Pursuing Progress: Point Four in Ethiopia," *Diplomatic History* 32(3) (2008): 373; Department of State, "A United States Assistance Strategy for India," November 8, 1965, NSF, NSC History, Indian Famine, Vol. 2, Tab 4, LBJL.

10. Congressional Research Service, *Fifty Five Years of Foreign Aid by the United States, 1917–1971* (Washington, DC, 1972).

11. Margaret Mead, *Cultural Patterns and Technical Change* (New York, 1955), 181–182.

12. Eric Hobsbawm, *The Age of Extremes: A History of the World, 1914–1991* (New York, 1994), 292.

13. Barack Obama, *Dreams from My Father: A Story of Race and Inheritance* (New York, 1995), 32, 37, 50; Barack Obama, Inaugural Address, January 21, 2009, www.whitehouse.gov.

I. THE WORLD FOOD PROBLEM

1. The Wesleyan Calorimeter," *NYT,* April 5, 1896, 5; "Occupants of the Wesleyan Glass Cage Changed," *CT,* March 24, 1896, 10; "The Human Body," *LAT,* May 3, 1896, 22; "Conservation of Energy in the Human Body," *Scientific American,* August 5, 1899, 85; "Almost a Hero," *Boston Daily Globe,* March 22, 1896, 1.

2. "Human Body and Food," *NYT,* March 23, 1899, 3; "The Man in the Copper Box," *Century Illustrated Magazine,* June 1897, 314; "The Food Test at Middletown," *NYT,* March 25, 1896, 1; "The People's Food—A Great National Inquiry," *Review of Reviews* 13 (June 1896): 679–690; W. O. Atwater, "How Food Is Used in the Body: Experiments with Men in a Respiration Apparatus," *Century Illustrated Magazine,* June 1897, 246.

3. "Cyclist to Aid Cause of Science," *CT,* October 30, 1904, A4; "Nine Days in a Sealed Box," *CT,* March 21, 1899, 1; "New Test in Examinations," *CT,* February 13, 1905, 3; "The Human Machine," *WP,* December 29, 1904, 6; "Will Fight Alcohol as Food," *NYT,* June 30, 1900, 3; "Declares War: Connecticut W.C.T.U. Is against Atwater," *Boston Daily Globe,* February 5, 1900, 3.

4. "Machine to Test Food," *WP,* January 10, 1910, E1; C. F. Langworthy and R. D. Milner, *Investigations on the Nutrition of Man* (Washington, DC, 1904); Mildred R. Ziegler, "The History of the Calorie in Nutrition," *The Scientific Monthly* 15 (1922): 520–526; Russell H. Chittenden, *Physiological Economy in Nutrition* (New York, 1913); "Plan Energy Test," *WP,* December 30, 1908, 1; "Measures Human Energy," *NYT,* December 21, 1908, 3; "Mystery of Body Read Like a Book," *CT,* December 21, 1908, 1; W. O. Atwater, "What the Coming Man Will Eat," *Forum,* June 1892, 498; "The People's Food," 687–689.

5. Thomas Malthus, *An Essay on the Principle of Population* (Washington, DC, 1809), 2: 344; Kenneth Pomerantz and Steven Topik, *The World That Trade Created* (Armonk, NY, 2006), 187–188.

6. Thomas Jefferson, *Notes on the State of Virginia* (New York, 2002), 139; Matthew C. Perry, *Narrative of the Expedition of the American Squadron to the China Seas and Japan* (New York, 1856), 512; Mike Davis, *Late Victorian Holocausts: El Niño Famines and the Making of the Third World* (London, 2001), 5.

7. Albert J. Beveridge, "The Development of a Colonial Policy for the United States," *AAA* 30 (1907): 3; Sun Yat-sen, *The International Development of China* (New York, 1922); Sugata Bose, "Instruments and Idioms of Colonial and National Development," in Frederick Cooper, ed., *International Development and the Social Sciences* (Berkeley, 1997), 49; Michael Hogan, *Informal Entente* (Columbia, MO, 1977), 212.

8. J. George Harrar, "Nutrition and Numbers in the Third World," *BioScience* 24 (1974): 514; Deborah Fitzgerald, *Every Farm a Factory: The Industrial Ideal in American Agriculture* (New Haven, 2003), 48; James C. Whorton, *Crusaders for Fitness: The History of American Health* (Princeton, 1982); Dana Jean Simmons, "Minimal Frenchmen: Science and Standards of Living, 1840–1960" (PhD diss., University of Chicago, 2004), 171–172; Anson Rabinbach, *The Human Motor:*

Energy, Fatigue, and the Origins of Modernity (New York, 1990); "About Experiments," *Dallas Morning News,* May 30, 1896, 8.

9. Lawrence Glickman, "Inventing the 'American Standard of Living': Gender, Race, and Working Class Identity, 1880–1925," *Labor History* 34(2) (1993): 221–235; Victoria de Grazia, *Irresistable Empire* (Cambridge, MA, 2005), 75–129; Naomi Aronson, "Nutrition as a Social Problem: A Case Study of Entrepreneurial Strategy in Science," *Social Problems* 29 (1982): 474–487; and "Social Definitions of Entitlement: Food Needs 1885–1920," *Media, Culture, and Society* 4 (1982): 51–61; Harvey Levenstein, "The New England Kitchen and the Origins of Modern American Eating Habits," *American Quarterly* 32 (Autumn 1980): 369–386; John Coveney, *Food, Morals, and Meaning: The Pleasure and Anxiety of Eating* (London, 2000), 72–78; Rabinbach, *The Human Motor,* 120–133.

10. "Statue of Germania Dedicated," *CT,* May 26, 1893, 2; Mary E. Green, *Food Products of the World* (Chicago, 1895), 3–4; "America's Vast Resources," *NYT,* December 3, 1893, 13; "French Agricultural Display," *CT,* May 17, 1893, 9; "Tea Is Their Text," *CT,* June 18, 1893, 12; Henry Adams, *The Education of Henry Adams* (Boston, 1961), 342.

11. "New System Devised to Prevent Figures from Telling Lies," *CT,* November 28, 1898, 10; Alain Desrosières, *The Politics of Large Numbers: A History of Statistical Reasoning* (Cambridge, MA, 1998); Theodore M. Porter, *The Rise of Statistical Thinking, 1820–1900* (Princeton, 1986); Ian Hacking, *The Taming of Chance* (Cambridge, UK, 1990).

12. Winthrop More Daniels, "Divination by Statistics," *The Atlantic Monthly,* January 1902, 101; Carroll D. Wright, "The Limitations and Difficulties of Statistics," *Yale Review* 3 (1894): 121; Eugene Richard White, "The Plague of Statistics," *The Atlantic Monthly,* December 1901, 842–843.

13. Hillel Schwartz, *Never Satisfied: A Cultural History of Diets, Fantasies, and Fat* (New York, 1986), 87; Aronson, "Social Definitions," 53.

14. C. F. Langworthy and R. D. Milner, "The Respiration Calorimeter and the Results of Experiments with It," in *Yearbook of the United States Department of Agriculture, 1910* (Washington, DC, 1911), 307–318; C. F. Langworthy, *Food, Customs, and Diet in American Homes,* Office of Experiment Stations Circular 110 (Washington, DC, 1911); "World's Finest Food Supply," *LAT,* April 30, 1911, 19.

15. W. O. Atwater, *Methods and Results of Investigations on the Chemistry and Economy of Food* (Washington, DC, 1895), 9, 214–218; C. F. Langworthy and R. D. Milner, *Investigations on the Nutrition of Man* (Washington, DC, 1904).

16. "Beware the Calorie," *Literary Digest,* December 8, 1917, 27; "Food Control," *TNR,* March 10, 1917, 155.

17. "How Germany's Food Problem Was Met," *NYT,* April 16, 1916, 6; "Germany's Food Problem," *Literary Digest,* February 24, 1917, 454; Sarah T. Barrows, "A Triumph of Scientific Housekeeping," *Journal of Home Economics* 8 (1916): 495–498; "How European War Departments Solve the Food Problems of Armies in the Field," *Current Opinion,* October 1914, 257; Robinson Smith, *Food Values and the Rationing of a Country* (London, 1917), 5.

18. United States Food Administration, *Food and the War* (Boston, 1918), 129–130; Herbert Hoover, *The Memoirs of Herbert Hoover: Years of Adventure, 1874–1920* (New York, 1961), 279.

19. George H. Nash, *The Life of Herbert Hoover: Master of Emergencies, 1917–1918* (New York, 1996), 206, 232; Lulu Hunt Peters, *Diet and Health with a Key to the Calories* (Chicago, 1918), 24.

20. Lyman Abbott, "The Pernicious Habit of Self-Examination," *Outlook,* May 30, 1917, 185; Harry A. Williams, "On the Way to Berlin," *LAT,* March 31, 1918, 10; "Herbie Hoover," *Philadelphia Inquirer,* September 29, 1917, 10.

21. Jean Brumberg, *Fasting Girls: The Emergence of Anorexia Nervosa as a Modern Disease* (Cambridge, MA, 1988); Michel Foucault, *Discipline and Punish* (New York, 1995), 214–224; Richard Norton Smith, *An Uncommon Man: The Triumph of Herbert Hoover* (New York, 1984), 88; "500 Hotels to Stop Serving Wheat," *NYT,* March 30, 1918, 9; Nash, *Hoover,* 232; T. T. C. Gregory, "Stemming the Red Tide," *World's Work,* May 1921, 95–97.

22. Herbert Hoover, *An American Epic* (Chicago, 1960), 2: 248; Hoover, *Memoirs,* 398.

23. Frank Ninkovich, *Modernity and Power: The History of the Domino Theory in the Twentieth Century* (Chicago, 1990), 76.

24. Charles S. Maier, "Between Taylorism and Technocracy: European Ideologies and the Vision of Industrial Productivity in the 1920s," *Journal of Contemporary History* 5 (1970): 27–61; Martin Fine, "Albert Thomas: A Reformer's Vision of Modernization, 1914–1932," *Journal of Contemporary History* 12 (1977): 545–564; Jean Monnet, *Memoirs* (Garden City, NY, 1978), 95–98.

25. Herbert Hoover, "The Paramount Business of Every American Today," *System,* July 1920, 24; Hoover, *American Individualism* (Garden City, NY, 1922); Smith, *Uncommon Man,* 93–94; Hoover, "The Nation and Science," *Science* 65 (January 14, 1927): 26–29.

26. Frank A Vanderlip, "Some Aspects of the So-Called Japanese Problem," *Outlook,* June 23, 1920, 380; Herbert Hoover, "The Battle Line of Hunger," *McClure's Magazine,* July 1920, 27–30; Burwell S. Cutler, "International Rationing," *AAA* 74 (1917): 34–42; G. B. Roorbach, "The World's Food Supply," *AAA* 74 (1917): 1–33; O. E. Baker, "The Potential Supply of Wheat," *Economic Geography* 1 (1925): 15–52.

27. Halford John Mackinder, *Democratic Ideals and Reality: A Study of the Politics of Reconstruction* (New York, 1919), 110–112; John Lossing Buck, *Chinese Farm Economy* (Chicago, 1930); Buck, "Agriculture and the Future of China," *AAA* 152 (1930): 109–115.

28. Pearl S. Buck, *The Good Earth* (New York, 1931).

29. John M. Jordan, "'To Educate Public Opinion': John D. Rockefeller Jr. and the Origins of Social Scientific Fact-Finding," *New England Quarterly* 64 (1991): 294; Robert Arnove, ed., *Philanthropy and Cultural Imperialism* (Boston, 1980), 8; Inderjeet Parmar, "'To Relate Knowledge and Action': The Impact of the Rockefeller Foundation on Foreign Policy Thinking during America's Rise to Globalism, 1939–1945," *Minerva* 40 (2002): 237; Ron Robin, *The Making of the Cold War*

Enemy: Culture and Politics in the Military-Intellectual Complex (Princeton, 2001), 33–35; Peter Collier and David Horowitz, *The Rockefellers: An American Dynasty* (New York, 1977), 62.

30. Frederick Taylor Gates, *Chapters in My Life* (New York, 1977), 206; Barbara Howe, "The Emergence of Scientific Philanthropy: Origins, Issues and Outcomes," in Arnove, ed., *Philanthropy*, 38–39.

31. "1930 Farm Census to Cover the World," *NYT,* October 7, 1928, xx8; "Making the World Safer," *NYT,* December 7, 1928, 28; John Ensor Harr and Peter J. Johnson, *The Rockefeller Century* (New York, 1988), 188; George E. Vincent, *The Rockefeller Foundation: A Review for 1922* (New York, 1923), 41; George E. Vincent, "Making the Whole World Well: What the Rockefeller Foundation Is Doing for Humanity," *The Independent,* June 14, 1919, 406; Robert L. Duffus, "Knights-Errant Inc., Part I, the Rockefellers," *The Independent,* July 11, 1925, 39.

32. Emily S. Rosenberg, *Financial Missionaries to the World: The Politics and Culture of Dollar Diplomacy, 1900–1930* (Durham, NC, 2003), 192; Anne O'Hare McCormick, "Hoover Molds a Foreign Policy," *NYT Magazine,* June 16, 1929, 1; Michael Adas, *Dominance by Design: Technological Imperatives and America's Civilizing Mission* (Cambridge, MA, 2006), 203; Robert Redfield, *Tepoztlan: A Mexican Village* (Chicago, 1930), 222.

33. Raymond B. Fosdick, *Letters on the League of Nations: From the Files of Raymond B. Fosdick* (Princeton, 1966), 9, 22; "Raymond B. Fosdick Dies at 89, Headed Rockefeller Foundation," *NYT,* July 19, 1972, 41; Fosdick, "The League of Nations Is Alive," *The Atlantic Monthly,* June 1920.

34. League Health Organization, *Report on the Physiological Bases of Human Nutrition* (Geneva, 1935); Fine, "Albert Thomas," 556; ILO, *Monthly Summary* 7 (July 1929): 40.

35. Raymond B. Fosdick, "Our Machine Civilization, A Frankenstein Monster?" *Current Opinion,* September 1922, 367; Fosdick, "The International Implications of the Business Depression," *Carnegie Endowment Studies in World Economy I* 267 (1931): 20–34; Fosdick, *The Rockefeller Foundation: A Review for 1936* (New York, 1937), 31–32; Fosdick, *The Rockefeller Foundation: A Review for 1937* (New York, 1938), 37–38; Lily E. Kay, "Rethinking Institutions: Philanthropy as an Historiographic Problem of Knowledge and Power," *Minerva* 35 (1997): 288–230.

36. Raymond B. Fosdick, *The Old Savage in the New Civilization* (Garden City, NY, 1931), 177–180; "Population Rise No Menace, He Says," *NYT,* March 27, 1925, 8.

37. George E. Vincent, *The Rockefeller Foundation: A Review for 1926* (New York, 1927), 42–43; League of Nations Health Organization, *Progress of the Science of Nutrition in Japan* (Geneva, 1926); League of Nations Health Organization, *Audit of the Accounts of the Rockefeller Foundation Grants to the Health Organization* (Geneva, 1926); Vincent, *The Rockefeller Foundation: A Review for 1925* (New York, 1926), 41–43; Raymond B. Fosdick, *The Story of the Rockefeller Foundation* (New York, 1952), 182–183; Jonathan Harwood, "Europe's Green

Revolution: Peasant-Oriented Plant Breeding in Central Europe, 1890–1945," paper presented at the meeting of the International Society for the History, Philosophy, and Social Studies of Biology, University of Guelph, July 2005; Fosdick, *The Rockefeller Foundation: A Review for 1937,* 52–53; Frank Ninkovich, "The Rockefeller Foundation, China, and Cultural Change," *Journal of American History* 70 (1984): 799–820.

38. W. K. Hancock, *Survey of British Commonwealth Affairs,* vol. 2: *Problems of Economic Policy, 1918–1939* (London, 1942), pt. 2: 267; J. Oldham, "Kenya and Its Problems," *TL,* June 10, 1926, 17; "Dual Policy in India," *TL,* January 26, 1932, 12.

39. J. L. Gilks and J. B. Orr, "The Nutritional Condition of the East African Native," *The Lancet,* March 12, 1927, 560–562; Royal Commission on Agriculture in India, *Evidence of the Officers Serving under the Government of India,* vol. 1, part 2 (Calcutta, 1927), 96; H. D. Kay, "John Boyd Orr, Baron Boyd Orr of Brechin Mearns, 1880–1971," *Biographical Memoirs of Fellows of the Royal Society* 18 (1972): 43–81; Michael Warboys, "The Discovery of Colonial Malnutrition between the Wars," in David Arnold, ed., *Imperial Medicine and Indigenous Societies* (Manchester, 1988), 208–225; David Arnold, "The 'Discovery' of Malnutrition and Diet in Colonial India," *The Indian Economic and Social History Review* 31 (1994): 1–26; S. R. Christophers, "What Disease Costs India: Being a Statement of the Problem before Medical Research in India," *Indian Medical Gazette* 59 (1924): 196–200; "Development of the Empire: A Higher Standard of Living," *TL,* November 26, 1937, 11.

40. M. K. Gandhi, *Diet and Diet Reform* (Ahmedabad, 1949); M. K. Gandhi, *Food Shortage and Agriculture* (Ahmedabad, 1949); Joseph S. Alter, *Gandhi's Body: Sex, Diet, and the Politics of Nationalism* (Philadelphia, 2000); Gandhi to Vijaypal Singh, July 17, 1927, in Gandhi, *Collected Works* (Delhi, 1958–1984), 34: 184–185; Ashis Nandy, *The Savage Freud* (Delhi, 1998), 182.

41. Bose, "Instruments," 45–63; Sunil S. Amrith, "Food and Welfare in India, c. 1900–1950," *Comparative Studies in Society and History* 50 (2008): 1021–1023; National Planning Committee, *Population* (Bombay, 1947), 44–49.

42. "A Nutrition Policy," *The Spectator,* July 24, 1936, 129; "The Staff of Nations," *NYT,* September 4, 1937, 4; Norris E. Dodd, *The United Nations Food and Agriculture Organization* (San Francisco, 1953), 15; Ralph Wesley Phillips, *FAO: Its Origins, Formation, and Evolution, 1945–1981* (Rome, 1981), 4.

43. F. L. McDougall, "Food and Welfare," *Geneva Studies* 9 (1938): 10; League of Nations, *Nutrition: Report of the Mixed Committee of the League of Nations on the Relation of Nutrition to Health, Agriculture, and Economic Policy,* 4 vols. (Geneva, 1936), 2A: 11; 3: 270; Amy L. S. Staples, "To Win the Peace: The Food and Agriculture Organization, Sir John Boyd Orr, and the World Food Board Proposals," *Peace & Change* 28 (2003): 495–523; "The Standard of Living Way to Economic Appeasement," *TL,* September 8, 1937, 9.

44. Timothy Egan, *The Worst Hard Time* (Boston, 2006), 146; "Canadian Wheat Policy," *TL,* February 16, 1935, 23; "French Wheat Surplus," *TL,* February 4, 1935, 11; "Reduction in Surplus Supplies," *TL,* February 12, 1935, "Seek Way to Avoid Dumping of Wheat," *NYT,* May 8, 1934, 40.

45. Alan P. Dobson, "'A Mess of Pottage for Your Economic Birthright?' The 1941-42 Wheat Negotiations and Anglo-American Economic Diplomacy," *The Historical Journal* 28 (1985): 739-750; Roosevelt, "State of the Union," January 6, 1941, www.americanrhetoric.com; Russell B. Porter, "Food Conferees Depict World of Cooperation," *NYT,* May 30, 1943, E7.

46. Matthew Connelly, *Fatal Misconception: The Struggle to Control World Population* (Cambridge, MA, 2008), 77-78.

47. Gunnar Myrdal, "Population Problems and Policies," *AAA* 197 (May 1938): 200, 215; Louis I. Dublin, "America Approaching Stabilized Population," *NYT,* May 4, 1930, E3; "Recent Social Trends Shaping the Course of the Nation's Development," *NYT,* January 2, 1933, SE1; Harold Collander, "When Populations Become Stationary," *NYT Magazine,* February 24, 1935, 7; A. B. Wolfe, "The Theory of Optimum Population," *AAA* 188 (1936): 243; J. M. Keynes, "Some Economic Consequences of a Declining Population," *The Eugenics Review* 29 (1937): 13-17; J. R. Hicks, *Value and Capital* (Oxford, 1938), 302.

48. Edmund Ramsden, "Carving Up Population Science: Eugenics, Demography, and the Controversy of the 'Biological Law' of Population Growth," *Social Studies of Science* 32 (2002): 857-899; Simon Szreter, "The Idea of Demographic Transition and the Study of Fertility Change: A Critical Intellectual History," *Population and Development Review* 19 (1993): 659-701.

49. See reviews by C. E. McGuire, *Political Science Quarterly* 46 (1931): 269-299; O. E. Baker, *American Journal of Sociology* 36 (1930): 300-302; Frank W. Notestein, *American Economic Review* 33 (1943): 937-940.

50. Harold Ickes, *The Secret Diary of Harold L. Ickes* (New York, 1954), 2: 281; Henry L. Stimson, *The Far Eastern Crisis: Recollections and Observations* (New York, 1936), 11-18; Ninkovich, *Modernity,* 112-120; Melvyn Leffler, *A Preponderance of Power* (Stanford, 1992), 20.

51. Edward H. Berman, *The Influence of the Carnegie, Ford, and Rockefeller Foundations on American Foreign Policy* (Albany, 1983), 44; "Rockefeller Foundation President Deplores Repressive Nations Suppression of Truth," *WP,* March 25, 1938, 5; Fosdick, *The Rockefeller Foundation: A Review for 1936,* 13-17; William S. Dutton, "Battling Diseases around the World," *Collier's,* May 5, 1951, 23; Fosdick to Thomas Parran, October 3, 1946, RFAC, RG 3.2, series 900, box 57, folder 310.

52. "Doctor Alfred Lotka, Statistician, Dies," *NYT,* December 7, 1949, 31; Louis Dublin, Statistician, Dies; At Metropolitan Life 51 Years," *NYT,* March 9, 1969, 88.

53. Warren Weaver, *The Scientists Speak* (New York, 1945), 5-6; Frank W. Notestein and Clyde V. Kiser, "Factors Affecting Variations in Human Fertility," *Social Forces* 14 (1935): 32-41; John R. Weeks, "Vignettes of PAA History: Milbank, Princeton, and the War," *PAA Affairs,* Fall 1997, www.pop.psu.edu/general/pubs/PAA_Affairs; Notestein, "Memories of the Early Years of the Association," *Population Index* 47 (1981): 484-488.

54. Frank W. Notestein, "Intrinsic Factors in Population Growth," *Proceedings of the American Philosophical Society* 80 (1939): 511; Notestein, "Population, the

Long View," in Theodore W. Schultz, ed., *Food for the World* (Chicago, 1945), 36–57; Notestein, "Population and Power in Europe," *Foreign Affairs* 22 (1944): 389–404; Notestein, "The Economics of Population and Food Supplies," in *Proceedings of the Eighth International Conference of Agricultural Economists* (London, 1952), 13–31.

55. Dudley Kirk, "Population Changes in the Postwar World," *American Sociological Review* 9 (1944): 28l; Rupert B. Vance, "Malthus and the Principle of Population," *Foreign Affairs* 26 (1948): 682–692; Warren Weaver, "Population and Food," July 17, 1949, RFAC, RG 3, series 915, box 3, folder 23.

56. Notestein to Roger Evans, June 28, 1948, RFAC, RG 1.2, series 600, box 1.

57. Department of State, "Population Problems in the Far East," July 1, 1949, Population Council Papers, RFAC, RG 4.2, general file, box 1, folder 3; Notestein to Joseph Willits, November 1, 1948, RF Papers, RG 1.2, series 600, box 1; Marshall C. Balfour, *Public Health and Demography in the Far East* (New York, 1950); Notestein et al., "Discussion: Human Readjustments," *Proceedings of the American Academy of Political Science* 21 (1945): 109–110; Notestein, "Economics of Population," 20.

58. Gilbert Rist, *The History of Development: From Western Origins to Global Faith* (London, 1997), 73; Hogan, *Informal Entente*, 212.

2. MEXICO'S WAY OUT

1. *Harvest,* directed by Willard van Dyke, 1961, film made for the Rockefeller Foundation, RFAC; Kenneth W. Thompson, "The Green Revolution: Leadership and Partnership in Agriculture," *Review of Politics* 34(4) (1972): 172.

2. John J. Haggerty, "Wartime Shifts in Latin American Agriculture," *Foreign Agriculture* 9(5) (1945): 75; Kathryn Wylie, "Agricultural Relations with Mexico," *Foreign Agriculture* 8(11) (November 1942): 365; Mexico, Dirección General de Estadística, *6⁰ Censo de Población, 1940, Resumen General* (México City, 1943); Survey Commission, "Summary of Recommendations and Conclusions," September 1941, RFAC, RG 1.1, series 323, box 1, folder 2.

3. Borlaug Oral History, June 1967, RFAC; "Mexican Food Project Called Model for World," *Novedades* (Mexico City), April 27, 1945, 1; George W. Gray, "Blueprint for Hungry Nations," *NYT Magazine,* January 1, 1950, 93–99; Study of the Ford Foundation on Policy and Program [Gaither Report], Conservation of Resources, Committee Report #6, January 1950, FFA; Edward E. Bomar, "Indo-China Grants Due to Increase," *WP,* April 13, 1953, 2.

4. John H. Perkins, *Geopolitics and the Green Revolution: Wheat, Genes, and the Cold War* (New York, 1997), 104.

5. "Grain Prices Rise as Rust Affects Wheat Crop Area," *WP,* August 7, 1927, 15; Elvin C. Stakman, "Spores in the Upper Air," *Journal of Agricultural Research* 24 (April 1923): 599; Stakman, "Relation of Barberry to the Origin and Persistence of Physiologic Forms of Puccinia Graminis," *Journal of Agricultural Research* 48 (January 1934): 953; Norman Borlaug, *The Composite Wheat Variety* (New York, 1958), 1; "Barberry Conference," *Indiana Farmer's Guide,* December 2, 1922, 1246; David

E. Hamilton, *From New Day to New Deal: American Farm Policy from Hoover to Roosevelt* (Chapel Hill, NC, 1991), 12; *Congressional Record,* December 28, 1932, 72nd Cong., 2nd sess., 1045–1046; Deborah Fitzgerald, "Exporting American Agriculture: The Rockefeller Foundation in Mexico, 1943–1953," *Social Studies of Science* 16 (1986): 463; Jack Ralph Kloppenberg Jr., *First the Seed: The Political Economy of Plant Biotechnology, 1492–2000* (Cambridge, MA, 1988), 84–87.

6. "New Leadership Is Urged," *NYT,* June 3, 1931, 1; Sarah T. Phillips, "Acres Fit and Unfit: Conservation and Rural Rehabilitation in the New Deal Era" (PhD diss., Boston University, 2004), 22, 88–89.

7. "Farmer Strike Move Spreads," *LAT,* August 2, 1932, 3; Great Plains Committee, *The Future of the Great Plains* (Washington, DC, 1936), 67; Ernie Pyle, *Ernie's America: The Best of Ernie Pyle's 1930s Travel Dispatches* (New York, 1989), 125–126.

8. Robert Redfield and W. Lloyd Warner, "Cultural Anthropology and Modern Agriculture," in *USDA Yearbook of Agriculture, 1940* (Washington, DC, 1940), 988.

9. Raymond Moley, *After Seven Years* (New York, 1939), 12; John C. Culver and John Hyde, *American Dreamer: The Life and Times of Henry Wallace* (New York, 2000), 128.

10. Henry Wallace, "The Year in Agriculture," in *USDA Yearbook of Agriculture, 1934* (Washington, DC, 1934), 6–7, 25, 27; Wallace, "In Search of New Frontiers," *Vital Speeches,* July 29, 1935, 705–710; Wallace, "The Farmer and Social Discipline," *Journal of Farm Economics* 16(1) (January 1934): 1–12; Wallace, "America Must Choose," *Rural America* 12(3) (March 1934): 3–4; Wallace, "A Working Balance Between Agriculture and Industry," *Rural America* 13(1) (January 1935): 3–4.

11. H. A. Wallace, "The Engineering-Scientific Approach to Civilization," *Rural America* 12(4) (1934): 3–6; Wallace, "Give Research a Chance," *Country Gentleman,* September 1934, 5; T. Swann Harding, "Science and Agricultural Policy," in *Yearbook of Agriculture, 1940* (Washington, DC, 1940), 1103; C. M. Christensen, *E. C. Stakman, Statesman of Science* (St. Paul, 1984), 96, 110, 113.

12. E. C. Stakman, "The Promise of Modern Botany for Man's Welfare through Plant Protection," *Scientific Monthly* 44(2) (1937): 117, 130; Lennard Bickel, *Facing Starvation: Norman Borlaug and the Fight against Hunger* (New York, 1974), 85–86; Norman Borlaug, oral history interview, February 1984, Cushing Memorial Library, Texas A&M University, College Station, 99; Perkins, *Geopolitics,* 102–103; William C. Cobb, "The Historical Backgrounds of the Mexican Agricultural Program," March 1956, RFAC, RG 1.2, series 323, 19.

13. Daniels to Hull, November 1, 1933, in Department of State, *FRUS, 1933* (Washington, DC, 1952), 5: 808; Daniels to Messersmith, December 6, 1933, in Department of State, *FRUS, 1933,* 5: 811; John J. Dwyer, "Diplomatic Weapons of the Weak: Mexican Policymaking During the U.S.-Mexican Agrarian Dispute, 1934–1941," *Diplomatic History* 26(3) (Summer 2002): 375–396; "Trouble in Mexico," *TNR,* May 25, 1938, 62; Ralph Bates, "The Future of Mexico," *TNR,* October 19, 1938, 298; Fitzgerald, "Exporting," 462.

14. Charles A. Thomson, "Mexico's Social Revolution," *Foreign Policy Reports* 13(10) (August 1, 1937): 114–124; Frank Tannenbaum, *The Mexican Agrarian Revolution* (Washington, DC, 1929), 393.

15. Alan Knight, *U.S.-Mexican Relations, 1910–1940: An Interpretation* (San Diego, 1987), 10; Frank Kluckhohn, "Revolution on a Silver Platter," *Saturday Evening Post,* February 5, 1938, 16; Maurice Halperin, "What about Mexico?" *TNR,* January 12, 1938, 271; Roberto Piña, "Mexico's Runaway New Deal," *American Mercury,* February 1939, 176–182; Prendergast, "New Deal in Mexico," *Nation,* September 4, 1937, 237–239.

16. Clayton Koppes, "The Good Neighbor Policy and the Nationalization of Mexican Oil," *JAH* 69(1) (June 1982): 69; Freidrich E. Schuler, *Mexico between Hitler and Roosevelt* (Albuquerque, 1998), 133.

17. Charles S. Maier, "The Politics of Productivity: Foundations of American International Economic Policy after World War II," *International Organization* 31 (Autumn 1977): 607–633; Michael A. Butler, *Cautious Visionary: Cordell Hull and Trade Reform, 1933–1937* (Kent, OH, 1998), 83–84; Arthur M. Schlesinger Jr., *The Coming of the New Deal* (Cambridge, MA, 1958), 188, 191; Catherine Anne Grollman, "Cordell Hull and His Concept of a World Organization" (PhD diss., University of North Carolina, 1965), 165–166; Raymond Moley, *After Seven Years* (New York, 1939), 115; Wallace, "Year in Agriculture," 7.

18. Richard Slotkin, *Gunfighter Nation: The Myth of the Frontier in Twentieth Century America* (New York, 1992), 311; Jeffrey Paul, "All Mexico Prepares for Tourist Invasion," *Washington Post,* May 10, 1936, B7; T. Philip Tery, *Terry's Guide to Mexico* (Boston, 1935), iii; Pablo C. de Gante, "Mexico as a Tourist Resort," *Banker's Magazine,* January 1936, 75.

19. Ernest Gruening, "The Meaning of Mexico," in Hubert Herring, ed., *Renascent Mexico* (New York, 1935), 1–8; Stuart Chase, "Machineless Men," *Forum and Century,* December 1930, 379.

20. John Steinbeck, *The Forgotten Village* (New York, 1941), 9; Daniel Cooper Alarcón, *The Aztec Palimpsest: Mexico in the Modern Imagination* (Tucson, 1997); Anita Brenner, "Mexico Shatters the Mold of Centuries," *NYT Magazine,* August 28, 1938, 19.

21. Stephen R. Niblo, *War, Diplomacy and Development: The United States and Mexico, 1938–1954* (Wilmington, DE, 1995), 66; Leslie B. Rout Jr. and John F. Bratzel, "Origins: US Intelligence in Latin America," CIA report, 1986, *DDRS,* ck3100239642; "Communazi Columnists," *Time,* June 3, 1940, 35; Lloyd C. Gardner, *Economic Aspects of New Deal Diplomacy* (Madison, WI, 1964), 117–122.

22. Nathaniel and Sylvia Weyl, *The Reconquest of Mexico: The Years of Lázaro Cárdenas* (New York, 1939), 176–177; Josephus Daniels, *Shirt Sleeve Diplomat* (Chapel Hill, NC, 1947), 201; Ralph Bates, "The Future of Mexico," *TNR,* October 19, 1938, 296.

23. George F. Kennan, *Sketches from a Life* (New York, 1989), 134; William Parker, "Juan Hangs Up His Gun," *Current History,* August 1939, 28–30, 54; Max

S. Handman et al., "The Chief Economic Problems of Mexico," *The American Economic Review* 20(1) (1930): 63–72; George Creel, "Can We Prevent Chaos in Mexico?" *Collier's,* July 23, 1938, 12–13, 50–51; Robert Redfield, *Chan Kom: A Maya Village* (Washington, DE, 1934); Redfield, *Tepoztlan, A Mexican Village* (Chicago, 1930), 222; Waldo Frank, "Cardenas of Mexico," *Foreign Affairs* 18 (1939): 91–101.

24. Nelson Rockefeller, "A Cárdenas Trip to the United States," April 15, 1943, State Department Central Files, 812.001, RG 59, box 4113, NARA.

25. Fosdick to Wallace, January 29, 1941, RFAC, RG 1.1, series 323, box 1, folder 2; Eyler N. Simpson, *The Ejido: Mexico's Way Out* (Chapel Hill, NC, 1937), esp. 496–501, 558–581.

26. Henry A. Wallace, "Wallace in Mexico," *Wallace's Farmer and Iowa Homestead,* February 22, 1941, 1, 10–11; Betty Kirk, *Covering the Mexican Front* (Norman, OK, 1942), 254, 257, 261–262; "Record Rains Hit Texas Panhandle," *NYT,* November 25, 1940, 36; "Crowds Cheer Wallace," *LAT,* November 27, 1940, 3; Robert Kleiman, "New Era of Friendship Dawns," *WP,* December 1, 1940, B5.

27. Henry A. Wallace, "Wallace in Mexico," *Wallace's Farmer and Iowa Homestead,* February 22, 1941, 1, 10–11; J. A. Ferrell, "Vice President Wallace, RBF and JAF, Regarding Mexico, Its Problems and Remedies," February 31, 1941, RFAC, RG 1.1, series 323, box 1, folder 2.

28. Cobb, "Historical Backgrounds," Chapter 2, 6; "Staff Conference," February 18, 1941, RFAC, RG 1.1, series 323, box 1, folder 2; James E. Austin and Gustavo Esteva, *Food Policy in Mexico: The Search for Self-Sufficiency* (Ithaca, NY, 1987), 35.

29. William P. Blocker to Hull, May 19, 1939, State Department Central Files, 812.001/169, RG 59, box 5334, NARA.

30. Enrique C. Ochoa, *Feeding Mexico: The Political Uses of Food Since 1910* (Wilmington, DE, 2000), 50–57.

31. Survey Commission, "Summary of Recommendations and Conclusions," September 1941, RFAC, RG 1.1, series 323, box 1, folder 2; Stakman to Rusk, December 22, 1953, RFAC, RG 3, series 915, box 3, folder 21.

32. Henry R. Luce, "The American Century," *Life,* February 17, 1941, 61–65; Culver and Hyde, *American Dreamer,* 275–277; Wallace, "Foundations of the Peace," *Atlantic Monthly,* December 1941; "Text of Vice President Wallace's Address on This Nation's War Aims," *NYT,* April 9, 1941, 18; Wallace, "Mexican Independence and New World Ideals," *Vital Speeches,* October 1, 1942, 740–743.

33. "Back to the Earth," *Time,* April 19, 1943, 33–38; Robert Kleiman, "New Era of Friendship," *WP,* Dec 1, 1940, B5; Raleigh Gibson to Secretary of State, "Report on the Accomplishments of Manuel Avila Camacho's First Year," December 9, 1941, State Department Central Files, 812.01/171, RG 59, box 4113, NARA; Jack O'Brine, "U.S. Bankers Offer to Put $100,000,000 Into Mexico," *WP,* December 11, 1940, 1; George S. Messersmith, "Mexico's War Contribution Has Been Great," *Ladies' Home Journal,* June 1944, 132.

34. Joseph Cotter, *Troubled Harvest: Agronomy and Revolution in Mexico, 1880–2002* (Westport, CT, 2003), 148–149; "Money and Mexico," *Newsweek,* August 16, 1943, 34–35; "Mexico: One Year at War," *Fortune,* August 1943, 120–121; Verna Carleton Millan, "What Has Happened to Mexico's Food?" *Inter-American,* March 1944, 13–15, 45; Kathryn Wylie, "Agricultural Relations with Mexico," *Foreign Agriculture* 6(11) (November 1942): 365–373; John J. Haggerty, "Wartime Shifts in Latin American Agriculture," *Foreign Agriculture* 9(5) (May 1945): 75–80; "Celebrations and Hunger," *Inter-American,* November 1943, 8; Niblo, *War, Diplomacy,* 130–131.

35. Stakman to Frank Hanson, February 10, 1943, RFAC, RG 1.1, series 323, box 1, folder 4; E. C. Stakman, Richard Bradfield, and Paul C. Mangelsdorf, *Campaigns against Hunger* (Cambridge, MA, 1967), 39.

36. Hanson to Stakman, April 11, 1944, RFAC, RG 1.1, series 323, box 1, folder 7; Hanson to Harrar, June 19, 1944, RFAC, RG 1.1, series 323, box 1, folder 7; Hanson to Harrar, October 28, 1942, RFAC, RG 1.1, series 323, box 1, folder 3, RFAC.

37. Cotter, *Troubled Harvest,* 180, 199; Fitzgerald, "Exporting," 467.

38. Vance Bourjaily, "One of the Green Revolution Boys," *Atlantic,* February 1973, 68.

39. Bickel, *Facing Starvation,* 108; Borlaug oral history, June 1967, BP, 7.

40. Cotter, *Troubled Harvest,* 185.

41. Comments of Norman E. Borlaug, The Borlaug Global Rust Initiative (BGRI) 2009 Technical Workshop, Ciudad Obregón, Sonora, Mexico, March 2009, www.globalrust.org; Rodomiro Ortiz, David Mowbray, Christopher Dowswell, and Sanjaya Rajaram, "Dedication: Norman E. Borlaug, the Humanitarian Plant Scientist Who Changed the World," *Plant Breeding Reviews* (2007): 1–37; Fitzgerald, "Exporting," 466; Stakman, "Report on RF Mexican Program based on visit from April 25 to May 17, 1949," RFAC, RG 1.2, series 323, Box 10, folder 60.

42. Borlaug oral history, June 1967, BP, 155–158; FBH to Fosdick, "E. C. Stakman," March 4, 1942, RFAC, RG 1.1, series 323, box 1, folder 3.

43. G. S. Messersmith to Hull, September 1, 1942, State Department Central Files, 812.001/268, RG 59, Box 4113, NARA; Cotter, *Troubled Harvest,* 189; Borlaug oral history, June 1967, BP, 66–70.

44. Niblo, *War, Diplomacy, and Development,* 23–28.

45. Michael Scully, "New Life in Old Mexico," *Reader's Digest,* February 1946, 45–48; "Mexico on the March," *Business Week,* March 10, 1945, 113–114; Henry Hazlitt, "Boom in Mexico," *Newsweek,* February 17, 1947, 80; Feliz Belair, "Truman Wins Triumph as Good-Will Envoy," *NYT,* March 9, 1947, E3; Raymond B. Fosdick, *The Rockefeller Foundation: A Review for 1945* (New York, 1945), 10–15, 28–32.

46. "Mexico in 1947," *Life,* February 24, 1947, 93; Draft of suggestions for the President's message to Congress in regard to the Greek situation, March 3, 1947, Joseph M. Jones Papers, HSTL; "Texts of Addresses of Aleman and Truman," *NYT,* March 4, 1947, 2; Lawrence Burd, "Work for Peace or Fall to Ruin, Truman Warns," *CT,* March 6, 1947, 2.

47. William Vogt, "A Continent Slides to Ruin," *Harper's,* June 1948, 481; Chester Barnard to Warren Weaver, "'Road to Survival,' by William Vogt," August 31, 1948, RFAC, RG 3.2, series 900, box 57, folder 310.

48. George Gallup, "World Explosion by Misuse of Atom Feared," *LAT,* September 16, 1945, 4; Jessica Wang, *American Science in an Age of Anxiety* (Chapel Hill, NC, 1999), 10–43; Daniel Lee Kleinman, *Politics on the Endless Frontier: Postwar Research Policy in the United States* (Durham, NC, 1995), 75–99.

49. William Vogt, *Road to Survival* (New York, 1948); Fairfield Osborn, *Our Plundered Planet* (New York, 1948), 137.

50. Amy L. Bentley, "Uneasy Sacrifice: The Politics of United States Famine Relief, 1945–1948," *Agriculture and Human Values* 11(4) (Fall 1994): 1; George Kennan, "United States Policy toward China," September 7, 1948, PPS/39, in Department of State, *The State Department Policy Planning Staff Papers* (New York, 1982), 2: 413; Senate Committee on Foreign Relations, *Reviews of the World Situation: 1949–1950,* 81st Cong., 1st and 2nd sess., [Historical Series], 1974, 86; David W. Elwood, *Rebuilding Europe: Western Europe, America, and Postwar Reconstruction* (London, 1992), 54; Walter Millis, ed., *The Forrestal Diaries* (New York, 1951), 311.

51. Notestein to Willits, November 1, 1948, RFAC, RG 1.2, series 600, box 1; Willits to Notestein, December 7, 1948, RFAC, RG 1.2, series 600, box 1; John Ensor Harr and Paul Johnson, *The Rockefeller Century* (New York, 1988), 459–460; N. S. Haseltine, "Dire State of the Future World Pictured by Scientists Here," *WP,* September 15, 1948, 6.

52. Barnard to Weaver, "'Road to Survival,' by William Vogt," August 31, 1948, RFAC, RG 3.2, series 900, box 57, folder 310; Chester I. Barnard, *The Rockefeller Foundation: A Review for 1948* (New York, 1948), 14–20.

53. William L. Laurence, "Scientists Promise More Food for All," *NYT,* December 28, 1949, 27; Weaver, "Population and Food," July 17, 1949, RFAC, RG 3, series 915, box 3, folder 23; Weaver to Barnard, June 21, 1951, RFAC, RG 3, series 915, box 3, folder 23; Weaver, "Human Ecology," May 4, 1955, RFAC, RG 2, series 100, box 6, folder 30; Weaver, "People, Energy and Food," *Scientific Monthly* 78(6) (June 1954): 359–364.

54. Barnard, *The Rockefeller Foundation: A Review for 1948,* 21; Lorimer to Weaver, "WFL Notes on World Population and World Food Supplies," November 22, 1949, RFAC, RG 3, series 915, box 3, folder 20.

55. "Mexico's Private Point Four," *NYT,* October 11, 1952, 18; Sydney Gruson, "Rockefeller Unit Widens Mexico Aid," *NYT,* October 10, 1952, 6; Jules DuBois, "U.S. Helps Mexico Build Better Citizens," *CT,* December 25, 1952, A8; Morris Kaplan, "A U.S. Foundation Aids Latin Farms," *NYT,* December 9, 1956, 13; Lula Thomas Holmes, "Pablo Is Eating Better Now," *Independent Woman,* November 1952, 331–332; J. Strohm, "Mexico Closes the Food Gap," *Reader's Digest,* June 1966, 32–37; J. G. Harrar, *Mexican Agricultural Program* (New York, 1950); Harrar, *The Agricultural Program of the Rockefeller Foundation* (New York, 1956).

56. Gladwyn Hill, "Mexican Wetbacks a Complex Problem," *NYT,* January 18, 1953, E6; Gladwyn Hill, "Peons in the West Lowering Culture," *NYT,* January 18,

1951, 31; George I. Sánchez and Lyle Saunders, "'Wetbacks': A Preliminary Report to the Advisory Committee, Study of Spanish Speaking Peoples," University of Texas, 1949.

57. Angus Wright, *The Death of Ramón González: The Modern Agricultural Dilemma* (Austin, TX, 1990); David Sonnenfeld, "Mexico's 'Green Revolution,' 1940–1980: Towards an Environmental History," *Environmental History Review* 16(4) (Winter 1992): 29–52; Jeffrey Pilcher, *¿Que Vivan los Tamales! Food and the Making Mexican Identity* (Albuquerque, 1998); Cynthia Hewitt de Alcántara, *Modernizing Mexican Agriculture* (Geneva, 1976); Borlaug, "A Review by Norman E. Borlaug of the Report: The Social and Economic Implications of Large Scale Introductions of New Varieties of Food Grain," September 17, 1975, BP, box 7.

58. Joseph A. Schumpeter, *Business Cycles* (New York, 1939); Wassily Leontief, *The Structure of American Economy, 1919–1929* (Cambridge, MA, 1941); John Louis von Neumann and Oskar Morgenstern, *Theory of Games and Economic Behavior* (Princeton, 1944); Harold D. Lasswell, "Strategies of Inquiry: The Rational Uses of Observation," in Daniel Lerner, ed., *Human Meaning of the Social Sciences* (New York, 1959), 89; Max Black, *Models and Metaphors: Studies in Language and Philosophy* (Ithaca, NY, 1962), 223; Lasswell, "The Semantics of Political Science—A Discussion," *American Political Science Review* 44(2) (June 1950): 422–425; Tim Mitchell, "America's Egypt: Discourses of the Development Industry," *Middle East Report* 21(2) (March 1991): 29–30; Ron Robin, *The Making of the Cold War Enemy: Culture and Politics in the Military Intellectual Complex* (Princeton, 2001) 59–71; Norman E. Borlaug and Ignacio Narvaez, "Progress Report: Accelerated Wheat Improvement Program in West Pakistan, and the Revolution in Agriculture," March 30, 1966, Wichita State University Library, Wichita, Kansas.

59. Melvyn P. Leffler, *The Specter of Communism* (New York, 1994), 50–57; Stewart Alsop, "Matter of Fact," *WP*, June 8, 1949, 11.

60. CIA, "Review of the World Situation," January 19, 1949, *DDRS*, ck3100371129; Ford Foundation, *Gaither Report: Report of the Study for the Ford Foundation on Policy and Program* (New York, 1949), 23; Robert Payne, *The Revolt of Asia* (New York, 1947), 278.

3. A CONTINENT OF PEASANTS

1. Department of State, *FRUS, 1949* (Washington, DC, 1979), 8: 723; Jack Belden, "Mission: Murder," *Saturday Evening Post,* August 20, 1947, 15; Odd Arne Westad, *Decisive Encounters: The Chinese Civil War, 1946–1950* (Stanford, 2003), 110, 238–244.

2. Department of State, *The State Department Policy Planning Staff Papers, 1947–1949* (New York, 1983), 2: 449; Department of State, *FRUS, 1945–1950: Emergence of the Intelligence Establishment* (Washington, DC, 1996), 896; Senate Committee on Foreign Relations, *Reviews of the World Situation: 1949–1950,* 81st Cong., 1st and 2nd sess., [Historical Series], 1974, 131.

3. John K. Fairbank, "Competition with Communism, Not Containment," *Foreign Policy Reports,* March 15, 1949, 6; "Text of President's Message," *WP,* March 13, 1947, 1, 4; George Kennan, "Review of Current Trends: U.S. Foreign Policy," PPS 23, February 24, 1948, in Thomas H. Etzold and John L. Gaddis, eds., *Containment: Documents on American Policy and Strategy, 1945–1950* (New York, 1978), 226.

4. David M. Potter, *People of Plenty* (Chicago, 1954); David Riesman, *The Lonely Crowd: A Study of the Changing American Character* (New Haven, 1950), 43, 113; Richard Hofstadter, *The Age of Reform* (New York, 1955), 23, 328.

5. Reinhold Niebuhr, *The Irony of American History* (New York, 1952), 120, 125; Arthur M. Schlesinger Jr., *The Vital Center* (New York, 1949), 223; William J. Lederer and Eugene Burdick, *The Ugly American* (New York, 1958), 283.

6. Timothy Mitchell, *Rule of Experts: Egypt, Techno-Politics, Modernity* (Berkeley, 2002), 123–152; Teodor Shanin, *Peasants and Peasant Societies: Selected Readings* (New York, 1987); Harold R. Isaacs, *Scratches on Our Minds: American Images of China and India* (New York, 1958), 212; Fairbank, "Competition with Communism," 6–9; Pearl S. Buck, "American Imperialism in the Making," *Asia,* August 1945, 365–368.

7. Partha Chatterjee, "The Nation and Its Peasants," in Vinayak Chaturvedi, ed., *Mapping Subaltern Studies and the Postcolonial* (London, 2000), 8–23; Ranajit Guha, "The Prose of Counter-Insurgency," in *Subaltern Studies II: Writings on South Asian History and Society* (Delhi, 1983), 1–42; Gyan Prakash, "Subaltern Studies as Postcolonial Criticism," *AHR* 95(5) (1994): 1491–1515; Dipesh Chakrabarty, "A Small History of *Subaltern Studies,*" in *Habitations of Modernity* (Chicago, 2002), 3–19; Department of State, Bureau of Intelligence and Research, "The Soviet Threat to the United States," September 14, 1953, *DDRS,* ck3100324186.

8. "Point IV," *Fortune,* February 1950, 88; Louis J. Halle, "On Teaching International Relations," *Virginia Quarterly Review* 40(1) (1964): 11–25; Truman, "Remarks at the Women's National Democratic Club Dinner, November 8, 1949, in *Public Papers of the Presidents, Harry S Truman, 1949* (Washington, DC, 1950), 556–557; Henry A. Byroade, "The World's Colonies and Ex-Colonies: A Challenge to America," *DOSB,* November 16, 1953), 655; Jawaharlal Nehru, *The Discovery of India* (New York, 1960), 393.

9. "The Poor Countries," *The Economist,* June 2, 1951, 1277; John Kenneth Galbraith, *The Nature of Mass Poverty* (Cambridge, MA, 1979), 29; Nils Gilman, *Mandarins of the Future: Modernization Theory in Cold War America* (Baltimore, 2003), 158; CENIS, *United States Foreign Policy: Economic, Social and Political Change in the Underdeveloped Countries and Its Implications for United States Policy,* Senate Committee on Foreign Relations, 86th Cong., 2nd sess., March 30, 1960, 10.

10. Ron Robin, *The Making of the Cold War Enemy* (Princeton, 2001), 32; Gilman, *Mandarins of the Future,* 67; Mark E. Hefele, "Walt Rostow's Stages of Economic Growth: Ideas and Action," in David Engerman et al., eds., *Staging Growth: Modernization, Development, and the Global Cold War* (Amherst, MA, 2003), 199–224.

11. "India Opens Project with the Help of U.S.," *NYT,* October 2, 1952, 3; Arran Moore, "India Starts Five-Year Program of Development," *WP,* October 3, 1952, 4; Hugh Tinker, "Community Development: A New Philosopher's Stone," *International Affairs* 37(3) (July 1961): 309, 322; United Nations Economic and Social Council, "Community Development and Related Services," *Community Development Review,* December 1956, 7; Rosaleen Smith, "The Roots of Community Development in Colonial Office Policy and Practice in Africa," *Social Policy and Administration* 38(4) (2004): 418–436; C. W. Chang, *The Rural Community Development Movement in Asia and the Far East* (Bangkok, June 1955).

12. A. M. Rosenthal, "Indians to Press Quiet Revolution," *NYT,* February 26, 1956, 26; Chester Bowles, *Ambassador's Report* (New York, 1954), 197–198; "India Conference, Notes on Discussion," March 26, 1952, RFAC, RG 1.2, series 460, box 1.

13. Douglas Ensminger, *A Guide to Community Development* (New Delhi, 1957), 3; Government of India, Planning Commission, *The First Five-Year Plan: A Summary* (New Delhi, 1952), 47; J. C. Kavoori and Baij Nath Singh, *History of Rural Development in Modern India* (New Delhi, 1967), 117.

14. James Reston, "Dewey Talk Awaited for Key to Policy on Asia's Defense," *NYT,* January 24, 1952, 3; Senate Armed Services Committee, *Mutual Security Act of 1951,* 82nd Cong., 1st sess., 1951, 458; Harry W. Blair, "The Green Revolution and 'Economic Man': Some Lessons for Community Development in South Asia?" *Pacific Affairs* 44(3) (1971): 358.

15. Melvyn P. Leffler, *A Preponderance of Power* (Stanford, 1992), 23, 35.

16. Isidor Lubin, "The World's Awakening Peoples and Their Demand for Human Betterment," *DOSB,* June 9, 1952, 935–936, quoted in Donald K. Faris, *To Plow with Hope* (New York, 1958), 107; Ashis Nandy, *An Ambiguous Journey to the City: The Village and Other Odd Ruins of the Self in the Indian Imagination* (New Delhi, 2001); David Ludden, "Subalterns and Others in the Agrarian History of South Asia," in James C. Scott and Nina Bhatt, eds., *Agrarian Studies: Synthetic Work at the Cutting Edge* (New Haven, 2001), 217.

17. D. Michael Shafer, *Deadly Paradigms: The Failure of U.S. Counterinsurgency Policy* (Princeton, 1988), 81; CIA, "Review of the World Situation," January 19, 1949, *DDRS,* ck3100371129; Lucian W. Pye, *Guerilla Communism in Malaya: Its Social and Political Meaning* (Princeton, 1956), 355; Senate Foreign Relations Committee, *Executive Sessions of the Committee,* 82nd Cong., 1st sess., 1951 [1976]), vol. 3, pt. 2, 396.

18. Alice O'Connor, "Community Action, Urban Reform, and the Fight against Poverty: The Ford Foundation's Gray Areas Project," *Journal of Urban History* 22(5) (1996): 586–626.

19. Albert Mayer, "Americans in India," *Survey Graphic,* March 1947, 202–206; Paul Goldberger, "Albert Mayer, 83, Architect and Housing Planner, Dies," *NYT,* October 16, 1981, B6.

20. Mayer to Nehru, December 19, 1945, Mayer Papers, Regenstein Library, University of Chicago, box 8, folder 1; Nehru to Mayer, May 1, 1946, Mayer Papers, box 8, folder 1; Alice Thorner quoted in F. Tomasson Jannuzi, *India's Persistent Dilemmma: The Political Economy of Agrarian Reform* (Boulder, CO, 1994),

90; Mayer, "Preliminary Outline for Village Planning and Reconstruction," December 2, 1946, Mayer Papers, box 2, folder 17; Mayer, "Proposal for Planning, Coordination, and Development for Immediate Application in One District," January 1, 1947, Mayer Papers, box 2, folder 17.

21. Albert Mayer, Henry Wright, and Lewis Mumford, *New Homes for a New Deal* (New York, 1939); Albert Mayer, "Attacking the City's Slum Problem: A New Approach," *NYT,* February 18, 1934, xx3; Albert Mayer, "New Towns and Defense," *The Survey,* February 1951, 64–65; Mayer and Julian Whittlesey, "Horse Sense Planning," *Architectural Forum* 79(5) (1943): 59–74.

22. Louis Wirth, "Urbanism as a Way of Life," *The American Journal of Sociology* 44(1) (1938): 1–24; Robert Redfield, *A Village That Chose Progress* (Chicago, 1950); Albert Mayer, *Pilot Project India: The Story of Rural Development at Etawah, Uttar Pradesh* (Berkeley, 1958), 333; Christopher Gray, "A Model of High-Density Residential Development," *NYT,* February 9, 1997, 47.

23. "Architect's Dream," *Time,* June 19, 1950, 37–38; "American to Plan New City for India," *NYT,* January 25, 1950, 4; Mayer, "Planning a New Capital," [*Lucknow*] *National Herald,* June 5, 1950, Mayer Papers, box 35, folder 6.

24. Eric Mumford, "The 'Tower in the Park' in America: Theory and Practice," *Planning Perspectives* 10(1) (1995): 17–41; Kermit C. Parsons, "British and American Community Design: Clarence Stein's Manhattan Transfer, 1924–74," *Planning Perspectives* 7(2) (1992): 181–210; Nicole Sackley, "Passage to Modernity: American Social Scientists, India, and the Pursuit of Development, 1945–1961" (PhD diss., Princeton University, 2004); Russell Walden,*The Open Hand: Essays on Le Corbusier* (Cambridge, MA, 1977), x; Christopher Rand, "City on a Tilting Plain," *The New Yorker,* April 30, 1955, 35–62.

25. N. V. Modak and Albert Mayer, *An Outline of the Master Plan for Greater Bombay* (Bombay, 1948), 5, 50–51; Mayer, *Pilot Project,* 18; Albert Mayer, "Social Analysis and National Economic Development in India," *Pacific Affairs* 35(2) (1962): 128.

26. Mayer, *Pilot Project,* 206; Mayer et al., *New Homes,* 36, 41; Mayer and Julian Whittlesey, "Horse Sense Planning," *Architectural Forum* 79(5) (1943): 68; Mayer, "Footholds for a New India," *Survey Graphic,* September 1947, 483.

27. Ronald Inden, *Imagining India* (Cambridge, MA, 1990), 131–161; David Ludden, "Orientalist Empiricism: Transformations of Colonial Knowledge," in C. A. Breckenridge, ed., *Orientalism and the Postcolonial Predicament* (Philadelphia, 1993), 251.

28. Mayer, *Pilot Project,* 20; F. L. Brayne, *Village Uplift in India* (Allahabad, 1927), 1, 4, 17; F. L. Brayne, *The Remaking of Village India* (London, 1929); Clive Dewey, *Anglo-Indian Attitudes: The Mind of the Indian Civil Service* (London, 1993), 61–100.

29. Mayer, "Report on Master Plan of the New Punjab Capital," May 12, 1950, Mayer Papers, box 18, folder 30; Sunil Khilnani, *The Idea of India* (New York, 1997), 130–133; Judith M. Brown, *Nehru: A Political Life* (New Haven, 2003), 201; Albert Mayer, "The New Capital of the Punjab," *Journal of the AIA* 14 (1950): 175; Mayer, "Footholds," 483.

30. Mayer, "New Capital," 173; Mayer, "Report on Master Plan."

31. Mayer, *Pilot Project,* 68–70; E. Holmes to Mayer, April 6, 1950, Mayer Papers, box 6, folder 16.

32. United Nations Economic and Social Council, "Community Development," 11; Ministry of Development and Co-Operation, *Kurukshetra: A Symposium* (New Delhi, 1961), 92.

33. Reinhard Bendix, *Nation-Building and Citizenship* (New Bruswick, NJ, 1996), 294; Bipan Chadra, Mridula Mukherjee, and Aditya Mukherjee, *India after Independence, 1947–2000* (New Delhi, 2002), 42–43, 60–61.

34. S. K. Dey, "Functional Democracy," *Kurukshetra* 7(10) (July 1959): 14; CIA, "The Community Development Experiment in India," 1960, CREST, box 5, folder 6, item 2–7.

35. Mayer, *Pilot Project,* 113, 200; "Kisan Special Leaves on Tour of India," *Overseas Hindustan Times,* September 29, 1955, 3; "Our Tourists," *Kurukshetra* 7(10) (July 1959): 4; Mayer, "Social Analysis," 139.

36. Ford Foundation, *Annual Report for 1953* (New York, 1953), 27–28; Mayer, *Pilot Project,* 207–209; Senate Armed Services Committee, *Mutual Security Act,* 470; Kavoori and Singh, *History of Rural Development,* 130.

37. Jawaharlal Nehru, *Selected Works* (Delhi, 1984), 2nd series, 1: 369; Senate Foreign Relations Committee, *Executive Sessions,* vol. 3, pt. 2, 430.

38. Jonathan B. Bingham, *Shirt Sleeve Diplomacy: Point 4 in Action* (New York, 1954), 45; Eleanor Roosevelt, *India and the Awakening East* (New York, 1953), 124; Elizabeth Converse, "Pilot Development Projects in India," *Far Eastern Survey* 20(3) (February 7, 1951): 23; Shyam S. Bhatia, "A New Measure of Agricultural Efficiency in Uttar Pradesh, India," *Economic Geography* 43(3) (1967): 244–260; Mayer, *Pilot Project,* 163.

39. Albert Mayer, "Nehru, the Man—and India's Travail," *The Survey,* December 1949, 661; Gorge Rosen, *Western Economists and Eastern Societies* (Baltimore, 1985), 11; Senate Foreign Relations Committee, *Executive Sessions,* vol. 3, pt. 2, 418; J. G. Harrar, Paul C. Manglesdorf, and Warren Weaver, "Notes on Indian Agriculture," March 1953, New Delhi Field Office Papers, RG 6.7, series II, box 26, folder 147, RFAC.

40. M. J. Akbar, *Nehru: The Making of India* (New Delhi, 2002), 472.

41. Senate Armed Services Committee, *Mutual Security Act,* 460–461.

42. Mayer, *Pilot Project,* 283; Mayer, *The Urgent Future: People, Housing, City, Region* (New York, 1967), 66–72.

43. John W. Mellor et al., *Developing Rural India: Plan and Practice* (Ithaca, NY, 1968), 36; Mayer, "Working with the People," February 24, 1952, Mayer Papers, box 35, folder 11; Mayer, "Community Development in India's Villages," July 7, 1960, Mayer Papers, box 35, folder 32.

44. Balvantray G. Mehta, *Report of the Team for the Study of Community Projects and National Extension Service* (Delhi, 1957).

45. Jane Jacobs, *The Death and Life of Great American Cities* (New York, 1961); William F. Whyte, *Street Corner Society: The Social Structure of an Italian Slum* (Chicago, 1955).

46. Maxwell Taylor to McGeorge Bundy, "Counterinsurgency Doctrine," USAM 182, August 13, 1962, *DDRS,* ck3100453890.

47. Bagley to Taylor, January 20, 1962, in Department of State, *FRUS, 1961–1963* (Washington, DC, 1994), 23: 899; Edward G. Lansdale, "Soldiers and the People," Lecture at the Special Warfare School, Fort Bragg, NC, August 30, 1962, in United States Operations Mission to Vietnam, Office of Rural Affairs, *Provincial Representative's Guide* (Saigon, 1963), 11; Michael Latham, *Modernization as Ideology* (Chapel Hill, NC, 2000).

48. Carl C. Taylor, *A Critical Analysis of India's Community Development Programme* (Delhi, 1956), 58; Joseph Burkholder Smith, *Portrait of a Cold Warrior* (Quezon City, 1976), 272; interview with Harold M. Jones, February 4, 1997, in Association for Diplomatic Studies and Training, *Frontline Diplomacy: The U.S. Foreign Affairs Oral History Collection* (Washington, DC, 2000 [CD-ROM]); Elizabeth Cobbs Hoffman, *All You Need Is Love: The Peace Corps and the Spirit of the 1960s* (Cambridge, MA 1998), 67; Mayer, *Pilot Project,* 333.

49. Henry L. Stimson, *Diaries,* March 26, 1936 (New Haven, 1973); Heald oral history, January 7, 1972, FFA; Forrest Hill, "Notes on Economic Development," December 10, 1958, Report 010459, FFA; Lyndon Johnson, "Statement before House Foreign Affairs Committee," June 5, 1961, *DDRS,* ck3100384487.

50. "New East Harlem Plaza a Boom to City," *New Pittsburgh Courier,* January 18, 1960, 4.

51. Senate Armed Services Committee, *Mutual Security Act,* 468.

52. James Rorty, "The Dossier of Wolf Ladejinsky," *Commentary,* April 1955, 326–334.

53. Mary S. McAuliffe, "Dwight D. Eisenhower and Wolf Ladejinsky: The Politics of the Declining Red Scare, 1954–1955," *Prologue* 14(3) (Fall 1982): 109–127; "The Case of Wolf Ladejinsky," *NYT,* December 20, 1954, 28; Aubrey Graves, "Land Reform in Japan," *WP,* January 5, 1955, 11; "Agrarian Reformers for Export," *CT,* December 28, 1954, 12; "Ladejinsky as a Symbol," *WP,* December 23, 1954, 26.

54. H. W. Arndt, *Economic Development: The History of an Idea* (Chicago, 1987), 6; Frederick Cooper and Randall Packard, *International Development and the Social Sciences: Essays on the History and Politics of Knowledge* (Berkeley, 1997), 29; John Harriss, "Great Promise, Hubris, and Recovery: A Participant's History of Development Studies," in Uma Kothari, ed., *A Radical History of Development Studies* (London, 2005), 17–46; Colin Leys, *The Rise and Fall of Development Theory* (Bloomington, IN, 1996); Gilman, *Mandarins,* 21; Wolf Ladejinsky, "Agrarian Reforms in Asia," *Foreign Affairs* 42(3) (1964): 455.

55. R. E. Pahl, "The Rural-Urban Continuum," *Sociologia Ruralis* 6(3–4) (1966): 299–326; Eugen Lupri, "The Rural Urban Variable Reconsidered: The Cross-Cultural Perspective," *Sociologia Ruralis* 7(1) (1967): 1–17; Edward Shils, "Centre and Periphery," in *The Logic of Personal Knowledge* (Glencoe, IL: Free Press, 1961), 117–130; Deborah Fitzgerald, *Every Farm a Factory: The Industrial Ideal in American Agriculture* (New Haven, 2003).

56. Michael Harringon, "The New Physiocrats," *NYT Book Review,* April 9, 1978, 4.

57. Rorty, "Dossier," 331.

58. Jeong Koo Kang, "Rethinking South Korean Land Reform: Focusing on U.S. Occupation as a Struggle against History" (PhD diss., University of Wisconsin, 1988), 323; Steven Schwartzberg, "The 'Soft Peace Boys': Presurrender Planning and Japanese Land Reform," *Journal of American-East Asian Relations* 2(2) (1993): 185–216; Stanley Andrews to Philip C. Jessup, September 25, 1950, Department of State Central Files, 890.16/8–1850, box 5530, RG59, NARA; U.S. Department of State, *Land Reform: A World Challenge* (Washington, DC, February 1952).

59. Joseph and Stewart Alsop, "The Orient's New Deal," *WP,* February 17, 1946, B5; "An Ally in Asia: Land Reform," *Fortune,* November 1950, 74; Barbara Ward, "Recipe for Victory in the Far East," *NYT Magazine,* March 25, 1951, 26; Aubrey Graves, "Conflict Rises in Ladejinsky 'Risk' Ouster," *WP,* December 23, 1954, 2.

60. W. Ladejinsky, "From a Landlord to Land Reform," June 1, 1951, Ladejinsky Papers, Library of Congress [microfilm]; George White, "Wolf Ladejinsky, Land Reformer, Dies," *WP,* July 5, 1975, C3; Paul L. Montgomery, "Wolf Ladejinsky, Land Reformer, Dies," *NYT,* July 4, 1975, 26; David C. Engerman, *Modernization from the Other Shore: American Intellectuals and the Romance of Russian Development* (Cambridge, MA, 2003), 208–211; Wolf Ladejinsky, "Soviet State Farms II," *Political Science Quarterly* 53(2) (1938): 231; Ladejinsky, "Collectivization of Agriculture in the Soviet Union II," *Political Science Quarterly* 49(2) (1934): 251; Ladejinsky, "Soviet Collective Farms," *NYT,* August 11, 1934, 12.

61. Wolf Ladejinsky, "Agriculture in Manchuria," *Foreign Agriculture,* April 1937, 157–182; "Agriculture of the Netherlands Indies," *Foreign Agriculture,* September 1940, 511–574; "Agriculture in Japan, Prewar," *Foreign Agriculture,* September 1945, 130–142; Edgar Snow, *The Battle for Asia* (New York, 1941); Wendell Willkie, *One World* (New York, 1943); James F. Byrnes, *Speaking Frankly* (New York, 1947), 204; Wolf Ladejinsky, "Too Late to Save Asia?" *Saturday Review,* July 22, 1950, 7; Darrell Berrigan and W. I. Ladejinsky, "Japan's Communists Lose a Battle," *Saturday Evening Post,* January 8, 1949, 102.

62. M. P. Cowen and R. W. Shenton, *Doctrines of Development* (London, 1996), 433; James A. Michener, *The Voice of Asia* (New York, 1951), 284; Wolf Ladejinsky, "Agrarian Revolution in Japan," *Foreign Affairs* 37(4) (1959): 103; Ladejinsky, "Too Late," 36; E. Herbert Norman, *Soldier and Peasant in Japan* (New York, 1943).

63. Berrigan and Ladejinsky, "Japan's Communists," 28; William M. Gilmartin and W. I. Ladejinsky, "The Promise of Agrarian Reform in Japan," *Foreign Affairs* 26(2) (1948): 313; Owen Lattimore, *The Situation in Asia* (Boston, 1949), 69, 73; W. O. Douglas, "Revolution Is Our Business," *The Nation,* May 31, 1952, 517; Mark Gayn, *Japan Diary* (New York, 1948), 311; Ladejinsky to Ken Iverson, "Paper on What Constitutes Human Welfare in the Broadest Sense of the Term," 1954, Ladejinsky reports, 002593, FFA; Ladejinsky, "Too Late," 37.

64. Toby Dodge, *Inventing Iraq: The Failure of Nation Building and a History Denied* (New York, 2003), 69; Richard Slotkin, *Gunfighter Nation* (New York, 1993), 449; Ladejinsky, "Too Late," 36; Ladejinsky, "Social Welfare"; Howard P. Jones to Department of State, "Conversation between Premier Ch'en and Mr. Ladejinsky on Formosan Conditions," August 8, 1952, *DDRS*, ck3100446307.

65. Berrigan and Ladejinsky, "Japan's Communists," 101; Ladejinsky, "Agrarian Revolution," 97, 100.

66. Lloyd Gardner, *Approaching Vietnam* (New York, 1988), 337; Senate Committee on Foreign Relations, *Mutual Security Act of 1955,* 84th Cong., 1st sess., 1955, 109; Jannuzi, *India's Persistent Dilemma, 56,* 99–126; Zubeda M. Ahmad, *Land Reform In Asia, With Particular Reference to Pakistan, The Philippines, and Thailand* (Geneva, 1976), 20–22, 82; Bowles, *Ambassador's Report,* 182; USAID, *Land Reform in Iran, Iraq, Pakistan, Turkey, and Indonesia* (Washington, DC, 1970).

67. USAID, *Land Reform,* 20–22; T. H. Shen, *The Sino-American Joint Commission on Rural Reconstruction* (Ithaca, NY, 1970), 56–67; Chen Cheng, *Land Reform in Taiwan* (Taipei, 1961), 76; Thomas E. Dewey, *Journey to the Far Pacific* (Garden City, NY, 1952), 109.

68. Ronald P. Dore, *Land Reform in Japan* (New York, 1959), 150; Al McCoy, "Land Reform as Counter-Revolution," *Bulletin of the Concerned Asia Scholars,* Spring 1971, 24.

69. Ladejinsky, "Human Welfare," 1; Barbara Ward, "These Are Days for Poetry, Not Statistics," *NYT Magazine,* July 30, 1950, 5.

70. Wolf Ladejinsky, "Self-Description/Appraisal," in *Agrarian Reform as Unfinished Business: The Selected Papers of Wolf Ladejinsky* (New York, 1977), 289; Gilmartin and Ladejinsky, "Promise," 321.

71. "Farmers and the Land," *Foreign Policy Reports* 27(6) (June 1, 1951): 72; House Committee on International Relations, *United States Policy in the Far East, Part I,* Selected Executive Session Hearings, Historical Series, 1976, 7: 461; Eugene Staley, *The Future of Underdeveloped Countries* (New York, 1954), 252–253.

72. Barbara Ward, "A Crusading Faith to Counter Communism," *NYT Magazine,* July 16, 1950, 32; Susan Deborah Chira, *Cautious Revolutionaries: Occupation Planners and Japan's Post-War Land Reform* (Tokyo, 1982), 44; Willard Thorp, "Land and the Future," in U.S. Department of State, *Land Reform,* 63.

73. Jackson V. McElveen, "Farm Numbers, Farm Size and Farm Income," *Journal of Farm Economics* 45(1) (1963): 1–12; John C. Ellickson and John M. Brewster, "Technological Advance and the Structure of American Agriculture," *Journal of Farm Economics* 29(4) (1947): 827–847.

74. "Text of Eisenhower's Address at Omaha," *NYT,* September 19, 1952, 14.

75. Edward L. and Frederick H. Schapsmeier, *Ezra Taft Benson and the Politics of Agriculture* (Danville, IL, 1975); Ezra Taft Benson, *Freedom to Farm* (Garden City, NY, 1960); House Committee on Agriculture, *Farm Proposals of the Administration,* 86th Cong., 1st sess, 1959; J. K. Galbraith, "How Fares the Land?" *The Reporter,* April 14, 1953, 23.

76. Schapsmeier, *Benson*, 224; Ezra Taft Benson, *Cross Fire: The Eight Years with Eisenhower* (Garden City, NY 1962), 57.

77. Schapsmeier, *Benson*, 90, 79–80, 255.

78. McAuliffe, "Eisenhower," 119–120; Senate Special Committee to Study the Foreign Aid Program, *The Foreign Aid Program*, 85th Cong., 1st sess., 1957, 720–721; "Agrarian Reformers for Export," *CT*, December 28, 1954, 12.

79. *Congressional Record*, May 19, 1950, 81st Cong., 2nd sess., 6811; Benson, *Cross Fire*, 227; Clark Mollenhoff, "Benson Gives Ladejinsky a Chance at Job," *Des Moines Register*, December 25, 1954, 5; Aubrey Graves, "Conflict Rises in Ladejinsky 'Risk' Ouster," *WP*, December 23, 1954, 2.

80. Schwartzberg, "Soft Peace Boys," 212; Aubrey Graves, "Land Reform in Japan," *WP*, January 5, 1955, 11; E. T. Benson, *Farmers at the Crossroads* (New York, 1956), 9; Douglas H. Mendel, "The Ladejinsky Case and Land Reform," *LAT*, January 4, 1955, A4.

81. Rostow, "Marx Was a City Boy," *Harper's*, February 1955, 25–30; P. N. Rosenstein-Rodan, "Remarks on the Economic Effects of Agrarian Reform," CENIS mimeograph, May 12, 1954.

82. Tillman Durdin, "Ladejinsky Finds Vietnam Paradox," *NYT*, April 5, 1955, 1; Hoard Jones, *Death of a Generation* (New York, 2003), 33; CIA, "Prospects in South Vietnam," April 17, 1963, NIE 53–63, *Digital National Security Archive*, http://nsarchive.chadwyck.com, item VI02405; Colin Jackson, "Ladejinsky on Land Reform in Viet-Nam," *TNR*, August 29, 1955, 10; interview with Ambassador Otto J. Reich, August 31, 1991, and interview with Richard S. Welton, January 6, 1996, in Association for Diplomatic Studies and Training, *Frontline Diplomacy;* USAID, *Land & Conflict: A Toolkit for Intervention* (Washington, DC, 2005); Ghazala Mansuri and Vijaendra Rao, *Community-Based (and Driven) Development: A Critical Review* (Washington, DC, 2004).

4. WE SHALL RELEASE THE WATERS

1. Mildred Caudill, *Helmand-Arghandab Valley, Yesterday, Today, Tomorrow* (Lashkar Gah, 1969), 55–59; Hafizullah Emadi, *State, Revolution, and Superpowers in Afghanistan* (New York, 1990), 41; Arnold J. Toynbee, *Between Oxus and Jumna* (New York, 1961), 12, 67–68.

2. David E. Lilienthal, *TVA: Democracy on the March* (New York, 1944).

3. Quoted in Alonzo L. Hamby, *Liberalism and Its Challengers: FDR to Reagan* (New York, 1985), 72–73; Robert H. Ferrell, ed., *The Diary of James C. Hagerty* (Bloomington, IN, 1983), 62–63; "New Rules Will Cut U.S. Dam Building," *Business Week*, December 25, 1954, 22; Department of State, "Foreign Policy: Basic Principles and Programs," undated c. 1954, *DDRS*, ck3100191301; Carroll Kirkpatrick, "Kennedy Asks Greater TVAs," *WP*, July 12, 1961, A5; Julius Duscha, "Annual Report of TVA Tries to Refute Critics," *LAT*, January 18, 1963, 13; "President's Remarks on TVA," *WP*, May 19, 1963, A8; David E. Lilienthal, *The Journals of Davie E. Lilienthal*, 3 vols. (New York, 1966), 3: 65.

4. David E. Lilienthal, "The Road to Change," *International Development Review* 6 (1964): 13. On Lilienthal's role as global spokesman, see David Ekbladh, "'Mr. TVA': Grass-Roots Development, David Lilienthal, and the Rise and Fall of the Tennessee Valley Authority as a Symbol of U.S. Overseas Development, 1933–1973," *Diplomatic History* 26(3) (2002): 335–374; Steven M. Neuse, *David E. Lilienthal: The Journey of An American Liberal* (Knoxville, 1996), 264–291.

5. Jawaharlal Nehru, "Speech at the Opening of the Nangal Canal," July 8, 1954, in *Jawaharlal Nehru's Speeches,* 4 vols. (Delhi, 1958) 3: 353.

6. Edward Goldsmith and Nicholas Hildyard, *The Social and Environmental Effects of Large Dams* (San Francisco, 1984); Ashis Nandy, *Bonfire of Creeds* (New Delhi, 2004), 394–419; Julian Huxley, "TVA: An Achievement of Democratic Planning," *The Architectural Review,* June 1943, 160; Desai quoted in Arundhati Roy, *The Cost of Living* (New York, 1999), 13.

7. United Nations, ECAFE, *A Case Study of the Damodar Valley Corporation and Its Projects* (Bangkok, 1960), 5; P. C. Mahalanobis, *Talks on Planning* (New York, 1961), 7; Lloyd I. Rudolph and Susan Hoeber Rudolph, *In Pursuit of Lakshmi: The Political Economy of the Indian State* (Chicago, 1987), 313; Erwin C. Hargrove, *Prisoners of Myth: The Leadership of the Tennessee Valley Authority, 1933–1990* (Princeton, 1994), 61.

8. Huxley, "TVA," 166; Caudill, *Helmand,* 6–8; Damodar Valley Corporation, *DVC in Prospect and Retrospect* (Calcutta, 1958), 1; Lilienthal, *Journals,* 3: 65.

9. Christopher Rand, "Constructing Bhakra Dam," *The New Yorker,* December 8, 1956, 66; Arthur Schlesinger Jr., *The Vital Center* (Boston, 1962), 233; Lilienthal, *TVA,* 217; Robert Trumbull, "Indians Criticize U.S. Experts' Pay," *NYT,* May 29, 1954, 1; "U.S. Construction Experts Take on Far-Flung Jobs," *Business Week,* April 14, 1956, 134–136; Henry R. Lieberman, "U.S. Cuisine Found in Afghan Valley," *NYT,* September 15, 1957, 31; David Klingensmith, "'One Valley and a Thousand': Remaking America, India, and the World in the Image of the Tennessee Valley Authority, 1945–1970" (PhD diss., University of Chicago, 1998), 150.

10. Hargrove, *Prisoners of Myth,* 58; Max F. Millikan and Walt Rostow, *A Proposal: Key to an Effective Foreign Policy* (New York, 1957), 4.

11. David E. Lilienthal, "Another Korea in the Making?" *Collier's,* August 4, 1951, 22–23, 56–58; Ekbladh, "Mr. TVA," 353; "Asian Rivals End Old Dispute," *Business Week,* September 3, 1960, 29; Marquis Childs, "The Receiving End of Foreign Aid," *WP,* December 14, 1964, 16; Kai Bird, *The Color of Truth: McGeorge Bundy and William Bundy, Brothers in Arms* (New York, 1998), 315–316.

12. Curzon, quoted in Cuthbert Collin Davies, *The Problem of the North-West Frontier, 1890–1908* (Cambridge, UK, 1932), 153; John Cowles Prichard, *Researches into the Physical History of Mankind,* 4 vols. (London, 1844), 4: 81–91; H. G. Raverty, "The Independent Afghan or Patan Tribes," *Imperial and Asiatic Quarterly Review* 7 (1894): 312–326; R. C. Temple, "Remarks on the Afghans Found along the Route of the Tal Chotiali Field Force in the Spring of 1879," *Journal of the Asiatic Society of Bengal* 49(1) (1880): 91–106; H. W. Bellew, *The Races of Afghanistan* (Calcutta, 1880).

13. George McMunn, *Afghanistan from Darius to Amanullah* (London: G. Bell, 1929), 225–228; Sultana Afroz, "Afghanistan in U.S. Pakistan Relations, 1947–1960," *Central Asian Survey* 8(2) (1989): 133; Davies, *Problem,* 162–163; Arthur Sulzberger, "Nomads Swarming over Khyber Pass," *NYT,* April 24, 1950, 6; Nigel J. R. Allan, "Defining Place and People in Afghanistan," *Post-Soviet Geography and Economics* 41(8) (2001): 545–560.

14. W. K. Fraser-Tytler, *Afghanistan: A Study of Political Developments in Central and Southern Asia* (London, 1953), 332; India Army, General Staff, *A Dictionary of the Pathan Tribes* (Calcutta, 1910), 34; J. G. Elliott, *The Frontier, 1839–1947* (London, 1968), 53; Hasan Kakar, "Trends in Modern Afghan History," in Louis Dupree and Linette Albert, eds., *Afghanistan in the 1970s* (New York, 1974), 31; McMunn, *Afghanistan from Darius,* 228.

15. Akbar S. Ahmend, "An Aspect of the Colonial Encounter in the North-West Frontier Province," *Asian Affairs* 9(3) (1978): 319–327; Rudyard Kipling, *The One Volume Kipling* (New York, 1932), 735; Olaf Caroe, *The Pathans, 550* B.C.– A.D. 1957 (Karachi, 1958), 429–430; Dupree, "Landlocked Images: Snap Responses to an Informal Questionnaire," *American Universities Field Staff Reports,* South Asia Series, 4(5) (June 1962): 51–73.

16. Arnold Fletcher, *Afghanistan: Highway of Conquest* (Ithaca, NY, 1965), 245; Alfred Janata, "Afghanistan: The Ethnic Dimension," in Ewan W. Anderson and Nancy Hatch Dupree, eds., *The Cultural Basis of Afghan Nationalism* (New York, 1990), 62; "Eleven Afghans Blown from Guns at Kabul," *NYT,* April 6, 1930, 8; "Afghan Revolt Reported," *NYT,* November 21, 1932, 7; Vladimir Cervin, "Problems in the Integration of the Afghan Nation," *Middle East Journal* 6(4) (1952): 407; Bhalwant Bhaneja, *Afghanistan: Political Modernization of a Mountain Kingdom* (New Delhi, 1973), 20; Sara Koplik, "The Demise of Afghanistan's Jewish Community," *Iranian Studies* 36(3) (September 2003): 353–379.

17. Louis Dupree, "A Note on Afghanistan," *American Universities Field Staff Reports,* South Asia Series, 4(8) (August 1960): 13; James C. Scott, *Seeing Like a State* (New Haven, 1999), 77–78; Rosita Forbes, "Afghan Dictator," *Literary Digest,* October 16, 1937, 29.

18. Wilber, *Afghanistan,* 238–243.

19. "Karakul Sheep," *Life,* July 16, 1945, 65–68; Peter G. Franck, "Problems of Economic Development in Afghanistan," *Middle East Journal* 3(3) (July 1949): 302; Abdul Haj Kayoumy, "Monopoly Pricing of Afghan Karakul in International Markets," *Journal of Political Economy* 77(2) (March/April 1969): 219–237; Ali Mohammed, "Karakul as the Most Important Article of Afghan Trade," *Afghanistan* 4(4) (December 1949): 48–53.

20. Najibullah Khan, "Speech Delivered over the Radio," *Afghanistan* 3 (April–June 1948): 13.

21. Ian Stephens, *Horned Moon* (Bloomington, IN, 1955), 263; Louis Dupree, "'Pushtunistan': The Problem and its Larger Implications," *American Universities Field Staff Reports,* South Asia Series, 2-4 (November–December 1961): 19–51; S. M. M. Quereshi, "Pakhtunistan: The Frontier Dispute between Afghanistan and

Pakistan," *Pacific Affairs* 39(1) (1966): 99–144; Afroz, "Afghanistan in U.S.-Pakistan Relations," 138–140.

22. Paul Overby, *Holy Blood: An Inside View of the Afghan War* (Westport, CT, 1993), 30; Louis Dupree, "An Informal Talk with Prime Minister Daoud," September 13, 1959, *American Universities Field Staff Reports,* South Asia Series, 3 (1959): 18.

23. "Builder Harry Morrison," *Time,* May 3, 1954, cover; Robert De Roos, "He Changes the Face of the Earth," *Collier's,* August 2, 1952, 28–30.

24. A. H. H. Abidi, "Irano-Afghan Dispute over the Helmand Waters," *International Studies (India)* 16(3) (1977): 358–359; Fraser-Tytler, *Afghanistan,* 8; Aloys Arthur Michel, *The Kabul, Kunduz, and Helmand Valleys and the National Economy of Afghanistan: A Study of Regional Resources and the Comparative Advantages of Development* (Washington, DC, 1959), 153.

25. Harold Isaacs, *Scratches on Our Minds* (New York, 1958), 44; State Department Office of Intelligence and Research, "The Far East and South Asia," June 23, 1955, OIR Rept. 6972, RG 59, NARA; *That Touch of Mink,* directed by Delbert Mann, Universal Pictures, 1962; Karl A. Wittfogel, *Oriental Despotism* (New Haven, 1957).

26. Goldsmith and Hildyard, *Social and Environmental Effects,* 51–224; Egil Skofteland, *Freshwater Resources: Environmental Education Module* (Paris, 1995); France Bequette, "Large Dams," *UNESCO Courier* 50(3) (1997): 44–46; Robert S. Divine, "The Trouble with Dams," *Atlantic,* August 1995, 64–74; Peter Coles, "Large Dams—The End of an Era," *UNESCO Courier* 53(4) (April 2000): 10–11; Roy, *Cost of Living,* 68; Vandana Shiva, *The Violence of the Green Revolution* (London, 1997), 121–39; Michel, *Kabul, Kunduz, and Helmand,* 152–153.

27. John Hlavacek, *United Press Invades India: Memoirs of a Foreign Correspondent, 1944–1952* (New York, 2006), 124; Michel, *Kabul, Kunduz, and Helmand,* 154.

28. Arthur Sulzberger, "Afghan Shah Asks World Bank Loan," *NYT,* April 20, 1950, 15; Cynthia Clapp-Wincek and Emily Baldwin, *The Helmand Valley Project in Afghanistan,* AID Evaluation Special Study #18 (Washington, DC, December 1983); Lloyd Baron, "Sector Analysis—Helmand Arghandab Valley Region: An Analysis," typescript, February 1973, Library of Congress, Washington, DC, 15; Donald N. Wilber, ed., *Afghanistan* (New Haven, 1956), 169; Emadi, *State, Revolution, and Superpowers,* 53; Nake M. Kamreny, *Peaceful Competition in Afghanistan: American and Soviet Models for Economic Aid* (Washington, DC, 1969), 29.

29. Senate, U.S. Congress, Special Committee to Study the Foreign Aid Program, *South Asia: Report on U.S. Foreign Assistance Programs,* 85th Cong., 1st sess., 1957, 23; Baron, "Sector Analysis," 17, 31.

30. Ira Moore Stevens and K. Tarzi, *Economics of Agricultural Production in Helmand Valley, Afghanistan* (Denver: U.S. Department of the Interior, Bureau of Reclamation, 1965), 30, 38.

31. Department of State, "Elements of U.S. Policy toward Afghanistan," March 27, 1962, 17, *DDRS,* item CK3100383246; Clapp-Wincek, *Helmand,* 5.

32. Louis Dupree, "An Informal Talk with Prime Minister Daoud," September 13, 1959, *American Universities Field Staff Reports,* South Asia Series, 3(3) (1959): 4, 19; State Department, Bureau of Intelligence and Research, "Biographic Report: Visit of Afghanistan's Prime Minister Sardar Mohammad Daud," June 13, 1958, *DDRS,* CK3100067545; National Security Council, "Progress Report on South Asia," July 24, 1957, in Department of State, *FRUS, 1955–1957* (Washington, DC, 1985), 13: 49; Dupree, "Afghanistan, the Canny Neutral," *The Nation,* September 21, 1964, 134–137.

33. Leon B. Poullada, *The Pushtun Role in the Afghan Political System* (New York, 1970), 22; Angus C. Ward to Department of State, December 14, 1955, in Department of State, *FRUS, 1955–1957,* 8: 204; Wilber, *Afghanistan,* 103.

34. Dulles to Embassy in Pakistan, July 12, 1955, in Department of State, *FRUS, 1955–1957,* 8: 189; Editorial note, in Department of State, *FRUS, 1955–1957,* 8: 202.

35. Franck, "Problems," 425; Clapp-Wincek, *Helmand,* 8; "Export-Import Bank Loan to Afghanistan," *DOSB,* May 31, 1954, 836; Tudor Engineering Company, *Report on Development of Helmand Valley Afghanistan* (Washington, DC, November 1956), 16, 90; Richard Tapper, "Nomadism in Modern Afghanistan," in Dupree and Albert, *Afghanistan in the 1970s,* 126–143; Vladimir Cervin, "Problems in the Integration of the Afghan Nation," *Middle East Journal* 6(4) (Autumn 1952): 400–416; James W. Spain, *The Way of the Pathans* (Karachi, 1962), 126.

36. Ann Morrison, "Mad Nomads Battle for a Bridge," *The Em-Kayan,* October 1951, 16–17, 21; Willem van Schendel, ed., *Illicit Flows and Criminal Things: States, Borders, and the Other Side of Globalization* (Bloomington, IN, 2005).

37. Baron, "Sector Analysis," 18; Ritchie Calder, "Hope of Millions," *The Nation,* August 1, 1953, 87–89; Wilber, *Afghanistan,* 222; Emadi, *State, Revolution, and Superpowers,* 41.

38. Dana Reynolds, "Utilizing Religious Principles and Leadership in Rural Improvement," [1962], box 125, John H. Ohly Papers, HSTL; National Security Council, "Progress Report on NSC 5409," November 28, 1956, in Department of State, *FRUS, 1955–1957,* 8: 15; Bureau of Intelligence and Research, "Biographic Report."

39. Robert J. McMahon, "The Illusion of Vulnerability: American Reassessments of the Soviet Threat, 1955–56," *International History Review* 18(3) (August 1996): 591–619; "Soviet-Afghan Communique," *Pravda,* April 30, 1965, in *Current Digest of the Soviet Press* 17(17) (May 19, 1965): 26; Hamilton Fish Armstrong, "North of the Khyber," *Foreign Affairs,* July 1956, 603–619.

40. Henry A. Kissinger, "Military Policy and Defense of the 'Gray Areas,'" *Foreign Affairs,* April 1955, 416–428; "Strange Kind of Cold War," *US News and World Report,* November 15, 1957, 160; "Atlantic Report: Afghanistan," *Atlantic,* October 1962, 26; Department of State, Office of Intelligence and Research, "Communist Economic Diplomacy in the Underdeveloped Areas," April 2, 1956, *DDRS,* CK310017186; Senate, Special Committee to Study the Foreign Aid Program, *The Foreign Aid Program,* 85th Cong., 1st sess, 1957, 404.

41. James A, Michener, *Caravans* (New York, 1963), 161; see also Michener, "Afghanistan: Domain of the Fierce and the Free," *Reader's Digest,* November 1955, 161–172.

42. Embassy Afghanistan to Department of State, March 3, 1965, in Department of State, *FRUS, 1964–1968* (Washington, DC, 1992), 25: 1051.

43. Peggy and Pierre Streit, "Lesson in Foreign Aid Policy," *NYT Magazine,* March 18, 1956, 56; Baron, "Sector Analysis," 55; Stevens and Tarzi, *Economics of Agricultural Production,* 29; Department of State, "Elements of U.S. Policy."

44. Gustav Ranis, "A Theory of Economic Development," *American Economic Review* 51 (1961): 533–565; Dale W. Jorgensen, "The Development of a Dual Economy," *Economic Journal* 66 (1961): 309–334; W. W. Rostow, "Some Lessons of Economic Development since the War," *DOSB,* November 9, 1964, 664–665; see also Rostow, *View From the Seventh Floor* (New York, 1964), 124–131.

45. "Tangible Tokens," *Time,* April 7, 1967, 18; Lester R. Brown, *Seeds of Change: The Green Revolution and Development in the 1970s* (New York, 1970), 19; Public Administration Service, *A Final Report on the Land Inventory Project of Afghanistan* (Chicago, January 1972), 9; Baron, "Sector Analysis," 44.

46. Clapp-Wincek, *Helmand,* 5; Baron, "Sector Analysis," 50, 53; Shafie Rahel, ed., *The Kabul Times Annual, 1970* (Kabul, 1970), 359.

47. Louis Dupree, "The Decade of Daoud Ends," *American Universities Field Staff Reports,* South Asia Series, 7 (May 1963): 7; Janata, "Ethnic Dimension," 62; U.S. Embassy Kabul to Department of State, "Afghanistan's Clerical Unrest: A Tentative Assessment," June 24, 1970, in William Burr, ed., *National Security Archive Electronic Briefing Book No. 59,* October 26, 2001, http://www.gwu.edu/~nsarchiv/NSAEBB/NSAEBB59.

48. Baron, "Sector Analysis," 50; Mike Davis, *Late Victorian Holocausts: El Nino Famines and the Making of the Third World* (London, 2001), 244; Kamreny, *Peaceful Competition,* 36; Clapp-Wincek, *Helmand,* 4; Robert A. Flaten, "Afghan Politics, the Creeping Crisis," May 31, 1972, in Burr, *National Security Archive Electronic Briefing Book.*

49. Clapp-Wincek, *Helmand,* 6.

50. Lloyd Baron, "The Water-Supply Constraint: An Evaluation of Irrigation Projects and the Role in the Development of Afghanistan" (PhD thesis, McGill University, 1975), 2; Clapp-Wincek, *Helmand;* Fletcher, *Highway of Conquest,* 268.

51. M. Hassan Kakar, *Afghanistan: The Soviet Invasion and the Afghan Response, 1979–1982* (Berkeley, 1995), 203; Ahmed Rashid, *Taliban: Militant Islam, Oil and Fundamentalism in Central Asia* (New Haven, 2000), 20.

52. Christopher Grey-Wilson, *Poppies: A Guide to the Poppy Family in the Wild and in Cultivation* (Portland: Timber Press, 2000), 24; James Wolf and Barry Hack, "Rehabilitation Assessment of the Helmand-Arghandab Valley Irrigation Scheme in Afghanistan," *Water International* 19(3) (1994): 121–128; United Nations Office on Drugs and Crime, *Afghanistan Opium Survey 2008* (New York, 2008), vii; Richard Lloyd Parry, "Campaign against Terrorism: Warning—UN Fears 'Disaster' over Strikes Near Huge Dam," *The Independent (London),* November 8, 2001, 4.

53. Afzal Khan, "USAID Funds Program to Boost Afghan Agriculture," State Department Press Release, December 23, 2003, www.factiva.com; Rajiv Chandrasekaran, "A Major Push into Taliban Bulwark," *WP*, February 10, 2010, A7.

54. Walden Bello and Shalmali Guttal, "The Limits of Reform: The Wolfensohn Era at the World Bank," *Race and Class* 47(3) (2006): 73; "Dams Back in Fashion," *Economist,* April 9, 2005, 34.

5. A VERY BIG, VERY POOR COUNTRY

1. Robert L. Beisner, *Dean Acheson: A Life in the Cold War* (New York, 2006), 507; National Security Council, "NSC-48, the Position of the United States with Respect to Asia," December 30, 1949, in Thomas Etzold and John L. Gaddis, eds., *Containment: Documents on American Policy and Strategy* (New York, 1978), 265.

2. W. W. Rostow, *Eisenhower, Kennedy, and Foreign Aid* (Austin, TX, 1986), 8–9; John F. Kennedy, "If India Falls," *The Progressive,* January 1958, 8–11; Michael Latham, *Modernization as Ideology* (Chapel Hill, NC, 2000), 86–87; Nils Gilman, *Mandarins of the Future* (Baltimore, 2003), 44–45; Walter Lippmann, "India, the Glorious Gamble," *Ladies' Home Journal,* August 1959, 48–49.

3. CIA, "Analysis of Possible Political Developments of Strategic Significance That May Occur between 1951 and 1954," February 28, 1950, *DDRS,* CK3100296001; Gary R. Hess, *America Encounters India, 1941–1947* (Baltimore, 1971), 162–172; H. W. Brands, *India and the United States: The Cold Peace* (Boston, 1990), 42; JSPC 814/3, December 11, 1947, in Etzold and Gaddis, *Containment,* 296.

4. Andrew Rotter, *Comrades at Odds: The United States and India, 1947–1964* (Ithaca, NY, 2000), 32; Office of Intelligence and Research, South Asia Branch, "The Need for and Possibility of Economic Development in India," March 2, 1951, Far East Program Division, South Asia Country Subject Files, 1951–1952, India, box 13, RG 469, NARA; Milton Katz to Richard Bissell, April 21, 1951, Office of the Deputy Administrator, Country Files, 1950–1951, box 2, RG 469, NARA.

5. CIA, "Comprehensive Plan of Requirements for Production of National Intelligence on the Far East," June 15, 1950, CIA-RDP79, CREST.

6. William C. Bullitt, "The Old Ills of Modern India," *Life,* October 1, 1951, 111–112; Dennis Merrill, *Bread and the Ballot: The United States and India's Economic Development, 1947–1963* (Chapel Hill, NC, 1990), 55; Acheson to Truman, "Indian Request for Food Grains," February 2, 1951, *DDRS,* CK3100407683; Ferdinand Kuhn, "Truman Asks Foreign Grant of $8.5 Billion," *WP,* May 25, 1951, 1.

7. Robert J. McMahon, *The Cold War on the Periphery: The United States, India, and Pakistan* (New York, 1994), 107; "GOP Demands India Vow Aid against Russia," *CT,* May 24, 1951, D6; Willard Edwards, "Denounce Bill to Give India Grain as 'Phony,'" *CT,* March 7, 1951, 5; "How Real Is India's Famine?" *CT,* February 19, 1951, 16; M. J. Akbar, *Nehru: The Making of India* (New Delhi, 2002), 491.

8. Jawaharlal Nehru, *The Discovery of India* (New York, 1960), 386; India Planning Commission, *Our Plan* (Delhi, 1953), 27–29; Harlan Cleveland to Wil-

liam C. Foster and Richard Bissell, "Aid to India," January 19, 1951, Records of the U.S. Foreign Assistance Agencies, RG 469, Country files, Box 1, NARA.

9. Oscar Calvo-Gonzalez, "Neither a Carrot Nor a Stick: American Foreign Aid and Economic Policymaking in Spain during the 1950s," *Diplomatic History* 30(3) (June 2006): 409–438; Senate Committee on Foreign Relations, *Development of Technical Assistance Programs: Background Information and Documents,* 83rd Cong., 2nd sess., 1954, 60; George V. Allen to Dulles, July 26, 1953, in Department of State, *FRUS, 1952–1954* (Washington, DC, 1986), 9: 1699; Dulles to Allen, September 3, 1953, in Department of State, *FRUS, 1952–1954,* 9: 1717.

10. James Michener, "The Riddle of Pandit Nehru," *Reader's Digest,* July 1956, 96–102; Norman Cousins, "What about Nehru?" *Saturday Review,* April 10, 1954, 24; Eleanor Roosevelt, *India and the Awakening East* (New York, 1953), 113–114; W. O. Douglas, "Way to Win in the East," *Rotarian,* June 1951, 6–53; Margaret Bourke-White, *Interview with India* (London, 1950), 175; Commager, "Acid Test for the American Character," *NYT Magazine,* April 29, 1951, 8.

11. Barbara Ward, "The Fateful Race between China and India," *NYT Magazine,* September 20, 1953, 9–67; Bowles, "New India," *Foreign Affairs* 31(1) (October 1952): 80; *Congressional Record,* 89th Cong., 2nd sess., March 25, 1966, 6822; Yuan-li Wu and Robert C. North, "China and India: Two Paths to Industrialization," *Problems of Communism* 4(3) (May–June 1955): 13–19; W. Rostow, The *Diffusion of Power* (New York, 1972), 104.

12. For the text of the *Panchsheel,* see G. V. Ambekar, *Documents on China's Relations with South and South-East Asia* (Bombay, 1964), 7–8; Nehru, "The Concept of Panchsheel," September 17, 1955, in *India's Foreign Policy* (Delhi, 1961), 100; Judith M. Brown, *Nehru: A Political Life* (New Haven, 2003), 269.

13. *Congressional Record,* 84th Cong., 1st sess., June 29, 1955, 9536; *Congressional Record,* 84th Cong., 1st sess., July 11, 1953, 10234.

14. NSC 5409, "United States Policy toward South Asia," February 19, 1954, in Department of State, *FRUS, 1952–1954,* 11: 1098; NSC 5701, Statement of Policy on U.S. Policy toward South Asia," January 10, 1957, in Department of State, *FRUS, 1955–1957* (Washington, DC, 1987), 8: 31; Yves Moroni, "India's Second Five Year Plan," May 22, 1956, Records of the Federal Reserve, country files, Asia, Australia, and New Zealand, general, FRBA; Kissinger, "Reflections on American Diplomacy," *Foreign Affairs* 35 (1956): 37.

15. Ward, "Race," 64; J. K. Galbraith, "Conditions for Economic Change in Underdeveloped Countries," *Journal of Farm Economics* 33(4) (1951): 689–696; Senate Committee on Foreign Relations, *Mutual Security Act of 1955,* 84th Cong., 1st sess., 1955, 520.

16. Helen C. Farnsworth, "Response of Wheat Growers to Price Changes: Appropriate or Perverse?" *The Economic Journal* 66(262) (1956): 271–287; John Kerry King, "Rice Politics," *Foreign Affairs* 31 (1953): 458; Galbraith, "Conditions," 691; Galbraith, "Making Point 4 Work," *Commentary,* October 1950, 229.

17. State Department, OIR, "The Far East and South Asia," June 23, 1955, OIR Report 6972, RG 59, NARA; Senate, *Mutual Security Act of 1955,* 8.

18. W. W. Rostow, "Marx Was a City Boy or, Why Communism May Fail," *Harper's Magazine,* February 1955, 26–29.

19. "Model for Asia—China or India," *Far Eastern Economic Review,* February 10, 1955, 161; Senate Foreign Relations Committee, *Mutual Security Act of 1955,* 93; Stassen meeting with Planning Commission, March 1, 1955, Records of U.S. Foreign Assistance Agencies, RG 469, Mission to India, Director Subject Files, box 2, NARA.

20. "Army Doubles GI Milk Ration to Help Ease Surplus," *WP,* October 8, 1954, 55; Aubrey Graves, "Farm Price Support Debate Gets Hotter," *WP,* August 6, 1954, 2.

21. *Congressional Record,* September 4, 1959, 86th Cong., 1st sess., 18056; *Congressional Record,* May 27, 1957, 85th Cong., 1st sess., 7716; Elmer L. Menzie and Robert G. Crouch, "Political Interests in Agricultural Export Surplus Disposal through Public Law 480," *Arizona Experiment Station Technical Bulletin* 161 (1964): 15, 28.

22. Merrill, *Bread and the Ballot,* 126–130; James Warner Bjorkman, "Public Law 480 and the Policies of Self-Help and Short-Tether: Indo-American Relations, 1965–68," in Lloyd I. and Susanne H. Rudolph, eds., *The Regional Imperative* (Atlantic Highlands, NJ, 1980), 201–262; State Department, Bureau of Intelligence and Research, "Food-for-Peace and Freedom-from-Hunger," August 23, 1960, Policy Planning Staff Records, Lot 67D548, RG 59, box 118, NARA.

23. P. C. Mahalanobis, *The Approach of Operational Research to Planning in India* (Calcutta, 1963), 6–7; Nehru, Press Conference, May 31, 1955, in *Selected Works of Jawaharlal Nehru,* 2nd series (Delhi, 2001), 28: 384–385; Minister of Food, "Impact of Wheat and Rice from the USA under Fresh P.L. 480," 1957, Ministry of Food and Agriculture Papers, FIMP-110(61)I, NAI; William F. Hall, *P.L. 480's Contribution to India's Economic Development* (Washington, DC, 1961), 10.

24. Nehru to Chief Ministers, August 12, 1956, in *Selected Works,* 34: 51; H. V. R. Iengar, *Inflation, the Food Crisis, and the Fourth Five Year Plan* (Madras, 1965), 16, 21; Foodgrains Enquiry Committee, *Report* (Delhi, 1957), 93; Nilakanth Rath and V. S. Patvardhan, *Impact of Assistance under P.L. 480 on Indian Economy* (Bombay, 1967), vi; "Modern Bakeries," *LT,* November 30, 1970, 4.

25. Deena R. Khatkhate, "Some Notes on the Real Effects of Surplus Disposal in Underdeveloped Countries," *Quarterly Journal of Economics* 76(2) (May 1962): 186–196; Christoph Beringer, "A Comment," *Quarterly Journal of Economics* 77(2) (May 1963): 317–323; Uma Kant Srivastava, "The Impact of Public Law 480 Imports on Prices and Domestic Supply of Cereals in India: A Comment," *American Journal of Agricultural Economics* 50(1) (1968): 143–145; B. K. Nehru, "P.L. 480—Aid to India," July 11, 1957, Ministry of Food and Agriculture Papers, FIMP-110(61)I, NAI; Rath and Patvardhan, *Impact of Assistance,* 79, 155.

26. Nehru, Press Conference, May 31, 1955, in *Selected Works,* 28: 388; Nehru to Chief Ministers, November 20, 1957, in Nehru, *Letters to Chief Ministers* (Delhi, 1988), 4: 600–601; S. R. Sen, "Impact and Implications of Foreign Surplus

Disposal on Underdeveloped Economies, the Indian Perspective," *Journal of Farm Economics* 42(5) (1960): 1031–1042; Foodgrains Enquiry, *Report,* 95; B. B. Ghosh, "Further P.L. 480 Agreement for Import of Wheat and Rice from USA," April 30, 1957, Food Ministry Papers, INA, FIMP-110(61)I, NAI; Bjorkman, "Public Law 480," 227.

27. A. M. Rosenthal, "Food Now Scarce in India's North," *NYT,* April 21, 1957, 11; Chunilal B. Mehta to Federal Reserve, May 2, 1957, Country Files, India, Federal Reserve Board Records, Washington, DC; Edna E. Erlich, "India's Payments Difficulties under the Second Plan," January 8, 1958, Federal Reserve Records, Asia, Australia, New Zealand, general, FRBA; Foodgrains, *Report,* 57–58.

28. Memo of Conversation, "The Ford Foundation," April 3, 1951; B. Evans to Acheson, September 26, 1952, Department of State, Bureau of Intelligence and Research, Subject Files, Lot 58D776, RG 59, box 5, NARA.

29. CIA, "Economic and Political Consequences of India's Financial Problems," NIE 51–58, September 2, 1958, in Department of State, *FRUS, 1958–1960* (Washington, DC, 1992), 15: 452–453; Engerman, "West Meets East," in *Staging Growth,* 212; "The Poor Countries," *The Economist,* June 2, 1951, 1277.

30. "Ragnar Nurkse, Economist, Dead," *NYT,* May 7, 1959, 33; "Paul Rosenstein-Rodan Dies," *NYT,* April 30, 1985, A26.

31. Ragnar Nurkse, "Foreign Aid and the Theory of Economic Development," *Scientific Monthly* 85(2) (1957): 81–85; Nurkse, "Reflections on India's Development Plan," *Quarterly Journal of Economics* 71(2) (1957): 188–204; Rosenstein Rodan, "Disguised Employment and Underemployment in Agriculture I," CENIS mimeograph, October 30, 1956.

32. P. N. Rosenstein-Rodan, "The International Development of Backward Areas," *International Affairs* 20(2) (1944): 157–165; Theodore W. Schultz, *Transforming Traditional Agriculture* (New Haven, 1964), 59.

33. Sir Arthur Lewis, "Autobiography," 1979, http://nobelprize.org; W. Arthur Lewis, "Economic Development With Unlimited Supplies of Labor," *The Manchester School of Economic and Social Studies* 22 (1954): 139–192; see also United Nations, Department of Economic Affairs, *Measures for the Economic Development of Under-Developed Countries* (New York, 1951), 45–48; Ansley J. Coale and Edgar M. Hoover, *Population Growth and Economic Development in Low-Income Countries* (Princeton, 1958), 128–131; P. C. Mahalanobis, *Talks on Planning* (New York, 1961), 136.

34. "Korea—Two Comments," *NYT,* April 15, 1951, 136; Nurkse, *Problems of Capital Formation in Underdeveloped Countries* (Oxford, 1953), 37–46; Nurkse, "Reflections," 200; Rosenstein-Rodan, "International Development," 163.

35. Mallory Browne, "Conversations with Dr. Millikan, Dr. Rostow, and Others at MIT Center for International Studies," July 14, 1952, *DDRS,* CK3100329230; Gilman, *Mandarins,* 160–190.

36. Donald L. M. Blackmer, *The MIT Center for International Studies: The Founding Years, 1951–1969* (Cambridge, MA, 2002), 40–41; CENIS, "A Plan of Research in International Communication: A Report," *World Politics* 6(3) (1954): 358–377.

37. Max F. Millikan and W. W. Rostow, *A Proposal: Key to an Effective Foreign Policy* (New York, 1957), 4–5, 19–23.

38. W. W. Rostow, "The Take-Off to Self-Sustained Growth," *Economic Journal* 66(261) (1956): 25–48; Gilman, *Mandarins*, 179.

39. Kimber Charles Pearce, *Rostow, Kennedy, and the Rhetoric of Foreign Aid* (East Lansing, MI, 2001), 38–42, 80–81.

40. Karl Wittfogel, "Food and Society in China and India," in Iago Galdston, ed., *Human Nutrition, Historic and Scientific* (New York, 1960), 61–77; Robert N. Bellah, "Reflections on the Protestant Ethic Analogy in Asia," *Journal of Social Issues* 19(1) (1963): 52–60.

41. Senate Foreign Relations Committee, *Review of Foreign Policy, 1958*, 85th Cong., 2nd sess., 1958, 283; Louis J. Halle, "Rostow: The Intellectual Fortinbras," *TNR*, July 25, 1964, 21; Senate Special Committee to Study the Foreign Aid Program, *The Objectives of United States Economic Assistance Programs*, Part 1, 85th Cong., 1st sess., 1957, 20–22, 57.

42. *Congressional Record*, March 17, 1958, 85th Cong., 2nd sess., 4544; *Congressional Record*, March 25, 1958, 85th Cong., 2nd sess., 5246–5253.

43. William J. Lederer and Eugene Burdick, "The Ugly American, Part 1," *Saturday Evening Post*, October 4, 1958, 19–20, 108–113.

44. William J. Lederer and Eugene Burdick, *The Ugly American* (New York, 1958), 284, 24; Thomas W. Wilson Jr., "How to Make a Movie Out of *The Ugly American*," *Harper's*, June 1959, 16; Jonathan Nashel, "The Road to Vietnam: Modernization Theory in Fact and Fiction," in C. Appy, ed., *Cold War Constructions: The Political Culture of United States Imperialism, 1945–1966* (Amherst, MA, 2000), 132–154.

45. Lederer and Burdick, *Ugly American*, 47; Rostow, *Eisenhower, Kennedy*, 155–162; Barbara Ward, "The Great Challenge Is Not the Sputniks," *NYT Magazine*, February 23, 1958, 15–17; Lippmann, "India, The Glorious Gamble," 48–49.

46. George Gallup, "Gallup Finds Majority for Foreign Aid," *LAT*, March 30, 1958, 27; Willard Johnson, "Foreign Aid Cut Opposed," *LAT*, April 17, 1960, E8; "388th Meeting of the NSC," December 3, 1958, in Department of State, *FRUS, 1958–1960*, 4: 438; Eisenhower to Swede Hazlett, August 3, 1956, Ann Whitman File, Name Series, Eisenhower Library, Abilene, Kansas.

47. President's Committee to Study the United States Military Assistance Program, *Composite Report* (Washington, DC, 1958), 1: 97, 2: 24.

48. Ford Foundation, *Report on India's Food Crisis & Steps to Meet It* (New Delhi, April 1959), 11–12; George Rosen, *Western Economists and Eastern Societies* (Baltimore, 1985), 74–75; Coale and Hoover, *Population Growth*; Ansley J. Coale, *An Autobiography* (Philadelphia, 2000), 34–36.

49. John M. Keynes, "Some Economic Consequences of a Declining Population," *Eugenics Review* 29(1) (1937): 13–17; Allen C. Kelley, "Economic Consequences of Population Change in the Third World," *Journal of Economic Literature* 26 (1988): 1698; Eugene R. Black, *The Diplomacy of Economic Development* (Cambridge, MA, 1961), 7; "US Policy Liberalized on Aid to Foreign Agricul-

ture," July 7, 1959, in Department of State, *FRUS, 1958–1960,* 4: 337; "388th Meeting of the NSC," December 3, 1958, in Department of State, *FRUS, 1958–1960,* 4: 439.

50. John Kenneth Galbraith, *Letters to Kennedy* (Cambridge, MA, 1998), 134; "Nixon Would Aid Nations Asking Birth Control Data," *NYT,* April 9, 1960, 1; Rostow, *Eisenhower, Kennedy,* 171; Latham, *Modernization as Ideology,* 57–58; Arthur Schlesinger Jr., *A Thousand Days* (Boston, 1965), 523; George W. Ball, *The Past Has Another Pattern* (New York, 1982), 183.

51. Bowles to Rusk, "A Coordinated Approach to Rural Development," August 17, 1961, PPS Records, Lot 67D548, RG 59, box 115, NARA; Taylor to Bundy, "US Overseas Internal Defense Policy," August 1, 1962, *DDRS,* CK3100428299; McMahon, *Cold War,* 273.

52. Thomas P. Bernstein, "Mao Zedong and the Famine of 1959–1960: A Study of Willfulness," *China Quarterly* 186 (2006): 421–445; CIA, "The Chances of a Chinese Communist Military Move in Southeast Asia," May 11, 1961, *DDRS,* ck3100341193; Lansdale to McNamara, April 3, 1961, in Department of State, *FRUS, 1961–1963* (Washington, DC, 1996), 22: 38–39; News Conference No. 10, April 21, 1961, in William Leuchtenberg, ed., *John F. Kennedy's Office Files, 1961–1963* (Bethesda, MD, 1989), part 1, reel 18, frame 578; "Starvation in China," *US News and World Report,* May 15, 1961, 48–50; Matthew S. Young, "When Your Enemy Hungers: The Kennedy Administration, Public Opinion, and the Famine in China, 1961–2" (PhD diss., Bowling Green State University, 2000), 109, 124–125.

53. "To World of Peace, Text of the Address," *WP,* September 26, 1961, A1; Editorial Note, in Department of State, *FRUS, 1961–1963,* 19: 317; Coombs to Bowles, "The 'New Look' in Foreign Assistance," May 5, 1961, in Department of State, *FRUS, 1961–1963,* 9: 236–237; Orville Freeman Diary, April 16, 1961, vol. 1, Freeman Papers, box 8, LBJL.

54. Nicole Sackley, "Passage to Modernity: American Social Scientists, India, and the Pursuit of Development, 1945–1961" (PhD diss., Princeton University, 2004), 206; Galbraith, *A Life in Our Times* (Boston, 1981), 418.

55. Dean Rusk, "The Tragedy of Cuba," *Vital Speeches,* February 15, 1962, 258–262; Barbara Ward, *India and the West* (New York, 1961), 181, 227.

56. "Speech at the Opening Ceremony of the World Food Congress," June 4, 1963, in *JFK Office Files,* part 1, reel 11, frame 1018; JFK, Speech to the National Academy of the Sciences, October 22, 1963, copy in Daniel Bell Papers, series IV, box 26, FFA.

6. A PARABLE OF SEEDS

1. Joseph Lelyveld, "Philippines Tries New Rice Strain," *NYT,* December 18, 1966, 11; F. F. Hill Oral History, April 20, 1973, FFA.

2. Thomas R. Hargrove, *A Dragon Lives Forever* (New York, 1994), 13; Gyan Prakash, *Another Reason: Science and the Imagination of Modern India* (Princeton, 1999), 47.

3. Martin Heidigger, *The Question Concerning Technology and Other Essays* (New York, 1977), 14–35; Reiner Schürmann, "Technicity, Topology, Tragedy: Heidigger on 'That Which Saves' in the Global Reach," in Arthur M. Melzer, Jerry Weinberger, and M. Richard Zinman, eds., *Technology in the Western Political Tradition* (Ithaca, NY, 1993), 190–213.

4. "Text of Address by Robert McNamara, World Bank's New President," *NYT,* October 1, 1968, 58; House Subcommittee on National Security Policy and Scientific Developments, *The Green Revolution: Symposium on Science and Foreign Policy,* 91st Cong., 1st sess., 1969, 30.

5. Daniel Lerner, "Modernization," in David L. Sills, ed., *International Encyclopedia of the Social Sciences* (New York, 1968), 10: 387; Gilbert Rist, *The History of Development: From Western Origins to Global Faith* (London, 1999).

6. Harrison E. Salisbury, "Nixon and Khruschev Argue in Public as U.S. Exhibit Opens," *NYT,* July 25, 1959, 1–2; House Special Subcommittee to Study the Foreign Aid Program, *Southeast Asia: Report on United States Foreign Assistance Programs,* 85th Cong., 1st sess., 1957, 6; Fowler Hamilton to Walt W. Rostow, "Back to the Sears Roebuck Catalog," August 13, 1962, State Department Policy Planning Staff files, Lot 69D121, box 211, NARA; David Halberstam, *The Best and the Brightest* (New York, 1972), 123.

7. Ford Foundation, *A Richer Harvest* (New York, 1967), 3.

8. H. Rowan Gaither, "Interview with Mr. Allen Dulles," April 15, 1955, Report 005611, FFA; F. F. Hill, "Notes on Economic Development," December 1958, 010459, Hill Papers, FFA; Hill, "Purposes of the Proposed Rice Research Foundation," 1959, Hill Papers, box 14564, FFA; A. Colin McClung, "Accelerated Rice Research Program for E. Pakistan in Cooperation with the IRRI," May 1965, report 001616, FFA; Walter A. McDougall, *The Heavens and the Earth: A Political History of the Space Age* (Baltimore, 1997); Robert F. Chandler, "On Rice Research," July 1960, Chandler speech file, IRRILA; Forrest F. Hill, "The Human Factor in Economic Development," October 14, 1957, Hill Papers, 003698, FFA; Robert S. Anderson, "The Origins of the International Rice Research Institute," *Minerva* 29(1) (Spring 1991): 61–89; Robert F. Chandler Jr., *An Adventure in Applied Science: A History of the International Rice Research Institute* (Manila, 1992).

9. J. G. Harrar to F. F. Hill, December 23, 1959, FF grant files, 06000178, FFA; Walker to J. G. Harrar, January 26, 1961, FF grant files, 06000178, FFA; Chandler to Harrar, February 17, 1960, FF grant files, 06000178, FFA; Ralph T. Walker, *Ralph T. Walker, Architect, of Voorhees, Gmelin, and Walker* (New York, 1957), 225; Ron Robin, *Enclaves of America: The Rhetoric of American Political Architecture Abroad, 1900–1965* (Princeton, 1992), 151.

10. Harry L. Case to George F. Gant, "International Rice Research Institute Budget," October 12, 1966, FF grant files, PA06500055, FFA; Robert F. Chandler Jr., "The Rockefeller Foundation and the International Agricultural Research Centers," undated, IRRILA; Chandler, "Case History of IRRI's Research Management during the Period from 1960 to 1972," undated, IRRILA; Chandler, *Adventure,* 94.

11. Robert F. Chandler oral history, 1967, IRRILA, Los Baños, 26; Paul Deutschman, "IRRI Fills Empty Rice Bowls," *Saturday Review,* August 6, 1966, 17.

12. George W. Ball, *The Past Has Another Pattern* (New York, 1982), 183; Hill, "The Human Factor," 8; Zbigniew Brzezinski, "The Politics of Underdevelopment," *World Politics* 9(1) (1956): 57–59; Lucian W. Pye, *Guerilla Communism in Malaya: Its Social and Political Meaning* (Princeton, 1956), 344–346; Daniel Lerner, *The Passing of Traditional Society* (New York, 1958); Chester Bowles, *Ambassador's Report* (New York, 1954), 90.

13. R. F. Chandler oral history, July 29, 1966, RFAC.

14. E. J. Kahn, "Rice, Rice, Rice," *New Yorker,* October 23, 1965, 172; *Beach Red,* directed by Cornel Wilde, 1967; Robert F. Chandler oral history, January 25, 1967, RFAC, 88; Ladejinsky to Walter A. Rudlin, January 17, 1963, Ladejinsky Papers, FFA, 006102; Chandler, *Adventure,* 86.

15. Chandler, *Aventure,* 166; Richard Handler and Eric Gable, *The New History in an Old Museum* (Durham, NC, 1997), 64; IRRI, *International Rice Research Institute* (film), 1965, RFAC.

16. Alfonso J. Aluit, *Galleon Guide to Manila and the Philippines* (Manila, 1968), 135–136; Resil B. Mojares, "Waiting for Mariang Makiling: History and Folklore," *St. Louis University (Baguio City) Research Journal* 19(2) (1988): 205–215; Jose Rizal, "Mariang Makiling," in *Rizal's Prose* (Manila, 1990), 86–92; Reynaldo C. Ileto, *Pasyon and Revolution* (Quezon City, 1989), 206, 210; Zacarias Saran, "FM Reaps Miracle Cereal," *Manila Chronicle,* November 16, 1966, 1; Edward R. Kiunisala, "The More Miraculous Rice," *Philippines Free Press,* October 11, 1969, 10–11.

17. FAO, *Report of the Rice Study Group, Trivandrum, Travancore State, India* (Washington, DC, 1947), 20–21; Kathleen McLaughlin, "UN to Establish Rice Research Center in Thailand," *NYT,* July 27, 1962, 29, 32; Hill to Chandler, October 2, 1962, Hill Papers, box 14564, FFA; Edmund K. Oasa, "The International Rice Research Institute and the Green Revolution: A Case Study in the Politics of Agricultural Research" (PhD diss., University of Hawaii, 1981), 201.

18. "Breeders Determine Desired Plant Characteristics," *IRRI Reporter,* January 1965, 2; IRRI, *Annual Report for 1961–1962* (Los Baños, 1962), 13; H. M. Beachell and J. E. Scott, "Breeding Rice for Desired Plant Type," in *Proceedings of the Rice Technical Working Group* (Houston, 1962), 15–16; Oasa, "International Rice," 183.

19. Oasa, "International Rice," 194–197; Anderson, *Rice Science,* p. 177.

20. John H. Perkins, *Geopolitics and the Green Revolution* (New York, 1997), 119–120; Frank Lorimer to Warren Weaver, "WFL Notes on 'World Population and World Food Supplies,'" November 22, 1949, Rockefeller Foundation Papers, RG 3, series 915, box 3, RFAC; Kennedy, "Statement at the Opening Ceremony of the World Food Congress," June 4, 1963, in William Leuchtenberg, ed., *John F. Kennedy's Office Files, 1961–1963* (Bethesda, MD, 1989), part 1, reel 11, frame 1018.

21. Simon Kuznets, *Modern Economic Growth: Rate, Structure, and Spread* (New Haven, 1966), 2; Albert O. Hirschman, *The Strategy of Economic Development* (New Haven, 1958); House Committee on Foreign Affairs, *The Green Revolution,* 91st Cong., 1st sess., December 5, 1969, 63; Nils Gilman, "Paving the World with Good Intentions: The Genesis of Modernization Theory, 1945–1965"

(PhD diss., University of California, Berkeley, 2000); Pierre Brocheaux, "Moral Economy or Political Economy? The Peasants Are Always Rational," *Journal of East Asian Studies* 42(4) (1983): 791–803; James C. Scott, "Everyday Forms of Peasant Resistance," *Journal of Peasant Studies* 13(2) (1986): 5–35; Bernard Fall, "A Grain of Rice Is Worth a Drop of Blood," *NYT Magazine* July 12, 1964, 10.

22. Mike Davis, *Late Victorian Holocausts: El Niño Famines and the Making of the Third World* (London, 2001), 245–248; CIA, "Communist Troop Movements in Laos," January 13, 1965, *DDRS,* ck3100355812; John M. Cabot, "Wise Distribution of U.S. Food Surpluses in Latin America," *DOSB,* April 1, 1959, 636; Douglas Dillon, "Building Growth in Freedom," *DOSB,* December 14, 1959, 856; Dean Rusk, "The Tragedy of Cuba," *Vital Speeches,* February 15, 1962, 259; Walt W. Rostow, *The Diffusion of Power* (New York, 1972), 422; "What's Happening to the Weather?" *US News and World Report,* August 30, 1965, 49–50; Perkins Committee, "Minutes of Meeting with McGeorge Bundy," October 12, 1965, in Department of State, *FRUS, 1964–1968* (Washington, DC, 1997), 9: 117.

23. National Academy of the Sciences, *Prospects of the World Food Supply: Proceedings of a Symposium* (Washington, DC, 1966), 2; Chandler oral history, 1967, IRRILA; IRRI, *Annual Report for 1965* (Los Baños, 1966), 15; USAID Philippines, *The Philippine Story of IR-8 The Miracle Rice* (Manila, 1967), 3.

24. Napoleon G. Rama, "Miracle Rice—Instant Increase," *Philippines Free Press,* August 6, 1966, 5; Wesley C. Haraldson, "The World Food Situation and Philippine Rice Production," *Journal of the American Chamber of Commerce (Philippines),* February 1966, 59; USAID, *The Philippine Story;* Harry M. Cleaver Jr., "The Contradictions of the Green Revolution," *Monthly Review* 24(2) (1972): 80–111; Claude Alvares, "The Great Gene Robbery," *The Illustrated Weekly of India,* March 23, 1986, 6–17; "CGIAR: Agricultural Research for Whom?" *The Ecologist* 26(6) (1996): 259–289; Quijano de Manila, "New Rice Bowls?" *Philippines Free Press,* April 29, 1967, 47; Victoria Arcega, "Technocrats as Middlemen and Their Networks in the Philippine Rice Project: The Case of the Masagana 99" (PhD diss., Michigan State University, 1976), 237.

25. CIA, "India's New Prime Minister," January 20, 1966, *DDRS,* ck3100375139; Bureau of Public Affairs, "Public Comment on Manila Conference and President's Trip," October 19, 1966, Department of State, Office of Public Opinion Studies, RG 59, NARA, box 44; Pedrino O. Ramos, "LBJ Country Hops," *Manila Chronicle,* October 27, 1966, 1.

26. IRRI, "Institution Names New Rice Variety," November 28, 1966, Hill Papers, FFA, box 14564; IRRI, *IR8 & Beyond* (Los Baños, 1977), 1.

27. IRRI, *Annual Report for 1968* (Los Baños, 1968), 13; CIA, "Intelligence Memorandum: Philippine Economic Problems," August 1968, *DDRS,* ck3100239916: 2690; Philip Bowring, "Rice: Manila's Facts and Fantasy," *Far Eastern Economic Review,* March 28, 1975, 43–45; Col. Osmundo Mondoñedo, "The Rise of the Miracle Men," *The Sunday (Manila) Times Magazine,* October 1, 1967, 30.

28. Akhil Gupta, *Postcolonial Developments: Agriculture in the Making of Modern India* (Durham, NC, 1998), 59–71; USAID, *Philippine Story,* 5; Rolando

B. Modina and A. R. Ridao, *IRRI Rice: The Miracle That Never Was* (Quezon City, 1987), 19.

29. CIA, "Philippine President Marcos' Problems at Midterm," December 7, 1967, in Department of State, *FRUS, 1964-1968,* 26: 805; Rostow to Johnson, "Indonesia," June 8, 1966, in Department of State, *FRUS, 1964-1968,* 26: 436-437; Edward Shils, "Political Development in the New States: II," *Comparative Studies in Society and History* 2(4) (1960): 409; Mutual Security Program, "Operations of the MSP, January 1-July 30, 1959," *DOSB,* February 1, 1960, 160; W. W. Rostow, *The Stages of Economic Growth: A Non-Communist Manifesto* (Cambridge, UK, 1960), 30-31.

30. "Director Scoffs at Miracle Rice Criticism," *Bangkok Post,* May 13, 1969, 2; "Rice of the Gods," *Time,* June 14, 1968, 69; "Breakthrough against Hunger: Miracle Rice for Far East," *US News and World Report,* December 4, 1967, 68-69; Kahn, "Rice, Rice, Rice," 160.

31. Bowles, *Ambassador's Report,* 247-248; Fall, "A Grain of Rice," 10; Paul Dean, "Viet's 'David' Adored in Goliath's World," *Indianapolis Star,* September 19, 1965, 22; Embassy of Vietnam, *Vietnamese Agriculture: A Progress Report* (Washington, DC, 1972), 5.

32. R. W. Komer to Johnson, "Second Komer Trip to Vietnam, 23-29 June 1966," July 1, 1966, in Department of State, *FRUS, 1964-1968,* 4: 480; Richard A. Hunt, *Pacification: The American Struggle for Vietnam's Hearts and Minds* (Boulder, CO, 1995), 134; U.S. Department of Defense, *The Pentagon Papers,* Gravel Edition (Boston, 1972), 2: 596; Robert W. Komer, *Bureaucracy at War: U.S. Performance in the Vietnam Conflict* (Boulder, CO, 1986), 120-121.

33. C. J. Zwick, C. A. Cooper, H. Heymann Jr., and R. H. Moorsteen, *U.S. Economic Assistance in Vietnam: A Proposed Reorientation,* July 1964, DDRS, ck3100101325.

34. Peter R. Kann, "Miracle in Vietnam: New Rice May Be Key to Economic Stability after War Ends in Land," *WSJ,* December 18, 1968, 1; Mark Kurlansky, *1968: The Year That Rocked the World* (New York, 2005), 49-50; James P. Grant to Orville Freeman, "Silver Lining to Disaster or How IR-8 Came to Vietnam in a Big Way," November 17, 1967, in Robert E. Lester, ed., *The Johnson Administration and Pacification in Vietnam: The Robert Komer-William Leonhart Files, 1966-1968* (Bethesda, MD, 1993 [microfilm]), reel 1, frame 37.

35. J. W. Holmes to Department of State, "Rice Policy Committee," January 6, 1968, State Department files, INCO RICE VIETS, NARA, box 1142; George L. McColm, "IR-8 and the Rice Revolution in Vietnam," November 6, 1967; and "Cultural Requirements for IR-8 Rice," December 20, 1967, McColm Papers, U.S. Army Military History Institute, Carlisle Barracks, PA.

36. Rusk to Bunker, "Land Reform Step Up," October 19, 1968, DDRS, ck3100061538.

37. Bunker to LBJ, "36th Weekly Message," January 24, 1968, DDRS, ck3100121660; Kann, "Miracle in Vietnam," 26; Defense Department, *Pentagon Papers,* 2: 552; Gene Roberts, "Lack of Security Upsets South Vietnam Rice Plan," *NYT,* April 10, 1968, 4.

38. Senate Committee on Foreign Relations, *Foreign Assistance Act of 1968,* pt. 2, 90th Cong., 2nd sess., March 13, 1968, 332; University of Hawaii/AID, Asia Training Center, *Debrief of an Agricultural Adviser, Quang Tri, Vietnam, 1967–68,* 1968, [typescript], Hamilton Library, University of Hawaii, Manoa, 13–15.

39. Bunker to AID, "New Pacification Concepts," September 26, 1968, *DDRS,* ck3100051342; William Colby, *Lost Victory: A Firsthand Account of America's Sixteen-Year Involvement in Vietnam* (Chicago, 1989), 266; Major General Nguyen Duy Hinh, *Vietnamization and Cease Fire* (Washington, DC, 1980), 88; "A Rice Goal in Sight," *Vietnam Magazine* 2(5) (1969): 17; Berger to SecState, "Rice," January 25, 1969, Department of State Central File, INCO RICE 17 VIET US, NARA, box 1142; Robert W. Chandler, *War of Ideas: The U.S. Propaganda Campaign in Vietnam* (Boulder, CO, 1981), 108–109.

40. Harriman to SecState, October 17, 1968, *DDRS,* ck3100021685; Hedrick Smith, "Harriman Suggests a Way out of Vietnam," *NYT Magazine,* August 24, 1969, 74; Hill to W. M. Myers, "RF and FF Financial Support for IRRI," March 4, 1969, FFA, PA06500055.

41. Hargrove, *Dragon Lives Forever,* 162; "Reds May Be Growing Miracle Rice," *Bangkok Post,* December 22, 1969, 2; House Committee on Foreign Affairs, *Green Revolution,* 37; Buy Huy Dap, *Khoa Hoc Ky Thuat Nong Nghiep,* July 1968, Joint Publication Research Service, Translations on North Vietnam 47179, January 3, 1969; CIA, "National Intelligence Survey: North Vietnam," January 1972, *DDRS,* ck3100275809.

42. Chandler to Thomas R. Hargrove, October 12, 1989, Chandler personnel file, IRRILA; Vo Nguyen Giap, *Essential Tasks of the Scientific and Technological Revolution in Agriculture* (Hanoi, 1979), 21–22; interview with Dat Van Tran, International Rice Commission, May 8, 2000, Rome, Italy.

7. YOU CAN'T EAT STEEL

1. Ministry of Food and Agriculture, *Indian Agriculture in Brief,* 6th ed. (Delhi, 1963), 39.

2. Ludwig Weindling, *Long Vegetable Fibers* (New York, 1947), 206–215; "The Birla Empire," *Business Week,* July 30, 1955, 90–94; Medha M. Kudaisya, *The Life and Times of G. D. Birla* (Delhi, 2003), 44–49.

3. B. Sivaraman, *Bitter Sweet: Governance of India in Transition* (Delhi, 1991), 346.

4. Gordon T. Stewart, *Jute and Empire* (Manchester, 1998), 141–142; George K. Chacko, *International Trade Aspects of Indian Burlap* (New York, 1961), 26–31.

5. Brown to Coombs, "India's Balance of Payments," December 15, 1960, Asia, General Federal Reserve Board Papers, U.S. Federal Reserve, Washington, DC; J. G. Harrar, Paul C. Mangelsdorf, and Warren Weaver, "Notes on Indian Agriculture," April 11, 1952, RG 6.7, series 2, box 26, RFAC; Ford Foundation Agricultural Production Team, *Report on India's Food Crisis and Steps to Meet It* (Delhi, 1959); Gunnar Myrdal, *Asian Drama: An Inquiry into the Poverty of Nations* (New York, 1968), 2: 1241.

6. Gwynn Garnett, *Observations on Indian Agriculture* (Washington, DC, 1956), 25; P. C. Mahalanobis, "The Approach of Operational Research to Planning in India," *Sankhya* 16 (December 1955): 10; Francine Frankel, *India's Political Economy: The Gradual Revolution* (Princeton, 1978), 123.

7. Jawaharlal Nehru, *The Discovery of India* (New York, 1960), 386.

8. Ford Foundation, *Roots of Change: The Ford Foundation in India* (New York, 1961), 11; Fredric Jameson, *A Singular Modernity: Essay on the Ontology of the Present* (London, 2002), 40.

9. Myrdal, *Asian Drama,* 2: 711–712; Pitamber Pant, "The Development of India," *Scientific American,* September 1963, 196.

10. Judith Brown, *Nehru: A Political Life* (New Haven, 2003), 238.

11. C. Subramaniam, *Hand of Destiny: Memoirs* (Bombay, 1993), 1: 174–175; P. C. Mahalanobis, *Talks on Planning* (New York, 1961), 7; Lloyd I. Rudolph and Susanne Hoeber Rudolph, *In Pursuit of Lakshmi: The Political Economy of the Indian State* (Chicago, 1987), 1.

12. T. T. Krishnamachari, *Speeches of T. T. Krishnamachari* (Delhi, 1957), 104; Frankel, *India's Political Economy,* 139–142.

13. S. R. Sen, "The Strategy for Agricultural Development," *ASI* 15(1) (January 1960): 1068; P. C. Mahalanobis, "The Asian Drama: An Indian View," *Sankhya* 31 (1969): 443; Frankel, *India's Political Economy,* 142.

14. Brown, *Nehru,* 238, 270; Frankel, *India's Political Economy,* 118; M. J. Akbar, *Nehru: The Making of India* (Delhi, 2002), 477; Michael Brecher, *Nehru's Mantle: The Politics of Succession in India* (New York, 1966), 145–146; Edward R. Dean, "Implementing India's Second Five-Year Plan," *Far Eastern Survey* 25(12) (1956): 184–191; "The Second Five-Year Plan: Basic Considerations Relating to the Plan-Frame," *Sankhya* 16 (December 1955): 112–130.

15. "Extracts from the Second Five-Year Plan: A Tentative Frame-Work," *Sankhya* 16 (December 1955): 91–110; Sen, "Strategy for Agricultural Development," 1072–1073; Radhe Shiam, "Rural Industrialization," *ASI* 13(10) (October 1958): 631–636; "Considerations Relating to the Plan Frame," 118.

16. Krishnamachari, *Speeches,* 26; Ramachandra Guha, *India after Gandhi* (New York, 2007), 218.

17. Weaver, "Human Ecology," January 3, 1952, RFAC, RG 2, series 100, box 6; Compton to Weaver, November 3, 1949, RFAC, RG 1.2, series 460, box 1; Warren Weaver to Chester Barnard, "The World Food Problem, Agriculture, and the Rockefeller Foundation," June 21, 1951, RFAC, RG 3, series, 915, box 3.

18. "Report of the Natural Sciences Division," November 1949, Gaither Report Supporting Documents, vol. 2, 29, FFA; "Conservation of Resources," Committee Report #6, January 1950, Gaither Report Supporting Documents, vol. 3, FFA.

19. Warren Weaver, "People, Energy and Food," *Scientific Monthly* 78(6) (1954): 359–364.

20. Warren Weaver to Chester Barnard, "The World Food Problem, Agriculture, and the Rockefeller Foundation," June 21, 1951, RFAC, RG 3, series, 915, box 3.

21. Weaver to Barnard, "The World Food Problem"; Weaver, "Human Ecology," January 3, 1952, RFAC, RG 2, series 100, box 6; John D. Rockefeller III, "Objective and Focus of My Asian Interest," November 17, 1953, John D. Rockefeller III Papers, RFAC, box 39; John Ensor Harr and Peter Johnson, *The Rockefeller Century* (New York, 1988), 466–467.

22. Weaver, "World Food Problem"; Roger Evans, "Round the World Trip," December 12, 1950, RFAC, RG 1.2, Series 600, box 1; Weaver, "Human Ecology," January 3, 1952, RFAC, RG 2, series 100, box 6; Compton to Weaver, November 3, 1949, RFAC, RG 1.2, series 460, box 1; Compton to Barnard, June 25, 1951, RFAC, RG 3, series 915, box 3.

23. Gaither and Price, "Interview with Mr. Allen Dulles," April 15, 1955, report 005611, FFA; "Philanthropoid No. 1," *Time,* June 10, 1957, 65; Weaver, "World Food Problem."

24. Harrar et al., "Notes on Indian Agriculture," April 11, 1952, RFAC.

25. Ellen Herman, *The Romance of American Psychology: Political Culture in the Age of Experts* (Berkeley, 1996), 137.

26. Richard Bradfield, "Report on Trip to Mexico," October 24, 1953, RFAC, RG 1.2, series 323, box 10; Borlaug oral history, June 12, 1967, RFAC, 198.

27. L. P. Reitz and S. C. Salmon, "Origin, History, and Use of Norin 10 Wheat," *Crop Science* 8 (1968): 686–689; Hitoshi Kitara, "Origin and History of Daruma, a Parental Variety of Norin 10," *Proceedings of the Sixth International Wheat Genetics Symposium* (Kyoto, 1983), 13–19.

28. Borlaug oral history, June 12, 1967, RFAC, 201, 205–206; Lennard Bickel, *Facing Starvation: Norman Borlaug and the Fight against Hunger* (Pleasantville, NY, 1974), 216–217.

29. Stakman, "Report on Mexico, Based on Visit April 16–May 14, 1954," RFAC, RG 1.2, series 323, box 10; Borlaug oral history, June 12, 1967, RFAC, 215–216; Marvin Alisky, "U.S. Helps Improve Mexican Food," *Christian Science Monitor,* May 20, 1961, 11.

30. Stakman, "Report on Mexico, January 8–April 9, 1960," RFAC, RG 1.2, series 323, box 10; "Hunger Reshapes Pakistani Policy," *NYT,* January 3, 1957, 60; Memcon, "US Economic Aid to Pakistan," July 10, 1957, in Department of State, *FRUS, 1955–1957* (Washington, DC, 1985), 8: 481–482; Bartlett to Rountree, "Political Evolution in Pakistan," October 7, 1958, and Langley to Department of State, October 8, 1958, in Department of State, *FRUS, 1958–1960* (Washington, DC, 1992), 15: 668–672; Borlaug to Fei, July 1, 1963, BP, box 1.

31. Bickel, *Facing Starvation,* 233; Borlaug oral history, RFAC, 206; Borlaug oral history, April 1, 1985, Cushing Library, College Station, TX, 26.

32. Stakman, "Report on Trip to India, Africa, and Europe, January 6–June 19, 1959," RFAC, RG 1.2, series 464, box 27; Harrar et al., "Notes on Indian Agriculture"; M. S. Swaminathan, "Benjamin Peary Pal," *Biographical Memoirs of Fellows of the Royal Society* 42 (1996): 266–274.

33. Indian Environmental Society, *Economic Ecologists of India: M. S. Swaminathan* (Delhi, 1982), 2–10; "Indo-AgroScientist Hounded Out of Job," *Blitz,*

October 31, 1970, 10; Nehru to CM, November 20, 1957, in Nehru, *Letters to Chief Ministers* (Delhi, 1988), 4: 600–601.

34. M. S. Swaminathan, *Wheat Revolution: A Dialogue* (Delhi, 1993), 10; M. S. Randhawa, *Green Revolution* (New York, 1974), 67; "Incentives to Agricultural Scientists," *ASI* 16(2) (February 1961): 1340; "Agricultural Research," *ASI* 14(1) (January 1959): 890–893.

35. J. P. Bhattacharjee, "Changing Characteristics of the Flow of Foodgrains Supplies from the Farmers," *ASI* 15(1) (January 1960): 1079; "Monthly News-Letter," *ASI* 14(4) (April 1959): 1; Ram Dayal, "Monopoly Procurement in Foodgrains," *ASI* 13(7) (October 1958): 631–636.

36. Jawaharlal Nehru, "A Long-Term Problem," December 8, 1959, in *India's Foreign Policy* (Delhi, 1961), 373; Brecher, *Nehru's Mantle*, 139; Steven A. Hoffman, *India and the China Crisis* (Berkeley, 1990), 49, 67; Planning Commisson, *Third Five-Year Plan: A Draft Outline* (Delhi, 1960), 11; "Agriculture in the Third Plan," *Eastern Economist* 34(11) (March 11, 1960): 630.

37. "Text of Kennedy's Message," *NYT,* March 23, 1961, 14; Ball to Kennedy, April 19, 1961, in Department of State, *FRUS, 1961–1963* (Washington, DC, 1996), 19: 33.

38. Swaminathan, *Wheat Revolution,* 11, 23; M. S. Randhawa, *A History of Agriculture in India* (Delhi, 1986), 4: 368–369.

39. John K. Knaus, *Orphans of the Cold War: America and the Tibetan Struggle for Survival* (New York, 1999), 255; Chen Jian, "The Tibetan Rebellion of 1959 and China's Changing Relations with India and the Soviet Union," *Journal of Cold War Studies* 8(3) (2006): 54–101; Hoffman, *India and the China Crisis,* 165, 219; Galbraith, *Ambassador's Report,* 487; V. S. Naipaul, *An Area of Darkness* (London, 1964), 248.

40. Subramaniam, *Hand of Destiny,* 2: 48; Hoffman, *India and the China Crisis,* 165, 219; Galbraith, *Ambassador's Report,* 487; "Prime Minister's Reply to Lok Sabha Debate," *Foreign Affairs Record* 9(2) (February 1963): 60; H. Venkatasubbiah, "State Plans and the Emergency," *The Hindu Weekly Review,* November 19, 1962, 11.

41. B. K. Nehru, interview on *Meet the Press* (NBC-TV), November 18, 1962, 2 (transcript); Frankel, *India's Political Economy,* 217; H. Venkatasubbiah, "State Plans and the Emergency," *The Hindu Weekly Review,* November 19, 1962, 1.

42. Brecher, *Nehru's Mantle,* 7; "Changes in Political Spectrum," *LT,* January 1, 1963, 11; "Statement of Principles of the Swatantra Party," *The Economic Weekly,* July 1959, 894; C. Rajagopalachari, "The Case for the Swatantra Party," *Illustrated Weekly of India,* August 16, 1959, 10–11; Frankel, *India's Political Economy,* 208–209.

43. Robert McMahon, "Choosing Sides in South Asia," in Thomas Paterson, ed., *Kennedy's Quest for Victory* (New York, 1989), 213; Kaysen to Kennedy, November 3, 1962, in Department of State, *FRUS, 1961–1963,* 19: 365; Rusk to Diplomatic Posts, December 8, 1962, in Department of State, *FRUS, 1961–1963,* 19: 426; Rusk to Kennedy, April 25, 1963, in Department of State, *FRUS, 1961–1963,*

19: 559; Meeting on India, April 25, 1963, in Department of State, *FRUS, 1961–1963*, 19: 563; Galbraith, *Ambassador's Journal*, 549.

44. Randhawa, *History of Agriculture*, 4: 369; Bickel, *Facing Starvation*, 244; M. S. Swaminathan, "Dr. Norman E. Borlaug," *Indian Farming* 20(9) (December 1970): 45.

45. "New Variety of Wheat Grown at Pusa Institute," *Times of India*, March 15, 1964; "Mexical Wheat under Cultivation at Pusa," *Sunday Standard*, March 15, 1964; "Dwarf with High Wheat Yield," *Sunday Statesman*, March 15, 1964; Sharada Prasad, "Story of a Giant and a Dwarf," *Yojana*, March 29, 1964, 1–4.

46. Swaminathan, *Wheat Revolution*, 117; Bickel, *Facing Starvation*, 245, 260.

47. "Indians Protest Rising Food Costs," *NYT*, February 23, 1964, 5.

48. "Why Fertilizers?" *Eastern Economist* 5(8) (June 3, 1960): ii–iii; F. W. Parker, "Positive Achievements in the Fight against Hunger," October 11, 1961, RFAC, RG 6.7, series 2, box 31; "Fertilisers: Sisyphus in India," *Economist*, January 26, 1963, 345; Galbraith, *Ambassador's Journal*, 468; "A Hard Core for Agricultural Development: 1961–1966," *Eastern Economist* 6(3) (March 6, 1961): iii–vi; Stephen Merrett, "The Growth of Indian Nitrogen Fertilizer Manufacture: Some Lessons for Industrial Planning," *Journal of Development Studies* 8(4) (1972): 395–410.

49. "Foreign Trade," *The Eastern Economist* 5(12) (January 6, 1961): x; Galbraith to Kennedy, November 13, 1962, in Department of State, *FRUS, 1961–1963*, 19: 382; CIA, "The People around Indian Prime Minister Shastri," June 26, 1964, *DDRS*, item ck3100352924; TTK to Shastri, November 23, 1965, Krishnamachari Papers, Nehru Memorial Library, Teen Murthi House, Delhi.

50. Sidney W. Mintz, *Tasting Food, Tasting Freedom: Excursions into Eating, Culture, and the Past* (Boston, 1996), 84–91; Kenneth Pomerantz and Steven Topik, *The World That Trade Created: Society, Culture, and the World Economy*, 2nd ed. (Armonk, NY, 2006), 187.

51. Salim-ur Rehman, "Chapatti Quality from British Wheat Cultivar Flours," *Lebensmittel Wissenschaft & -Technologie/Food Science & Technology* 40(5) (2007): 775–784; Borlaug, "Indian Wheat Research Designed to Increase Wheat Production," April 11, 1964, RFAC, RG 6.7, series 4, subseries 6, box 84; Glenn Anderson, "Organization through Coordination," 1969, NDFO Papers, RG 6.7, series II, box, 29, folder 167, RFAC; Borlaug 1985 oral history, April 1, 16; Borlaug to Swaminathan, June 24, 1964, BP, Correspondence Files, Box 1.

52. B. S. Minhas and T. N. Srinivasan, "New Agricultural Strategy Analysed," *Yojana*, January 26, 1966, 20–24; Borlaug oral history, April 1, 1985, University of Texas, 40.

53. Borlaug to Moseman, December 21, 1966, and Borlaug to Oddvar Aresevik, December 13, 1966, BP, Correspondence Files, box 1.

54. Borlaug oral history, RFAC, 256; Swaminathan, *Wheat Revolution*, 19, 105.

55. Swaminathan, *Wheat Revolution*, xi; Swaminathan, "The Punjab Miracle," *Illustrated Weekly of India*, May 11, 1969, 32.

56. CIA, "Lal Bahadur Shastri," June 1, 1964, *DDRS*, item ck3100352923; Rusk to Bowles, May 8, 1965, in Department of State, *FRUS, 1964–1968* (Washington, DC, 2000), 25: 253; Guha, *India after Gandhi*, 403; Shastri, "The New

Agricultural Strategy," October 1, 1964, in *Selected Speeches of Lal Bahadur Shastri* (Delhi, 1974), 102; Gucharan Das, *India Unbound* (New York, 2002), 130.

57. House Committee on Agriculture, *World War on Hunger,* 89th Cong., 2nd sess., February 14–18, 1966, 93–94; Pant, "The Development of India."

58. Thorner, *The Shaping of Modern India* (Delhi, 1980), 245–246; Neville Maxwell, "Will India Seek an Alternative to Parliamentary Democracy?" *LT,* February 10, 1967, 13.

59. Ronald Segal, *The Anguish of India* (New York, 1965), 273; Haravu Iengar, *Inflation, the Food Crisis, and the Fourth Five Year Plan* (Madras, 1965), 21.

8. THE MEANING OF FAMINE

1. M. S. Swaminathan, ed., *Wheat Revolution: A Dialogue* (Madras, 1993), 67, 87.

2. Government of India, *Review of the Food and Scarcity Situation in India* (Delhi, 1967); Alan Berg, "Famine Contained: Notes and Lessons from the Bihar Experience," in *Famine: A Symposium* (Uppsala, 1971), 113–129; "The Famine That Never Was," *Economist,* April 13, 1968, 34–37; Lyndon B. Johnson, *The Vantage Point* (New York, 1971), 228.

3. Subramaniam to T. T. Krishnamachari, July 1, 1964, T. T. Krishnamachari Papers, correspondence file, NMML; C. Subramaniam, *Hand of Destiny: Memoirs* (Bombay, 1993), 2: 116.

4. "RFF-IAP, 1957–1971," NDFO Papers, RG 6.7, box 5, folder 33, series I, RFAC; A. H. Moseman, "Increasing Food Grain Production—India," January 14, 1965, NDFO Papers, RG 6.7, series II, box 33, folder 209, RFAC; Johnson E. Douglas, "Summary of Seeds Act Development," December 13, 1969, NDFO Papers, RG 6.7, series II, box 26, folder 145, RFAC; Norman Borlaug, "World Food Security and the Legacy of Canadian Wheat Scientist R. Glenn Anderson," *Canadian Journal of Plant Pathology* 14 (1992): 253–266; Ministry of Food and Agriculture, *Modernising Indian Agriculture: Report on the Intensive Agricultural Districts Programme* (Delhi, 1968); "More Food, Less Dogma," *Economist,* April 24, 1965, 410.

5. "Atlantic Report," *The Atlantic,* May 1965, 20; R. G. Anderson, "Organization through Coordination," 1969, NDFO Papers, RG 6.7, series II, box, 29, folder 167, RFAC; Ronald Segal, *The Anguish of India* (New York, 1965), 208; Subramaniam, "Agriculture, the Hand Maid of Industry," *Industrial India Annual* (1965): 33–40.

6. Subramaniam, *Hand of Destiny,* 2: 117; Ministry of Food, *Report of the Committee on Fertilisers* (Delhi, 1965); William D. Smith, "India Is Pushing New Fertilizer Plan," *NYT,* January 10, 1965, F1; Thomas E. Brady, "Fertilizer Plant Delayed in India," *NYT,* April 12, 1965, 58; Francine Frankel, *India's Political Economy* (Princeton, 1978), 280–281; Committee on Plan Projects, *Review of the Construction of the Trombay Fertilizer Project* (Delhi, November 1965); Bechtel, *Fertilizer for India* (San Francisco, 1965).

7. Matthew Connelly, *Fatal Misconception* (Cambridge, MA, 2008), 217–218; Anderson, "Organization though Coordination"; Leland Hazard, "Strong

Medicine for India," *The Atlantic,* December 1965, 45; "India Plans for Survival," *Economist,* September 24, 1966, 1266–1267.

8. Moseman, "Increasing Food Grain Production—India."

9. Norman K. Nicholson, "Political Aspects of Indian Food Policy," *Pacific Affairs* 41(1) (1968): 48; "Return to New Delhi," *Economist,* March 28, 1964, 1193; Ashutosh Varshney, "Ideas, Interests, and Institutions in Policy Change: Transformation of India's Agricultural Strategy in the Mid-1960s" (unpublished manuscript, MIT Library, October 1968); Frankel, *India's Political Economy,* 283; "To Those That Have Not," *Economist,* November 20, 1965, 834; "15 Million Tons of Poison," *Blitz,* December 25, 1965, 2–3; M. Brecher, *Nehru's Mantle* (New York, 1966), 148–149; Ajit Prasad Jain, "The Food Crisis in Kerala," *Illustrated Weekly of India,* September 12, 1965, 15; "Maharashtra's Food Difficulties," *Hindu Weekly Review,* July 19, 1965, 11.

10. Subramaniam, *Hand of Destiny,* 2: 114–115; K. C. Arora, *V. K. Krishna Menon: A Biography* (New Delhi, 1998), 265; Margaret Parton, *The Leaf and the Flame* (New York, 1959), 215; Brecher, *Nehru's Mantle,* 149.

11. James Reston, "New Delhi: The Real War on Poverty," *NYT,* December 15, 1965, 46; Rusk to Bowles, May 8, 1965, in Department of State, *FRUS, 1964–1968* (Washington, DC, 2000), 25: 253; Selig Harrison, *India: The Most Dangerous Decades* (Princeton, 1960), 177, 338.

12. CIA, "The People around Indian Prime Minister Shastri," June 26, 1964, *DDRS,* ck3100352924; CIA, "Lal Bahadur Shastri," June 1, 1964, *DDRS,* ck3100352923; Freeman to Johnson, "Report on Review of Indian Agriculture," April 27, 1964, NSF, History, Indian Famine, box 25, LBJL; Freeman and Gaud to Johnson, "Food Aid for India in 1968," October 10, 1967, NSF, NSC Meeting 1/11/67, box 2, LBJL; Rusk, "A United States Assistance Strategy for India," November 8, 1965, NSF, NSC History, Indian Famine, vol. 2, box 25, LBJL; B. K. Nehru, *Nice Guys Finish Second* (Delhi, 1997), 470.

13. Robert A. Caro, *The Path to Power* (New York, 1990), 10; Joseph A. Califano Jr., *The Triumph and Tragedy of Lyndon Johnson* (New York, 1991), 150; "Lyndon's Other Bible," *Time,* September 3, 1965, 19; "Washington Outlook," *Business Week,* May 30, 1964, 40; Johnson to Ward, April 15, 1965, White House Central File, Name file, Jackson, Barbara, LBJL; Barbara Ward, *The Rich Nations and the Poor Nations* (New York, 1962); Ward, *India and the West* (New York, 1961), 13.

14. Ward, *India and the West,* 286–287; Ward, *The Rich Nations and the Poor Nations,* 87, 91–92; George C. McGhee, "The United States and Germany: Our Mutual Responsibilities and Our Mutual Dependence," *DOSB,* April 25, 1966, 662.

15. Lewis to Bell, "Betting on India," January 14, 1965, Indian Famine, vol. 2, Tab 4a, NSC History, box 25, LBJL; Chester Bowles, *Promises to Keep: My Years in Public Life, 1941–1969* (New York, 1971), 556; "Chester Bowles's Suggestion," *The Hindu Weekly Review,* July 26, 1965, 2; Komer to Cook, June 3, 1965, NSC History, Indian Famine, vol. 1, Tab 1, box 25, LBJL.

16. Murray Kempton, "No Miracles for Mr. Johnson," *Spectator,* December 27, 1963, 842; "Should Foreign Assistance Be Substantially Reduced?" *Congressional Digest,* June–July 1965, 176–190; Willard Edwards, "Polls Show Rights

Tactics Sour North," *CT,* March 11, 1964, 3; Johnson to Ball, May 13, 1964, in Department of State, *FRUS, 1964–1968,* 9: 22.

17. Robert McMahon, *The Cold War on the Periphery* (New York, 1994), 329; Senate Foreign Relations Committee, *Executive Sessions,* 89th Cong., 1st sess., 1965, 27: 1094; "Activities Scheduled in Congress," *WP,* June 8, 1968, A20; Nick Kotz, *Judgment Days: Lyndon Baines Johnson, Martin Luther King, and the Laws That Changed America* (New York, 2005), 330–331.

18. C. Subramaniam, *The New Strategy in Indian Agriculture: The First Decade and After* (Delhi, 1979), 47; Borlaug to Cummings, August 20, 1965, and Borlaug to Guy Baird, September 17, 1965, RG 6.7, series IV, subseries 6, box 83, folder 536, RFAC.

19. Randall Woods, *LBJ: Architect of American Ambition* (New York, 2006), 589–590; "Los Angeles Riots," *Times of India,* August 21, 1965, 6.

20. Vance Bourjaily, "One of the Green Revolution Boys," *Atlantic,* February 1973, 66–76; "The Bombay Beat," *Illustrated Weekly of India,* September 26, 1965, 51; "Diary of Conflict," *Himmat,* September 17, 1965, 7; Stanley Wolpert, *India* (Berkeley, 2005), 234–235.

21. "Springs of Strength," *Blitz,* November 14, 1965, 8; Lal Bahadur Shastri, "Produce More Food and Preserve Our Freedom," *Indian Farming* 15(7) (1965): 3–4, 52; C. Subramaniam, "India on the Eve of Breakthrough in Agriculture," *Indian Farming* 15(8) (1965): 7; "Delhi's New Look," *Monthly Commentary in Indian Economic Conditions* 7(3) (October 1965): 6–7.

22. Bell to Johnson, "Proposed New Aid Commitments through December 21, 1965," October 21, 1965, in Department of State, *FRUS, 1964–1968,* 9: Doc. 44; John W. Finney, "An Irked US Bars Ghana Food Plea," *NYT,* November 25, 1965, 3; Bundy to Rusk and McNamara, "Presidential Decisions on Aid to India/Pakistan," June 9, 1965, in Department of State, *FRUS, 1964–1968,* 25: 274; "US Food Aid Not Used to Pressurise India," *Hindu Weekly Review,* November 22, 1965, 2.

23. Department of State, *FRUS, 1964–1968,* 25: 392, 408, 554–555, 594; John Lewis, *India's Political Economy: Governance and Reform* (Delhi, 1995), 94–99.

24. Robert B. McKay, "Reapportionment: Success Story of the Warren Court," *Michigan Law Review* 67(2) (1968): 230; Charles M. Hardin, "Present and Prospective Policy Problems of U.S. Agriculture," *Journal of Farm Economics* 47(5) (1965): 1091–1115.

25. Vernon W. Ruttan, ed., *Why Food Aid?* (Baltimore, 1993), 88; "Johnson May Revise Food Aid Policy," *NYT,* November 8, 1965, 1, 39; John A. Schnittker, "Farm Policy—Today's Direction," *Journal of Farm Economics* 48(5) (1966): 1091; Freeman to Johnson, "Weekly Report," September 24, 1965, Freeman Papers, chron file, box 3, LBJL.

26. Department of State, "A United States Assistance Strategy for India," November 8, 1965, NSF, NSC History, Indian Famine, vol, 2, Tab 4, LBJL; Rusk to Bowles, November 10, 1965, in Department of State, *FRUS, 1964–1968,* 25: 461.

27. Komer, "President's Talk with Ambassador B. K. Nehru," July 16, 1965, NSF, NSC History, Indian Famine, vol. 1, box 25, LBJL; Nehru, *Nice Guys Finish Second,* 430–31.

28. Subramaniam, *New Strategy,* 53; Orville Freeman Diary, November 24, 1965, LBJL; Lewis, *India's Political Economy,* 126.

29. "Cabinet Agenda," November 19, 1965, Cabinet Papers, box 4, LBJL; Johnson to Freeman, "Critical Indian Food Situation," NSAM 339, December 17, 1965, in Department of State, *FRUS, 1964-1968,* 25: 513-514; Komer, "President's Meeting with Subramaniam," December 20, 1965, NSF, Komer Files, box 24, LBJL; Thomas J. Foley, "Famines May Alter Farm Policy," *WP,* December 12, 1965, R5.

30. Foreign Agricultural Service, *The World Food Deficit: A First Approximation* (Washington, DC, March 1961), 1; Economic Research Service, *The World Food Budget, 1962 and 1966* (Washington, DC, October 1961), 69; ERS, *The World Food Budget 1970* (Washington, DC, October 1964); Lester Brown, *An Economic Analysis of Far Eastern Agriculture* (Washington, DC, November 1961); Lester R. Brown, *Man, Land, and Food: Looking Ahead at World Food Needs* (Washington, DC, November 1963), 130; "Administrative History of the Department of Agriculture," vol. 1, chapter 4, box 1, LBJL; CIA, "The 1954-55 Food Situation in the Sino-Soviet Bloc," March 9, 1956, www.foia.cia.gov.

31. Niall Ferguson, "Home Truths about Famine, War and Genocide," *The Independent,* June 14, 2006; Cornelius Walford, *The Famines of the World: Past and Present* (London, 1879), 2, 89-90; George Hamilton, "Measures Taken by Government for the Prevention of Famine in India," *Journal of the Society of Arts* 45 (March 19, 1897): 369.

32. Bombay Presidency, *Famine Relief Code* (Bombay, 1904), 22; Bengal, *Bengal Famine Code* (Calcutta, 1908), 14; *The Bihar and Orissa Famine Code 1930* (Patna, 1930), 2, 11, 15; Dana Simmons, "Starvation Science: From Colonies to Metropole," in Alexander Nützenadel and Frank Trentmann, eds., *Food and Globalization: Consumption, Markets, and Politics in the Modern World* (Oxford, 2008), 176.

33. Michael Watts, "Heart of Darkness: Reflections on Famine and Starvation in Africa," in R. E. Downs, Donna O. Kerner, and Stephen P. Reyna, eds., *The Political Economy of African Famine* (Philadelphia, 1991), 23-68; Amartya Sen, "Famines," *World Development* 8(9) (1980): 613-621; Rolando V. Garcia, *Drought and Man,* vol. 1: *Nature Pleads Not Guilty* (Oxford, 1981).

34. Senate Subcommittee on Foreign Aid, *Population Crisis,* 90th Cong., 2nd sess., pt. 2, 1968, 312; Barbara Tufty, "Analysis of Famine," *Science News,* July 30, 1966, 74-75; "Food Is Politics," *Economist,* February 5, 1966, 503; Thomas L. Hughes to Rusk, "Some Political Implications of the Indian Food Shortage," December 21, 1965, NSF, Files of Robert Komer, India—Food 1964-1965, box 24, LBJL; CIA, "Indo-Pakistani Reactions to Certain US Courses of Action," December 7, 1965, Special National Intelligence Estimate 31-32-65, in Department of State, *FRUS, 1964-1968,* 25: 489-490; Carolyn Castore, "The United States and India: The Use of Food to Apply Economic Pressure—1965-67," in Sidney Weintraub, ed., *Economic Coercion and U.S. Foreign Policy: Implications of Case Studies from the Johnson Administration* (Boulder, CO. 1982), 137.

35. P. N. Dhar, *Indira Gandhi, the "Emergency" and Indian Democracy* (New Delhi, 2000), 108; B. S. Minhas and T. N. Srinivasan, "The New Agricultural Strat-

egy Analysed," *Yojana* 10(1) (January 26, 1966): 20–24; "TTK Discounts Fears of Rise in Prices," *Hindu Weekly Review,* August 30, 1965, 2; T. T. Krishnamachari to Shastri, December 1, 1965, correspondence file, NMML; Subramaniam, *Hand of Destiny,* 2: 135; B. Sivaraman, *Bitter Sweet: Governance of India in Transition* (Delhi, 1991), 277; T. T. Krishnamachari to Subramaniam, July 2, 1964, correspondence file, NMML.

36. "Violent Demonstrations in Kerala," *Hindu Weekly Review,* February 7, 1966, 3; Rajni Kothari, "India: The Congress System on Trial," *Asian Survey* 7(2) (1967): 84–86; "Sovereignty for Nagaland," *Hindu Weekly Review,* February 28, 1966, 6; "Army Sent to Crush Mizo Violence," *Hindu Weekly Review,* March 7, 1966, 3; W. W. Rostow, "The Sharing of the Good Life," *DOSB,* May 23, 1966, 809–810; Subramaniam, *Hand of Destiny,* 2: 135; CIA, "India under Indira Gandhi," February 25, 1966, *DDRS,* ck3100375152; Komer to Johnson, "Final Notes on Gandhi's Visit," March 27, 1966, in Department of State, *FRUS, 1964–1968,* 25: 593.

37. "Johnson Asks Aid for 'Life of Man,'" *NYT,* January 22, 1966, 1; Freeman, "Telephone Call from the Ranch," December 13, 1965, Freeman Papers, box 3, LBJL; Treadmill to Starvation," *NYT,* January 4, 1966, 26; Senate Subcommittee on Foreign Aid Expenditures, *Population Crisis,* 89th Cong., 2nd sess., 1966, 16; Komer, "President's Meeting with Indian Food Minister Subramaniam," December 20, 1965, NSF, Komer Files, India Food 1964–1965, box 24, LBJL.

38. "Food Deficit in Southern States," *Eastern Economist,* March 4, 1966, 366; "Food, 1966," *Yojana,* March 20, 1966, 1; "Shortage Not of Food But of Money," *Yojana,* May 29, 1966, 2; Bowles, *Promises to Keep,* 530; "American Trap behind Famine Scare," *Blitz,* November 20, 1965, 10–11; CIA, "Excerpts from Communist Media Exploitation of Food Shortage in India," January 17, 1966, CREST; Kingsley Martin, "A Famine in India?" *New Statesman,* March 4, 1966, 286; Chanchal Sarkar, "Below the Wheatline," *Spectator,* March 4, 1966, 255–256; "Transcript of President's Press Conference on Indian Famine," *NYT,* February 5, 1966, 8; "Food Ships Streaming into Famine-Free India," *LT,* February 22, 1966, 8.

39. "Pope Asks World Give Famine Aid," *NYT,* February 10, 1966, 26; "Joint Appeal by U Thant and Dr. Sen," *Hindu Weekly Review,* February 21, 1966, 3; "Pupils Fast," *WP,* February 10, 1966, A25; "Italian Drive Raises $1.5 Million," *WP,* February 16, 1966, A13; "Millions May Starve," *NYT,* February 15, 1966, 1; "Indo-U.S. Talks: Food, Disarmament, and Nuclear Policy," March 29, 1966, in Department of State, *FRUS, 1964–1966,* 25: 599; "Riceless in Kerala," *Eastern Economist,* February 11, 1966, 211; Gaud to Califano, "Proposed Message on India's Food Needs," March 25, 1966, White House Aides, Bob Hardesty file, box 10, LBJL; R. Komer, "President's Meeting with Indian Ambassador Nehru," February 3, 1966, NSF, NSC History, vol. 1, box 25, LBJL.

40. Philip Geyelin, *Lyndon B. Johnson and the World* (New York, 1966), 157; "Quotation of the Day," *NYT,* April 1, 1966, 37; Homer Bigart, "Mrs. Gandhi Sees Visit as Triumph," *NYT,* April 2, 1966, 6; Indira Gandhi, *A Journey of Friendship* (Delhi, 1966), 41; Betty Friedan, "How Mrs. Gandhi Shattered 'The Feminine Mystique,'" *Ladies' Home Journal,* May 1966, 167; James Warner

Bjorkman, "Public Law 480 and the Policies of Self-Help and Short Tether," in Lloyd Rudolph and Susanne Rudolph, eds., *The Regional Imperative: The Administration of U.S. Foreign Policy toward South Asian States* (Atlantic Highlands, NJ, 1980), 234.

41. Senate Agriculture Committee, *Emergency Food Relief for India,* 89th Cong., 2nd sess., 1966; "Johnson Asks Billion Food Aid for India," *CT,* March 31, 1966, 2; R. Guha, *India after Gandhi* (New York, 2003), 410; "Indo-U.S. Talks: Food, Disarmament and Nuclear Policy," in Department of State, *FRUS, 1964–1968,* 25: 599; Indira Gandhi, interview on *Meet the Press* (NBC-TV), April 3, 1966; "Death in Orissa," *Himmat,* April 8, 1966, 3; G. S. Bhargava, "Starvation vs. Malnutrition," *Yojana,* May 15, 1966, 27.

42. Freeman to Johnson, "Review of the India Food Situation," March 4, 1966, in Department of State, *FRUS, 1964–1968,* 25: 581; Rusk to Johnson, "Briefing Papers for the Visit of India's Prime Minister," March 21, 1966, NSF, NSC History, Indian Famine, vol. 2, LBJL, box 25; "Devaluation—Resolve and Challenge," *Thought,* June 11, 1966, 3; Inder Malhotra, *Indira Gandhi: A Personal and Political Biography* (London, 1989), 96.

43. V. Rastyannikov, "To Raise a Giant: The Food Problems of the Developing Countries Can Be Solved," *Literaturnaya Gazeta* 17 (April 24, 1968), 1, 15; I. Sinyagin, "Labor and Soil Fertility," *Literaturnaya Gazeta* 17 (April 24, 1968), 12; Telephone conversation with Freeman, February 2, 1966, in Department of State, *FRUS, 1964–1968,* 25: 554; Rusk to McConaughy, November 10, 1965, in Department of State, *FRUS, 1964–1968,* 25: 459; telephone conversation between Johnson and Freeman, November 11, 1966, in Department of State, *FRUS, 1964–1968,* 25: 758.

44. Subramaniam, *Hand of Destiny,* 2: 153–160; Borlaug, "Brief Report on Progress Being Made by the Indian Coordinated Wheat Improvement Program," April 12, 1966, RG 6.7, series IV, subseries 6, box 84, RFAC.

45. India, *Food and Scarcity Situation,* 11–17; Government of Bihar, *Bihar Famine Report, 1966–67* (Patna, 1973), 85; Arthur J. Dommen, "Thousands in India Face Starvation," *LAT,* November 10, 1966, 9; Morris Kaplan, "One Fourth Face Starvation," *NYT,* October 19, 1966, 3; Maggie Black, *A Cause for Our Times: Oxfam: The First 50 Years* (Oxford, 1992), 113; Rostow to Johnson, December 8, 1966, NSF, NSC History, Indian Famine, vol. 3, box 26, LBJL; Paul R. Brass, "The Political Uses of Crisis: The Bihar Famine of 1966–1967," *Journal of Asian Studies* 45(2) (1986): 255; telephone conversation between Johnson and Freeman, November 27, 1966, in Department of State, *FRUS, 1964–1968,* 25: 764–765.

46. Bowles, *Promises to Keep,* 534; "Harvest of Mercy," *Bulletin of the Atomic Scientists,* February 1967, 3–4.

47. Johnson, "Two Threats to Peace: Hunger and Aggression," *DOSB,* July 25, 1966, 115; Schnittker, "India Discussions in Late 1966," January 10, 1967, NSF, NSC History India Famine, vol. 5, box 26, LBLJ; Norman Palmer, "India's Fourth General Election," *Asian Survey* 7(5) (1967): 275–291; "C. Subramaniam Loses to DMK Candidate," *Hindu Weekly Review,* February 27, 1967, 2; "Will Fight to Put Down Regional Imbalance," *Hindu Weekly Review,* April 3, 1967, 3.

48. Government of Bihar, *Bihar Famine Report*, 99; "In the States," *Hindu Weekly Review*, March 6, 1967, 8; "Center Increases Grain Allotment to Bihar," *Hindu Weekly Review*, April 24, 1967, 2; Brass, "Political Uses of Crisis"; "Changed Political Pattern Is a Sign of Our Commitment," *India News*, April 21, 1967, 5.

49. "The Disaster That Never Was," *Economist*, April 13, 1968, 34–35; Berg, "Famine Contained," 120–122; Jean Drèze and Amartya Sen, *The Political Economy of Hunger* (Oxford, 1990), 2: 59–60; Tim Dyson and Arup Maharatna, "Bihar Famine 1966–67 and Maharashtra Drought 1970–73: The Demographic Consequences," *Economic and Political Weekly*, June 27, 1992, 1325–1332; Bowles to Rusk, November 4, 1966, NSF, NSC History, Indian Famine, vol. 3, box 26, LBJL; Rostow to Johnson, "India Food," August 31, 1967, in Department of State, *FRUS, 1964–1968*, 25: 883.

50. NSC, "NSC History, India's Food Crisis, 1965–67," 1968, NSF, Indian Famine, vol. 5, box 26, LBJL.

51. Nehru, *Nice Guys Finish Second*, 430–431; House Committee on Foreign Affairs, *Foreign Assistance Act of 1968*, 90th Cong., 2nd sess., 1968, 55.

52. Gregg Easterbrook, "Forgotten Benefactor," *Atlantic*, January 1997, 75; J. M. Roberts, *Twentieth Century: The History of the World, 1901–2000* (New York, 1999), 118; Paul Kennedy, *The Rise and Fall of the Great Powers* (New York, 1987), 440; Eric Hobsbawm, *The Age of Extremes: A History of the World, 1914–1991* (New York, 1991), 292, 366.

9. THE CONQUEST OF HUNGER

1. "Record Food Production Forecast for 1967–68," *India News*, January 5, 1968, 1; Indira Gandhi, "Country Going through Dynamic Changes," *India News*, February 23, 1968, 1.

2. Weathersby to Rusk, "Unseasonal Rains Complicate Wheat Market," June 13, 1968, State Department Central Files, Inco-Wheat-India, box 1175, NARA; Ohelert to State, "Wheat Production Final Estimate, State Department Central Files, Inco-Wheat-Pak, box 1175, NARA; "Wheat Procurement Is 11.5% above Last Year in Punjab," *Times of India*, May 30, 1968, 5; "Wheat Deluge in Punjab Mandis," *The Statesman*, June 13, 1968, 1; "Rain Ravages Wheat Piled in Mandis," *The Statesman*, June 13, 1968, 3; Rawalpiindi Embassy to Rusk, April 26, 1967, State Department Central Files, Inco-Wheat 17 Pak-Mex, box 1175, NARA; Norman Borlaug, "The Accelerated Crop Improvement and Production Programs," October 1968, FFA, report 001624; "Good News from the Farms," *Economist*, July 18, 1968, 25–26.

3. "The Revolution of Falling Expectations," *Economist*, July 6, 1968, 45; "Don't Feed the Starving Millions," *Economist*, September 28, 1969, 60; Felix Belair, "Farming Revolution in Poorer Lands Is Held Near," *NYT*, May 14, 1968, 8.

4. Eric Wentworth, "Aid Chief Protests Program Cutbacks," *WP*, March 9, 1968, A5; Warren Unna, "Green Revolution to Fight Hunger," *WP*, April 11, 1968, A20; T. J. Byres, "The Dialectic of India's Green Revolution," *South Asian Review*

5(2) (1972): 100; Caroll Kilpatrick, "US Aid Results Are Standing Out," *WP,* July 1, 1968, A20.

5. Rockefeller Foundation, *Strategy for the Conquest of Hunger: Proceedings of a Symposium* (New York, 1968), 112; House Committee on Foreign Affairs, *The Green Revolution: Symposium on Science and Foreign Policy,* 91st Cong., 1st sess., 1969, 3, 10, 13.

6. Senate Committee on Foreign Relations, *Foreign Assistance Act of 1968,* 90th Cong., 1st sess., part 1, March 12, 1968, 332; House Committee on Foreign Affairs, *Foreign Assistance Act of 1968,* 90th Cong., 2nd sess., 1968, 58; Special Report of the Rockefeller Foundation, quoted in *War on Hunger* (White House Office on War on Hunger), May 1971, 18; Lester Brown, *Seeds of Change: The Green Revolution and Development in the 1970s* (New York, 1970), 10.

7. "Commemorative Stamp on Wheat," *Hindu Weekly Review,* July 22, 1968, 16; *Blitz,* August 3, 1968, 23; "UP Bumper Crop May Benefit All But Farmer," *Times of India,* May 28, 1968, 1; CIA, "India's Foodgrain Situation: Progress and Problems," August 1972, *DDRS,* ck3100381157.

8. Summary Notes of 576th NSC Meeting, October 11, 1967, NSC Meetings, vol. 4, box 2, LBJL; "Food for Rats?" *Blitz,* April 20, 1968, 2; Rahul Mukherji, "India's Aborted Liberalization, 1966," *Pacific Affairs* 7(3) (2000): 375–392; "We Have Not Given Up on Planning," *Blitz,* June 29, 1968, 5.

9. Gunnar Myrdal, *Asian Drama* (New York, 1971), 1: 413; Senate Committee on Foreign Relations, *Foreign Assistance Act of 1968,* 5; "Text of Address by Robert McNamara," *NYT,* October 1, 1968, 58.

10. State Department, Bureau of Intelligence and Research, "South and Southeast Asia: "Miracle" Seeds Have Postponed, But Not Eliminated, Region's Population Problem," April 16, 1970, State Department Central Files, AGR 12 ASIA, 1970–73, box 466, NARA; Edmundo Flores, "The Big Threat Is Not Hunger," *Ceres,* May–June 1969, 19–21; Richard Critchfield, "Feeding the Hungry," *TNR,* October 26, 1969, 16.

11. Lowell Hardin, "Economic, Political and Social Implications of the Green Revolution," January 28, 1971, report 4022, FFA.

12. Lowell S. Hardin, "Bellagio 1969: The Green Revolution," *Nature,* September 2008, 470–471; Bell to Bundy, "Follow Up to Bellagio," June 25, 1970, Bell Papers, series IV, box 30, folder 744, FFA.

13. Martha Finnemore, "Redefining Development at the World Bank," in Frederick Cooper and Randall Packard, eds., *International Development and the Social Sciences: Essays on the History and Politics of Knowledge* (Berkeley, 1997), 203–227.

14. Addeke H. Boerma, "A World Agricultural Plan," *Scientific American,* August 1970, 54–69; "U.S. Bars F.A.O. Proposal to Cut Food Output," *NYT,* November 18, 1969, 17; Dick Wilson, "The Legacy of Miracles," *Far Eastern Economic Review,* September 4, 1969; "Global Fallacies," *Economist,* November 15, 1969.

15. Richard Nixon, "Special Message to Congress on Foreign Aid," May 28, 1969, in *Public Papers of the Presidents of the United States, Richard Nixon, 1969* (Washington, DC, 1971), 414; William Rogers, "Viet-Nam in the Perspective of East Asia," *DOSB,* May 12, 1969, 308.

16. "28 Are Burned to Death in Madras Farm Clash," *NYT,* December 27, 1968, 3; Norman Borlaug and Oddvar Aresvik, "The Accelerated Crop Improvement and Production Programs and the Agricultural Revolution," October 1968, report 001624, FFA; "And Now?" *Economist,* April 13, 1968, 48; "Bleak Hope for Opponents of Ayub Khan," *LT,* October 14, 1967, 4; "Opening of Huge Indus Project," *LT,* November 23, 1967, 7; "Ayub Khan Describes His Revolution," *LT,* September 5, 1967, 9; "Pakistan's Fate," *WP,* March 27, 1969, A22; Selig Harrison, "Military Takes Pakistan Reins as Ayub Quits," *WP,* March 26, 1969, A1; Borlaug oral history, Cushing Library, Texas A&M University, April 1, 1985, 2.

17. Martin H. Billings and Arjan Singh, *Conventional Energy as a Constraint to the Green Revolution, 1964–1984: The Punjab Case* (New Delhi, April 15, 1969), 59; Economic Research Service, Department of Agriculture, *The Impact of New Grain Varieties in Asia* (Washington, DC, 1969), 21; Clifton R. Wharton Jr., "The Green Revolution: Cornucopia or Pandora's Box?" *Foreign Affairs,* April 1969, 467.

18. Richard Critchfield, "Feeding the Hungry," *TNR,* October 25, 1969, 16–19; Justus M. van der Kroef, "Communism and Reform in the Philippines," *Pacific Affairs* 46(1) (1973): 29–58; Southeast Asia Treaty Organization, *The Maoist Communist Party of the Philippines* (Bangkok, 1971), 43–44; Inder Malhotra, "Ayub's Fall Has Many Useful Lessons for India," *Statesman Weekly,* March 1, 1969, 2; Hubell to AID, "Rural Income Equality," October 17, 1969, State Department Central Files, Agr-India, SNF 67–69, box 420, NARA.

19. Wolf Ladejinsky, "The Green Revolution in Bihar," *Economic and Political Weekly,* September 1969, A147–A162; Francine Frankel, "Agricultural Modernisation and Social Change," *Mainstream,* November 29, 1969, 9–12; Richard Critchfield, "The New World Food Crisis," *The Nation,* September 10, 1973, 208.

20. Daniel Thorner, "Gentlemen Farmers, the New Rich of India," *LT,* September 9, 1968, 7; Norman Kipping, "How the Indian Farmer Is Living with His New-Found Wealth," *LT,* May 6, 1968, 3; Barbara J. Culliton, "The Rich Get Richer," *Science News,* April 5, 1969, 336; T. K. Oomen, "Green Revolution and Agrarian Conflict," *Economic and Political Weekly,* June 26, 1971, A99–A103; New Delhi to AID, "Rural Income Inequality," October 14, 1969, State Department Central Files, AGR-India, SNF 67–69, Box 420, NARA; Ashok Rudra, A. Majid, and B. D. Talib, "Big Farmers of Punjab," *Economic and Political Weekly,* September 27, 1969, A144.

21. Frank Lorimer to Warren Weaver, "WFL Notes on 'World Population and World Food Supplies,'" November 22, 1949, RG3, series 915, box 3, RFAC; Samuel P. Huntington, "The Bases of Accommodation," *Foreign Affairs,* July 1968, 649; IAP Staff Minutes, June 10, 1968, RG 1.2, series 464, box 27, folder 199, RFAC.

22. Amrit Lall, "India's Urbanization," *Focus,* September 1968, 1–7; Michael Perelman, "Second Thoughts on the Green Revolution," *TNR,* July 17, 1971, 21; Osgood to Kissinger, "Overview of World Situation," August 20, 1969, *DDRS,* ck3100566100; United Nations, Department of Economic and Social Affairs, *Urbanization in the Second United Nations Development Decade* (New York, 1970), 5.

23. Borlaug, oral history, Cushing Library, April 1, 1985, 2; Corry to Rusk, "Aid to Ceylon," May 17, 1968, and Lyon to State, "Aid Commodity Loan,"

February 27, 1967, State Department Central Files, AID(US)9Ceylon, RG 59, box 465, NARA; T. D. S. A. Dissanayake, *Dudley Senanayake of Sri Lanka* (Colombo, 1975), 101–105.

24. Robert S. Anderson, Edwin Levy, and Barrie M. Morrison, *Rice Science and Development Politics: Research Strategies and IRRI's Technologies Confront African Diversity, 1950–1980* (Oxford, 1991), 176; Frank J. Moore to George F. Gant, "IRRI Projects in Ceylon," January 24, 1968, report PA06700244, FFA; Staples to Bell, March 14, 1969, report PA06700244, FFA; Lucien Rajakaruna, "Rain Wrecks Ceylon's 5-Year Rice Plan," *Bangkok World,* January 15, 1970, 1.

25. *Congressional Record,* 91st Cong., 1st sess., May 26, 1969, 13720; Arnold to Secretary of State, March 24, 1970, State Department Central Files, POL2Ceylon, RG 59, box, 2172, NARA; Dissanayake, *Dudley Senanayake,* 125; Arnold to Secretary of State, "Ceylonese General Election, Predictions," May 25, 1970, State Department Central Files, POL14Ceylon, RG 59, Box 2172, NARA; "Overturn in Ceylon," *NYT,* May 30, 1970, 22.

26. F. Marcos, "Text of Proclamation 1081," September 21, 1972, www.filipiniana.net; Victoria Arcega, "Technocrats as Middlemen and Their Networks in the Philippine Rice Project: The Case of the Masagana 99" (PhD diss., Michigan State University, 1976), 39; R. Guha, *India after Gandhi* (New York, 2003), 491; John Bresnan, *Managing Indonesia: The Modern Political Economy* (New York, 1993), 123; Jim Schiller and Barbara Martin Schiller, eds., *Imagining Indonesia: Cultural Politics and Political Culture* (Athens, OH, 1997), 292.

27. Ian Westergren, "Nobel Peace Prize Winner, Dr. Norman Ernest Borlaug," *Wilmington Star,* October 22, 1970, 1; "Prix Nobel," *Le Monde,* December 12, 1970, 26; "Foundations of Subversion," *Blitz,* December 12, 1970, 15; "Revolutionist," Syracuse *Herald-Journal,* October 25, 1970, 8; "Timely Recognition," LaCrosse *Tribune,* 6.

28. McGeorge Bundy to Borlaug, October 23, 1970, Bell Papers, Series IV, box 26, folder 681, FFA.

29. Norman Borlaug, "The Green Revolution, Peace, and Humanity," December 11, 1970, RG 6.7, series IV, subseries 6, box 88, RFAC.

30. Ian McDonald, "The Man behind the Green Revolution," *LT,* November 13, 1970, 10.

31. Michael Allaby, "Why Not Ban DDT?" *The Ecologist,* April 1972, 4–6; Senate Committee on Government Operations, *Interagency Environmental Hazards Coordination, Pesticides and Public Policy* [Ribicoff Report], 89th Cong., 2nd sess., July 21, 1966.

32. Norman Borlaug, "Mankind and Civilization at Another Crossroad," November 8, 1971, FAO Library; Michael McGuire, "Agricultural Expert Criticizes Nobel Winner's Defense of DDT," *CT,* November 11, 1971, A14.

33. Norman Borlaug, "DDT, The First Domino," *NYT,* November 21, 1971, E13; *Congressional Record,* 92nd Cong., 1st sess., November 1, 1971, 38678; "Norman Borlaug, DDT," *NYT,* November 26, 1971, 36; Asger Christensen, "The Green Revolution and the Multinational Corporation" (Copenhagen, 1970); Harry M. Cleaver Jr., "The Contradictions of the Green Revolution," *Monthly Review,*

June 1972, 89; Andre Gunder Frank, "Reflections on Green, Red, and White Revolutions in India," *Economic and Political Weekly*, January 20, 1973, 119.

34. Paul Ehrlich, "Population, Food and Environment," *Texas Quarterly*, Summer 1968, 46.

35. Georg Bergstrom, *Gränser för vår Tillvaro* (Stockholm, 1964); René Dumont and Bernard Rosier, *Nous Allons à la Famine* (Paris, 1966); Paul Ehrlich, *The Population Bomb* (New York, 1968); Garrett Hardin, "The Tragedy of the Commons," *Science*, December 13, 1968, 1243–1248; Francis Moore Lappé, *Diet for a Small Planet* (New York, 1971); Barry Commoner, *The Closing Circle* (New York, 1971).

36. Kennon to Department of State, "NCAER Finds Green Revolution Real," February 23, 1973, State Department Central Files, Agr2India, RG59, box 470, NARA; Directorate of Intelligence, "India's Foodgrain Situation: Progress and Problems," August 1972, *DDRS*, ck3100381157; CIA, "India: Developing Power or Developing Power Vacuum," June 1, 1974, *DDRS*, ck3100174788.

37. Kennon, "NCAER Finds Green Revolution Real"; Philip Maxwell, "The Shape of Things to Come?" *Internationalist*, May 1972, 6–12.

38. Robert Reinhold, "Mankind Warned of Perils of Growth," *NYT*, February 27, 1972, 1; Henry C. Wallich, "More on Growth," *Newsweek*, March 13, 1972, 86; Simon Kuznets, "Population Trends and Modern Economic Growth," in *The Population Debate: Dimensions and Perspectives* (New York, 1975), 1: 425–433; Paul N. Edwards, "The World in a Machine: Origins and Impacts of Early Computerized Global Systems Models," in Agatha C. Hughes and Thomas P. Hughes, eds., *Systems, Experts, and Computers* (Cambridge, MA, 2000), 221–254.

39. Julian Simon, "Economic Effects of Population Change," *UNESCO Courier*, May 1974, 23–32; Simon, "Resources, Population, and Environment, an Oversupply of False Bad News," *Science*, June 27, 1980, 1431–1437; "Letters," *Science*, December 19, 1980, 1296–1306; John Tierney, "Betting the Planet," *NYT Magazine*, December 2, 1990, 52–79; Paul R. Ehrlich, "Environmental Disruption: Implications for the Social Sciences," *Social Science Quarterly* 62(1) (1981): 7–22; Julian Simon, "Environmental Disruption or Environmental Improvement?" *Social Science Quarterly* 62(1) (1981): 30–43; Simon, "Paul Ehrlich Saying It Is So Doesn't Make It So," *Social Science Quarterly* 63(2) (1982): 381–384.

40. Paul Ehrlich, "An Economist in Wonderland," *Social Science Quarterly* 62(1) (1981): 44–49.

41. Michael Watts, "Heart of Darkness: Reflections on Famine and Starvation in Africa," in R. E. Downs, Donna O. Kerner, and Stephen P. Reyna, eds., *The Political Economy of African Famine* (Philadelphia, 1991), 23–68; Amartya Sen, "Famines," *World Development* 8(9) (1980): 613–621; Jean Drèze and Amartya Sen, *The Political Economy of Hunger*, vol. 2: *Famine Prevention* (Oxford, 1990); Rolando V. Garcia, *Drought and Man*, vol. 1: *Nature Pleads Not Guilty* (Oxford, 1981); G. A. Harrison, *Famine* (Oxford, 1988).

42. Bernard D. Nossiter, "The Death of Slogans," *WP*, April 18, 1973, A23; M. R. Bhagavan et al., *The Death of the Green Revolution* (London, 1973); Douglas Brinkley, *The Unfinished Presidency* (New York, 1998), 185; Gregg Easterbrook, "Forgotten Benefactor of Humanity," *Atlantic*, January 1997, 80; Frosty

Hill, Hill oral history, April 20, 1973, FFA; Senate Subcommittee on Foreign Agriculture Policy, *Foreign Food Assistance and Agricultural Development*, 94th Cong., 1st sess., 1975, 40.

43. "Research Unit Seeks Green Revolution in Nigeria," *NYT*, September 13, 1972, 16; Leon Dash, "Urban Renewal Is a Target of a Thriving Cameroon," *WP*, August 31, 1979, A19; G. Hans Holmén, "The State and Agricultural Intensification in Sub-Saharan Africa," in Göran Djurfeldt et al., eds., *The African Food Crisis: Lessons from the Asian Green Revolution* (Cambridge, MA, 2005), 68–70.

44. Rockefeller Foundation, *Annual Report* (New York, 1977), 34–35.

45. "The Price of Optimism," *Time*, August 1, 1969; NBC News, "Speaking Frankly: Foundations and Philanthropy," February 23, 1969, RFAC; "Report Millions Starve in U.S.," *CT*, April 23, 1968, A4; Senate Committee on Labor and Public Welfare, *Hunger in America*, 90th Cong., 1st sess., 1968; Citizens Board of Inquiry into Hunger and Malnutrition, *Hunger U.S.A.* (Washington, DC, 1968), 4.

46. House Foreign Affairs Committee, *United States Policy toward Asia*, 89th Cong., 2nd sess., 1966, pt. 2, 539; Henry A. Kissinger, "Central Issues of American Foreign Policy," 1968, in Department of State, *FRUS, 1969–1976* (Washington, DC, 2003), 1: 39–40.

47. "The Undernourished Generation," *Blitz*, December 12, 1970, 13; Hans Singer, "The Riderless Horse," *Internationalist*, November 1972, 26–27; A. D. Horne, "Aid at Crossroads: A Lively Encounter," *WP*, March 10, 1970, A16.

48. Gregg Easterbrook, "The Most Powerful Nobody in Washington," *The Washington Monthly*, September 1980, 57; Nick Eberstadt, *Foreign Aid and American Purpose* (Washington, DC, 1988), 34–36; Mark Hulbert, "Will the U.S. Bail Out the Bankers?" *Nation*, October 16, 1982, 364–366; Jack Anderson, "US Retreats from Goals It Once Set Self as Nation," *WP*, March 3, 1972, A28; "Mr. Nixon and Foreign Aid," *WP*, September 20, 1970, 38.

49. Kissinger to Nixon, October 20, 1969, in Department of State, *FRUS, 1969–1976*, 1: 127; Jeremi Suri, *Henry Kissinger and the American Century* (Cambridge, MA, 2007), 235–236; Joan Hoff, *Nixon Reconsidered* (New York, 1994), 158–159.

50. Lucian W. Pye, "Foreign Aid and America's Involvement in the Developing World," in Anthony Lake, ed., *The Vietnam Legacy* (New York, 1976), 379; Rashid Khalidi, *Sowing Crisis: The Cold War and American Dominance in the Middle East* (Boston, 2009), 122; Kissinger press briefing, August 14, 1970, in Department of State, *FRUS, 1969–1976*, 1: 235.

51. MemCon, "President's Task Force on Foreign Aid," September 2, 1969, in Department of State, *FRUS, 1969–1976*, 1: 102–104; Michael Marchino and Robert K. Musil, "Food for Peace or Food for Power?" *Christian Century*, August 17, 1977, 714; Vernon Ruttan, *United States Development Assistance Policy* (Baltimore, 1996), 279.

52. "Rationing the Soviets," *Time*, August 25, 1975, 50–51; Joel Solkoff, "No Choice But to Sell the Russians Grain," *TNR*, September 6, 1975, 16–19; Stephen S. Rosenfeld, "The Politics of Food," *Foreign Policy*, Spring 1974, 17–29.

53. Kathleen Teltsch, "U.S. Shortages Peril World Food Aid Plan," *NYT,* August 19, 1973, 1; "GAO Asserts Food Program for Poor Abroad Is Disrupted," *NYT,* April 23, 1975, 17; "Michael Maren, "The Food Aid Racket," *Harper's,* August 1993, 10–12; Rahul Mukherji, "India's Aborted Liberalization—1966," *Pacific Affairs* 73(3) (2000): 380.

54. Susan R. Abbasi, *Issues Related to Hunger in Africa: Drought, Population Growth, Environment, Natural Resources and Agricultural Development* (Washington, DC, April 1986), 28.

55. Organization for African Unity, *Lagos Plan of Action for the Economic Development of Africa, 1980–2000* (Addis Ababa, 1980); World Bank, *Accelerated Development in Sub-Saharan Africa: An Agenda for Action* (Washington, DC, 1981); "Boom Again," *Economist,* November 29, 1980, 60; "Africa's Growing Pains," *Economist,* October 16, 1981, 90–91; William Raspberry, "Big Aid for Small Farms," *WP,* November 2, 1981, A15.

56. Rostow, "Some Lessons in Economic Development since the War," *DOSB,* November 9, 1964, 664.

57. House Committee on Foreign Affairs, *Feeding the World's Population,* 98th Cong., 2nd sess., 1984, 88–89; George Schultz, "Mobutu Tour d'Horizon," September 3, 1985, *DDRS,* ck3100498991; Holmén, "The State and Agricultural Intensification," 94–95.

58. Bob Geldof, *Is That It?* (New York, 1986), 216, 282–283, 313.

59. David Fricke, "Bob Geldof, Rock & Roll's World Diplomat," *Rolling Stone,* July 18, 1985, 18; Richard Harrington, "Geldof's Plea for the Starving," *WP,* July 24, 1985, A1; Christopher Dickey, "Rains Crimp Sudan's Famine Relief," *WP,* July 22, 1985, A1; Dennis McDougal, "USA for Africa: New Heights of Affluence," *LAT,* September 1, 1985, N3; Steve Coll, "How to Spend $58 Million," *WP,* September 5, 1985, C1; Jeffrey Sachs, *The End of Poverty: Economic Possibilities for Our Time* (New York, 2005); William Easterly, "The Utopian Nightmare," *Foreign Policy,* September 2005, 61.

60. UN General Assembly, *United Nations Millennium Declaration,* September 18, 2000, A/Res/55/2; Elisabeth Bumiller, "Bush Plans to Raise Foreign Aid and Tie It To Reforms," *NYT,* March 15, 2002, 8; International Monetary Fund, *Global Monitoring Report, 2005, Millenium Development Goals: From Consensus to Momentum* (Washington, DC, 2005); Nina Munk, "Jeffrey Sachs's $200 Million Dream," *Vanity Fair,* July 2007, 140–147; Commission for Africa, *Our Common Interest* (London, 2005).

10. PRESENT AT THE RE-CREATION

1. Barack Obama, Inaugural Address, January 21, 2009, www.whitehouse.gov; "Previewing Ghana," July 8, 2009, www.whitehouse.gov.

2. "New Government, New Spirit," *Life,* January 19, 1953, 18; Douglas Brinkley, *The Unfinished Presidency* (New York, 1998), 185; Richard Critchfield, "Bring the Green Revolution to Africa," *NYT,* September 14, 1992, A19.

3. Abel Mboozi, "Halt Mealie-Meal Exports," *The Times of Zambia,* February 26, 2006; "Tanzania Suspends Food Exports over Looming Famine," BBC, January 8, 2006; Daphne Eviatar, "Spend $150 Billion per Year to Cure World Poverty," *NYT Magazine,* November 7, 2004, 47; Rockefeller Foundation Press Release, September 8, 2006, www.rockfound.org/initiatives/agra; World Bank, *Agriculture for Development: World Development Report 2008* (Washington, DC, 2007); Missy Ryan, "Food Crisis Requires New Green Revolution," Reuters, May 14, 2008; Chicago Council on Foreign Affairs, *Renewing America's Leadership in the Fight against Global Hunger and Poverty* (Chicago, 2009); David Twiddy, "USDA to Up International Food Aid," Associated Press, April 7, 2009.

4. U.S. Congress, Senate, *Appropriations for FY 2010 through 2014 to Provide Assistance to Foreign Countries to Promote Food Security,* 111th Cong., 1st sess., 2009, S. 384; Michael Gerson, "Gates's Field of Dreams," *WP,* October 16, 2009.

5. Carlotta Gall, "Deep in Taliban Territory, a Push for Electricity," *NYT,* November 9, 2008, 5; Media Newswire, "Team Borlaug Helps Iraqis Build a Future through 4-H Style Program," February 23, 2009, media-newswire.com/release_1086543.html; Chicago Council on Foreign Affairs, *Renewing America's Leadership,* 17; Hillary Clinton, "Remarks on Trilateral Discussions with Afghanistan and Pakistan," May 6, 2009, www.state.gov.

6. "If Words Were Food, Nobody Would Go Hungry," *Economist,* November 19, 2009,

7. UN News Centre, "Migiro Urges Sustainable African Green Revolution to Tackle Food Crisis," May 4, 2009, www.un.org; Rockefeller Foundation, "Frequently Asked Questions about the Original Green Revolution," October 2006, www.rockfound.org.

8. Food and Agriculture Organization, *Pathways to Success: Success Stories in Agricultural Production and Food Security* (Rome, 2009); Food and Agriculture Organization, *Food Security Statistics, 2008* (Rome, 2008).

9. Daniel Zwerdling, "India's Farming Revolution Headed for Collapse," National Public Radio, April 14, 2009, www.npr.org; Daniel Pepper, "The Toxic Consequences of the Green Revolution," *U.S. News and World Report,* July 8, 2008; Jane Perlez, "Taliban Exploit Class Rifts in Pakistan," *NYT,* April 16, 2009, A1; GMA News, "CBCP: Int'l Study Debunks Benefits of Chemical Agriculture," April 17, 2009, www.gmanews.tv/story/157449; "Sowing Seeds of a Green Revolution," *Times of India,* April 6, 2009; "Bill Gates Calls for United Action to Support World's Poorest Farmers," October 14, 2009, www.gatesfoundation.org.

10. Vance Borjaily, "One of the Green Revolution Boys," *The Atlantic,* February 1983, 67; House Committee on Foreign Affairs, *Foreign Assistance Act of 1968,* 90th Cong., 2nd sess., 1968, 58; David J. Speilman, *Highlights from Millions Fed: Proven Successes in Agricultural Development,* www.gatesfoundation.org; World Bank, *Agriculture for Development,* 247; Chicago Council on Foreign Affairs, *Renewing America's Leadership,* 110.

11. State Department, "Global Hunger and Food Security Initiative," September 28, 2009, http://www.state.gov/s/globalfoodsecurity/129952.htm; Ha-joon Chang, "Hamlet without the Prince of Denmark: How Development Has Disappeared

from Today's 'Development' Discourse," in S. Khan and J. Christiansen, eds., *Towards New Developmentalism: Market as Meansrather than Master* (London, forthcoming).

12. World Bank, *Agriculture for Development,* 227.

13. Robert Paarlberg, *Starved for Science: How Biotechnology Is Being Kept Out of Africa* (Cambridge, MA, 2008), 164.

14. Paul Collier, "The Politics of Hunger," *Foreign Affairs,* December 2008.

15. Narcís Serra and Joseph Stiglitz, "The Barcelona Development Agenda," in Serra and Stiglitz, eds., *The Washington Consensus Reconsidered* (Oxford, 2008), 56–60; Robert M. Solow, "The Last 50 Years in Growth Theory and the Next 10," *Oxford Review of Economic Policy* 23 (2007): 3–14; William Easterly, "The Anarchy of Success," *New York Review,* October 8, 2009, 28–30; Dambisa Moyo, *Dead Aid: Why Aid Is Not Working and How There Is a Better Way for Africa* (New York, 2009), 9.

Cushing Library, Texas A&M University, College Station, TX
  Borlaug Oral History

Federal Reserve Board Records, Federal Reserve, Washington, DC
  Country Files

Food and Agriculture Organization Archives, Rome, Italy
  Binay R. Sen Papers
  Monlik Subject File

Ford Foundation Archive, New York, NY
  Daniel Bell Papers
  Forrest Hill Papers
  Grant Files
  Lowell S. Hardin Papers
  Reports
  Wolf Ladejinsky Papers

Harry S Truman Library, Independence, MO
  John H. Ohly Papers
  Joseph M. Jones Papers

International Rice Research Institute Library and Archives, Los Baños,
  Philippines

Lyndon Baines Johnson Library, Austin, TX
  Bob Hardesty File
  Cabinet Papers
  National Security Council Records
  Orville Freeman Papers
  Robert Komer Files
  White House Central File

National Archives of India, New Delhi, India
    Ministry of Food and Agriculture Records

Nehru Memorial Museum and Library, Teen Murthi House, New Delhi, India
    Asok Mitra Papers
    T. T. Krishnamachari Papers

Regenstein Library, University of Chicago, Chicago, IL
    Albert Mayer Papers

Richard B. Russell Library, University of Georgia, Athens, GA
    Dean Rusk Papers

Rockefeller Foundation Archive Center, Tarrytown, NY
    John D. Rockefeller III Papers
    New Delhi Field Office Papers
    Population Council Papers
    Rockefeller Foundation Papers

Seeley G. Mudd Manuscript Library, Princeton, NJ
    Frank W. Notestein Papers
    John Foster Dulles Papers

University of Minnesota Library, Special Collections, Minneapolis, MN
    Norman Borlaug Papers

U.S. Army Military History Institute, Carlisle Barracks, PA
    George L. McColm Papers

U.S. National Archives, College Park, MD
    CIA Records Search Tool (CREST)
    RG59 Records of the Department of State
        Bureau of Intelligence and Research Records, Lot 58D776
        Central Files
        Office of Public Opinion Studies
        OIR Reports
        Policy Planning Staff Records, Lot 67D548, Lot 69D121
    RG469, Records of the U.S. Foreign Assistance Agencies
        Country Subject Files
        Director Subject Files